Lecture Notes in Computer Science   10694

Commenced Publication in 1973
Founding and Former Series Editors:
Gerhard Goos, Juris Hartmanis, and Jan van Leeuwen

More information about this series at http://www.springer.com/series/7409

Nora Cuppens · Frédéric Cuppens
Jean-Louis Lanet · Axel Legay
Joaquin Garcia-Alfaro (Eds.)

Risks and Security of Internet and Systems

12th International Conference, CRiSIS 2017
Dinard, France, September 19–21, 2017
Revised Selected Papers

 Springer

Editors
Nora Cuppens
IMT Atlantique
Cesson Sévigné
France

Frédéric Cuppens
IMT Atlantique
Cesson Sévigné
France

Jean-Louis Lanet
LHS Rennes
Rennes
France

Axel Legay
Inria
Rennes
France

Joaquin Garcia-Alfaro 🆔
Télécom SudParis
Evry Cedex
France

ISSN 0302-9743   ISSN 1611-3349   (electronic)
Lecture Notes in Computer Science
ISBN 978-3-319-76686-7   ISBN 978-3-319-76687-4   (eBook)
https://doi.org/10.1007/978-3-319-76687-4

Library of Congress Control Number: 2018934357

LNCS Sublibrary: SL3 – Information Systems and Applications, incl. Internet/Web, and HCI

Printed on acid-free paper

This Springer imprint is published by the registered company Springer International Publishing AG
part of Springer Nature
The registered company address is: Gewerbestrasse 11, 6330 Cham, Switzerland

Preface

This volume contains the papers presented at the 12th International Conference on Risks and Security of Internet and Systems (CRISIS 2017), which was held in Dinard, France, September 19–21, 2017. Each submission was reviewed by at least three committee members. The review process was followed by intensive discussions over a period of one week. The Program Committee selected 17 regular papers. The accepted papers cover diverse research themes, ranging from classic topics, such as vulnerability analysis, access control and filtering, or cloud security to emerging issues, such as cyber threat intelligence, human-centric security, or apps security. The program was completed with three excellent invited talks given by Thomas Jensen (Inria Rennes), Gérard Le Comte (Société Générale), and Arnaud Tisserand (Lab-STICC Lorient) and one thrilling tutorial by Ronan Lashermes (Inria Rennes). Finally, the conference included a panel between the four Brittany chairs on cybersecurity: Chair CNI on Cybersecurity of Critical Infrastructures, Chair Cyberdefense and Cybersecurity of Saint-Cyr-Sogeti-Thales, Chair Cyberdefense of Naval Systems, and Chair on Threat Analysis.

Many people contributed to the success of CRISIS 2017. First, we would like to thank all the authors who submitted their research results. The selection was a challenging task and we sincerely thank all the Program Committee members, as well as the external reviewers, who volunteered to read and discuss the papers. We greatly thank the tutorial and publication chair, Joaquin Garcia-Alfaro (Telecom SudParis), and the publicity chairs, Ronan Lashermes (Inria) and Reda Yaich (IMT Atlantique). We would like to thank most warmly the local organization chair, Ghislaine Le Gall (IMT Atlantique), for her great efforts to organize and manage the logistics during the conference. We also cannot forget our sponsors including the Brittany Region, the Chair Cyber CNI on Cybersecurity of Critical Infrastructures and the *Laboratoire de Haute Sécurité* for their support. Last but not least, thanks to all the attendees. As security becomes an essential property in the information and communication technologies, there is a growing need to develop efficient methods to analyze risks and design systems providing a high level of security and privacy. We hope the articles in this proceedings volume will be valuable for your professional activities in this area.

January 2018

Nora Cuppens
Frédéric Cuppens
Jean-Louis Lanet
Axel Legay

Organization

General Chairs

Nora Cuppens   IMT Atlantique, France
Jean-Louis Lanet   LHS Rennes, France

Program Co-chairs

Frédéric Cuppens   IMT Atlantique, France
Axel Legay   Inria, France

Publications Chair

Joaquin Garcia-Alfaro   Télécom SudParis, France

Publications Chairs

Ronan Lashermes   Inria, France
Reda Yaich   IMT Atlantique, France

Program Committee

Esma Aimeur   University of Montreal, Canada
Luca Allodi   Eindhoven University of Technology, The Netherlands
Jocelyn Aubert   Luxembourg Institute of Science and Technology,
                               Luxembourg
Christophe Bidan   Centrale-Supelec, France
Fabrizio Biondi   Inria Rennes, France
Anis Bkakria   IMT Atlantique, France
Yu Chen   State University of New York - Binghamton, USA
Jorge Cuellar   Siemens AG, Germany
Frédéric Cuppens   IMT Atlantique, France
Nora Cuppens   IMT Atlantique, France
Roberto Di Pietro   Bell Labs, France
José M. Fernandez   Ecole Polytechnique de Montreal, Canada
Simone Fischer-Hübner   Karlstad University, Sweden
Simon Foley   IMT Atlantique, France
Joaquin Garcia-Alfaro   Telecom SudParis, France
Bogdan Groza   Politehnica University of Timisoara, Romania
Ruan He   Orange Labs, France
Christos Kalloniatis   University of the Aegean, Greece

Sokratis Katsikas	Center for Cyber and Information Security, NTNU, Norway
Nizar Kheir	Thales Group, France
Barbara Kordy	INSA Rennes, France
Igor Kotenko	St. Petersburg Institute for Informatics and Automation of the Russian Academy of Sciences (SPIIRAS), Russia
Marc Lacoste	Orange Labs, France
Costas Lambrinoudakis	University of Piraeus, Greece
Jean-Louis Lanet	Inria Rennes, France
Axel Legay	Inria Rennes, France
Javier Lopez	University of Malaga, Spain
Raja Natarajan	Tata Institute of Fundamental Research, India
Stephen Neville	University of Victoria, Canada
Kai Rannenberg	Goethe University Frankfurt, Germany
Michael Rusinowitch	Inria Nancy, France
Ketil Stoelen	SINTEF, Norway
Nadia Tawbi	Laval University, Canada
Lingyu Wang	Concordia University, Canada

Additional Reviewers

Cristina Alcaraz	Christos Lyvas
Andrew Bedford	Patrick Murmann
Olivier Decourbe	Maria Mykoniati
Mike Enescu	Aida Omerovic
Gencer Erdogan	Atle Refsdal
David Harborth	Stavros Simou
Majid Hatamian	Ahmed Seid Yesuf
Angeliki Kitsiou	Nikos Yfantopoulos

Contents

Cloud Security

Cyber-Insurance and Cyber Threat Intelligence

Human-Centric Security and Trust

Risk Analysis

Vulnerability Analysis and Classification

Automatic Vulnerability Classification Using Machine Learning

Marian Gawron$^{(\boxtimes)}$, Feng Cheng, and Christoph Meinel

Hasso Plattner Institute (HPI), University of Potsdam, 14482 Potsdam, Germany
{marian.gawron,feng.cheng,christoph.meinel}@hpi.de

Abstract. The classification of vulnerabilities is a fundamental step to derive formal attributes that allow a deeper analysis. Therefore, it is required that this classification has to be performed timely and accurate. Since the current situation demands a manual interaction in the classification process, the timely processing becomes a serious issue. Thus, we propose an automated alternative to the manual classification, because the amount of identified vulnerabilities per day cannot be processed manually anymore. We implemented two different approaches that are able to automatically classify vulnerabilities based on the vulnerability description. We evaluated our approaches, which use Neural Networks and the Naive Bayes methods respectively, on the base of publicly known vulnerabilities.

Keywords: Vulnerability analysis · Security analytics · Data mining
Machine learning · Neural Networks

1 Introduction

Nowadays, the overall number of possible combinations of applications and operating systems and the complexity of each piece of software results in an inability to manually survey the configuration of modern systems. Thus, the maintenance and recognition of all components and their reported vulnerabilities requires a tremendous effort. In the current situation, the huge amount of vulnerabilities complicates the administration and protection of modern IT infrastructures. Therefore, it is desirable to automatically process vulnerability information. Common Vulnerability Scoring System (CVSS) parameters [7] of the vulnerability are usually used to enrich vulnerability information with additional metrics that allow automatic processing. Some of the parameters can be used to derive an estimation of the severity and the effect of a vulnerability. In particular, the attack range and the impact on the basic security principles, namely `availability`, `confidentiality`, and `integrity`, are crucial to analyze the vulnerability.

The identification and assignment for the CVSS [7] base metrics is a time-consuming action that requires expert knowledge. Usually, professional analysts

© Springer International Publishing AG, part of Springer Nature 2018
N. Cuppens et al. (Eds.): CRiSIS 2017, LNCS 10694, pp. 3–17, 2018.
https://doi.org/10.1007/978-3-319-76687-4_1

from the National Institute of Standards and Technology (NIST) have to perform this scoring manually [4]. They try to match the new vulnerability to a predefined template. But if the description of the vulnerability is ambiguous, an even more time consuming manual analysis has to be performed. Then, already analyzed vulnerabilities are identified that have similar information or keywords in their descriptions. The scores and attributes of these vulnerabilities are used as a guidance to perform the final evaluation and scoring of the new vulnerability. This process [4] reveals that also the human experts start their investigation with the textual description of the vulnerability. Commonly used services to report newly identified vulnerabilities, e.g. the vulnerability report form of Carnegie Mellon [2], limit the information to a textual description. So, the human experts do not initially receive more comprehensive information. Although they might benefit from additional background information from the common knowledge, we can identify a direct dependency between textual description and CVSS attributes within the evaluation procedure of a new vulnerability.

Since this scoring method requires advanced knowledge and a manual investigation, the scoring procedure sometimes leads to a delay in the attribution. Consequently, there are vulnerabilities, which have been released without CVSS metrics. The missing metrics are usually integrated later. This duration could be crucial for analytic systems that rely on these metrics to evaluate or even detect the vulnerability. The delay of the scoring could amount to several days. For example, the vulnerability in OpenSSH with the identifier CVE-2016-0777 was published on the 14th of January in 2016, whereas the CVSS attributes were released on the 19th of January 2016. Thus, there have been 5 days without the possibility of a classification or an automatic processing of the vulnerability. This delay could also not be explained with the low usage and minor distribution of the software, since OpenSSH is a commonly used program, which is also pre-installed in many Linux distributions. We believe that this delay and the manual workload of the vulnerability analysts could be dramatically reduced with an automatic classification of the vulnerability. Therefore, we will propose machine learning approaches to perform the classification based on the textual description.

The paper will begin with an introduction to illustrate the problem and its importance. Afterwards, some related ideas and approaches will be introduced and described. However, the problem is currently not widely explored, which results in the lack of numerous approaches that tackle the problem. Then, our own approaches will be explained in Sect. 3. We will describe a Neural Network approach and the Naive Bayes approach that both learn to classify the vulnerabilities based on extracted features of the description. In Sect. 4 our evaluation results are presented and illustrated. Thereafter, we will mention additional steps, which we plan to pursue in the future. Finally, we will conclude our work and summarize the contributions.

2   Related Work

Early ideas to use textual data, which is accumulated in vulnerability databases was already presented in [15]. The authors refer to different data mining algorithms to benefit from the diverse knowledge inside various vulnerability databases. However, they state that immense effort should be invested into the normalization and compatibility to benefit from vulnerability information of different sources. Furthermore, they want to use data mining to be able to predict and avoid vulnerabilities in future software products. The authors of [15] claim that learned classifiers should be able to identify vulnerability patterns in software before the code is included in productive software. Therefore, formal vulnerability characteristics should be constructed to train the mining algorithms.

Another application of machine learning to the field of vulnerabilities could be observed in [13]. The authors applied text mining algorithms to the source code of different software components. Then, they predict the likelihood of each component to contain vulnerabilities. This method allows them to highlight components that should be reviewed by security analysts, since it is very likely that the components are vulnerable. In [6], another method to identify vulnerabilities in software is presented. Beside the source code evaluation, the authors of [6] also propose the usage of metrics of version control systems and the architecture of the software itself to improve the prediction of vulnerabilities. The authors of [10] also investigated the possibility to apply machine learning algorithms on vulnerabilities. They tried to predict vulnerabilities in software components based on similarities to other software components. They also integrated the approach into an existing tool, which is called Vulture. The major difference is that they used vulnerability databases as a source to find vulnerabilities in programs, which they identified by using the CPE-IDs (Common Platform Enumeration IDs) [8]. They did not try to predict characteristics of the vulnerability itself.

Another paper utilized machine learning approaches to predict the likelihood for the existence of an up-to-now undiscovered vulnerability in a piece of software using data from the National Vulnerability Database (NVD) [9]. The authors of [18] applied several machine learning algorithms, but concluded that the prediction capability of their models based on the data from NVD is poor. Their goal to build a prediction model for the time-to-next disclosed vulnerability per application was unfeasible as they encountered several problems. For instance, they found that new vulnerabilities affect all previous versions, which results in an unusable `versiondiff` feature. Finally they conclude that the data from NVD might not be designed to be used for machine learning approaches at all.

Furthermore, an interesting approach of vulnerability classification and identification is presented in [17]. The authors utilized text mining methods to identify characteristics in the description of vulnerabilities and bugs. Their idea is to classify bug reports in two categories, namely regular bugs and hidden impact bugs. The major difference is that the hidden impact bugs could violate security policies. Thus, these hidden impact bugs are usually related to vulnerabilities. So, the procedure can be used to identify vulnerabilities from bug reports.

The classification of vulnerabilities was also investigated in [1]. The authors tried classify vulnerabilities based on the fact if the vulnerability was exploited or not. In contrast to our approach they based their findings on a different subset of vulnerabilities and used the OSVDB (Open Source Vulnerability Database). They concentrated on the fact if an exploit is available or if it is rumored or unavailable, which dramatically decreases the amount of usable data. In addition, they also regarded textual features as binary representations in a bag-of-words style. So they will have a high-dimensional vector for textual attributes that represents the words that are present in the corresponding field. This approach is similar to our approach, which was used in the preprocessing step for Naive Bayes. For our Neural Network we did not simply chose a binary representation for the words but the GloVe [11] tool to also retain semantic meanings.

3   Classification Approach

The classification of vulnerability information is a fundamental step in the process of an automatic processing. As it was described, the information about newly identified vulnerabilities rarely contains sufficient details to automatically process the impact of an exploit or fully understand the prerequisites. Usually the reports contain a description of the vulnerability, information about the affected software, and a rough textual description about a possible impact or even less information. The descriptions are submitted in natural language and information about the affected product could be specified by CPE-IDs (Common Platform Enumeration Identifiers) [8] or by keywords. A well-known example is the submission form of the CERT [2]. This process requires a manual investigation and translation to formal vulnerability attributes, such as CVSS metrics [7]. The formal metrics could then be used in an automatic analysis of existing vulnerabilities, since the information can be interpreted by machines.

Our idea aims at an automation of this translation to formal attributes. Therefore, we wanted to investigate the possibilities of a machine-learning approach to derive the formal attributes from the description of the vulnerability. We wanted to solve two interesting questions. The first question was if it is possible to derive the previously mentioned characteristics. The other question was, if the accuracy of the automated approach is sufficient to classify the vulnerability autonomously. We implemented two different classification methods to evaluate the accuracy and discuss advantages between the approaches. We will begin with our Neural Network approach and introduce the Naive Bayes classification afterwards.

3.1   Neural Network

We chose a Neural Network as one of our approaches, since it is a common choice for multi-label classification and classification problems with a high complexity. We believe that the approach is well suited to work with descriptions in natural

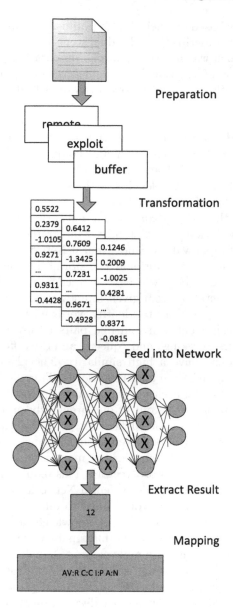

Fig. 1. Workflow of the classification

language if the domain is limited and a sufficient amount of training data is available. In our case both requirements can be met with already classified vulnerabilities. We can use the descriptions of 72,000 older vulnerabilities to train our network. Additionally, we found that the number of distinct words in all descriptions accumulate to 104,000 words. Thus, we could build our limited vocabulary and collected already classified data for our training set. The overall workflow to classify vulnerabilities based on their description using Neural Networks is illustrated in Fig. 1. We will describe the individual steps according to the illustration.

The first step, which was illustrated as the preparation phase in Fig. 1, was to remove unnecessary information from the descriptions. Since the description is created with natural language, it contains words that do not provide any additional benefit to the overall meaning. Thus, we removed stop words with the help of a predefined list of well-known stop words that we gathered from [16]. Furthermore, we used word stemming methods to overcome the differences of words that are produced by declination and conjugation. Additionally, every word with capital characters is transformed to lower case. This will resolve any differences that arise from word orders inside the sentences. So, every description is transformed into a list of substantial words.

In the next step the input data for our network has to be derived from the preprocessed descriptions. This step was integrated into our workflow as the transformation of input values. Since Neural Networks are usually not able to work on textual data, this additional transformation has to be performed. Therefore, we chose GloVe [11], which is an unsupervised learning algorithm to derive vector representation from given input words. The distinctive feature of this algorithm is the capability to identify words with similar meanings and to retain the relationship between multiple pairs of words. For example the difference of the vectors for "king" and "queen" and the difference of the vectors for "man" and "woman" have a high similarity. The algorithm assigns a 50 dimensional vector to each of the identified words. This dictionary can then be used to replace the vectors for each word in the description. In the final step, this algorithm creates a list of vectors out of our previously processed descriptions. Thus, each description consists of 50 floating point values multiplied by the number of words in the description. Even though the average number of words per description is 37, we have to consider the maximum number of words of all descriptions to create our list of word vectors. This requirement arises from the condition of uniform input values to the Neural Network. If we would work with the average number of words, we would have to omit several words for some descriptions, which could lead to a loss of knowledge about those. Thus, we decided to expand all descriptions to the maximum word count. Therefore, we enlarge the shorter descriptions with null vectors to equalize the different lengths of the individual descriptions. For our experiments we identified a maximum length of around 400 words and enlarged smaller descriptions accordingly. So we end up with around 2,000 input values per description that originate from 400 words and 50 floating point values for each word.

Finally, we only have to translate the formal values of the CVSS [7] attributes to numbers to completely work in the numerical space and feed the data into our Neural Network.

This final translation strongly depends on the attributes which should be predicted. First we need to identify all possible values for the selected attribute. Then we can simply enumerate the possible values and use this mapping to translate the textual information to numbers. For the single attribute predictions, such as integrity or attack-range, we identified the distinct values None, Partial, Complete and Unknown, Local, Adjacent Network, Network respectively.

For our combined predictions the possible combinations of the selected attributes had to be considered. So the combination of confidentiality, integrity, and availability (CIA) results in 27 distinct values. For our overall combination we added the attack-range which means that we would have to work with 108 different values. The mapping itself has to be persisted to allow the back translation, which we perform as our final step of the workflow 1.

At this point we can feed our data into the Neural Network. We decided to use 80% of the data to train the network and the remaining 20% for testing. The Neural Network was configured with a learning rate of 0.001 and it runs for 100 epochs. Additionally, we tested various configurations for the number of hidden layers as well as the number of units per layer. The most promising results have been achieved with a network of 3 layers and 1200, 700, and 50 units for the respective layers. During the evaluation, which will be described in the next chapter, we encountered the problem of overfitting of our network. We tackled the problem with the specification of a dropout rate. This rate describes a probability that an individual node is kept or dropped from propagation. Thus, not all nodes of each layer influence the output anymore. This method is also illustrated in the Neural Network of our workflow in Fig. 1. It is shown that the nodes marked with an "X" do not propagate their results to the following layers of the network.

Afterwards the results are extracted and the numerical values can be mapped back to human readable values of the CVSS attributes. Thus, we can create the single attribute value or the combination of attributes from a description. So we can use the approach to automatically classify vulnerabilities according to the specified attribute. This final step concludes the workflow that is illustrated in Fig. 1.

3.2 Naive Bayes

Beside Neural Networks, we implemented another method to derive CVSS [7] attributes of vulnerabilities automatically. We implemented a Naive Bayes [12] classifier that can predict the selected attribute based on the associated description. We chose the Naive Bayes classification method, since we believe that it is a widely known and applied algorithm for classification problems. It was already thoroughly studied and investigated and could therefore serve well as a comparison and reference value to the Neural Network approach.

First of all, we have to perform some preparation steps similar to the Neural Network approach. We determine the most meaningful words of the descriptions from all vulnerabilities depending on the individual feature. Therefore, we choose to create our features based on a bag-of-words model that uses the existence of words in descriptions. The overall dictionary was created out of 72,000 descriptions resulting in a list of around 104,000 words. In an initial training round the meaningful words are collected automatically. Hence, the corpus of all vulnerability descriptions has to be cleansed from stop-words and we also use word stemming to resolve differences that arise by declination and conjugation. Afterwards the remaining words are ranked by importance, which is measured by the impact that an existence of a word in a vulnerability description has to the classification result. Therefore, we separated the previously cleansed descriptions based on the value of the attribute that should be predicted. So we create one set of descriptions that is correlated with a remote attack range and a different set that is correlated with a local attack range for example. Afterwards, we compute the term frequency and the inverse document frequency to find the most promising candidates that could indicate a special value of the attribute. We believe that the term frequency is a well suited method to find these candidates, since it is more likely that a word has a higher impact on the characteristic if it appears more often in the respective set of descriptions. Another observation was based on the differentiation of descriptions based on the attribute that should be investigated. We found that words with a high frequency in one group of descriptions and a low frequency in the other group of descriptions have a strong impact on the classification. This observation can also be generalized since we know of the effect of domain specific vocabulary and keyphrase extraction [3]. In natural languages we usually use a specific vocabulary to describe scenarios in a certain domain. Thus, it is possible to evaluate the utilized vocabulary to derive the domain and try to predict the meaning of the description. So we compared the term frequencies group wise and selected the words with the highest discrepancies. For example, words like "remote", "message", or "connection" have a strong indication that the attack range of a vulnerability is remote. Whereas, words, such as "crash" or "denial" suggest a violation of availability.

For the final classification we found out that using the 500 most significant words per attribute is sufficient to achieve satisfying results. This limitation also reduces the computation time dramatically. The approach of an automatically generated list of meaningful words has the benefit that the features are comprehensible and a manual verification is possible. The final features that are used within the Naive Bayes classifier are binary representations of the existence of the previously identified meaningful words. So we iterate through the list of our previously created set of meaningful words and flag the existence or the non-existence. These features are then passed to the Naive Bayes classifier to train the model.

The workflow for each description is similar to our Neural Network approach. First we prepare the descriptions by removing stop-words and applying word stemming. Afterwards we transform the individual words to numerical features, which are binary in the Naive Bayes approach. The transformation will produce a binary vector that represents the existence of each meaningful term. Finally we feed the vector into our classifier and receive the classification result in a textual format.

4   Classification Results

We used real descriptions of already published vulnerabilities for our experiment. So we gathered all available vulnerabilities with their descriptions and CVSS [7] attributes that have been published before the 1st of January 2016. Thus, the collection consists of 72,490 vulnerabilities with known CVSS attributes. We used 80% to train the algorithm and 20% of the descriptions as a testing set. The division between training and testing data is performed with a shuffling before the partition to let the algorithm train independent of the chosen training data. Because of this random arrangement in the data the test results may vary for each classifier creation. Thus we executed our classifier creation several times and used the average measurements for our evaluation. Additionally, we used 2,400 vulnerabilities that have been published in 2016 as a validation set to evaluate the trained algorithm. This allows us to test our classifiers more thoroughly on data that was definitely not used in any of the training steps. It is even more important in the Neural Network approach since the testing data will be used to adjust and fine-tune the parameters in each iteration of the network. So the descriptions of the validation set did not have any impact on the training of the Neural Network. When the network has to predict the selected attributes the result represents the accuracy that can also be achieved on newly discovered vulnerabilities.

Our CVSS attribute prediction focused on the most important attributes `attack range`, `availability`, `confidentiality`, and `integrity`. We built separate classifiers for each of these attributes. Furthermore, we implemented a classifier for a combination of confidentiality, integrity, and availability, which we refer to as `CIA` classifier. Finally, a classifier for the combination of all attributes was constructed as well. The combined classifiers were created with separate Neural Networks or Naive Bayes classifiers respectively. We combined the primary values of each attribute that is part of the combination and derived a list of possible value combinations for each attribute. Then, the combinations and the vulnerability descriptions are fed into our algorithms to build the combined classifiers.

Because of the different distributions of the attribute values in our data set, we had to adjust the training data to end up with a balanced set of descriptions for the selected attributes. For example the availability attribute divides the overall amount of around 72,000 vulnerabilities into 17,700 vulnerabilities with a `complete`, 31,900 vulnerabilities with a `partial`, and 22,800 vulnerabilities with a `unaffected` specification. The difference is even more significant in the attack range. More than 80% of the vulnerabilities can be exploited remotely. This imbalance results in a major problem of machine learning capabilities. Usually, the application of machine learning algorithms requires the precondition of a well-balanced set of training data. So, that the algorithm is not influenced by the pure majority of attribute characteristics during the classification process. Thus, we adjust our training set to be more balanced and reduce the number of considered vulnerabilities. For example, our availability classifier will not use all 72,000 descriptions, but it will use 17,700 descriptions from each of the characteristics, namely `complete`, `partial`, and `unaffected`, because of the before mentioned balancing method. This leads to the final training set of 53,100 vulnerabilities, which is well-balanced. Hence, the classification should only depend on the descriptions themselves and not on the difference in the amount.

Furthermore, our results mainly focus on the accuracy of the tested approaches, which slightly varies from the accuracy of a linear classifier that has to decide in a two-dimensional space. Therefore, our accuracy computation was derived from the Hamming score. The classifier accuracy is computed over all labels to correctly evaluate the effectiveness of our multi-label classification as also described in [14]. The formula to compute the accuracy is shown in Eq. 2.

$$CorrectlyClassified = \bigcap_{Label \in SelectedLabels} \{v \in Vulns | v.Label = result\}$$

$$(1)$$

$$ClassificationAccuracy = \frac{|CorrectlyClassified|}{|AllDescriptions|}$$

$$(2)$$

4.1 Naive Bayes

The first results and the initial impression, if it is possible to create an automatic classification approach for vulnerability descriptions was produced by a Naive Bayes classification. We chose the Naive Bayes approach because this method is commonly used for classification problems. Additionally, Naive Bayes could also be used to perform a multi-label classification, which was one of our requirements. We also believe that the Naive Bayes with its wide distribution is well suited to be a candidate to compare results from other approaches. We applied the Naive Bayes classification as it was described in Sect. 3.2.

So we created 4 separate classifiers that apply the Naive Bayes approach to each single attribute of our data set. The results are shown in Table 1. As we already expected the results of the training data are similar to the results of the test data. Because we randomly select the 20% test data at the beginning of each execution anew, there is no difference between test and training data. Furthermore, the validation set also produces similar results, which are also promising.

Table 1. Accuracy of the Naive Bayes approach

CVSS attribute	Train data	Test data	Validation data
Attack vector	89.9%	90.8%	92.3%
Availability	68.4%	68.0%	70.0%
Confidentiality	73.2%	72.4%	69.1%
Integrity	74.2%	73.6%	68.3%

Besides the mentioned results, the Naive Bayes classifier also offers an additional metric that describes the confidence of the classification result. We modified our algorithm to only perform the classification if the confidence value amounts to at least 0.75. The results that have been produced using the confidence do not differ significantly from the already listed findings in Table 1. We found that the accuracy of the attack vector classification drops by 2%, whereas the accuracy of the availability, confidentiality, and integrity classifiers increases by 3%. But the modified version omits 56, 419, 428, 321 vulnerabilities respectively. Nevertheless if the Naive Bayes approach would be used to automatically classify the descriptions in practice the confidence value should be included. If the confidence is not satisfying a manual classification should be considered to achieve accurate results.

4.2   Neural Networks

As it was already described in Sect. 3, we implemented a second approach that is based on Neural Networks. Our Neural Network was created with Tensorflow version 0.10[1] and Glove 1.2 [11]. Since we wanted to produce comparable results to our first approach we created different networks for the individual attributes. So, at first we also created one network for each of the four CVSS attributes. Each experiment was executed 10 times and we computed the accuracy according to the formula of Eq. 2. In the case of a single attribute the formula can be reduced to the fraction of correctly classified descriptions and overall number of descriptions. For the Neural Network we divided our input data set into training data and test data, similar to out Naive Bayes approach. We chose 80% of the data for the training set and the remaining 20% for the test data set. The difference is that the test data is already considered during the training of the model. We configured our network to run for 100 epochs. The network itself consists of 3 hidden layers with 1200, 700, and 50 units respectively. The classification results are illustrated in Table 2.

Table 2. Accuracy of the Neural Network approach

CVSS attribute	Train data	Test data	Validation data
Attack vector	99%	88.9%	80.3%
Availability	99%	80.7%	70.0%
Confidentiality	99%	81.1%	70.2%
Integrity	99%	81.9%	69.8%

The results also indicate the problem that arose with the Neural Network approach. As it was already mentioned in Sect. 3, we encountered the overfitting effect that often occurs with Neural Network approaches. The algorithm has

---

[1] https://www.tensorflow.org/.

been able to adjust too much to the training data. Thus, the high accuracy for the training data results in a poor accuracy of the test data. A commonly used method against overfitting is the utilization of a dropout rate. We described the working principle of the dropout rate in Sect. 3 and it is also illustrated in Fig. 1.

4.3 Combined Classifiers

We described the results for the two implemented classifiers in the previous sections and the comparison shows that both approaches are capable to classify vulnerabilities in consideration of single CVSS attributes. The two results for each of the attributes are comparable and therefore neither the Naive Bayes nor the Neural Network could achieve significantly better results than the other approach. But, our overall goal was to create an approach that is able to perform a detailed classification of multiple CVSS attributes. Therefore, we considered the attribute triple of confidentiality, integrity, and availability, which is commonly abbreviated as CIA. The results for the CIA-classification are illustrated in Table 3. We produced the results according to previously described methods. The major difference was to create the different value combinations of the attribute triples. Those combinations are considered to construct the possible labels for our data. Then, the workflow will be similar to the single-attribute based approach that was described earlier. So we trained our two classification methods on our training data set and applied the resulting models to the evaluation data set. The process was reiterated 10 times and the average accuracy was computed. Now the computation has to consider the individual number of Labels to compute the correct accuracy, which means we now use the MultiLabelAccuracy from Eq. 2.

Table 3. Accuracy of Naive Bayes and Neural Network on combined attributes

CVSS attribute combination	Naive Bayes	Neural Network
CIA test data	63.9%	71.2%
CIA validation data	51.6%	53.4%
Overall test data	61.4%	59.3%
Overall validation data	48.1%	49.1%

Moreover, the Overall classification includes the attack range in the process. Then we are able to produce predictions for availability, integrity, confidentiality, and attack range, which is usually sufficient for a deep analysis of the requirements and impacts of a vulnerability. The results are illustrated in Table 3. Finally, we can observe that it is possible to use machine learning techniques for an automated vulnerability classification to save processing time for vulnerability experts. In addition, we can see that the Neural Network performs slightly better in the combined classification.

5   Future Work

The presented approaches represent the first attempts to automatically classify vulnerabilities. This would allow a faster analysis of requirements and impacts of known vulnerabilities. Usually, the time period that is required to manually process the information from the description is crucial, since attackers could also use the information in this time frame. Therefore, we plan to continue this work to achieve still higher accuracy rates and enhance the classification process that it could be applied on public vulnerability databases, such as, National Vulnerability Database (NVD) [9], HPI-VDB [5]. The possibility of an automatic classification of incoming vulnerability descriptions should increase processing performance, because the experts still manually extract the attributes. Then, delays, as the delay of vulnerability CVE-2016-077, should not occur to often anymore.

Furthermore, we could use the trained models on public security forums to find discussions and insights about vulnerabilities. From time to time the community discusses information about vulnerabilities before the vulnerability itself becomes officially or publicly known. Thus, the attackers might have an advantage, since they could already interpret the content and benefit from the gained information. We believe that the trained models could be applied on natural language posts, discussions, or other texts. If a vulnerability classification was possible or if the used vocabulary is similar to the already known vocabulary from other vulnerability descriptions, it is very likely that the topic of the discussion or the text is a vulnerability. Finally, one could use the classification results to evaluate if the discussed vulnerability describes an already known vulnerability or if the description belongs to an unknown vulnerability, which increases the importance considerably.

6   Conclusion

This paper describes an approach to deal with delay in vulnerability classification that is caused by manual interaction. The problem arises because the report about a newly detected vulnerability contains human readable information about the vulnerability. This information will be converted to the vulnerability description in natural language. Nevertheless most of the analytic tools require formal attributes to determine the requirements and the impact of the vulnerability. We propose an automatic approach to classify vulnerabilities and their natural language descriptions into those formal attributes. Therefore, the first goal was to investigate the feasibility of an automated approach and secondly evaluate the accuracy. Thus, we implemented two different approaches that are capable of an automated classification. We used Naive Bayes [12] as one approach, since it is a widely distributed method to solve classification problems. For the other approach we rely on Neural Networks, as modern natural language processing systems utilize Neural Networks as well.

At first, we identified the most important characteristics of vulnerabilities, namely the CVSS attributes `availability`, `integrity`, `confidentiality`, and

attack range. Then we created our training, testing, and validation data sets and trained our model on the vulnerability description. Both approaches required some additional preprocessing steps, as it was already described in Sect. 3. The application of the Naive Bayes classification has the advantage that it could directly work with natural language, whereas the Neural Network required one additional transformation step. After the training we evaluated the two approaches on the test data set. In addition to the test data set we also created one validation data set, since the Neural Network approach also uses the test data to train the model or adjust the parameters. So the most important evaluation metric is the accuracy of the validation data set, since it was not used during the training procedure. We found that the automated classification is possible and the accuracy for single attributes, which was around 70% to 90% depending on the attribute and the data set, is also satisfying. The important metric of the combined attributes results in lower accuracy, but it was still possible to achieve an accuracy of 60% to 70% on the test data and around 50% on the validation data. Since those attribute combinations accumulate to more than 100 possible combinations we believe that an accuracy of around 50% is an acceptable result. Furthermore it turned out that the result between test data and validation data differ for both methods. This fact could also indicate that the language of vulnerability descriptions in those sets differ as well. It could be possible that the vulnerabilities that have been published later use a different style to describe the impact of the vulnerability. Nevertheless the possibility to benefit from an automated classification approach has been shown.

References

1. Bozorgi, M., Saul, L.K., Savage, S., Voelker, G.M.: Beyond heuristics: learning to classify vulnerabilities and predict exploits. In: Proceedings of the 16th ACM SIGKDD International Conference on Knowledge Discovery and Data Mining, pp. 105–114. ACM (2010)
2. Carnegie Mellon University: Cert/cc vulnerability report form (2017). Accessed 12 Mar 2017
3. Frank, E., Paynter, G.W., Witten, I.H., Gutwin, C., Nevill-Manning, C.G.: Domain-specific keyphrase extraction. In: 16th International Joint Conference on Artificial Intelligence (IJCAI 99), vol. 2, pp. 668–673. Morgan Kaufmann Publishers Inc., San Francisco (1999)
4. Franklin, J., Wergin, C., Booth, H.: CVSS implementation guidance. Nat. Inst. Stand. Technol. NISTIR-7946 (2014). http://nvlpubs.nist.gov/nistpubs/ir/2014/NIST.IR.7946.pdf
5. Hasso Plattner Institute: HPI vulnerability database (2017). Accessed 26 Mar 2017
6. Hein, D., Saiedian, H.: Predicting attack prone software components using repository mined change metrics. In: Proceedings of the 2nd International Conference on Information Systems Security and Privacy, ICISSP, vol. 1, pp. 554–563 (2016)
7. Mell, P., Scarfone, K., Romanosky, S.: Common vulnerability scoring system. Secur. Priv. IEEE **4**(6), 85–89 (2006)
8. Mitre Corporation: CPE - Common Platform Enumeration (2017). Accessed 11 Mar 2017

9. National Institute of Standards and Technology: National vulnerability database (2017). Accessed 22 Feb 2017
10. Neuhaus, S., Zimmermann, T., Holler, C., Zeller, A.: Predicting vulnerable software components. In: Proceedings of the 14th ACM Conference on Computer and Communications Security, pp. 529–540. ACM (2007)
11. Pennington, J., Socher, R., Manning, C.D.: GloVe: global vectors for word representation. In: Empirical Methods in Natural Language Processing (EMNLP), pp. 1532–1543 (2014)
12. Russell, S.J., Norvig, P., Canny, J.F., Malik, J.M., Edwards, D.D.: Artificial Intelligence: A Modern Approach, vol. 2. Prentice Hall, Upper Saddle River (2003)
13. Scandariato, R., Walden, J., Hovsepyan, A., Joosen, W.: Predicting vulnerable software components via text mining. IEEE Trans. Softw. Eng. **40**(10), 993–1006 (2014)
14. Schapire, R.E., Singer, Y.: Improved boosting algorithms using confidence-rated predictions. Mach. Learn. **37**(3), 297–336 (1999)
15. Schumacher, M., Haul, C., Hurler, M., Buchmann, A.: Data mining in vulnerability databases. Comput. Sci., 12–24 (2000)
16. Text Fixer: Common English Words List (2017). Accessed 11 Mar 2017
17. Wijayasekara, D., Manic, M., McQueen, M.: Vulnerability identification and classification via text mining bug databases. In: IECON 2014–40th Annual Conference of the IEEE Industrial Electronics Society, pp. 3612–3618. IEEE (2014)
18. Zhang, S., Ou, X., Caragea, D.: Predicting cyber risks through national vulnerability database. Inf. Secur. J. Glob. Perspect. **24**(4–6), 194–206 (2015)

A Semantic Approach to Frequency Based Anomaly Detection of Insider Access in Database Management Systems

Muhammad Imran Khan[1(✉)], Barry O'Sullivan[1], and Simon N. Foley[2]

[1] Insight Centre for Data Analytics, Department of Computer Science,
University College Cork, Cork, Ireland
{imran.khan,barry.osullivan}@insight-centre.org
[2] IMT Atlantique, LabSTICC, Université Bretagne Loire, Rennes, France
simon.foley@imt-atlantique.fr

Abstract. Timely detection of an insider attack is prevalent among challenges in database security. Research on anomaly-based database intrusion detection systems has received significant attention because of its potential to detect zero-day insider attacks. Such approaches differ mainly in their construction of normative behavior of (insider) role/user. In this paper, a different perspective on the construction of normative behavior is presented, whereby normative behavior is captured instead from the perspective of the DBMS itself. Using techniques from Statistical Process Control, a model of DBMS-oriented normal behavior is described that can be used to detect frequency based anomalies in database access. The approach is evaluated using a synthetic dataset and we also demonstrate this DBMS-oriented profile can be transformed into the more traditional role-oriented profiles.

Keywords: Anomaly detection · Database intrusion detection
Insider threats · Cybersecurity

1 Introduction

Database Management Systems (DBMS) is one of the essential elements of an organization that enables management and storage of personal data. However, management and storage of such data raises privacy concerns. As has been routinely demonstrated in the popular press, a data breach can cause an organization to suffer from damages in-terms of reputation and financial loss, when an individual's privacy is compromised. Data breaches can be caused by an external attacker (outsider attack) or an internal attacker (insider attack). Many security defenses have been proposed to deal with outsider attack, including host-based access controls, intrusion detection systems, and access control mechanisms.

Internal attacks, on the other hand, are caused by an insider, a member of an organization who is authorized to access a range of data and services. It is

© Springer International Publishing AG, part of Springer Nature 2018
N. Cuppens et al. (Eds.): CRiSIS 2017, LNCS 10694, pp. 18–28, 2018.
https://doi.org/10.1007/978-3-319-76687-4_2

reported that malicious insiders are the cause of the costliest cybercrimes [1], and in one study 89% of respondent organizations were vulnerable to insider attacks [3]. A further study reports that a significant level (43%) of data exfiltration was caused by insiders and half of which was intentional [2]. A challenge in insider attack detection is that they often go unnoticed for months and years [4]. An Intrusion Detection System (IDS) can play a role in detecting insider attacks. Misuse detection systems (misuse-based IDSs) are helpful in detecting previously known attacks by looking for well-known attack patterns [10]. Anomaly detection systems (anomaly-based IDSs) [7,11], on the other hand, have the potential to detect previously unknown, or zero-day, attacks [15] by looking for deviation from normal behavior. We are interested in the latter to detect insider attacks.

In this paper, we are interested in detecting *frequent observation attacks* by insider(s). A frequent observation attack is an attack whereby an insider, or group of insiders, has made numerous malicious accesses to same record in the DBMS. Real-world examples of frequent observation attacks [5,16] report insiders (hospital staff) looking up the medical records of patients in the public-eye. In the context of frequent observation attacks, determination of an exact attack pattern before the attack is carried out is a challenging task. The frequent observation attack does not follow a concrete pattern, as an attacker can devise multiple ways to access a record by constructing same effective query in different ways. Our hypothesis is that an anomaly-based IDS can be used to detect such attacks. In an anomaly-based IDS, a *profile* of a user or a role is constructed. This profile is an approximation of normative behavior of a user or a role. The effectiveness of an anomaly-based IDS relies on what behavior is captured in a user's or role's profile. Existing anomaly-based IDS, while constructing user/role profiles, misses aspects of user's behavior that enable the detection of frequent observation attacks thus existing techniques are unable to detect frequent observation attacks carried out by insiders.

In this paper, we propose the notion of *DBMS-oriented profiles*, as compared to traditional *role/user-oriented profiles*. The goal of constructing a DBMS-oriented profile is to capture an approximate normal behavior of the DBMS, whereas the goal of role/user-oriented profile is to have an approximation of normative behavior of a user or a role.

The majority of anomaly-based IDSs consider *syntax-centric* features when constructing role/user-oriented profiles [6,12,17]. Syntax-centric features are based on syntax of the SQL query, and include but are not limited to, the attributes in a projection clause, the relations queried, the attributes in a selection clause, and the type of SQL command. However, as mentioned above, a query can be articulated in many different ways to get the same result and this is a major drawback of anomaly-based IDSs based on syntax-centric features. Thus we are interested in constructing DBMS-oriented profiles by considering *data-centric* features that include the data returned in the response to a query. Data-centric features include, but are not limited to, the amount of data returned or any other statistics related to the resultant data. Profiles constructed by considering data-centric features can be referred to as *semantic approaches*.

In order to detect frequent observation attacks by insiders, we propose an anomaly-based IDS that constructs DBMS-oriented profiles by considering data-centric features that are based on the frequency of records being accessed. Thus, we refer to the constructed profiles as *data-centric DBMS-oriented* profiles. Statistical Process Control (SPC) [14] is used in the construction of our model. We also demonstrate that one can transform the data-centric DBMS-oriented profile construction model into a *data-centric Role-oriented* profile construction model. The paper is organized as follows. Section 2 describes the related work. Section 3 outlines the proposed model, followed by the discussion in Sect. 4. We demonstrate the model in Sects. 5 and 6 concludes the paper.

2   Related Work

Several anomaly-based IDS construct user/role-oriented profiles [6,8,11,17]. As mentioned above, most anomaly-based IDSs construct user/role-oriented profiles by considering syntax-centric features [8]. However, there are few anonmaly-based IDS that construct user/role-oriented profiles by considering context-centric features [6] and data-centric features [13] (sometimes referred to as result-centric in the literature). In the case of syntax-centric features, the constructed profiles are based on the syntax of the SQL query, for example, the attributes in a projection clause, the relations queried, the attributes in a selection clause, or the type of SQL command. In case of data/result-centric features, the constructed profiles are based on the data returned in response to a SQL query. For example, one could use the amount of information returned in response to a query or the returned values of attributes to generate profiles. In the case of context-centric features, profiles are based on information related to the context of a query. For example, the time of access or the time at which the query was made, the user ID of the person making the query, or the number of queries made in a specified time period. There are techniques in literature that consider a combination of data-centric, context-centric and syntax-centric features to construct profiles [6,17].

The approach in [17] considers syntax-centric and data-centric features to construct profiles during the training phase from logs containing user/role activities. The proposed approach transforms a SQL query into a SQL query signature/abstraction called a *quadruplet Q* which is composed of the following elements $Q(C, P_R, P_A, S_R)$: C is the command type; P_R and P_A are lists of accessed relations and attributes, respectively; S_R represents the amount of selected information from a relation. Naive Bayesian classifier was used to predict the role of a user submitting queries while multi-labeling classifier was used in case of an overlap of roles that results in more than one role. In the case where there are no roles, *COWEB* clustering algorithm was employed. An approach considering data-centeric features is proposed [13] where it was argued that syntax-centric features of a query alone are a poor discriminator of intent. Syntactically different queries can give the same result while syntactically similar queries can yield different results, resulting in an increase in false positives and false negatives respectively [13]. User profiles are user clusters that are specified in terms of an *S-Vector* that provides a statistical summary of results (tuples/rows) from columns accessed. An S-Vector represents statistical measurements for queried attributes in the relation. In the case of numeric attributes, the S-Vector consists of maximum value, minimum value, standard deviation, median and mean for each numeric attribute in the query. In the case of non-numeric attributes, the S-Vector consists of the total count of values, along with the number of distinct values. In the detection phase, if the query belongs to the cluster then it is considered normal, otherwise it is considered anomalous.

Existing anomaly-based IDSs can certainly be used to detect individual queries or query sequences that are different from normal (similar queries or similar query sequences), however, they are unable to detect frequent observation attacks by insiders in their user/role-oriented profiles: queries made to access records in frequent observation attacks by insiders appear as normal queries.

In this paper, we propose the construction of DBMS-oriented profiles that capture the frequency of records being accessed in profiles of normal behavior. Compared to existing approaches in literature, the proposed DBMS-oriented approach has the advantage that anomalies can be detected if multiple roles or users are accessing the same record while individually they are not raising any alarm.

3   DBMS-Oriented Model for Normative Behavior

In this section, we propose a model for DBMS-oriented profiles of normal behavior. Let $\mathbb{D}$ represent a relational database with a table $\mathbb{T}$. For ease of exposition, we assume that each record/tuple $\mathbf{r}$ in $\mathbb{T}$ is unique. The proposed approach consists of a learning phase (alternatively known as training phase) and a detection phase. In the learning phase, a DBMS-oriented normal profile is constructed by determining a range for the number of times records are accessed in $\mathbb{T}$. A time period $\mathbf{t}$ is user-defined which is dependent on the nature of the target application.

For example, in the case of an hospital where a record of a specific patient is queried frequently compared to an electricity billing system where a specific record might be queried twice or thrice in a six months period. For the purposes of this paper we assume that the time-period is user-defined.

We wish to determine the number of times a record (or any attribute of the record) is queried in the time period $\mathbf{t}$. Let $\mathcal{F}_i$ be a numeric counter for the ith record $\mathbf{r}_i$ in $\mathbb{T}$. When the ith record, or any attribute value in the ith record, is accessed then the value of $\mathcal{F}_i$ is incremented by one. We store these values of $\mathcal{F}_i$ for each day. The decision of selecting the value of time period $\mathbf{t}$ is left on the organization and the nature of the application where the mechanism is deployed. For the purposes of exposition, we set the time period to 24 h. We collect values of $\mathcal{F}_i$ over the time period in order to get an approximation of the times a record is accessed and this provides a training set. The collection of the values of $\mathcal{F}_i$ can be done for a longer duration (for multiple days).

In this paper, we assume that the frequency at which each record is accessed in table $\mathbb{T}$ is uniformly distributed. However, in the case where the frequency at which each record is accessed in table $\mathbb{T}$ is not uniformly distributed then one variant of the model we are proposing can be to collect values of $\mathcal{F}_i$ for a couple of days, then taking an average of these values over the number of days to get an approximation of the number of time a record is accessed. This can be one variant of the model we are proposing in this paper, however to present our basic model we exclude this variant of the model.

We call the set of values generated for the training data-set (learning phase) $\mathcal{L}$, and $\mathcal{L}_i$ is the frequency value of the ith record in the training data-set. Here, an outlier is a value of $\mathcal{F}_i$ that is significantly different from the rest of the values of $\mathcal{F}_i$. The aim of the training phase is to have a fair approximation of normal behavior from this training set $\mathcal{L}_i$. It is possible that we may miss behaviors (values of $\mathcal{F}_i$), but it is also possible that we may include those behaviors that are unusual and infrequent (unusual values for $\mathcal{F}_i$) that we call outliers. Thus, in order to determine the spectrum of normal values for $\mathcal{F}_i$, we consider two scenarios, one that is free from outliers and the other that is susceptible to (with) outliers.

3.1   With-Outlier Scenario

In this scenario, where data is influenced by outliers, Median Absolution Deviation (MAD) is used to determine the spectrum of normal values for $\mathcal{F}_i$. MAD is based on the median and this is typically preferred to other measures of central tendency in the case of outliers. Let $\mathbf{m}(\mathcal{L})$ denote the median value for training set $\mathcal{L}$. Let $\mathbf{m}_{AD}(\mathcal{L})$ denote the median absolute deviation for $\mathcal{L}$.

Statistical Process Control (SPC) [14] originated from performance monitoring in manufacturing processes. Control charts are at the heart of SPC and provide the history of a running process about which decision are made. Different types of control charts have been studied in the literature. We use Shewhart chart [14] for the outlier-free scenario. Shewhart charts rely on the mean and standard deviation for their specification limits (upper and lower specification limits). For training data with-outliers we generate a modified version of a control chart using median and median absolute deviation as upper/lower specification limits. The modified control chart is generated for each record. A sample modified control chart is shown in Fig. 3. In the detection phase, for this scenario, the counter $\mathcal{F}_i$ for each record starts with the value zero at the beginning of a day and is then reset to zero at the end of the day. Every time a record $\mathbf{r}_i$ or any attribute in the record is accessed, the value of the associated counter with that record $\mathcal{F}_i$ is incremented by one. The values of $\mathcal{F}_i$ are plotted on the modified control chart. For with-outlier scenario, we chose upper specification limits and lower specification limit $+2\mathbf{m}_{AD}(\mathcal{L})$ and $-2\mathbf{m}_{AD}(\mathcal{L})$, respectively. Thus, any value of $\mathcal{F}_i$ above and below $+2\mathbf{m}_{AD}(\mathcal{L})$ and $-2\mathbf{m}_{AD}(\mathcal{L})$, respectively, are an indication of an anomaly.

3.2 Outlier-Free Scenario

For the outlier-free scenario, the mean μ and standard deviation σ are used to determine the upper/lower specification limits. We have functions $\mu()$ and $\sigma()$ that compute the mean and standard deviation, respectively. Thus $\mu(\mathcal{L})$ and $\sigma(\mathcal{L})$ gives us the mean and standard deviation for $\mathcal{L}$, respectively. As compared to the with-outlier scenario, in this scenario, we use mean and standard deviation, instead of median and median absolute deviation. A control chart is generated for each record, sample chart is shown in Fig. 2. Similar to the above scenario, in the detection phase for this scenario, the counter $\mathcal{F}_i$, starts with the value zero at the beginning of the day and is reset to zero for each record at the end of the day. Value for $\mathcal{F}_i$ are plotted for each day on the control chart. For upper specification limit and lower specification limit, we chose $+3\sigma(\mathcal{L})$ and $-3\sigma(\mathcal{L})$, respectively. Values of $\mathcal{F}_i$ above and below $+3\sigma(\mathcal{L})$ and $-3\sigma(\mathcal{L})$, respectively, are an indication of an anomaly.

In both scenarios, the anomalies can be further inspected by a security officer. Reporting anomalies and anomaly response is a separate body of research [9] thus details regarding anomaly response are out of the scope of this work. The aim of the detection mechanism is to detect records that are frequently queried as appeared in incidents [5,16]. However, the proposed approach also enables the detection of records that are less frequently queried as compared to what is normal/usual. As a use-case for instance, it may be the scenario in a hospital where a doctor/nurse missed a daily check up of a patient.

In the above sections, an approach for modeling normative behavior of DBMS is presented. The DBMS-oriented profiles initially contains specification limits computed using training data-set for instance in outlier-free scenario the DBMS-oriented profiles contains the values for $\mu(\mathcal{L})$, $+3\sigma(\mathcal{L})$ and $-3\sigma(\mathcal{L})$. In the detection phase, control chart of each record is added to DBMS-oriented profile. In other words, the value for $\mathcal{F}$ for each record is added to DBMS-oriented profile. The reason to do so is to evolve the initially constructed DBMS-oriented profile. Let says, the values for $\mathcal{F}$ for a ith record is results in too many false positives thus one could re-compute the specification limits for i^{th} record by looking at the past values of $\mathcal{F}$, plotted on control chart, for this record.

3.3 Translating DBMS-Oriented Model into Role-Oriented Model

The above DBMS-oriented profile model does not consider roles, that is, which role is accessing the record. The advantage of the DBMS-oriented model is when several roles/users (employees) are accessing the same record, as in [5,16], it is easier to detect anomalous behavior of the collaboration. In other words, the DBMS-oriented model enables detection of collaborative frequent observation attacks. However, a fine-grained role-oriented profile construction model can be derived from the above model. The role-oriented construction of normative behavior can alternatively be considered the traditional approach to the construction of normal profiles.

With the DBMS-oriented construction of a profile, $\mathcal{F}$ provides a counter for each record. However in a role-oriented approach, each record $\mathbf{r}_i$ has several counters $\mathcal{F}_i^{role}$, one for each role. For example, $\mathcal{F}_i^{doctor}$ gives a count of accesses to record i by a user in the *doctor* role.

In the training phase, a normal profile is constructed by determining a range for the number of times records are accessed by a specific role, for instance it is determined how frequently the role *doctor* accesses $\mathbf{r}_3$ in $\mathbb{T}$. Similar to the above-mentioned DBMS-oriented profile construction approach, a time period $\mathbf{t}$ is defined. The number of times a record (or any of the attribute in the record) is queried in time period $\mathbf{t}$ by each role is determined. Every time a record or any attribute value in the record is queried, the value of $\mathcal{F}$ is incremented by one. The profiles are constructed in a similar manner as mentioned in the DBMS-oriented approach, with the difference in the DBMS-oriented profile construction approach is having a control chart for each record, however, in this approach a separate control chart for each role for every record is generated.

The detection phase is similar to the detection phase in the DBMS-oriented approach. For the with-outlier scenario, values of $\mathcal{F}_i^{role}$ above and below $+2\mathbf{m}_{AD}$ and $-2\mathbf{m}_{AD}$, respectively, are an indication of an anomaly and in outlier-free scenario, values of $\mathcal{F}_i^{role}$ above and below $+3\sigma$ and -3σ, respectively, are an indication of an anomaly.

4 Discussion

In this paper, we introduced the notion of DBMS-oriented profiles. The presented DBMS-oriented models of normative behavior is easy to be integrated with existing systems because of their simplicity, as well as they can compliment other detection systems. The proposed models enables the detection of frequent observation attacks, where these attacks can be carried out in isolation, that is, when an insider carries out the attack or collectively where several insiders carry out the attack. It is possible that these insider may not be collaborating while accessing a particular record with malicious intentions. Another base of this work is the utilization of control charts from SPC to build our model. SPC was originally proposed with its application in manufacturing industries where it was used to observe if the process is working as expected during production in order to detect defective products. SPC is a analytical decision making tool that enables monitoring the quality of the processes.

In SPC, measurements are computed from samples (that are subset of item produce/manufactured). These measurements are then used in establishing specification limits, that are, upper specification limits and lower specification limits. In our case, the samples are the values of the number of time each record is accessed. As mentioned in above section, control charts are the heart of SPC. Control charts are graphs that show measurements and variation among the measurements, that are plotted against predetermined specification limits, during a specific time period. This time period is the time during which the process was being observed. The purpose of control charts is to monitor processes, and the resultant information by monitoring the processes is then used to make improvements in-terms of quality. In our case, we computed specification limits using training data-sets and the measurements plotted against these predetermined specification limits are the values of number of times a specific record is accessed in a certain time period. Control charts are of various types, however, we utilized Shewhart chart, and a modified version of Shewhart chart in which median and median absolute deviation is used to compute specification limits.

Record (r)	Patient ID	First name	Last name	Date of birth	Gender	Room	Diagnosis
r_1	7301	Robert	Green	26-03-1964	Male	829	Diabetes
r_2	7302	Melvin	Allen	11-06-1972	Male	893	Flu
r_3	7303	Betty	Crain	03-09-1968	Female	824	Heart Disease
r_4	7304	Jonathan	Moro	20-11-1996	Male	854	Leg Fracture
r_5	7305	Nora	Vargas	17-08-1974	Female	890	Flu
.	.	.	.	.	.	.	.
.	.	.	.	.	.	.	.
.	.	.	.	.	.	.	.
.	.	.	.	.	.	.	.

Fig. 1. Sample table $\mathbb{T}$ from patients database.

In the detection phase of our approach, the graphical representation, in-terms of control chart, shows the pattern of access to a record over a horizon of time give us insights that can be subsequently be used to update the specification limits for a particular record. The concept is analogous to a feedback loops in control systems where feedback loops considers the output of the system thus enabling the system to fine-tune its performance. For example, lets say the mean, the upper specification limit and the lower specification limit for record r_7 were 33.5, 49.25 and 17.75, respectively. In the detection phase, the value of the number of times r_7 was accessed in one day was plotted each day up-till 30 days. After 30 days, a pattern emerged that the value for the number of times r_7 accessed was always above 40.25. Using this insight, specification limits for r_7 can be re-calculated using the values of number of times r_7 was accessed each day. Thus this approach of monitoring the past behavior even in detection phase enables to fine-tune existing DBMS-oriented profile.

5 Detecting Anomalies

In order to evaluate our work, we generated a synthetic training data-sets that are training data-set for the outlier-free scenario $\mathcal{L}^{OF}$, for the outlier-free scenario $\mathcal{L}^{WO}$, for the with-outlier scenario when roles are considered $\mathcal{L}^{OFR}_{RoleName}$

and for the with-outlier scenario when roles are considered $\mathcal{L}_{RoleName}^{WOR}$. The synthetic training data-sets consisted values for number of times each record in table $\mathbb{T}$ was accessed each day for the duration of 10 days. Where the patient record table $\mathbb{T}$ in the scenario of a hospital with roles including specialist, house officer, consultant, nurse, IT administrator, clinical specialist, and medical record clerk was generated with random attribute values. The sample table is shown in Fig. 1. Table $\mathbb{T}$ consisted of 100 randomly generated records, thus 100 values were contained in each training data-set.

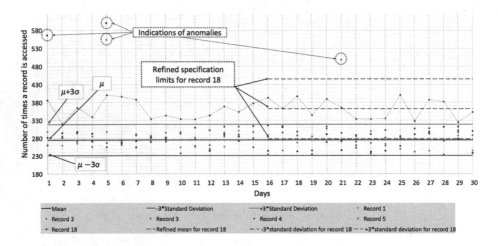

Fig. 2. A control chart for outlier-free training data is shown. Additionally, anomalies are indicated in red circles. (Color figure online)

We first demonstrate how an anomaly is detected for DBMS-oriented model without considering roles. We carried out experiment in order to construct an example DBMS-oriented normal profile for $\mathbb{T}$. The computed mean μ, +3*standard deviation $(+3 * \sigma)$ and −3*standard deviation $(-3 * \sigma)$ for $\mathcal{L}^{OF}$ are 274.7 , 318.4 and 231.2 respectively. We carried attacks where frequent observation accesses were made to specific records.

The control chart in Fig. 2 is generated with outlier-free training data-set $\mathcal{L}^{OF}$. Access to records 1 to 5 and record 18 for 30 days are shown for the purpose of demonstration in this paper. It can be seen that record 4 is accessed more than usual on day 1 and day 5 and record 3 is accessed more than usual on day 5 and 21. In the case of record 18, it is observed from days 1 to 15 that the number of times record 18 is accessed is above 330 or above $+3 * \sigma(\mathcal{L}^{OF})$. Refined specification limits for record 18 are computed by looking at the past behavior of record for days 1 to 15 provided that this behavior is inspected by the security officer and is concluded as a safe behavior. The refined specification limits for record 18 are $\mu(\mathcal{L}_{record18}^{OF}) = 361.6$, $+3 * \sigma(\mathcal{L}_{record18}^{OF}) = 444.9$ and $-3 * \sigma(\mathcal{L}_{record18}^{OF}) = 278.2$. These refined specification limits are used for record 18 from day 16 and on-wards.

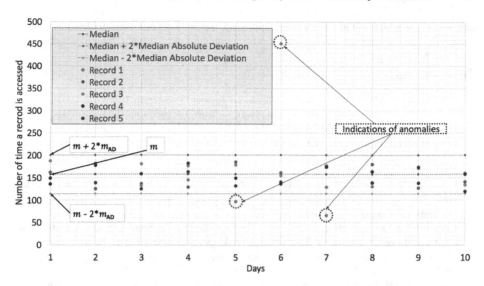

Fig. 3. A control chart for the role of *medical record clerk* is shown. The training data in this scenario is with-outliers.

Figure 3 show the control chart, for role of *Medical Record Clerk* in the with-outlier scenario. The control chart in Fig. 3 is generated with training data-set having outliers $\mathcal{L}_{MedicalRecordClerk}^{WOR}$ thus median and median absolute deviation are used for the determination of Upper Specification Limit and Lower Specification Limit. The computed median $\mathbf{m}$ and median absolute deviation $\mathbf{m}_{AD}$ for role of *Medical Record Clerk* in the with-outlier scenario are 157.5 and 43, respectively. We carried attacks where frequent observation accesses were made to specific records from the role *Medical Record Clerk*. Figure 3 shows anomalous access to record 3 on day 5 and day 6, record 1 on day 7.

6   Conclusions and Future Work

This paper introduced a novel notion of DBMS-oriented model of normative behavior for construction of normal profiles that considers data-centric features. The construction of the profiles utilizes Control Charts from Statistical Process Control as a way to detect anomalies. We considered two scenarios, in the first scenario, the training data contains outlier and in the second scenario the training data is free from outliers. The initial experiments have demonstrated the effectiveness of the proposed approach in the detection of frequent observation attacks as well as anomalies introduced due to human negligence/errors (that is the case where the doctor/nurse missed a the daily check up of a patient). It is also demonstrated, in the paper, that the proposed model for the construction of DBMS-oriented profiles can be transformed into a model for construction of role-oriented profiles. In future work, we plan to further evaluate these models using non-synthetic systems.

Acknowledgments. This work was supported by Science Foundation Ireland under grant SFI/12/RC/2289.

References

1. 2015 cost of cyber crime: global. Technical report, Ponemon Institute (2015)
2. Grand Theft Data. Data exfiltration study: actors, tactics, and detection. Technical report, Intel Security and McAfee (2015)
3. Insider threat report: insider threat security statistics, vormetric. Technical report, Vormetric (2015)
4. 2016 data breach investigations report. Technical report, Verizon (2016)
5. Carr, J.: Breach of britney spears patient data reported, SC magazine for IT security professionals (2008). https://www.scmagazine.com/breach-of-britney-spears-patient-data-reported/article/554340/
6. Costante, E., den Hartog, J., Petkovic, M., Etalle, S., Pechenizkiy, M.: A white-box anomaly-based framework for database leakage detection. J. Inf. Secur. Appl. **32**, 27–46 (2017). http://www.sciencedirect.com/science/article/pii/S221421261630 2629
7. Forrest, S., Hofmeyr, S.A., Somayaji, A., Longstaff, T.A.: A sense of self for unix processes. In: Proceedings 1996 IEEE Symposium on Security and Privacy, pp. 120–128, May 1996
8. Hussain, S.R., Sallam, A.M., Bertino, E.: Detanom: detecting anomalous database transactions by insiders. In: Proceedings of the 5th ACM Conference on Data and Application Security and Privacy, CODASPY 2015, pp. 25–35. ACM, New York (2015). https://doi.org/10.1145/2699026.2699111
9. Kamra, A., Bertino, E., Nehme, R.: Responding to anomalous database requests. In: Jonker, W., Petković, M. (eds.) SDM 2008. LNCS, vol. 5159, pp. 50–66. Springer, Heidelberg (2008). https://doi.org/10.1007/978-3-540-85259-9_4
10. Kemmerer, R.A., Vigna, G.: Intrusion detection: a brief history and overview. Computer **35**(4), 27–30 (2002)
11. Khan, M.I., Foley, S.N.: Detecting anomalous behavior in DBMS logs. In: Cuppens, F., Cuppens, N., Lanet, J.-L., Legay, A. (eds.) CRiSIS 2016. LNCS, vol. 10158, pp. 147–152. Springer, Cham (2017). https://doi.org/10.1007/978-3-319-54876-0_12
12. Lee, S.Y., Low, W.L., Wong, P.Y.: Learning fingerprints for a database intrusion detection system. In: Gollmann, D., Karjoth, G., Waidner, M. (eds.) ESORICS 2002. LNCS, vol. 2502, pp. 264–279. Springer, Heidelberg (2002). https://doi.org/10.1007/3-540-45853-0_16
13. Mathew, S., Petropoulos, M., Ngo, H.Q., Upadhyaya, S.: A data-centric approach to insider attack detection in database systems. In: Jha, S., Sommer, R., Kreibich, C. (eds.) RAID 2010. LNCS, vol. 6307, pp. 382–401. Springer, Heidelberg (2010). https://doi.org/10.1007/978-3-642-15512-3_20
14. Oakland, J.S.: Statistical Process Control, 6th edn. Routledge, London (2011)
15. Pieczul, O., Foley, S.N.: Runtime detection of zero-day vulnerability exploits in contemporary software systems. In: Ranise, S., Swarup, V. (eds.) DBSec 2016. LNCS, vol. 9766, pp. 347–363. Springer, Cham (2016). https://doi.org/10.1007/978-3-319-41483-6_24
16. Report C: 27 suspended for Clooney file peek (2007). http://edition.cnn.com/2007/SHOWBIZ/10/10/clooney.records/index.html?eref=ew
17. Sallam, A., Fadolalkarim, D., Bertino, E., Xiao, Q.: Data and syntax centric anomaly detection for relational databases. Wiley Interdisc. Rev. Data Mining Knowl. Discov. **6**(6), 231–239 (2016). https://doi.org/10.1002/widm.1195

Towards a Security Event Data Taxonomy

Gustavo Gonzalez-Granadillo[1], José Rubio-Hernán[2],
and Joaquin Garcia-Alfaro[2(✉)]

[1] Atos Research & Innovation, Cybersecurity Laboratory,
C/ Pere IV, 291-307, 08020 Barcelona, Spain
gustavo.gonzalez@atos.net
[2] Institut Mines-Télécom, Télécom SudParis, CNRS UMR 5157 SAMOVAR,
9 Rue Charles Fourier, 91011 Evry, France
{jose.rubio_herman,joaquin.garcia_alfaro}@telecom-sudparis.eu

Abstract. The information required to build appropriate impact models depends directly on the nature of the system. The information dealt by health care systems, for instance, is particularly different from the information obtained by energy, telecommunication, transportation, or water supply systems. It is therefore important to properly classify the data of security events according to the nature of the system. This paper proposes an event data classification based on four main aspects: (i) the system's criticality, i.e., critical vs. non-critical; (ii) the geographical location of the target system, i.e., internal vs. external; (iii) the time at which the information is obtained and used by the attacker i.e., a priory vs. a posteriori; and (iv) the nature of the data, i.e., logical vs. physical. The ultimate goal of the proposed taxonomy is to help organizations in the assessment of their assets and events.

Keywords: Security event taxonomy · Data classification
Risk assessment · Countermeasure selection

1 Introduction

Visualization models have been widely proposed to help operators in the evaluation and selection of security countermeasures against cyber attacks [1–3]. Most of the approaches rely on statistical data and expert knowledge to fill the parameters composing the model. A great level of accuracy and detail is required to compute the impact of malicious actions detected on the target system and therefore, to determine the most suitable solution.

Geometrical models [4–6] have been previously proposed to represent graphically the impact of cyber security events (e.g., attacks, countermeasures), as geometrical instances (e.g., polygons, cubes, prisms). The approaches consider information of many kinds (e.g., logical, physical, internal, external, etc.) to fill up the model and compute the shape and size of the cyber event. As a result, it is possible to determine the impact (e.g., size, coverage, residual risk, collateral damage) of single and/or multiple events occurring on the target system through geometrical operations (e.g., union, intersection).

© Springer International Publishing AG, part of Springer Nature 2018
N. Cuppens et al. (Eds.): CRiSIS 2017, LNCS 10694, pp. 29–45, 2018.
https://doi.org/10.1007/978-3-319-76687-4_3

One issue that confronts the impact assessment of cyber security events is the identification of the type of information required to feed the model. Each system provides information according to the nature of the event (e.g., energy system provides data about power consumption, blackouts, voltage, etc.; Dam systems provide data related to the level of water, turbidity, volume, etc.). It is therefore important to properly classify the data of security events according to the nature of the system.

This paper is an attempt towards a security event data taxonomy. We propose to classify the information of events based on the criticality of the system (critical vs. non-critical), the time at which the information is obtained (a priory vs. a posteriori), the geographical location of the target system (internal vs. external), and the nature of the data itself (logical vs. physical). This classification is not intended to be exhaustive, but a guide to help organizations in the assessment of their assets and events.

The remaining of the paper is structured as follows: Sect. 2 defines security event data. Section 3 discusses about the information of critical and non-critical systems. Section 4 discusses about internal versus external data. Section 5 compares the a priori information versus the a posteriori information. Section 6 details logical versus physical data. Section 7 proposes a Security Event Data Matrix. Related work are presented in Sect. 8. Finally, conclusions and perspective for future work are presented in Sect. 9.

2   Security Event Data

Considering that an *event* is defined as any observable action in a system or network that indicates the occurrence of an incident; and *information* is defined as any communication or representation of knowledge (e.g., facts, data, opinions in any medium or form, including textual, numerical, graphic, cartographic, narrative, or audiovisual) [7], we define *Security event data* as all relevant information considered to have potential security implications to the system or network.

This article aims at organizing the information of security events based on their nature and usefulness. We consider any information that can potentially impact organizational operations (e.g., mission, functions, image, reputation), assets (physical or logical resources), or individuals (personnel, providers, customers) through an information system via unauthorized access, destruction, disclosure, modification of information, and/or denial of service.

Security event data are useful to identify threats, define risks, and determine the impact of malicious actions (e.g., attacks) and benign actions (e.g., countermeasures) in an information system. We identify relevant data for critical and non-critical systems. Information about critical systems is divided according to the system's nature (e.g., energy, water, telecommunications, finance, health, transportation), and further classified as *cyber systems* (based on ICT solutions); and *physical systems* (composed of physical processes managed by, e.g., control-theoretic solutions). Information about non-critical systems is divided into *internal information*, further classified as logical and physical data;

and *external information*, further classified as *a priori* and *a posteriori* data. The remaining of the paper details each type of data from our proposed classification.

3   Critical vs. Non-critical Systems Data

This section details the types of data required for critical and non-critical systems to analyze risks, assess events, draw conclusions, and select countermeasures.

3.1   Information About Critical Systems

Critical Infrastructures rely on the Supervisory Control And Data Acquisition (SCADA) technology to monitor industrial and complex infrastructures based on Networked Control Systems (NCSs). They include sectors that account for substantial portions of national income and employment such as energy, ICT, finance, health, food, water, transport, and government. Most of these sectors use Industrial Control Systems (ICSs), e.g., Supervisory Control And Data Acquisition (SCADA) in order to provide control of remote equipment (using typically one communication channel per remote station) [8]. For space constraints, we develop in this section the required and additional cyber and physical data for energy distribution and water supply infrastructures.

3.1.1   Energy Distribution

This category includes the production, storage, transportation, and refining of electrical power, gas and oil. The information used in the energy distribution process includes classification of losses as technical and non-technical. The former originates due to physical reasons and depend on the energy flowing through the network, the nature of transmission lines, and transformers. The latter includes measurement errors, recording errors, theft, and timing differences [9]. Examples of technical losses are underground cables and overhead lines. The information on this category includes the type of conductor (e.g., copper, aluminum); conductor temperature (e.g., 0 Celsius, resistance temperature, heating effect, losses due to heating); energy demand (e.g., 100 MWh/year); energy consumption (e.g., estimated annual consumption, real energy consumption, thresholds, kWh, kVAh); load (e.g., heating load, peak load, load factor); peak load times (e.g., winter afternoons). In addition, technical losses can be originated due to the fact that electricity is transported over long distances and the quality of records can be low. Examples of data retrieved in this category include transformer distance (e.g., Kms); transformer material (e.g., iron); power voltage (e.g., high voltage, medium voltage, 400/230 V, 132,000 V); transformer temperature (e.g., heating level, fixed losses, mean temperatures).

Examples of non technical losses include errors (e.g., reading errors, positive error, negative error, timeswitch errors); timing differences (e.g., meter reading period, meter reading frequency, absolute differences); profiling (e.g., profile coefficient, half hourly periods, street lighting profiles, domestic consumers profile, business consumers profile); data collection frequency (e.g., monthly, quarterly, annually); reconciliation (e.g., reconciliation run, settlement reconciliation, post-final reconciliation run); service status (e.g., active, idle, energisation).

Other types of data found in energy distribution systems include meter identification (meter point administration service, meter point administration number); meter type (e.g., passive, dynamic); Calculation Factor (Group Correction Factor, Loss Factor, Peak Load Factor, Power Factor, Half Hourly Consumers Factor); agents (e.g., distributors, suppliers, collectors); wiring system for supplying electricity (e.g., three phase, single phase); sources (source of technical losses, potential source of error); electrical equipment (e.g., transformers, electrical switches); media type (e.g., fiber optics, leased line, Public Switch Telephone Network - PSTN, Global System for Mobile communications - GSM, General Packet Radio Service - GPRS, Terrestrial Trunked Radio - TETRA); communication protocols (e.g., Long-Term Evolution - LTE, High Performance Radio LAN - Hyperlan); Human Machine Interface (e.g., video wall, client console); switch brand (e.g., Cisco, HP, DIGI); Distribution Management System (e.g., high voltage, medium voltage, low voltage), security device (e.g., firewall, load balancer, IDS, IPS, anti-virus, SIEM).

3.1.2 Water Supply

This category includes services that maintain, store, pump, and process water used primarily for drinking.

Several parameters are monitored to assess the safety of a water supply infrastructure (i.e., dam) and foresee possible failures or anomalies [10,11]. Each parameter is measured using different sensors (e.g., Wireless Sensor Networks - WSN). The most common sensors used in monitoring applications are: inclinometers and tiltmeters, used for the measurement of lateral earth movements and wall tilt/rotation which could result in walls failures; crackmeters, used to monitor movement of cracks and joints on the dam surface and are installed on opposite sides of wall cracks to foresee cracks enlargements; jointmeters, deployed across joints to monitor expansion and contraction of a joint, e.g., between adjacent blocks of a concrete dam; earth pressure cells, used to measure the total pressure for embankment dams; piezometers, used to measure fluids pressure in the embankments or in the boreholes, as well as to monitor the seepage, measure uplift pressure and evaluate the shear strength; turbidimeters, used to measure the water turbidity and to identify signs of internal erosion and piping that can lead to the failure of the dam's walls; thermometers, used to measure water temperature and for environmental thermal monitoring to prevent damages to the water life habitat.

In addition to sensors, other components take part of a water supply infrastructure. Examples of such components are: Programmable Logic Controllers - PLCs (e.g., integrated, compact, modular, small, medium-sized, large); data collectors (e.g., human machine interaction interfaces, data storing units, command and data gateways, signal buses); control devices (e.g., workstation, database, Human Machine Interface, shared resource); monitoring device (e.g., Master

Control Unit - MCU, Remote Master Unit - RMU). These components use standard protocols (e.g., TCP/IP, Collection Tree Protocol - CTP, USB serial communication port, Modbus, Distributed Network Protocol - DNP3, Inter-Control Center Communications Protocol - ICCP); they are connected to a public network for exchanging information and data with remote sites a connecting links (e.g., satellite and radio links, telephone lines, Internet). They are protected using security mechanisms (e.g., Firewalls, VPNs, Intrusion Detection Systems, Intrusion Protection Systems); such mechanisms allow for software controls (e.g., patching, automatic updates, component changes).

3.2 Information About Non-critical Systems

The primary data needed for a risk assessment should include the organization's mission statement, a list of programs they have developed in support of that mission, a list of assets by classification that support the programs, the organization's functional organization chart, the relationship between the business functions and the physical property, existing countermeasures used to protect those assets, and any historical data relating to past security events [12].

The identification of methods in the system are proposed by Howard et al. [13] and further detailed by Manadhata and Wing [14]. An information system communicates with its environment through methods. These latter are entry/exit points that receive/send data directly or indirectly from/to the environment. Examples of a web server's direct entry points are the methods in the web server's API and the web server's methods that read configuration files. An example of exit points are methods that write to a log file.

Other types of data in non-critical systems include penetrating methods (e.g., password cracking, social engineering, masquerading); biometrics and physical tokens (e.g., fingerprint, iris, voice recognition, signatures); defeating mechanisms and policies (e.g., challenges related to authentication, authorization, access controls and policies); and malicious code (e.g., virus, bugs, coding problems) [15].

For events originating in Mobile Ad hoc Networks (MANETs), data can be defined based on the legitimacy of attacking node (e.g., internal, external node); based on the number of nodes involved (e.g., single, multiple), based on the exploited vulnerability (e.g., lack of security boundaries, lack of central management, scalability, cooperativeness); based on the targeted victim (e.g., host, network); based on the security violation (e.g., availability, confidentiality, integrity). More details on each type of data can be found in the work of Noureldien [16].

Information about non-critical systems is further classified as *internal* and *external* data.

4   Internal vs. External Data

Internal and external information are required to analyze the impact of a cyber security event. Internal information represents all logical and physical data from the local network or from the information system, such as assets, vulnerabilities, defense mechanisms, etc. External information is related to entities outside the information system such as customers, providers, competitors, attackers. These latter can be identified according to their knowledge, motivation, and capabilities to exploit a given vulnerability from the target system. This section details both information from the target system and from outsiders.

4.1   Internal Data (Information About the Target)

Considering the characteristics of access control models [17], we identify three types of information associated to a particular event: User account - a unique identifier for users in the system that allows them to connect and interact with the system's environment (e.g., super admin, system admin, standard user, guest, internal user, nobody); Resource - either a physical component, (e.g., host, server, printer), or a logical component, (e.g., files, records, database), of limited availability within a computer system; and Channel - the way to execute actions, (e.g. connect, read, write, etc.). Channels can also regroup IP addresses, port numbers, protocols and all other kind of TCP/IP connections. More information about these data types are found in the research of Gonzalez-Granadillo et al. [4].

In addition, we consider the notion of contexts proposed in the Organization based Access Control (OrBAC) model [18], such as temporal conditions - granted privileges only during specific periods of time (working time, day time, night time, weekdays, weekends) or considering actions performed at a given time slot (e.g., connection time, detection time, time to react, time to completely mitigate the attack, recovery time, etc.); spatial conditions - granted privileges when connected within specific areas (e.g., user's location, security areas, specific buildings, a country, a network or sub-network); and historical conditions - granted privileges only if previous instances of the same equivalent events were already conducted. For instance, in order to access a web-server (resource) of a given organization, an external user (user account) connects remotely (spatial condition) to the system by providing his/her log-in and password (channel) at nights (temporal condition).

Information security properties (e.g., confidentiality, integrity, availability) are also a key aspect in the analysis of a cyber security event. An event can be associated to a particular issue compromising the system's confidentiality (e.g., unauthorized access to sensitive information, disclosure resources, etc.), integrity (e.g., unauthorized change of the data contents or properties, etc.), or availability (e.g., unavailable resources, denial of service, etc.).

Internal information is further classified as Logical and Physical. Section 6 details each type of data.

4.2   External Data (Information About the Attacker)

All information systems interact with people: internals, when they belong to the organization; and externals, otherwise. External people can have direct contact to the organization (e.g., vendors, visitors, customers) or indirect contact with the organization (e.g., competitors, intruders, attackers). For people with direct contact with the organization, we need to identify their occupancies (where they work and interact), the hours of occupancy, tasks, uses of hazardous materials or equipment, their needs for access, and their frequency of access [12]. It is also important to note any classic or specific threats against these people. People with indirect contact to the organization are seen as adversaries.

According to Krautsevich et al. [19], adversaries can be either (i) omniscient, when they know all vulnerabilities and all possible patches of the system; (ii) deterministic, when they have a belief knowledge of the system and they choose the best possible action to break into the system; or (iii) adaptive, when they adapt the strategy to complete the attack, using updated knowledge about the system. In reality, attackers do not have the knowledge of all the system's vulnerabilities. We concentrate, therefore, in deterministic and adaptive attackers. Data coming from these type of entities are considered in Sect. 5 as a priori and a posteriori data.

5   A Priori vs. A Posteriori Data

This section discusses two types of information that can be used for a malicious entity in the execution of an attack. *A priori data*, which considers information before the attack is realized, and *a posteriori data*, which considers information discovered by the attacker once the attack is in place. The remaining of this section presents examples of each data type.

5.1   A Priori Data

This classification considers the set of information about the system, possessed by an attacker before exploiting a given vulnerability. If the attacker has a priori knowledge about the operation of the entire system, he/she would be able to inflict a much severe attack. We distinguish two types of a priori knowledge: the knowledge about the information system, and the knowledge about the attack. The former considers the understandings that the attacker has about the system, whereas the latter considers the skills and experience of the attacker in executing a given attack.

About the information system: Following the common vulnerability system scoring method (CVSS) [20], we consider in this category, the known vulnerabilities of the information system that can be exploited by an attacker to access the system (e.g., access vector, complexity, authentication type, required privilege, exploitability, report confidence, potential collateral damage, user interaction).

The *access vector* category considers the way a vulnerability can be exploited by an attacker in the system (e.g., physical, local access, adjacent network access, network access). The *access complexity* includes the complexity level required for an attacker to exploit a vulnerability once he/she has gained access to the target system (e.g., high, medium, low). The *authentication type* category considers the number of times an entity must authenticate to a target in order to exploit a vulnerability (e.g., multiple, single, none). The *required privilege* category describes the level of privileges needed for an attacker to successfully exploit a vulnerability in the system (e.g., none, low, high). The *exploitability* category considers level of difficulty at which a vulnerability can be exploited (e.g., unproven, proof of concept, functional, high, not defined). The *report confidence* category identifies the degree of confidence in the existence of the vulnerability and the credibility of the known technical details (e.g., unconfirmed, uncorroborated, confirmed, not defined). The *potential collateral damage* category considers the potential for loss of life or physical assets through damage or theft of property or equipment (e.g., low, low-medium, medium, medium-high, high, not defined). The *user interaction* category considers the requirement for a user, other than the attacker, to participate in the successful exploitation of a vulnerability (e.g., none, required).

About the attack: Based on the taxonomy of cyber events proposed in [21], and the research proposed by Cayirci and Ghergherehchi [2], we consider in this category information about the attacker (e.g., type, location, quantity, motivation, technique, mobility), and the attack (e.g., cause, affected service, objective, impact).

The *attacker type* classification includes all threat agents that are primarily responsible for the cyber event (e.g., malicious agents, organizations, foreign governments, natural disasters, or human errors). In terms of *location*, attackers can be located within the network (i.e., insider), or outside the network (i.e., outsider). The *quantity* category defines three types of attackers: single, multiple, or coordinating multiple. These latter defines the case when multiple attackers collaborate with each other. The *attacker's motivation* as proposed by Bielecki and Quirchmayr [1], and Shinder [22] considers the different goals (motives) that can encourage an attacker to exploit a vulnerability on the system such as low (e.g., no motivation, just for fun), medium (e.g., political motives), and high (e.g., for monetary profit; anger, revenge and other emotional drivers; sexual impulses; psychiatric illness). The *technique* includes all types of actions used to achieve the attacker's objective (e.g., system compromise, protocol compromise, resource exhaustion, hardware failure, software crash). In terms of *mobility*, attackers can be fixed or mobile.

The *attack cause* classification differentiates between effects directly or indirectly caused by an event (e.g., disruption within service, cascade disruption from a service). The *affected services* classification considers the priority of service nodes (e.g., primary service node, intermediate service node, secondary service node). The *objective* of the attack considers how the malicious entity attempt to achieve its goal (e.g., data corruption, data fabrication, data destruction, data disclosure, data discovering, no objective). The *attack impact* considers the effects in terms of confidentiality, integrity and availability (e.g., none, low, medium, high, extreme).

5.2   A Posteriori Data

A set of information gained by the attacker after a successful exploitation of a system's vulnerability [19]. The system can release information that improves the attacker's knowledge to exploit vulnerabilities or to overcome the security controls set by the system, however, the adversary knowledge is generally incomplete. In this section we study the attacker's knowledge with respect to the system evolution (e.g., deployment of countermeasures).

About the countermeasures: From the adversary point of view, the ability to penetrate a system does not necessarily implies the ability to break into a system. Breaking a system means making the system to fail and keep on failing. It is more hostile, and more difficult than penetrating into the system, since it requires an understanding of what makes the system fail [23]. However, penetrating the system is the first step for an attacker to improve his/her knowledge about the system.

According to Krautsevich et al. [19], an attacker observes a system and can influence its behavior by making actions at a given moment. The system responds to an action probabilistically. Attackers do not make decisions about actions blindly. Instead, they take into account past, current, and possible future states of the system, as well as possible rewards that are connected with the actions. The goal of the attacker is to maximize the expected total reward according to a sole criterion.

We define the attacker's a posteriori knowledge based on the actions the defender performs to protect the system against a given attack (e.g., implementing security countermeasures). Security measures can be performed automatically by the system and can be soft (e.g., reducing credit limits, restarting the system, requesting password change), moderate (additional authentication method, temporal access denial, temporary fix, alarms) or aggressive (e.g., vulnerability patching, blocking user account, admin rights request). Depending on the decisions available to the attacker, he/she will be able to change its behavior and adapt to the system or quit his/her initial goal.

The Incident Object Description Exchange Format (IODEF) [24] classifies the actions taken a system as a defense mechanism. Examples of such actions are: nothing (i.e., no action is required); contact-source-site (i.e., contact the site identified as the source of the activity); investigate (i.e., investigate the systems listed in the event); block-host/network/port (i.e., block the host/network/port listed as sources in the event); status-triage (i.e., conveys receipts and the triaging of an incident).

In addition, physical countermeasures consider all security actions taken to prevent, protect, or react against a malicious physical event that originates in the system. Examples of physical countermeasures include blocking/opening doors, disabling/enabling hardware, disconnecting/connecting equipment, repairing/replacing hardware, turning on/off devices, posting banners and/or security messages within the organization's infrastructure, installing video surveillance and/or biometric systems.

6 Logical vs. Physical Data

As previously stated, internal information (i.e., related to the system and its entities) is classified according to its nature in *Logical* when the information is intangible (i.e., digital data) and *Physical* otherwise. This section details each type of data.

6.1 Logical Data

Logical information corresponds to all intangible data associated to the target system that can be used by an adversary to execute an attack. Examples of logical data are proposed by Howard et al. [13] as business records, application's information, and security issues. In terms of business records, we consider the organization's proprietary Information (e.g., proprietary business processes, strategic plans, customer lists, vital records, accounting records).

Application's information considers resource consumption (e.g., CPU cycles, memory capacity, storage capacity, and I/O bandwidth); communication channels (e.g., sockets, RPC connections, named pipes, files, directories, and registries); and process targets (e.g., browsers, mailers, and database servers).

Security issues consider alerts or alarm signals, access control violations, photo-ID alteration, noise in voice and video records. Examples of this category include the use of *security mechanisms* such as Transport Layer Security (TLS), expressing that the application uses HTTPS, or server side input validation; the use of *cookies* (considering the maximum number of cookies and the number of foreign cookies from other sites that the application sets during a session); the *access control method* required (e.g., unauthenticated, authenticated, or root); and the *access right* required (e.g., read, write, execute, root).

In addition, Howard et al. [13] have identified several attack vectors to determine a relative attack surface of different Windows applications. Examples of such vectors include open sockets (e.g., TCP or UDP sockets on which at least one service is listening), active web handlers (e.g., http, nntp), dynamic web pages (e.g., .exe files, .asp (Active Server Pages) files, and .pl (Perl script) files), VBScript enabled (whether applications, such as Internet Explorer and Outlook Express, are enabled to execute Visual Basic Script).

For event notification messages using the Syslog protocol [25], useful information is associated to the facility responsible of the message (e.g., kernel, user, mail system, clock daemon, log alert); to the severity associated to the message (e.g., emergency, alert, critical, error, warning, debug), to the identified machine that originally sent the message (e.g., Fully Qualified Domain Name, IP address, hostname), and to the time at which the message was originated (i.e., timestamp).

The Intrusion Detection Message Exchange Format (IDMEF) [26] identifies other fields of interest in the event data classification. The alert has been fired by an analyzer, from which we can derive the source, the target, the time at which the alert was created, the time at which the event was detected, the impact assessment, and information about the node or user that appears to be causing the event. In addition, we can also consider the information about the completion of the event (e.g., failed, succeeded); the confidence on the evaluation of the event (e.g., low, medium, high); and the algorithm used for the computation of the checksum (e.g., MD4, MD5, SHA1, SHA2-256, Gost).

6.2 Physical Data

Physical information corresponds to all tangible elements that interact directly or indirectly with the target system and whose intrinsec vulnerabilities can be used by an adversary to execute an attack. Examples of physical data are proposed by Norman [12] as people, technical and non-technical devices.

People, represents all internal user accounts (e.g., Key Senior Management, Management and Employees, Contractors, Vendors, Visitors, Customers).

Hi-tech devices correspond to information technology systems (e.g., PCs, servers, laptops, tablettes, pads, mobile phones); office equipment (e.g., copiers, printers, furniture, cash registers); and security devices (e.g., sensors, intrusion detection systems, security information and event management systems, biometrical systems, physical access control systems).

Non-technical devices represent documents or equipment with low or no technical attributes. Examples of such devices are: lo-tech devices (e.g., Access-controlled and non-access-controlled gates, doors, and barriers, lighting, signage, property-marking system, key-control system); no-tech devices (e.g., Policies and procedures, guard patrols and posts, investigation programs, law enforcement liaison program, security awareness program, emergency preparedness program, disaster recovery program).

In addition, it is useful to identify the physical location of people (e.g., network administrator's room, employees offices, guests rooms), physical location of high-tech devices (e.g., server's room, control operation center's location), physical location of network elements (e.g., router location, sensor's physical location), information about the network topology (e.g., interconnection of network elements), location of lo-tech devices (e.g., printer's location, lighting control room), location of no-tech devices (e.g., drawer that stores disaster recovery programs, policies and procedures).

7 Security Event Data Matrix

Based on the information presented in previous sections, we propose a matrix that organizes the event information based on four main aspects: (i) system criticality, (ii) asset location, (iii) event time, and (iv) event nature. Table 1 shows a cyber and physical-based data classification of two critical infrastructure systems (i.e., energy production, water distribution). Table 2 shows a logical and physical-based data classification of internal and external sources of non-critical infrastructure systems.

In order to illustrate the applicability of the event data classification, we consider an issue originated in an infrastructure-less network that uses a Mobile

Table 1. Critical infrastructure systems classification

	Energy distribution		Water supply	
	Required	Additional	Required	Additional
Cyber systems	Technical losses (e.g., circuits, meters, transformers); non-technical losses (e.g., errors, profiling); type of conductor (e.g., copper); data collection frequency (e.g., annually); reconciliation (e.g., settlement reconciliation); protocols (e.g., DNP3, IEC-60870 101, IEC-60870 104)	Transformer material (e.g., iron); timing differences (e.g., absolute differences); profiling (e.g., profile coefficient); meter identification (meter point administration number); meter type (e.g., passive); media type (e.g., fiber optics); communication protocols (e.g., Long-Term Evolution - LTE); Human Machine Interface (e.g., client console); switch brand (e.g., Cisco); security device (firewall)	Security logs (e.g., logs provided by firewall); protocols (e.g., Modbus); resources (e.g., available bandwidth); virtual distribution map (e.g., virtual district metering area)	PLC type (integrated PLC); data collectors (e.g., data storing units); connecting elements (e.g., satellite links); security mechanisms (e.g., Firewall); software controls (e.g., patching)
Physical systems	Load (e.g., heating load); peak load times (e.g., winter afternoons); conductor temperature (e.g., Celsius); energy demand (e.g., 100 MWh/year); Calculation Factor (e.g., Loss Factor); energy consumption (e.g., KW/h); transformer distance (e.g., Kms); power voltage (e.g., high voltage); service status (e.g., idle); errors (e.g., reading errors); sources (e.g., potential source of error); transformer temperature (e.g., heating level)	Electrical equipment (e.g., transformers); Distribution Management System (e.g., medium voltage); wiring system for supplying electricity (e.g., taree phase): agents (e.g., collectors); PMU (phasor measurement unit)	Sensors (e.g., WSN); inclinometer (e.g., lateral earth movements); tiltmeter (e.g., wall tilt/rotation level); crackmeter (e.g., movement of cracks and joints on the dam surface) jointmeter (e.g., expansion and contraction of a joint); earth pressure cell (e.g., total pressure for embankment dams); piezometer (e.g., fluids pressure in the embankments or in the boreholes); turbidimeter (e.g., water turbidity level); thermometer (e.g., water temperature)	Monitoring device (e.g., MCU); automated meter reading (ARM); acoustic measures (based on hydrophone sensors or on accelerometers, e.g., to determine leak positions); biosensors measures (e.g., behavior of living organisms in the water)

Table 2. Non-critical infrastructure systems classification

| | Internal | | External | | | |
| | Required | Additional | A priori | | A posteriori | |
			Required	Additional	Required	Additional
Logical	User account (e.g., admin); resource (e.g., file); Channel (e.g., IP address); unauthorized access); confidentiality (e.g., unauthorized access); integrity (e.g., unauthorized change of data content); availability (e.g., denial of service); security mechanisms (e.g., TLS); access control method (e.g., authenticated); access right (e.g., read); event severity (e.g., alert)	Temporal conditions (e.g., detection time); spatial conditions (e.g., user's location); proprietary Information (e.g., accounting records); resource consumption (e.g., memory capacity); process targets (e.g., browsers); cookies (e.g., number of foreign cookies); open sockets (e.g., TCP), active web handlers (e.g., http); dynamic web pages (e.g., .exe files); facility (e.g., kernel); sender (e.g., Fully Qualified Domain Name); analyzer (e.g. source); event completion (e.g., failed); confidence (e.g., high); algorithm used (e.g., SHA1)	Access complexity (e.g., high); authentication type (e.g., multiple); required privilege (e.g., high); user interaction (e.g., required); attacker type (e.g., malicious agents); attacker's location (e.g., insider); quantity (e.g., multiple); technique (e.g., resource exhaustion); affected services (e.g., primary); objective (e.g., data corruption); attack impact (e.g., extreme)	Exploitability (e.g., proof of concept); report confidence (e.g., unconfirmed); potential collateral damage (e.g., high); attacker's motivation (e.g., monetary profit); mobility (e.g., fixed); attack cause (e.g., disruption within service)	Defense mechanism (e.g., block-host/ network/ port); confirmation about the access complexity, authentication type, required privilege and the user interaction required by the system	Soft countermeasures (e.g., restarting the system), moderate countermeasures (temporal access denial); aggressive countermeasures (e.g., blocking user account), confirmation about the exploitability of the system's vulnerabilities
Physical	People (e.g., employees); hi-tech devices (e.g., servers); hi-tech accessories (e.g., USB driver) office equipment (e.g., printers); security devices (e.g., Intrusion Detection Systems), physical access controls (e.g., fingerprint scanners)	Lo-tech devices (e.g., lighting systems); no-tech devices (e.g., disaster recovery program)	Access vector (e.g., local access), physical location of people (e.g., network administrator's room), physical location of high-tech devices (server's room), physical location of network elements (e.g., router location)	Network topology (e.g., interconnection of network elements), location of lo-tech devices (lighting control room), location of no-tech devices (e.g., drawer that stores the disaster recovery program)	Countermeasures in place (e.g., replace hardware), confirmation about access vectors, location of people, location of hi-tech devices, and location of network elements	Confirmation about the network topology, the physical location of lo-tech and no-tech devices

ad-hoc Network to connect devices wirelessly in a continuing self-configuring way. A malicious event has been detected on 2017-03-23 T 15:22 UTC, from an external node that compromised two internal nodes from the network (i.e., Node1: WEB_SRV03, ID 718bc323-9d78-4ada-9629-8176f42a9703; and Node2: FTP_SRV01, ID e470baab-5d88-4b20-ac28-61ea42b37da3). The malicious node exploits a resource exhaustion vulnerability to originate a DoS attack. The source IP address is unknown, and the target IP addresses are identified as 192.168.1.125, and 192.168.4.315.

- Internal logical data (Required): channel (IP address); node IP address (192.168.1.125, 192.168.4.315); node identification (718bc323-9d78-4ada-9629-8176f42a9703, e470baab-5d88-4b20-ac28-61ea42b37da3); security violation (availability);
- Internal logical data (Additional): number of nodes involved (multiple); detect time (2017-03-23 T 15:22 UTC); targeted victim (Node1, Node2).
- Internal physical data (Required): technical device (web server, ftp server);
- External logical a priori data (Required): legitimacy of attacking node (external node); exploited vulnerability (resource exhaustion); consequence (denial of service).

8   Related Work

Classification of cyber and physical security events has been widely researched in the past two decades. While some researches propose attack taxonomies, some others concentrate in countermeasure taxonomies, and some others present formats and standards for event messages. Classification of attacks is extensively proposed in the bibliography. Noureldien [16], for instance, proposes a taxonomy of MANET attacks. Such classifications, although well developed, they lack on information about security actions to mitigate the attacks.

The classification of security countermeasures have been studied by Norman [12] and Abbas et al. [15]. The former proposes a classification of assets for physical security countermeasure analysis; the latter proposes an approach to designing internet security taxonomies. Both researches concentrate on logical and physical security controls, leaving aside different attack scenarios.

Few research works have been dedicated to the classification of both benign and malicious events. Harrison and White [21], for instance, propose a taxonomy of cyber events affecting communities. The taxonomy classifies threats and countermeasures based on multiple criteria but it does not provide information on cyber-physical systems as a whole, nor they consider the time at which the information is detected and used by the attacker.

Howard et al. [13] propose an attack surface model with several attributes to be used in the analysis of the criticality of similar operating systems. The approach has been extended by Manadhata et al. [14] to compare different software systems based on entry points, methods, and channels. More recently, Gonzalez-Granadillo et al. [5] propose a geometrical approach to evaluate the impact of security events based on a multi-dimensional tool. Even though the models are useful in the evaluation and analysis of the criticality of systems and events, they require to identify event relevant information to compute the results.

Based on the aforementioned limitations we propose an event data classification matrix that considers data formats, standards, and protocols (e.g., IDMEF [26], IODEF [24], Syslog [25], CVSS [20], as well as several other approaches used in the classification and assessments of cyber and physical events.

9   Conclusions and Future Work

We have proposed in this paper an event data taxonomy to be used in the identification of key axes and/or dimensions in the impact assessment of cyber security events. The taxonomy considers required and additional information about all entities involved in the identified event. As such, the proposed matrix separates critical from non-critical systems. The former details the useful data to model cyber and physical events in energy distribution systems and water supply infrastructures. The latter details the useful information related to internal and external entities affected to the events. The proposed matrix goes further by classifying the logical and physical data associated to internal entities (e.g., target system); as well as, the a-priori and a-posteriori data associated to external entities (e.g., attackers). As a result, it is possible to identify the main axes composing geometrical models to assess the impact of malicious and benign cyber security events.

Future work will focus on extending the classification matrix to other critical infrastructures (e.g., transportation, health, finance, etc.) and to use the outcome of this matrix to build and populate the axes of a geometrical model for impact assessment and countermeasure selection.

References

1. Bielecki, M., Quirchmayr, G.: A prototype for support of computer forensic analysis combined with the expected knowledge level of an attacker to more efficiently achieve investigation results. In: International Conference on Availability, Reliability and Security, pp. 696–701 (2010)
2. Cayirci, E., Ghergherehchi, R.: Modeling cyber attacks and their effects on decision process. In: Winter Simulation Conference (2011)
3. Kotenko, I., Doynikova, E.: Countermeasure selection in SIEM systems based on the integrated complex of security metrics. In: 23rd Euromicro International Conference on Parallel, Distributed, and Network-Based Processing (2015)
4. Granadillo, G.G., Garcia-Alfaro, J., Debar, H.: Using a 3D geometrical model to improve accuracy in the evaluation and selection of countermeasures against complex cyber attacks. In: Thuraisingham, B., Wang, X.F., Yegneswaran, V. (eds.) SecureComm 2015. LNICST, vol. 164, pp. 538–555. Springer, Cham (2015). https://doi.org/10.1007/978-3-319-28865-9_29

5. Gonzalez-Granadillo, G., Rubio-Hernan, J., Garcia-Alfaro, J., Debar, H.: Considering internal vulnerabilities and the attacker's knowledge to model the impact of cyber events as geometrical prisms. In: Conference on Trust, Security and Privacy in Computing and Communications (2016)

6. Gonzalez-Granadillo, G., Garcia-Alfaro, J., Debar, H.: An n-sided polygonal model to calculate the impact of cyber security events. In: Cuppens, F., Cuppens, N., Lanet, J.-L., Legay, A. (eds.) CRiSIS 2016. LNCS, vol. 10158, pp. 87–102. Springer, Cham (2017). https://doi.org/10.1007/978-3-319-54876-0_7

7. Kissel, R.: Glossary of key information security terms, Revision 2. National Institute of Standards and Technology. U.S. Department of Commerce (2013)

8. Gordon, K., Dion, M.: Protection of critical infrastructure and the role of investment policies relating to national security. OECD, White paper (2008)

9. Sohn Associates: Electricity Distribution System Losses. Non Technical Overview, White paper (2009)

10. Singapore, Public Utilities Board: Managing the water distribution network with a smart water grid. Int. J. @qua - Smart ICT Water (Smart Water) **1**(4), 1–13 (2016)

11. Coppolino, L., D'Antonio, S., Formicola, V., Romano, L.: Integration of a system for critical infrastructure protection with the OSSIM SIEM Platform: a dam case study. In: Flammini, F., Bologna, S., Vittorini, V. (eds.) SAFECOMP 2011. LNCS, vol. 6894, pp. 199–212. Springer, Heidelberg (2011). https://doi.org/10.1007/978-3-642-24270-0_15

12. Norman, T.L.: Risk Analysis and Security Countermeasure Selection. CRC Press, Taylor & Francis Group, Boca Raton (2010)

13. Howard, M., Pincus, J., Wing, J.M.: Measuring relative attack surfaces. In: Computer Security in the 21st Century, pp. 109–137 (2005)

14. Manadhata, P.K., Wing, J.M.: An attack surface metric. IEEE Trans. Softw. Eng. **37**(3), 371–386 (2010)

15. Abbas, A., Saddik, A.E., Miri, A.: A comprehensive approach to designing internet security taxonomy. In: Proceedings of the Canadian Conference on Electrical and Computer Engineering, pp. 1316–1319 (2006)

16. Noureldien, A.: A novel taxonomy of MANET attacks. In: Conference on Electrical and Information Technologies ICEIT (2015)

17. Li, N., Tripunitara, M.: Security analysis in role-based access control. Trans. Inf. Syst. Secur. **9**(4), 391–420 (2006)

18. Cuppens, F., Cuppens-Boulahia, N.: Modeling contextual security policies. Int. J. Inf. Secur. **7**(4), 285–305 (2008)

19. Krautsevich, L., Martinelli, F., Yautsiukhin, A.: Towards modelling adaptive attacker's behaviour. In: Garcia-Alfaro, J., Cuppens, F., Cuppens-Boulahia, N., Miri, A., Tawbi, N. (eds.) FPS 2012. LNCS, vol. 7743, pp. 357–364. Springer, Heidelberg (2013). https://doi.org/10.1007/978-3-642-37119-6_23

20. Mell, P., Scarfone, K., Romanosky, S.: Common vulnerability scoring system Version 2.0, Specification Document, June 2007

21. Harrison, K., White, G.: A taxonomy of cyber events affecting communities. In: Proceedings of the 44th Hawaii International Conference on System Sciences (2011)

22. Shinder, D.: Scenes of the Cybercrime. Computer Forensics Handbook. Syngress Publishing Inc., Burlington (2002)

23. Libicki, M.: Brandishing cyberattack capabilities. National Defense Research Institute, white paper (2013)

24. Danyliw, R., Meijer, J., Demchenko, Y.: The incident object description exchange format (IODEF), RFC5070, December 2007
25. Gerhards, R., Adiscon GmbH: The syslog protocol. Network Working Group (2009)
26. Debar, H., Curry, D., Feinstein, B.: The intrusion detection message exchange format (IDMEF), RFC4765 (2007)

Apps Security

Unraveling Reflection Induced Sensitive Leaks in Android Apps

Jyoti Gajrani[1]([⊠])[iD], Vijay Laxmi[1], Meenakshi Tripathi[1], Manoj S. Gaur[1],
Daya Ram Sharma[2], Akka Zemmari[3], Mohamed Mosbah[3], and Mauro Conti[4]

[1] MNIT, Jaipur, India
{2014rcp9542,vlaxmi,mtripathi.cse,gaurms}@mnit.ac.in
[2] GEC Ajmer, Ajmer, India
dayasharma96@gmail.com
[3] LaBRI, Bordeaux INP, CNRS, University of Bordeaux, Bordeaux, France
{zemmari,mohamed.mosbah}@labri.fr
[4] University of Padua, Padua, Italy
conti@math.unipd.it

Abstract. Reflection is a programming language feature that permits analysis and transformation of the behavior of classes used in programs in general, and in apps in particular at the runtime. Reflection facilitates various features such as dynamic class loading, method invocation, and attribute usage at runtime. These language features allow the development of apps that may obtain and exchange information that is unavailable at compile time. Unfortunately, malware authors leverage reflection to subvert the malware detection by static analyzers as reflection can hinder taint analysis used by static analyzers for analysis of sensitive leaks. Even the latest, and probably the best performing static analyzers are not able to detect information leaks in the malware via reflection. In this paper, we propose EspyDroid, a system that combines dynamic analysis with code instrumentation for a more precise detection of leaks in malicious apps via reflection with code obfuscation. The evaluation of EspyDroid on the benchmark, VirusShare, and Playstore apps shows substantial improvement in detection of sensitive leaks via reflection.

Keywords: Android · Instrumentation · Reflection · Runtime
Malware · Dynamic analysis · Leaks

1 Introduction

Reflection is the ability of an app to examine and modify the structure and behavior of an object at runtime. Reflection facilitates language features such as inspecting class of objects, constructing objects of class, examining fields of class, invoking methods of an object, changing accessibility flags of constructors, methods, and fields at runtime.

Unfortunately, malware authors are using reflection to subvert their detection by static analyzers. Through an analysis spanned across four years, Andrubis [18]

© Springer International Publishing AG, part of Springer Nature 2018
N. Cuppens et al. (Eds.): CRiSIS 2017, LNCS 10694, pp. 49–65, 2018.
https://doi.org/10.1007/978-3-319-76687-4_4

reported that reflection is employed by 57.08% of Android malware samples. Instead of utilizing usual programming language syntax, reflection passes class-name, methodname etc. as parameters to reflection APIs. Also, these parameters can be constructed dynamically or supplied at runtime. Malware families Obad and FakeInstaller are the two most sophisticated malware families that combine reflection and code obfuscation to hide their malicious behaviors from detection by static analysis techniques.

Moreover, Android provides Inter-Component Communication (ICC) feature for communication among components of the application. ICC is a feature provided by Android to encourage component reuse. Intent [5] is a message passing object to request an action from a component (from the same or different app) to facilitate ICC. Unfortunately, malware authors misuse the feature to distribute the leaks over multiple components of given apps [20]. Techniques developed for analyzing single component based leaks may not work for ICC based leaks [10].

Listing 1.1 shows the code of Onlytelephony_reverse[1] app from the well-known DroidBench [4] test-suite for Android. This app uses reflection APIs and ICC (lines 7-9). The class android.Telephony.TelephonyManager define the method getDeviceId(). MainActivity instantiates the object of this class using Class.forName reflection API (line 3). However, the method name is constructed dynamically by using the reverse() function (line 2). Then, it passes this dynamically constructed method name to getMethod() reflection API (line 5) which creates the method object. Finally, it invokes the method getDeviceId() using reflection API invoke() (line 6) which return IMEI value. MainActivity passes the IMEI value to Activity2 using Android Intent (lines 7-9), and Activity2 performs leakage of IMEI using SMS.

Listing 1.1. Exploitation of Reflection APIs for leaks

```
1    String cls="android.Telephony.TelephonyManager";
2    String reverse=new StringBuffer("dIeciveDteg").reverse().toString();
3    Class c=Class.forName(cls);
4    tM = (TelephonyManager) this.getSystemService (Context.TELEPHONY_SERVICE);
5    Method method = c.getMethod(reverse, new Class<?>[0]);
6    String id=(String) method.invoke(tM);
7    Intent i=new Intent(this, Activity2.class);
8    i.putExtra("imei", id);
9    startActivity(i);
                         $MainActivity$
10   Intent im = getIntent();
11   String value= getIntent().getExtras().getString("imei");
12   SmsManager sm = SmsManager.getDefault();
13   sm.sendTextMessage(phoneNo,null,value,null,null);
                         $Activity2$
```

The method reverse() here is just an example, where in other cases more complicated methods are applied such as encryption, substring, concatenation etc. to subvert static analysis. Analysis results of the example by FlowDroid [8],

---

[1] https://github.com/secure-software-engineering/DroidBench/tree/develop/apk/Reflection_ICC/OnlyTelephony_Reverse.apk.

IccTA [16], AmanDroid [25], and DroidSafe [14] static analysis tools do not capture any privacy leak as reflection hindered taint analysis. Reflection-aware static analysis approach DroidRA [17] also fails to identify the leak in application. This failure is because that app constructs the method name at runtime. The dynamic construction of targets of reflection APIs is very trivial and can be done using various ways like concatenation, encryption, statically unresolved Intents, and substring generation. Further, not only classes or methods can be called through reflection but `Intents` also. Listing 1.2 shows another motivating example from DroidBench[2] where `Intent` reflection is used.

Listing 1.2. Intent Reflection

```
1   Class<?> i = Class.forName("android.content.Intent");
2   Constructor c = i.getConstructor(Context.class, Class.class);
3   Object intent = c.newInstance(this, A2.class);
4   Method m = intent.getClass().getMethod("put"+"Extra", params);
5   Object[] obj = { "imei", id };
6   m.invoke(intent, obj);
7   startActivity((Intent) intent);
```

Instead of normal Intent creation as in Listing 1.1 (lines 7–9), this app creates object of `Intent` (lines 1–3), invoke the method to pass the IMEI to `A2` (lines 4–6), and starts `A2` Activity (line 7), all with reflection APIs. Intent reflection is used here by malware to hide the communication between two components.

Analysis results of various apps implementing any type of non-constant use of parameters in reflection concludes that even static reflection-aware analysis approaches based on constant string analysis of reflection APIs fail in identification of leaks. This highly imposes the requirement of a reflection aware runtime analysis approach with ICC support.

Contributions. The major contributions of this work are as follows:

- This paper proposes EspyDroid: A system that combines dynamic analysis with code instrumentation to unfold the hidden leaks performed by the app using reflection and obfuscation or encryption of parameters. EspyDroid resolves the actual parameters of reflection calls and automatically instruments the app with equivalent non-reflection calls using runtime parameters to produce an instrumented app.
- EspyDroid can detect leaks distributed over multiple components through Intents and also, where Intents themselves are called through reflection.
- We tested EspyDroid on widely used DroidBench [4] benchmark, 75 Play-Store apps, and 277 randomly selected apps from VirusShare [7]. The results show that analyzing EspyDroid's instrumented apps instead of original apps improves the precision and accuracy of static analyzers in finding information leaks.
- To facilitate the use by other researchers and practitioners in this direction, we plan to release EspyDroid as open-source tool with user documentation.

---

[2] https://github.com/secure-software-engineering/DroidBench/blob/develop/apk/Reflection_ICC/OnlyIntent.apk.

Organization. The rest of the paper is organized as follow: Sect. 2 provides the brief overview of the reflection APIs and categories. We discuss the proposed solution in Sect. 3. Section 4 reports evaluation results. Section 5 describes the limitations of our proposal. We include Related work in Sect. 6 and conclude the paper in Sect. 7.

2   Background

This section provides the classification of reflection APIs and examples of usages of these APIs for performing information leaks. A `source` is any method that accesses user's private data, and a `sink` is any method which can potentially leak this data outside the application. The malicious Android apps use reflection APIs for hiding invocation of sensitive sources and sinks. The reflection APIs belong to four major categories [1]. We next cover these categories and how each of this category can be used for leakage.

– **Constructing class's object or examining object's class**
  Malicious apps instantiate the classes corresponding to source and sink methods reflectively to hide the identification of leaks. An analysis technique must correctly identify instantiated classes to capture access to private information. Listing 1.3 reflectively creates the object of class `ConcreteClass` using `forName` reflection API and instantiates it using `newInstance` reflection API (line 2). The classname `ConcreteClass` is not present directly in app bytecode. It stores DeviceId to `imei` field of this class (line 3) to perform leak.

Listing 1.3. Reflective Class Instantiation

```
1   String cls = "preConcreteClasspost".substring(3, 16);
2   BaseClass bc = (BaseClass) Class.forName(cls).newInstance();
3   bc.imei = telephonyManager.getDeviceId(); //source
```

– **Examining or invoking class methods**
  Malicious apps use reflective invocation of methods to hide the sensitive sources (sinks) accessing (leaking) user's data. Listing 1.4 from DroidBench invokes `setImei` (lines 4 and 5) method reflectively using `getMethod` and invoke APIs. `setImei` method of ReflectiveClass calls the sink method `sendtextMessage()` to leak the DeviceId.

Listing 1.4. Reflective Method Invocations

```
1   String imei = telephonyManager.getDeviceId(); //source
2   Class c = Class.forName("ReflectiveClass");
3   Object o = c.newInstance(); //No class type information
4   Method m = c.getMethod("setIme" + "i", String.class);
5   m.invoke(o, imei);
```

– **Examining or setting fields of class**
  The value is assigned to the field of class through reflection API `set()` and the value is retrieved using reflection API `get()`.

Listing 1.5 first stores the sensitive value, i.e., `DeviceId` in `imei` field of class (lines 4–5) and then retrieves (lines 6–7) with reflection APIs. The application sends `refdeviceId` to sink instead of `deviceId` (the case where analysis will able to identify leak) to hide the leak.

Listing 1.5. Field-based reflective access

```
1   String deviceId = telephonyManager.getDeviceId(); //source
2   Class<?> c = this.getClassLoader().loadClass("ConcreteClass");
3   Object o = c.getConstructor(String.class).newInstance();
4   Field f1 = c.getField("imei");
5   f1.set(o, deviceid);
6   Field f2 = c.getField("imei");
7   String refdeviceId = (String) f2.get(o);
```

– **Getting constructor of class and instantiating constructor**
   The specific constructor of class may be obtained through `getConstructor()` API. Malicious apps store sensitive data in the class field through a constructor and later read out again and perform leaks. The analysis must be able to handle constructor-based reflective class instantiations. The example of Listing 1.6 reflectively instantiates the object of `BaseClass` using the constructor of `ConcreteClass` (line 3) and stores `deviceId` in it.

Listing 1.6. Constructor based Reflective Class Instantiation

```
1   String deviceId = telephonyManager.getDeviceId(); //source
2   Class<?> cls = Class.forName("ConcreteClass");
3   BaseClass bc = (BaseClass) cls.getConstructor(String.class).newInstance(deviceId);
```

We prepared list of various reflection APIs belonging to four categories. This is used in all phases of EspyDriod.

3   Proposed Solution: EspyDroid

EspyDroid is a system that combines dynamic analysis with code instrumentation to unravel the potential hidden leaks implemented through the use of reflection and runtime data dependency. The overall architecture of EspyDroid is as shown in Fig. 1. The complete system of EspyDroid consists of four main modules: App Hooking, Dynamic Analyzer, Log-Tracer, and Instrumentation.

EspyDroid first searches for the presence of reflection APIs in the apk. EspyDroid assumes that reflection APIs itself are not obfuscated. We use AndroGuard [3] for checking the presence of reflection, which is a static analysis tool written in Python and works directly on apk files. After the confirmation of the presence of reflection, the app undergoes further analysis. As seen from motivating examples, the information of parameters and return values of reflection APIs can not be inferred statically if parameters have any runtime dependency. The aim of App Hooking and Dynamic Analyzer is to get this information by monitoring the reflection APIs related to four categories mentioned in Sect. 2.

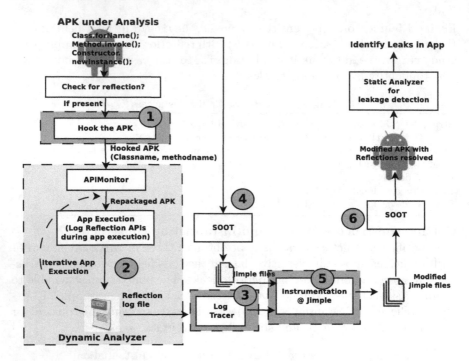

Fig. 1. EspyDroid system architecture

3.1 App Hooking and Dynamic Analyzer

The Dynamic Analyzer module uses APIMonitor [2] tool to add the monitoring code for the reflection APIs. The monitoring code is like a wrapper to the reflection APIs which logs the APIs in Android `logcat` along with pre-defined tag as and when the specified APIs are invoked during repackaged app execution. For automatic UI exploration of the app, Intelligent UI exploration module from our earlier work [13] is used which is Depth-First based black-box testing approach extended using Robotium framework [6]. The exploration time depends on the complexity of app GUI. The average exploration time for the experimental data-set of 40 apps worked in [6] is 6 min. Note that the detailed explanation is too large to be included in this paper. However, interested reader can refer to [13]. Various reflection APIs belonging to four reflection categories are given as input to APIMonitor and REFLECTIONCALL is set as the tag. The constraint of APIMonitor is that it logs the APIs with its parameters type, value and return type, value but it does not add any information regarding the calling (wrapper) class or method in which the APIs are present. The information of wrapper class and method of reflection APIs is necessary for instrumentation. The more details of why it is required are in next section. To achieve the same, EspyDroid first hooks the apk using Soot [15] such that whenever a reflection API got logged, the information of its wrapper class and method also gets logged with pre-defined tag WRACLASS-METHOD. The Fig. 2 shows the logs obtained corresponding to motivating example of Listing 1.1 after App Hooking and Dynamic Analysis. Runtime analysis and monitoring enables EspyDroid to resolve the reflection calls with runtime parameter dependency, encryption or obfuscation.

WRACLASS-METHOD: com.example.MainActivity/OnCreate
REFLECTIONCALL: Ljava/lang/Class;->forName(Ljava/lang/String;= android.telephony
    TelephonyManager)Ljava/lang/Class;=class android.telephony.TelephonyManager

WRACLASS-METHOD: com.example.MainActivity/OnCreate
REFLECTIONCALL: Ljava/lang/Class;->getMethod(Ljava/lang/String;= getDeviceId |
    [Ljava/lang/Class;={})Ljava/lang/reflect/Method;=public java.lang.String
    android.telephony.TelephonyManager.getDeviceId()

WRACLASS-METHOD: com.example.MainActivity/OnCreate
REFLECTIONCALL: Ljava/lang/reflect/Method;-->invoke(Ljava/lang/Object;=android.telephony.
    TelephonyManager|[Ljava/lang/Object;={})Ljava/lang/Object;=000000000000000

Fig. 2. Logs of motivating example

3.2   Log-Tracer

Log-Tracer processes raw logs and stores them in appropriate data structures in processed form. We use separate HashMap data structures for storing various runtime values belonging to four categories of reflection. Log-Tracer reads each line of log and checks for one of the two tags. If it finds WRACLASS-METHOD tag then saves the corresponding wrapper classname/methodname value as the key of HashMap. Next, it process the log statement with tag REFLECTION-CALL and stores the data in corresponding data structure. We use following six HashMap data structures:

```
<String, ArrayList<ArrayList<String>>> mapWraToClasses
<String, ArrayList<ArrayList<String>>>mapWraToMethodDeclared
<String, ArrayList<ArrayList<String>>> mapWraToFieldDeclared
<String, ArrayList<ArrayList<String>>> mapWraToFieldGetSet
<String, ArrayList<ArrayList<String>>> mapWraToConsGet
<String, ArrayList<ArrayList<String>>> mapWraToConsInstantiation
```

HashMaps `mapWraToClasses` for class reflection, `mapWraToMethodDeclared` for method declaration and invocation, `mapWraToFieldDeclared` for field declaration, and `mapWraToConsGet` for field value set/get, `mapWraToConsGet` for constructor reference creation, and `mapWraToConsInstantiation` for constructor instantiation related information storing are used.

Figure 3 shows the structure of these HashMaps in general. Here, the Jimple classname/methodname (e.g., JC1/M1) in which this reflection call is present serves as the key and various runtime values of the calls are stored in corresponding ArrayLists as values. The reason behind choosing key as wrapper classname/methodname is to assist at the time of instrumentation in the way that all reflections present in specific class and method will be resolved in that class only. The ArrayLists in HashMap are list of different parameters stored at runtime like reflectively called class or method name, method specifier, method parameters, etc. Figure 4 shows the HashMap data structures corresponding to logs of Fig. 2.

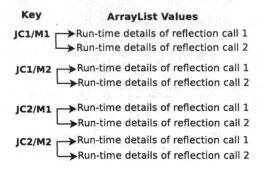

Fig. 3. Structure of HashMaps

com.example.MainActivity/OnCreate ──➤ android.telephony.TelephonyManager
(a) mapWraToClasses HashMap

com.example.MainActivity/OnCreate ──➤ getDeviceId
(b) mapWraToMethodDeclared HashMap

Fig. 4. HashMaps for Fig. 2

3.3 Instrumentation

The purpose of this module is to instrument reflection call with an equivalent non-reflection call to make the further analysis possible by static analyzers. We have chosen Jimple, an intermediate representation (IR) of Soot for instrumentation. Soot is a framework which was originally designed to analyze and transform Java bytecode and has also been extended to Android. The variables of Java correspond to Locals of Jimple. The original reflection calls are not eliminated to preserve the semantics. The important concept here is to construct the non-reflection statement in a way to maintain data-flow precision. For e.g., to be able to catch the leakage, it is necessary that non-reflection statement assigns results to same Local where reflection statement assigning its results. Also the Locals corresponding to parameters of reflection call must be same in instrumented non-reflection calls.

Soot translates all classes of apk to Jimple for instrumentation. Algorithm 1 depicts higher level concepts of instrumentation. The module traverses each Jimple of an apk and check for various reflection statements belonging to four reflection categories (lines 1–3). It constructs equivalent non-reflection statements in Jimple using runtime information of parameters and return values which are parsed from logs in HashMaps by Log-Tracer. The runtime construction of non-reflection statement depends on the category of reflection API. Therefore, it performs the check of category (lines 5, 9, 17, and 22). However, in all cases respective HashMap is used to get the runtime information. In all cases, key of HashMap is Jimple classname/methodname in which the reflection call is present to ensure that reflections belonging to any Jimple class/method will be resolved in that Jimple class only. Next, indices in ArrayList are used to ensure that within the method, information of same reflection statement is being accessed. Therefore, during instrumentation, we first obtain Jimple

---

Algorithm 1. EspyDroid's Instrumentation Algorithm

Result: Instrumented app

1 **for** *each Jimple class JC of apk* **do**
2   **for** *each statement S of JC* **do**
3   **if** *S is reflection call* **then**
4   Do instrumentation based on the category of reflection;
5   **if** *S is Class Reflection* **then**
6   Obtain aclassname from `mapWraToClasses` HashMap;
7   Instrument "$r = new aclassname" statement after S;
8   **end**
9   **if** *S is Method Declaration Reflection* **then**
10   Instrument "$r = new aclassname" statement before S;
11   Find the runtime details of actual methodname, parameter-types, return-types from `mapWraToMethodDeclared` HashMap ;
12   Find the locals corresponding to parameters by using backward flow analysis.;
13   Construct the non-reflection statement from the information obtained in above two steps;
14   Find the invoke statement in JC corresponding to this method declaration using data-flow analysis;
15   Instrument the constructed statement after this invoke statement in a way to maintain data-flow accurate;
16   **end**
17   **if** *S is Constructor Call Reflection* **then**
18   Find classname from `mapWraToConsGet` HashMap and parameter types using `mapWraToConsInstantiation` HashMap;
19   Find the locals corresponding to parameters by using backward flow analysis from S;
20   Construct and Instrument a non-reflection constructor call statement from the information obtained above after S;
21   **end**
22   **if** *S is Field Reflection* **then**
23   Find field-name, its classname from `mapWraToFieldDeclared` HashMap;
24   Construct non-reflection field access statement using the above information and based on whether field is static or non-static. Also the statement construction depends on whether the field's value is retrieved or assigned;
25   **end**
26   **end**
27   **end**
28 **end**

---

classname and methodname in which this reflection call is present with Soot APIs. This information is used as the key to map runtime values from corresponding HashMap.

The first category is class reflection where it can use any of `forName/loadClass/getClass` API for instantiating class. The class name is the parameter of these APIs which is generally obfuscated by malicious apps. The module uses `mapWraToClasses` HashMap to get actual runtime value `aclassname` of classname (line 6) and construct a "`$r = new aclassname`" statement and instrument it after class-reflection statement (line 7). Here, this is ensured that $r is Local of `aclassname` type. Therefore, this Local declaration statement also gets instrumented.

The second category is method reflection where it can use `getMethod/getDeclaredMethod` API for creating the object of method and then `invoke` API to invoke the method. To construct the non-reflection statement, runtime values of reflection call's, method's classname, specifier, return type, parameter type, Jimple Locals corresponding to parameters are required along with Jimple class and wrapper method. All the information except variables corresponding to parameters is obtained from `mapWraToMethodDeclared` HashMap. In method reflection statement, parameters to method are passed in the form of object array while in corresponding non-reflection, these are required as individual Local. To get these Locals, backward data-flow analysis is implemented which calculates individual Locals which constituted the object array (line 12). The non-reflection statement will be instrumented after the invoke of this method declaration. It may be the case that set of method declarations may be followed by the set of invokes. Also, these invokes may be interleaved. For e.g., declaration of methods M1, M2, M3 may be followed by invocation in order M3, M2, M1. To handle such interleaved invocations, we also implemented forward data-flow analysis which finds the invoke corresponding to current method declaration and instrument non-reflection statement after that invoke only. To perform accurate data-flow analysis by static analyzers, it is ensured that the non-reflection statement gets assign the result to Local where reflection statement was assigning the result.

The third category is constructor call reflection where the name of method is always `<init>` but its classname and parameters type, variables corresponding to parameters are required for construction of non-reflection statement. Classname is obtained from `mapWraToConsGet` and parameter type from `mapWraToConsInstantiation` HashMap. The similar approach of backward data-flow analysis is used for obtaining variables corresponding to method parameters.

The fourth category is field reflection where reflection APIs may be used either getting the value from the field or assigning the value to it. Construction of non-reflection statement require fieldname, its class and Jimple local corresponding to field. The first two pieces of information are obtained from HashMap while the last from current Jimple only. Instrumentation is done after current field reflection keeping data-flow accurate.

Intent reflection as shown in Listing 1.2, Intent itself is class whose method `putExtra` is used for sending data to another component. As seen from the approach, reflection belonging to any component will be done in that component of app only. Here, Intent reflection itself will be taken as class and method reflection and instrumentations will be done accordingly.

4 Evaluation

We evaluate EspyDroid against both open-source apps taken from benchmarks and apks available in bytecode format from PlayStore and VirusShare. The major usage of reflection in the experimental data-set is identified as follows:

1. Reflective instantiation of classes to hide sensitive leaks.
2. Reflective instantiation of constructors to hide leaks present in constructors.
3. Reflective invocations of methods to hide the malicious methods invoked.
4. Reflective access of fields to either set the fields with the malicious information to be leaked or to get malicious information from the fields.
5. For complicating analysis further, Inheritance feature is used where the class instantiated is derived while the fields/methods are accessed from base-class.
6. All above cases with leaks distributed over multiple components.
7. Reflective invocation of Intent to hide communication between components.
8. Obfuscated/runtime dependent parameters of reflective APIs to fail even reflection aware static analysis based techniques.

Furthermore, in the experimental dataset the leaks were also distributed over multiple components of the app. In multiple component based leaks, two or more components communicate through ICC mechanism.

4.1 Open-Source Apps

Open-source apps are selected from DroidBench benchmark, DroidRA - the most similar work in the field and some apps which are modified version of DroidRA to include encryption/obfuscation. DroidBench is an open test suite for evaluating the effectiveness of both static and dynamic tools specifically for Android apps. The benchmark is used by various research papers including recent works such as [21,24,26,27] for evaluation.

We use FlowDroid [8] static analyzer to find sources, sinks and leakage paths of apps both with and without EspyDroid. Table 1 shows the results of EspyDroid for open-source apps highlighting identified sources and sinks. The results depicts that FlowDroid missed to identify sources, sinks, and paths in original apps having reflection but the same tool could identify these missed leaks in instrumented apps. In the original representative dataset, FlowDroid could detect 19 leakage paths while the same tool could detect 51 leakage paths in the instrumented apps generated from EspyDroid. Not only the leakage paths, but the number of detected sources and sinks is also improved significantly. FlowDroid could detect 108 sources and 35 sinks while FlowDroid along with EspyDroid could detect 130 sources and 42 sinks. DroidRA could detect 119 sources, 39 sinks, and 38 leakage paths. The numbers show that DroidRA has less precision compared to EspyDroid. As the source code of these apps was available, we could verify that EspyDroid detected all sources, sinks, and paths for DroidBench apps. The information which missed by FlowDroid in the analysis of original apps is leaking private information of the user through sinks like SMS and Logs. The leaked data may further include user's sensitive information like financial details, location, etc. which, if exploited, may cause data ex-filtration and monetary loss. Except single app with reflection APIs called in loop, EspyDroid catched all leaks in DroidBench dataset.

Table 1. Results on open-source apps having confirm reflection

Sno	#App	Repository	FlowDroid			EspyDroid + FlowDroid		
			Sources	Sinks	Paths	Sources	Sinks	Paths
1	18	DroidBench	73	21	16	92	28	37
2	9	DroidRA	23	10	1	26	10	10
3	2	DroidRA with encryption	12	4	2	12	4	4
Total			108	35	19	130	42	51

4.2   APKs in Bytecode

We downloaded random 75 apps from playstore for analysis by EspyDroid. Espy-Droid could find two apps as shown in Table 2 in which FlowDroid captured additional leaks in instrumented apps. EspyDroid shows improvement in the results for the VirusShare apps. Out of 277 apps under analysis 167 apps are investigated which were using reflection. Although the results of these apps do not show improvements in leaks detection concerning sources, sinks, and paths because of complex obfuscation with multi-level of encryption and reflection. However, a significant improvement in forward edges, backward edges, and paths of call-graph is observed for three apps in EspyDroid's instrumented apps by FlowDroid. FlowDroid uses IFDS framework [22] to reduce the program analysis problem to graph reachability problem. IFDS framework first reduces the app into call-graph and calculates forward and backward edges and then builds the paths between sources and sinks. Table 3 show the improvement in results.

Table 2. Results on PlayStore apps

Sno	App name	FlowDroid			EspyDroid + FlowDroid		
		Sources	Sinks	Paths	Sources	Sinks	Paths
1	air.com.productmadness. atlas	119	59	23	119	59	25
2	com.productmadness. hovmobile	12	95	62	95	62	72

Table 3. Evaluation results on apps from VirusShare

App MD5	FlowDroid		EspyDroid + FlowDroid	
	Forward edges	Backward edges	Forward edges	Backward edges
0fa1d7a9ef7011ca 8976910b07347732	311748	115400	460679	181660
eedaf39b21aca987b 315f1e5d0e4cba6	108015	29017	110693	29441
ddc75a9aea5ac4933 bcdf6001c0ef817	323104	123781	343234	128386

The app[3] instantiates class `doom.androidquickfaster849.R$layout` reflectively and accesses its field where the classname is dynamically constructed. This runtime construction of classname requires an approach like EspyDroid involving dynamic analysis. FlowDroid missed the leak to sink `StartActivity()` from sources `getDeviceId()` and `getCountry()` in this app which EspyDroid could identify. FlowDroid constructed 20 connections between sources and sinks in original app while for EspyDroid's instrumented app, FlowDroid constructed 22 connections. The results demonstrate that with EspyDroid, the precision of static analysis tool gets improved for reflection-employed apps.

5   Limitations of EspyDroid

Despite the fact that EspyDroid can improve the state-of-art static analyzers by avoiding false negatives arising out of reflection, the technique has certain limitations. The proposed automatic dynamic analysis module may miss the coverage of some complex views like custom actionbars, custom views, etc. facilitated by Android for rich Graphical User Interface. Consequently, our proposal likely to miss some uses of reflection which are behind these views. In future work, we would develop and integrate improved intelligent techniques to achieve improved code coverage. In some cases, different runs may result in different runtime value for some parameters of reflection APIs. However, practically it may not be possible to get all possible values of these parameters dynamically. Another limitation is that currently, EspyDroid cannot resolve loop based invocation of reflection APIs.

6   Related Work

As on today, most of the best performing static analyzers [8,11,14,16,20,25] shown their limitation in handling reflection. Reflection aware analysis for Java applications is proposed by Bodden et al. in [9]. However, the solution can not be applied to Android apps directly as their approach is based on load-time instrumentation that the Android platform does not currently support. DroidRA [17]

---

[3] MD5-0fa1d7a9ef7011ca8976910b07347732.

models the identification of reflective calls as a composite constant propagation problem through the COAL declarative language [19]. However, dependency on constant string inference fails the approach when the parameters of reflection APIs have runtime dependency like passing `getDeviceId` indirectly as `dIeciveDteg.reverse()` has failed DroidRA in identification of leakages.

Ripple [28] is a reflection aware analysis technique that adds type inference in DroidRA to get more sound results in cases where direct string analysis of reflection parameters is not sufficient. However, being static in nature, Ripple will also fail when reflection combines with runtime dependency of parameters.

Hybrid analysis to handle reflection in Android has been performed in the past few years. Authors in StaDyna [29] focus on addressing dynamic code loading and reflection using the hybrid approach. The static analysis first constructs the Method Call Graph (MCG) of application, and then expands it with additional information captured at runtime. However, evaluation is done only in terms of increased number of nodes and edges without any focus to privacy leakage. It needs modified Android OS which makes it installation and use complex. At present implementation is only done for Android OS version 4.1.2 r2 which limits the scalability. It does not provide a way to directly benefit existing static analyzers, i.e., to support them in performing reflection-aware analyses. BPS Rocha et al. introduced lightweight hybrid static-runtime mechanism for information flow control [23].

Rasthofer et al. in [21] present harvester tool based on the hybrid approach to automatically extract runtime values from Android applications. First, it prepares a reduced apk using static backward slicing, and this reduced apk is executed on the emulator. Runtime values of reflective call targets resolved during the dynamic execution are manifested as ordinary method calls in the application's bytecode. The main limitation is that the current implementation of slicing is limited to single Android component. Therefore, any sample using inter-component communication (ICC) can not be analyzed. In contrast, EspyDroid's also work on malware using ICC. Due to unavailability of its source code, we are not able to practically work with Harvester[4].

This paper is an extension of our poster work in ASIACCS [12] with significant improvements. First, we added HashMap based data structures, forward data-flow analysis to make interleaved APIs instrumentation accurate. Second, we added App hooking module, which ensures reflection calls belonging to specific class and method will be non-reflectively instrumented in that class and method only. Third, we extended the evaluation dataset with PlayStore and VirusShare apps.

7   Conclusion

In this paper, we propose EspyDroid, a reflection aware hybrid analysis technique for Android app analysis. Through experimental evaluation, we demonstrate that

---

[4] We contacted authors for code. They mentioned that their legal department is working on a proper license for Harvester.

EspyDroid is resilient against encryption, obfuscation or any kind of runtime dependency of reflection parameters. The solution can also detect malware that uses Inter-Component Communication to distribute leaks over multiple components in a single application. The results demonstrate that static analyzers result in large number of false negatives in the presence of reflection. EspyDroid improves the precision by capturing the leaks missed by static analyzers alone. We plan to release EspyDroid as an open-source tool with benchmark results. In future work, we plan to develop and integrate improved intelligent techniques to achieve improved code coverage and thus reduce false negatives in capturing sensitive leaks done by malicious apps.

Acknowledgments. This work is partially supported by Security Analysis Framework for Android Platform (SAFAL, Grant 1000109932) by Department of Electronics and Information Technology, Government of India. The work is also partially supported by CEFIPRA project. Mauro Conti is supported by EU TagItSmart! Project (agreement H2020-ICT30-2015-688061) and IT-CNR/Taiwan-MOST 2016-17 "Verifiable Data Structure Streaming".

References

1. https://docs.oracle.com/javase/tutorial/reflect/
2. https://github.com/pjlantz/droidbox/tree/master/APIMonitor
3. Androguard. https://github.com/androguard/androguard
4. DroidBench. https://github.com/secure-software-engineering/DroidBench/tree/develop
5. Intents and Intent Filters. https://developer.android.com/guide/components/intents-filters.html
6. RobotiumTech/robotium. https://github.com/RobotiumTech
7. VirusShare. https://virusshare.com/
8. Arzt, S., Rasthofer, S., Fritz, C., Bodden, E., Bartel, A., Klein, J., Le Traon, Y., Octeau, D., McDaniel, P.: Flowdroid: precise context, flow, field, object-sensitive and lifecycle-aware taint analysis for android apps. ACM SIGPLAN Not. **49**(6), 259–269 (2014)
9. Bodden, E., Sewe, A., Sinschek, J., Oueslati, H., Mezini, M.: Taming reflection: aiding static analysis in the presence of reflection and custom class loaders. In: Proceedings of the 33rd International Conference on Software Engineering, pp. 241–250. ACM (2011)
10. Elish, K.O., Yao, D., Ryder, B.G.: On the need of precise inter-app icc classification for detecting android malware collusions. In: Proceedings of IEEE Mobile Security Technologies (MoST), in Conjunction with the IEEE Symposium on Security and Privacy (2015)
11. Feng, Y., Anand, S., Dillig, I., Aiken, A.: Apposcopy: semantics-based detection of android malware through static analysis. In: Proceedings of the 22nd ACM SIGSOFT International Symposium on Foundations of Software Engineering, pp. 576–587. ACM (2014)
12. Gajrani, J., Li, L., Laxmi, V., Tripathi, M., Gaur, M.S., Conti, M.: Poster: detection of information leaks via reflection in android apps. In: Proceedings of the 2017 ACM on Asia Conference on Computer and Communications Security, pp. 911–913. ACM (2017)

13. Gajrani, J., Tripathi, M., Laxmi, V., Gaur, M., Conti, M., Rajarajan, M.: Spectra: a precise framework for analyzing cryptographic vulnerabilities in android apps. In: 2017 14th IEEE Annual Consumer Communications & Networking Conference (CCNC), pp. 854–860. IEEE (2017)
14. Gordon, M.I., Kim, D., Perkins, J.H., Gilham, L., Nguyen, N., Rinard, M.C.: Information flow analysis of android applications in droidsafe. In: NDSS. Citeseer (2015)
15. Lam, P., Bodden, E., Lhoták, O., Hendren, L.: The soot framework for java program analysis: a retrospective. In: Cetus Users and Compiler Infastructure Workshop (CETUS 2011), vol. 15, p. 35 (2011)
16. Li, L., Bartel, A., Bissyande, T.F., Klein, J., Le Traon, Y., Arzt, S., Rasthofer, S., Bodden, E., Octeau, D., McDaniel, P.: IccTA: Detecting inter-component privacy leaks in android apps. In: Proceedings of the 37th International Conference on Software Engineering, vol. 1, pp. 280–291. IEEE Press (2015)
17. Li, L., Bissyandé, T.F., Octeau, D., Klein, J.: Droidra: taming reflection to support whole-program analysis of android apps. In: Proceedings of the 25th International Symposium on Software Testing and Analysis, pp. 318–329. ACM (2016)
18. Lindorfer, M., Neugschwandtner, M., Weichselbaum, L., Fratantonio, Y., Van Der Veen, V., Platzer, C.: Andrubis-1,000,000 apps later: a view on current android malware behaviors. In: 2014 Third International Workshop on Building Analysis Datasets and Gathering Experience Returns for Security (BADGERS), pp. 3–17. IEEE (2014)
19. Octeau, D., Luchaup, D., Jha, S., McDaniel, P.: Composite constant propagation and its application to android program analysis. IEEE Trans. Softw. Eng. **42**(11), 999–1014 (2016)
20. Octeau, D., McDaniel, P., Jha, S., Bartel, A., Bodden, E., Klein, J., Le Traon, Y.: Effective inter-component communication mapping in android: an essential step towards holistic security analysis. In: Presented as part of the 22nd USENIX Security Symposium (USENIX Security 2013), pp. 543–558 (2013)
21. Rasthofer, S., Arzt, S., Miltenberger, M., Bodden, E.: Harvesting runtime values in android applications that feature anti-analysis techniques. In: Proceedings of the Annual Symposium on Network and Distributed System Security (NDSS) (2016)
22. Reps, T., Horwitz, S., Sagiv, M.: Precise interprocedural dataflow analysis via graph reachability. In: Proceedings of the 22nd ACM SIGPLAN-SIGACT Symposium on Principles of Programming Languages, pp. 49–61. ACM (1995)
23. Rocha, B.P., Conti, M., Etalle, S., Crispo, B.: Hybrid static-runtime information flow and declassification enforcement. IEEE Trans. Inf. Forensics Secur. **8**(8), 1294–1305 (2013)
24. Rubinov, K., Rosculete, L., Mitra, T., Roychoudhury, A.: Automated partitioning of android applications for trusted execution environments. In: Proceedings of the 38th International Conference on Software Engineering, pp. 923–934. ACM (2016)
25. Wei, F., Roy, S., Ou, X., et al.: Amandroid: a precise and general inter-component data flow analysis framework for security vetting of android apps. In: Proceedings of the 2014 ACM SIGSAC Conference on Computer and Communications Security, pp. 1329–1341. ACM (2014)
26. Wong, M.Y., Lie, D.: Intellidroid: a targeted input generator for the dynamic analysis of android malware. In: Proceedings of the Annual Symposium on Network and Distributed System Security (NDSS) (2016)
27. Zhang, M., Duan, Y., Feng, Q., Yin, H.: Towards automatic generation of security-centric descriptions for android apps. In: Proceedings of the 22nd ACM SIGSAC Conference on Computer and Communications Security, pp. 518–529. ACM (2015)

28. Zhang, Y., Tan, T., Li, Y., Xue, J.: Ripple: reflection analysis for android apps in incomplete information environments. In: Proceedings of the Seventh ACM on Conference on Data and Application Security and Privacy, pp. 281–288. ACM (2017)
29. Zhauniarovich, Y., Ahmad, M., Gadyatskaya, O., Crispo, B., Massacci, F.: Stadyna: addressing the problem of dynamic code updates in the security analysis of android applications. In: Proceedings of the 5th ACM Conference on Data and Application Security and Privacy, pp. 37–48. ACM (2015)

Remotely Assessing Integrity of Software Applications by Monitoring Invariants: Present Limitations and Future Directions

Alessio Viticchié[✉], Cataldo Basile, and Antonio Lioy

Politecnico di Torino, Torino, Italy
{alessio.viticchie,cataldo.basile,lioy}@polito.it

Abstract. Invariants monitoring is a software attestation technique that aims at proving the integrity of a running application by checking likely invariants, which are predicates built on variables' values. Being very promising in literature, we developed a software protection that remotely checks invariants. However, we faced a series of issues and limitations. This paper, after presenting an extensive background on invariants and their use, reports, analyses, and categorizes the identified limitations. Our work suggests that, even if it is still promising, further studies are needed to decree if invariants monitoring could be practically used as a remote protection of software applications.

1 Introduction

Software attestation is a category of protection techniques that allows a monitoring system to verify that a program, which is running on another system, is behaving as expected. This verification is performed by checking the integrity of the program memory against modifications made by malicious code [3]. As opposed to the remote attestation defined by the Trusted Computing Group [9,28], software attestation does not rely on secure hardware to establish a root of trust, rather is built on peculiar properties of the software to monitor. Therefore, software attestation is better suited for scenarios where hardware is heterogeneous or when secure hardware features are not available, like often happens for embedded systems and Internet of Things devices.

Invariants monitoring (IM) is a technique proposed in literature to perform software attestation [22]. Invariants, borrowed from software engineering, are logical assertions that are held to be true during the execution of (some parts of) the application. Introduced and used for software maintenance and verification purposes (assertions, programming by contract) [16,20,21], invariants have been used to detect programming errors and incorrect implementations [10,19].

Unfortunately, user specified invariants are often nearly absent in applications [14], hence a defender wanting to protect selected code areas from tampering, may experience an insufficient number of invariants. For this reason, the works

© Springer International Publishing AG, part of Springer Nature 2018
N. Cuppens et al. (Eds.): CRiSIS 2017, LNCS 10694, pp. 66–82, 2018.
https://doi.org/10.1007/978-3-319-76687-4_5

in literature about IM resorted to dynamically-extracted likely-invariants. Likely invariants, as opposed to the "true" invariants described before, are inferred from the analysis of traces collected by executing the applications on selected inputs [14]. Usually, several likely invariants can be inferred for every part of the application whose integrity needs to be ensured.

Being very promising on paper, we have designed and implemented an IM technique. A client-side Attester sends to a trusted remote server the values of selected variables, among the ones in memory. On the server, an integrity Verifier uses the received values to check invariants and establish trustworthiness of the target application. Moreover, we have created a tool chain that, after having identified likely invariants, instruments target applications to be protected with IM. Apart from the selection of the invariants to use and the adaptation of the compilation options, which are human assisted, all the phases are automatically performed by the tool chain, which also generates all the server-side processes.

Unfortunately, we have soon experimented limitations of this protection. Some limitations are related to the use of invariants. For instance, likely invariants, which are true for the analysed traces, are not true in general. Therefore, for protection purposes, likely invariants generate false positives, i.e., violations of invariants are not related to attacks. Other limitations depend on the technology, mainly on the tool that extracts the invariants. For instance, the most known and used tool, Daikon [15], does not infer invariants on matrices, structures, and inner scope variables. Finally, additional issues relate to the assumptions to use IM for protection purposes. The assumption that a defender could tell compromised applications from original ones by verifying invariants is not proven. Determining a positive inference between attacks and invariants' violations would require an empirical assessment because invariants are also subject to false negatives, i.e., attacks may compromise applications without violating invariants.

This paper presents the following contributions. (1) It reviews the literature on invariants monitoring, presents and categorizes the limitations that affect this technique. (2) Then, it introduces the IM tool we have developed that checks the integrity application at runtime and presents how some limitations have been overcome. (3) Furthermore, it presents a tool chain that automatically applies IM to target applications. (4) Finally, especially for the limitations that have not been addressed, it discusses the issues to solve and research to perform to allow the use of IM to protect real applications from real attackers.

The paper is organized as follows. Section 2 introduces the background on invariants and limitations of likely invariants and Daikon. Section 3 presents the IM technique we have implemented and Sect. 4 shows how to instrument a target application to be protected with IM. Section 5 presents the use cases and Sect. 6 discusses the limitations of invariants monitoring. Finally, Sect. 7 draws conclusions and sketches future works.

2   Background on Invariants and Related Works

Invariants: definitions and early works. Invariants are known in computer science since long time, as they were used to identify program bugs before they revealed during application working, and to assist development and maintenance [20]. As Gries demonstrated, a program can be formally derived from its specifications [16], hence software engineers defined axioms that describe correct executions and properties in terms of constraints. Several works in literature exploited invariants as axioms to identify and locate faults and problems in software implementation [5,6,8,13,23]. Indeed, in these works invariants were explicitly deduced from the theoretical specifications of the program, then checked against the actual implementation.

Likely invariants and their use in non-security contexts. In practice, it could happen that invariants are absent or too little to be useful. Therefore, researchers proposed to dynamically extract invariants from target applications by observing the execution of an application and inferring a set of relations, which are then used as invariants. Dynamically extracted invariants are not axioms, rather constraints that can fail, by chance, even if the program is sound. Hence, the term *likely invariants* has been introduced to identify these empirically deduced constraints.

One of the most widespread tools for likely invariants detection is Daikon, which is free and open source[1]. Daikon tests potential invariants against observed runtime values, taken from traces collected trough a front-end instrumentation if the target application [14,15]. Daikon uses a statistical approach to minimize invariants that may generate false positives. That is, only the true relations whose probability to be a mere coincidence is under a user-definable threshold become invariants. Moreover, Daikon can improve its effectiveness with abstract type information [17].

Daikon has been used by several authors for software maintenance purposes. Xie *et al.* used Daikon to extract invariants for automatic unit test generation without any *a priori* specification [34]. Csallner *et al.* proposed DSD-Crasher, a tool that automatically finds software bugs by combining dynamic analysis (i.e., likely invariants inferred with Daikon) with static analysis and dynamic verification [11]. Schuler *et al.* proposed a tool to infer class contracts with Daikon [30]. Schiller *et al.* proposed VeriWeb, a web-based IDE that uses Daikon to infer clauses used to help users when they have to write verifiable specifications [29]. Sahoo *et al.* exploit Daikon-generated likely invariants to locate elements in the code that may lead to failures. Likelihood failure is assessed via dynamic backward slicing and heuristic filtering [27]. Lemieux *et al.* introduced Texada, a tool for extracting specifications in linear temporal logic that once combined with Daikon infers likely data-temporal properties [24].

---

[1] Daikon is the subject of a number of publications, which is maintained at https://plse.cs.washington.edu/daikon/pubs/.

Beside Daikon, several other tools and methodologies have been developed for likely invariant detection. DIDUCE by Hangal *et al.*, performs dynamic invariants detection on online Java applications at run time [19]. It automatically detects program errors and their causes (e.g., errors in handling corner cases, errors in inputs, and misuse of APIs) by analysing the detected invariants. Csallner *et al.* proposed DySy, a dynamic invariants detector that combines concrete executions and symbolic executions of test cases [12] to deduce *symbolic invariants*, which not only depend on execution traces but also on text structure of the program. Along with academic progresses, industrial invariants detection solutions have appeared: Ackermann *et al.* proposed a tool that infers invariants based on data-mining techniques [2], IODINE is a tool to detect invariants from hardware design [18], and Agitator is a commercial tool inspired by Daikon [7].

Invariants monitoring for software protection purposes. In terms of software security, invariants have been used as a measure of software integrity (data or code). Lorenzolli *et al.* proposed FFTV, a self-protecting technique that uses invariants to analyse and react to failures [25]. The technique infers likely invariants from the contexts that generate failures. Hence, whenever invariants from failing contexts are valid, FFTV applies a protection mechanism to prevent the failure either by correcting the execution issue or by avoiding the execution of the faulty code. Perkins *et al.* proposed ClearView which analyses a running system and uses Daikon to describe its behaviour in terms of likely invariants [26]. Clearview, in case of failures, automatically detects the failed invariants and proposes patches that re-establish the invariants' validity. Therefore, ClearView may protect from some attacks, such as code-injection.

Kil *et al.*, proposed ReDAS, a software attestation mechanism to monitor dynamic system properties [22]. ReDAS first extracts likely invariants from global variables values collected during system call invocations. Then, by evaluating invariants at runtime, they claim the system is able to offer protection from tampering and limited protection from runtime memory corruption. Beliga *et al.*, proposed Gibraltar, a solution to detect kernel-level rootkits based on violation of inferred likely invariants [4]. Gibraltar, during an inference phase, observes data structures and values (e.g., entropy pool, processes list, page sizes) of the Linux kernel, thus it deduces invariants that are monitored during the detection phase. Wei *et al.* proposed an attestation mechanism that uses "scoped invariants", likely invariants valid in specific scopes inside the program, to spot anomalies [33].

2.1   Limitations of Likely Invariants

The use of invariants is subject to limitations that depend on the technique itself, regardless of tool used to extract them, the reason for using invariants, and the target application.

First of all, for attestation purposes, likely invariants can generate *false positives* $(\mathcal{L}_1)^2$, which are failures of invariants for applications that are not

---

² All the found limitations have been labelled as $(\mathcal{L}_i)$ to ease reference.

compromised. While theoretically avoidable with complete execution traces, false positives are very "likely" in practice.

Then, the verification of invariants must be done with variable values taken from the memory at the same time ($\mathcal{L}_2$). Values from correct but different executions may invalidate invariants.

For instance, given the code snippet below:

```
for(i=0;i<100;i++){
    j=100-i;
    /* do something with i and j */}
```

A tool could deduce i+j==100, but this invariant can only be verified with values of i and j acquired from memory simultaneously. This also leads to classical concurrency issues: data consistency must be ensured when variable values are extracted from memory (e.g., by stopping the execution).

2.2 Limitations of Daikon

Daikon checks for invariants when procedures are entered and exited, likely invariants are thus *pre- and post-conditions* ($\mathcal{L}_3$). This is a feature for software maintenance purposes, but a limitation from the attestation point of view, as an attestation request may arrive in the mid of the procedure execution.

Furthermore, Daikon neglects the execution history. When a request arrives the application may have walked any path in its control flow graph, thus the call stack may contain data from several functions. Hence, it would be interesting evaluating invariants that involve variables from different functions ($\mathcal{L}_4$).

Daikon is unable to inspect all the variables ($\mathcal{L}_5$). It only considers global variables and variables passed as inputs to functions but it does not inspect the inner local variables. Furthermore, Daikon is unable to correctly manage data structures (struct), it only shows a minimum ability to treat mono-dimensional arrays, and it simply ignores multidimensional data structures ($\mathcal{L}_6$).

Daikon checks for 75 different *types of invariants* ($\mathcal{L}_7$), furthermore, additional types of invariants can be specified by expert users. Checking a large number of invariants increases the chances that the output contains the facts that are needed by a human or a tool; however, it also increases the run time of the invariant detector algorithm.

In addition, to improve the often very frustrating performance of the tool extracting traces (Kvasir for x86 platforms), Daikon invariants' research scope can be limited to specific portions of the application code ($\mathcal{L}_8$). Theoretically, the "quality" of invariants extracted should not be affected.

3 Remotely Monitoring Invariants at Runtime

We have designed an IM system where a client-side Attester is able to send the value of selected variables present in memory to a trusted remote server. On the server, a Verifier uses the received values to decree the integrity of the target application (see Sect. 3.1). Moreover, we have developed a tool chain to protect a client application with IM (see Sect. 4).

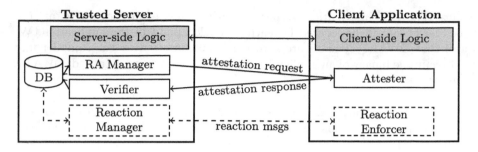

Fig. 1. Architecture of our IM implementation.

3.1   Our IM Implementation at Run-Time

Our implementation of the IM technique uses the architecture in Fig. 1. We assume that, when an application is launched, it notifies a server, regardless of the fact that it may need the execution of some server-side logic. We also assume that client and server perform a mutual authentication phase and, strongly suggested, negotiate a secure channel.

The *Remote Attestation Manager* (*imRAM*) is the server-side component that starts an attestation transaction with application client and logs all the transactions data in a local DB. Attestation requests are generated periodically at random time intervals (with a constant average time). An attestation request is a message that only conveys a random 256 bit nonce N.

The *Attester* (*imATT*) is the client-side component in charge of processing the attestation requests. It collects the values of selected variables among the ones available in memory at the moment of the attestation request. Then, it prepares the attestation responses that are sent to the server.

The *Verifier* (*imVER*) is the server-side component that uses the attestation responses received from the *imATT* to decree the integrity of the application. It extracts from the responses the variable values, use them to evaluate invariants, and logs into the DB all the evaluation results, both positives and negatives.

Since our research aims at investigating the detective abilities of invariants, we did not consider the reactions. However, we mention that a server-side component, the *Reaction Manager*, is needed to decide, according to a policy[3], when an application needs to be punished. Moreover, at client-side, a *Reaction Enforcer* may be useful to enforce the reactions that cannot be enforced on the server (e.g., graceful memory data corruption [31]).

The *imATT* needs to extract the value of the variables in memory. Variables can be stored in the stack, in the data segment, in a register, in a known location in memory, in a memory location referenced by a register, or it can be translated as a constant value. In addition, the storage location of a variable may change depending on the execution point of the program. To this purpose,

---

[3] The policy may take decisions based on the type of the invariants failed and the frequency of failure as well user and business information, like the type of contract.

we use DWARF[4] information, at instrumenting time, to predict where, at runtime, variables will be located for each execution point of the application. We recall that DWARF symbols are additional data inserted by the compiler into the executable binary of an application for debugging purposes. Indeed, DWARF symbols associate the location of a variable with an instruction pointer range, which specifies the code segment for which the location is valid. DWARF symbols depends on the compiler (e.g., `gcc` vs. `llvm`) and, obviously, the information associated to symbols depends on the destination platform of the application (e.g., x86 or ARM).

Moreover, variables are uniquely identified during the instrumentation phase to allow the *inVER* to unambiguously recognise them. Unique IDs and DWARF information are used to build the Variables Data Structure (VDS), injected during the instrumentation phase.

Therefore, based on the VDS, the *imATT*: (1) stops the execution of the target application; (2) unwinds the call stack and, for each stack frame, reads the instruction pointer and deduces the associated function; (3) for each deduced function and depending on the instruction pointer, identifies and locate the extractable variables; (4) collects the variables values. Finally, the *imATT* builds:

$$d = n \| (v_{ID}(v_i), \text{Value}(v_i)) \| \ldots \| (v_{ID}(v_i), \text{Value}(v_i))$$

where n is a 16 bit integer that counts the total number of collected variables, $v_{ID}(v_i)$ is the unique identifier of the variable and $\text{Value}(v_i)$ is the value of the variable found in memory and sends to the *inVER* the response:

$$r = d \| H \| (dN \| ID \mid S)$$

where H is a hash function of choice (we support SHA1, SHA256, and Blake2), ID are optional data that unequivocally identifies the running application, and S are data that relate the client to the server (e.g., secrets shared during the mutual authentication).

Then, during the verification, the *inVER* first checks the correctness of the received hash. Then, it reads the P_i in r, uses the $v_{ID}(v_i)$ to determine the invariants that can be verified (which are the ones for which all the variables v_{ID} are in r), then employs the values $\text{Value}(v_i)$ to actually evaluate the invariants.

3.2   Limitations of Monitoring Invariants at Runtime

Our implementation presents some limitations, mainly due to the fact that it is just a prototype we implemented to test IM.

First, the current implementation simply *sends all the variables values* ($\mathcal{L}_9$) available in memory that are involved in at least one invariant, that is, the variables in the VDS. This simplified approach introduces a risk: attestation responses may be too big, e.g., when the target application has too many global

---

[4] DWARF is a standard produced by the DWARF Standards Committee available at http://dwarfstd.org/.

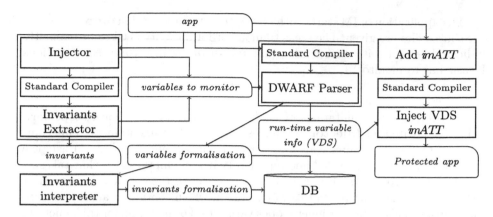

Fig. 2. IM tool chain.

variables (always accessible thus always sent by the *imATT*) and when the variable size is large (e.g., big data buffers or big data structures).

Furthermore, in our implementation the *imATT* needs to access the same memory areas as the original application, therefore, *the imATT cannot be an external entity* ($\mathcal{L}_{10}$), thus we injected it in the client application. To ease the implementation (i.e., avoid source code modifications), the *imATT* is launched before the main, thus immediately recognizable and easy to disable. Indeed, the *imATT* initialisation function is given the `constructor` attribute (which is valid both for `gcc` and `llvm`) and tells the compiler to insert the function invocation before the main function call or before the dynamic library is loaded ($\mathcal{L}_{11}$). It is worth mentioning, it is our first (not so) quick and dirty prototype implementation.

Moreover, another limitation is very important for the practical use invariants as a software attestation technique: there is not a precise link between attacks and invariants. That is, there is not a clear way to assume that an attack compromising the target application will violate invariants. This is a case of *false negatives* ($\mathcal{L}_{12}$), the most dangerous issue for a technique aiming at attesting the integrity of application from modifications. The presence of false negatives has been revealed also on the use cases we have instrumented and tested, as shown in Sect. 5. However, even though it has been discovered during the implementation, this is a general limitation of invariants.

4 Instrumenting an App to Be Protected with IM

We developed a tool chain to automatically apply the IM implementation presented in Sect. 3.1 to target applications, which is illustrated in Fig. 2. The tool chain identifies the invariants, generates the client- and server-side components, and prepares the necessary server-side infrastructure. This is a key point to make a protection technique usable, as it should be easy to apply also by software developers and not only for experts.

The application of IM starts with an unprotected application (**app**) for which the source files are given. The areas to monitor for integrity need to be explicitly indicated (either with source code annotation or by discarding the functions Kvasir has to monitor).

The app source code is taken as input by two processes: discovery of likely invariants, extraction of DWARF information.

To overcome the limitations of Daikon and monitor inner local scope variables, we created an **Injector**, as suggested by Daikon maintainers. This component analyses the source code and, for each inner scope found, it (1) lists the variables, (2) generates an ad hoc function (with an empty body) that takes as input all the listed variables, and (3) inserts a call to the generated function at the exit of the inner scope. In this way, Daikon, which considers values passed to functions, can also consider inner scopes variables. For instance, for this function:

```
double a(int a, int b){
    int c; double d;
    c=a+b;
    d=(double)a/c;
    return d;}
```

the Injector finds the c and d variables and generates the function:

```
void _____injectedFunction_rand (int c, double d){}
```

where **rand** is a random string added to make the function name unique. Finally, it injects a call in the original function and the function definition:

```
void _____injectedFunction_rand (int c, double d){}
double f(int a, int b){
    int c; double d;
    c=a+b;
    d=(double)a/c;
    _____injectedFunction_rand (c, d);
    return d;}
```

This component also outputs a description file where it links the injected functions to the function where they have been injected, to allow reconstructing each invariant from the output Daikon will produce in a later step.

The output of the Injector is then processed with the **standard compiler** to generate a binary that can be traced by Kvasir[5]. The compiler is run with debugging options enabled (i.e., `-g -gdwarf-2`) and optimisation options disabled (i.e., `-O0`). Then, the **Invariants Extractor** launches Kvasir to collect execution traces and, subsequently, it calls Daikon to analyse the traces. The Invariants Extractor produces two outcomes: the invariants detected by Daikon that serve for monitoring purposes, which can be (optionally) manually filtered

---

[5] Note that Kvasir works for x86 architectures, unfortunately, for other architectures we experienced major limitations in using Daikon.

by users, and the list of the variables to retrieve at runtime to verify the selected invariants.

The second process also starts from the unprotected application sources. The application, together with the *imATT* files, is compiled by standard compiler. Starting from the obtained binary, the **DWARF Parser** analyses the DWARF symbols and collects the information (location descriptions) needed to retrieve variables values at run-time. Furthermore, it assigns a unique ID (a progressive integer) to all the variables to monitor, and stores all these data in the DB (*variables formalisation*). The parser also produces the VDS as a binary file.

Finally, an **Invariant Interpreter** uses the output of the Invariants Extractor and variables' info to optimise the invariants representation for fast verification and obtain the *invariants formalisation* then stored in the DB.

In the end, the application is compiled without debugging symbols together with the *imATT* code (and the logic to communicate with the server). Then the VDS is injected in the resulting binary, thus delivering the protected application.

4.1 Limitations of our IM Application

The toolchain and our approach has an important limitation: *the instrumented application contains the VDS* ($\mathcal{L}_{13}$). Information about monitored variables is sensitive for an attacker trying to compromise IM.

Another limitation is related to the compilation. Our tool chain may automatically apply IM, but only after the *compiler options for Daikon* and its trace collection helpers have been properly identified ($\mathcal{L}_{14}$). Since there is not any standard way to build all kinds of C applications, these options can only be found manually for each application to protect (e.g., by analysing makefiles and scripts). Moreover, *compiler optimizations need to be disabled* to allow the *imATT* to deterministically find the location of variables ($\mathcal{L}_{15}$). Currently, we have no alternatives, even if we imagine that future advancements will allow the reconstruction of the variables' location also with optimization.

5 Use Cases

We protected with IM the following open source applications written in C: *Lynx*, a command line web browser (http://lynx.browser.org), *Bzip2*, a command line compression tool (http://www.bzip.org), and *MOC (Music On Console)*, a command line music player (http://moc.daper.net).

We just report here the analysis of MOC, which is representative of the others and highlights features and limitations of the IM. Table 1 reports the number of files and the LOCs of each use case, together with the invariants (total and distinct) discovered by Daikon with and without the injector enabled. Moreover, it reports the invariants we have manually selected for the IM.

MOC is made of 91 C source files, 43478 LOC. MOC plays and pauses songs that can also be organized in playlists reproduced in linear or random order. To have a more realistic use case, we modified the original MOC code to have two versions. We assumed that the original MOC application as a *Premium* version and created a *Free* version that introduces limitations: it only allows playing playlists in random order (shuffle mode always on), and it does not allow skipping tracks or navigating the playlists (inspired by Spotify). The changes have been implemented as if statements based on a preprocessor define, named PREMIUM:

```
if(PREMIUM){ /* perform original task */
}else{ /* write a message */ }
```

Both the unused branch of the statements and the PREMIUM define are removed by the compiler and do not appear in the final binaries. Practically, we prevented the execution of the *next, previous* and *toggle shuffle* commands at user interface level, where the requested operations are forwarded to the proper player component. Additionally, we modified the player; the branch of the function that jumps to the next song in a playlist points to the random skip.

First, by analysing the call graph, we identified the functions to monitor, starting from the modified ones[6]. We then protected with IM the *Free* version with our toolchain, executed on an i7-4910MQ@2.90 GHz with 16 GB RAM. We manually modified the original MOC makefile to adapt the Kvasir compilation parameters (added -gdwarf-2, substituted -O2 with -O0). Daikon discovered 8553 invariants, most of them were redundant (e.g., identically repeated pre-post-conditions). In the end, only 246 invariants were distinct, and most of them related to global variables. In fact, MOC largely uses global variables whose value do not change during the execution (thus not interesting for monitoring purposes). Running Kvasir with the option --ignore-globals reduced the traces collected, the collection time, and Daikon found only 24 invariants. In the end, we manually selected 38 invariants to monitor. Then, we ran Kvasir and Daikon with the Function Injector enabled. Unfortunately, Daikon was not able to infer additional invariants. We were expecting a limited number of new invariants, as MOC makes limited use of inner scope variables, but none at all was surprising. We have carefully debugged our code to exclude our responsibility then we investigated the reason for this result. We discovered that Kvasir correctly reports in the traces the call to the injected functions but Daikon is unable to infer more invariants with the injector also when we reduced the threshold for accepting invariants. We experienced the same issue with the other use cases.

Then we simulated an attacker wanting to use Premium features on a Free app. By attaching a debugger to the running application, we were able to test IM against two different attacks: (1) toggle the shuffle mode to enable ordered playlist reproduction (by forcing the value of the shuffle variable in the go_to_another_file function), and (2) enable the *next* function (by trapping the call to go_to_another_file function and executing the (previously remove) code to jump to the next track in the playlist).

We ran the attacks and then we analysed, for each one, 100 attestation responses. The first attack is always detected by IM: the alteration of the shuffle

---

[6] Namely, the functions are the main in main.c, go_to_another_file, audio_play, and audio_queue_move in audio.c, go_file, play_it, cmd_next, menu_key, and options_get_int in interface.c.

Table 1. Statistical information on the use cases (∅ indicates that no invariants were extracted after 24 h execution).

app	Files-functions-LOC	Invariants	Monitored
Lynx	264-1890-193625	∅ (585)	52
Bzip2	1-106-7010	5770 (193)	13
MOC	91-1215-43478	8553 (246)	38

value revealed the tampering (100% detection). On the other hand, the second attack is never detected by IM (100% false negatives). Indeed, the attack is mounted without altering variable values ($\mathcal{L}_{16}$).

By running our experiments, we discovered another limitation of IM. As said before, the inferred invariants are pre- post-conditions associated to functions, hence, they are only evaluable when the associated functions are executed, even for invariants only based on global variables. By chance, we have selected applications that are in the idle state most of the time waiting for user input. During the idle period, very few functions are being executed, often just the main (or the library functions that play tracks), thus few variables are in the call stack. Hence, the risk is that either IM evaluates almost always the same invariants, or checks no invariants at all, if the idle functions are not monitored ($\mathcal{L}_{17}$).

6   Discussion

We have categorized the limitation identified in the previous sections in two classes. Limitations that are Specific of invariants (labelled with S) are issues intrinsic to the use of invariants. In this class we have preferred to explicitly mark (with P) limitations related to the use of invariants for software protection. On the other hand, technological limitations (T) depend on the current technological infrastructure used to extract invariants and use them for remote monitoring purposes (extraction, evaluation, implementation details). We have associated every limitation to a severity level, in the high (h), medium (m), low (l) range, to express how hard should be to overcome it. In this way, we have a compact classification of limitations in the form [$\mathcal{L}_i =$ (classes; severity)].

[$\mathcal{L}_1 = (S; m)$]. *False positives* can be reduced by increasing the traces used to infer invariants. Theoretically, with full coverage no false positive should be found, however, the number of likely invariants could decrease.

[$\mathcal{L}_2 = (S; m)$]. Limitations on the *concurrent extraction* of variables' values could be mitigated by considering data dependency information. Our guess is that some invariants could be verified with values from different executions while others will only be evaluable with values taken at the same time, regardless of the technological improvements. Further research is needed in this field.

[$\mathcal{L}_3 = (S; m)$]. To overcome the limitation related to when Daikon collects variables' values (i.e., *only pre- and post-conditions*), invariants could be inferred within functions' body, e.g., by injecting code (as for the inner scope) or waiting for new tools to do it. However, the impact of this improvement needs an estimation. It may only be beneficial for large functions when variables have more complex lifecycles. Moreover, data dependency graph info should be considered.

$[\mathcal{L}_4 = (S; m)]$. Also lack of studies on *inter-function invariants* can be mitigated with further research that also considers data dependency. Indeed, evaluating invariants with variables from different functions may improve the quality of the verification (if values can be taken in different moments in time).

$[\mathcal{L}_5 = (S; m)]$. Limitations related to *variables' types* considered by Daikon (only global variables and inputs to functions, no data structures, no inner scope) are important but not severe, as enough invariants can be found already. Waiting for limitations to be eliminated in next versions of the extraction tools, our tool already tried (but failed) to overcome the limitation on inner scope variables and we are working to inject code to process structures.

$[\mathcal{L}_6 = (S; m)]$. Limitations related to the *impossibility to infer invariants on arrays* are more difficult to overcome. Indeed, despite the technological evolution, arrays and matrices may contain data that are difficult to correlate and may increase false positives. It some cases, it could be useful to instrument the application to flatten multi-dimensional arrays. Further studies are in order.

$[\mathcal{L}_7 = (S; m)]$. Limitations on the *inferred invariants types* are not alarming. The list of invariants types considered by Daikon is big enough and extensible.

$[\mathcal{L}_8 = (S; m)]$. Limitations related to the *invariants' research scope* are also not alarming, as they only depend on limits in the current trace extractor.

$[\mathcal{L}_9 = (S; m)]$. Since our *imATT sends all the variables* involved in invariants it may be problematic for bandwidth consumption, further research is needed. Attestation requests that explicitly ask for a set of variables have been considered but discarded. Indeed, all variables but the global ones are only available in memory when a specific part of the code is executed. Thus, the *imATT* is legitimate to answer that a variable is not in memory, and an attacker may legally bypass the protection by always answering that no variables are available in memory. Developing an *imATT* that only sends specific variables (e.g., only the ones that changed since the last attestation) or a subset of the global variables requires the solution of data dependency to allow sending values in different moments. Moreover, a security analysis must establish such an IM could be circumvented.

$[\mathcal{L}_{10} = (S; m)]$. Getting variables values with an *external imATT* requires a process working at higher level of privileges (e.g., with VM introspection). However, it looks feasible even if this introduces other security and privacy issues (may it monitor the whole client?).

$[\mathcal{L}_{11} = (S; m)]$. Also avoiding the use of the *constructor option* to load the *imATT* should be easily overcome with limited engineering (but it's not research).

$[\mathcal{L}_{12} = (S; m)]$. The most serious issue and the most difficult to overcome, is certainly related to *false negatives*, a fundamental limitation to use IM for protection purposes. Establishing a clear inference among violation of invariants and attacks that actually compromise application assets is a research issue of primary importance. An empirical assessment with humans (being or playing the role of hackers) can determine if successful attack may not be discovered with IM, as done with other techniques [32]. Additionally, a formal model of the assets to protect (e.g., with control and data flow graphs), and their relations to variables used by invariants can show what be monitored with IM. Such a model may help determining the functions to monitor and the ones that require different protections.

[$\mathcal{L}_{13} = (S; m)$]. We did not find an effective solution to avoid the *injection of the VDS*. Certainly, the VDS can be better hidden in the application binaries (e.g., with obfuscation) but needs to be made available at the client.

[$\mathcal{L}_{14} = (S; m)$]. The *manual effort* needed to compile for Kvasir and Daikon is not a major issue and appears sustainable (but boring).

[$\mathcal{L}_{15} = (S; m)$]. Analogously, overcoming the limitations on *compiler optimization* both for Daikon and memory management, seems feasible with better extractors or extensions of the existing ones, and with more modern standards.

[$\mathcal{L}_{16} = (S; m)$]. Unfortunately, there is nothing to do when attacks can be mounted by attaching a debugger without altering variables values.

[$\mathcal{L}_{17} = (S; m)$]. The limitation on the *availability of invariants* to monitor point seems possible to overcome with guidelines on the selection of the functions to monitor (like "include the functions executed during the idle phases").

We can conclude that, if the impact of false negatives on the effectiveness of the protection can be actually precisely estimated, all the other issues and limitations can be (completely or partly) addressed to make invariants monitoring a protection technique that can work in practice, provided it is associated to techniques that avoid attaching debuggers [1].

7   Conclusions and Future Work

This paper has presented the Invariants Monitoring protection technique, which aims at remotely monitoring the integrity of a running application by checking likely invariants. We have analysed the literature on invariants and presented the foundations of the invariants monitoring technique, our implementation of IM, and the tool chain we have used to automatically protect an arbitrary application. We have also analysed and categorised all the found limitations to identify the research and technology effort needed to overcome them. Our analysis confirmed that IM is a promising technique, as several practical and technological limitations can be overcome, for instance, by companies wanting to commercialise IM. However, our work identified the need for further studies to decree if invariants monitoring can be practically used to protect software applications, the most important issues being related to false negatives. From the theoretical point of view, a formalization of IM may allow better understanding and improvement of this protection technique.

As future work, we will improve IM to reduce the impact of its security weaknesses. We planned to empirically evaluate IM by means of experiments with participants trying to attack and circumvent IM. We expect to draw more solid conclusions on the benefits and limitations of IM, especially on the relations among assets to protect, invariants, and attacks to prevent. It could be worth investigating the use of data dependency and data flow analysis techniques to improve the semantic of the inferred statements. Moreover, IM must evolve to integrate with techniques aiming at modifying and reconfiguring applications at runtime (e.g., code mobility). Combining these techniques could be a valuable direction for improvements and practical application of IM.

References

1. Abrath, B., Coppens, B., Volckaert, S., Wijnant, J., De Sutter, B.: Tightly-coupled self-debugging software protection. In: Proceedings of the 6th Workshop on Software Security, Protection, and Reverse Engineering, SSPREW, pp. 7–10. ACM (2016)
2. Ackermann, C., Cleaveland, R., Huang, S., Ray, A., Shelton, C., Latronico, E.: Automatic requirement extraction from test cases. In: Barringer, H., Falcone, Y., Finkbeiner, B., Havelund, K., Lee, I., Pace, G., Roşu, G., Sokolsky, O., Tillmann, N. (eds.) RV 2010. LNCS, vol. 6418, pp. 1–15. Springer, Heidelberg (2010). https://doi.org/10.1007/978-3-642-16612-9_1
3. Armknecht, F., Sadeghi, A.-R., Schulz, S., Wachsmann, C.: A security framework for the analysis and design of software attestation. In: Proceedings of the 2013 ACM SIGSAC Conference on Computer & communications security, pp. 1–12. ACM (2013)
4. Baliga, A., Ganapathy, V., Iftode, L.: Detecting kernel-level rootkits using data structure invariants. IEEE Trans. Dependable Secure Comput. 8(5), 670–684 (2011)
5. Beyer, D., Henzinger, T.A., Majumdar, R., Rybalchenko, A.: Path invariants. In: ACM Sigplan Notices, vol. 42, pp. 300–309. ACM (2007)
6. Blanchet, B., Cousot, P., Cousot, R., Feret, J., Mauborgne, L., Miné, A., Monniaux, D., Rival, X.: A static analyzer for large safety-critical software. In: ACM SIGPLAN Notices, vol. 38, pp. 196–207. ACM (2003)
7. Boshernitsan, M., Doong, R., Savoia, A.: From daikon to agitator: lessons and challenges in building a commercial tool for developer testing. In: Proceedings of the 2006 International Symposium on Software Testing and Analysis, pp. 169–180. ACM (2006)
8. Cohen, E., Dahlweid, M., Hillebrand, M., Leinenbach, D., Moskal, M., Santen, T., Schulte, W., Tobies, S.: VCC: a practical system for verifying concurrent C. In: Berghofer, S., Nipkow, T., Urban, C., Wenzel, M. (eds.) TPHOLs 2009. LNCS, vol. 5674, pp. 23–42. Springer, Heidelberg (2009). https://doi.org/10.1007/978-3-642-03359-9_2
9. Committee, T., et al.: Trusted computing platform alliance (TCPA) main specification v1. Technical report, 1b TCPA Alliance (2002)
10. Cristian, F.: Exception handling and software fault tolerance. IEEE Trans. Comput. 31(6), 531–540 (1982)
11. Csallner, C., Smaragdakis, Y., Xie, T.: DSD-Crasher: a hybrid analysis tool for bug finding. ACM Trans. Softw. Eng. Methodol. (TOSEM) 17(2), 8 (2008)
12. Csallner, C., Tillmann, N., Smaragdakis, Y.: DySy. In: 30th ACM/IEEE International Conference on Software Engineering, ICSE 2008, pp. 281–290. IEEE (2008)
13. Delgado, N., Gates, A.Q., Roach, S.: A taxonomy and catalog of runtime software-fault monitoring tools. IEEE Trans. Softw. Eng. 30(12), 859–872 (2004)

14. Ernst, M.D., Cockrell, J., Griswold, W.G., Notkin, D.: Dynamically discovering likely program invariants to support program evolution. IEEE Trans. Softw. Eng. **27**(2), 99–123 (2001)
15. Ernst, M.D., Perkins, J.H., Guo, P.J., McCamant, S., Pacheco, C., Tschantz, M.S., Xiao, C.: The daikon system for dynamic detection of likely invariants. Sci. Comput. Program. **69**(1), 35–45 (2007)
16. Gries, D.: The Science of Programming. Springer, New York (1981). https://doi.org/10.1007/978-1-4612-5983-1
17. Guo, P.J., Perkins, J.H., McCamant, S., Ernst, M.D.: Dynamic inference of abstract types. In: Proceedings of the 2006 International Symposium on Software Testing and Analysis, pp. 255–265. ACM (2006)
18. Hangal, S., Chandra, N., Narayanan, S., Chakravorty, S.: IODINE: a tool to automatically infer dynamic invariants for hardware designs. In: Proceedings of the 42nd Annual Design Automation Conference, pp. 775–778. ACM (2005)
19. Hangal, S., Lam, M.S.: Tracking down software bugs using automatic anomaly detection. In: Proceedings of the 24th International Conference on Software Engineering, pp. 291–301. ACM (2002)
20. Hoare, C.A.R.: An axiomatic basis for computer programming. Commun. ACM **12**(10), 576–580 (1969)
21. Jazequel, J.-M., Meyer, B.: Design by contract: the lessons of Ariane. Computer **30**(1), 129–130 (1997)
22. Kil, C., Sezer, E.C., Azab, A.M., Ning, P., Zhang, X.: Remote attestation to dynamic system properties: towards providing complete system integrity evidence. In: Proceedings of the IEEE/IFIP International Conference on Dependable Systems and Networks, DSN 2009, pp. 115–124. IEEE (2009)
23. Klein, G., Elphinstone, K., Heiser, G., Andronick, J., Cock, D., Derrin, P., Elkaduwe, D., Engelhardt, K., Kolanski, R., Norrish, M., et al.: seL4: formal verification of an OS kernel. In: Proceedings of the ACM SIGOPS 22nd Symposium on Operating Systems Principles, pp. 207–220. ACM (2009)
24. Lemieux, C., Park, D., Beschastnikh, I.: General LTL specification mining (t). In: Proceedings of the 30th IEEE/ACM International Conference on Automated Software Engineering (ASE), pp. 81–92. IEEE (2015)
25. Lorenzoli, D., Mariani, L., Pezze, M.: Towards self-protecting enterprise applications. In: The 18th IEEE International Symposium on Software Reliability, ISSRE 2007, pp. 39–48. IEEE (2007)
26. Perkins, J.H., Kim, S., Larsen, S., Amarasinghe, S., Bachrach, J., Carbin, M., Pacheco, C., Sherwood, F., Sidiroglou, S., Sullivan, G., et al.: Automatically patching errors in deployed software. In: Proceedings of the 22nd ACM SIGOPS Symposium on Operating Systems Principles, pp. 87–102. ACM (2009)
27. Sahoo, S.K., Criswell, J., Geigle, C., Adve, V.: Using likely invariants for automated software fault localization. In: ACM SIGARCH Computer Architecture News, vol. 41, pp. 139–152. ACM (2013)
28. Sailer, R., Zhang, X., Jaeger, T., Van Doorn, L.: Design and implementation of a TCG-based integrity measurement architecture. In: USENIX Security Symposium, vol. 13, pp. 223–238 (2004)
29. Schiller, T.W., Ernst, M.D.: Reducing the barriers to writing verified specifications. ACM SIGPLAN Not. **47**(10), 95–112 (2012)
30. Schuler, D., Dallmeier, V., Zeller, A.: Efficient mutation testing by checking invariant violations. In Proceedings of the 18th International Symposium on Software Testing and Analysis, pp. 69–80. ACM (2009)

31. Tan, G., Chen, Y., Jakubowski, M.H.: Delayed and controlled failures in tamper-resistant software. In: Camenisch, J.L., Collberg, C.S., Johnson, N.F., Sallee, P. (eds.) IH 2006. LNCS, vol. 4437, pp. 216–231. Springer, Heidelberg (2007). https://doi.org/10.1007/978-3-540-74124-4_15

32. Viticchié, A., Regano, L., Torchiano, M., Basile, C., Ceccato, M., Tonella, P., Tiella, R.: Assessment of source code obfuscation techniques. In: 2016 IEEE 16th International Working Conference on Source Code Analysis and Manipulation (SCAM), pp. 11–20. IEEE (2016)

33. Wei, J., Pu, C., Rozas, C.V., Rajan, A., Zhu, F.: Modeling the runtime integrity of cloud servers: a scoped invariant perspective. In: Pearson, S., Yee, G. (eds.) Privacy and Security for Cloud Computing. CCN, pp. 211–232. Springer, London (2013). https://doi.org/10.1007/978-1-4471-4189-1_6

34. Xie, T., Notkin, D.: Tool-assisted unit test selection based on operational violations. In Proceedings of the 18th IEEE International Conference on Automated Software Engineering, pp. 40–48. IEEE (2003)

Using Data Integration to Help Design
More Secure Applications

Sébastien Salva[(✉)] and Loukmen Regainia

LIMOS CNRS UMR 6158, Clermont Auvergne University,
Clermont-Ferrand, France
{sebastien.salva,loukmen.regainia}@uca.fr

Abstract. Security patterns are reusable solutions, which enable the
design of maintainable systems or applications that have to meet security
requirements. The generic nature of security patterns and their growing
number make their choices difficult, even for experts in software design.
We propose to contribute in this issue by presenting a methodology of
security pattern classification based upon *data integration*. The classification exhibits relationships among 215 software attacks, 66 security
principles and 26 security patterns. It expresses pattern combinations,
which are countermeasures to a given attack. This classification is semi-
automatically inferred by means of a data-store integrating disparate
publicly available security data. Besides pattern classification, we show
that the data-store can be used to generate *Attack Defence Trees*. In our
context, these illustrate, for a given attack, its sub-attacks, steps, techniques and the related defences given under the form of security pattern
combinations. Such trees make the pattern classification more readable
even for beginners in security patterns.

Keywords: Security patterns · Classification · Attack
Attack defence tree

1 Introduction

In the domain of software security, many documents (knowledge bases, papers,
etc.) are now publicly available to help developers design and code more secure
applications. For instance, the notion of security patterns, which is one of the
topics of this paper, aims at providing guidelines to help in design secure systems
[17]. Schumacher postulates that *a security pattern intuitively relates countermeasures to threats and attacks in a given context* [11]. As developers cannot be
expert in all security fields, this plethora of (often complex) documents exposes
them to the difficult choice of the most suitable security solutions for a given
context. From these resources, several works recently proposed to organise them
in order to help developers in their understanding and usage. Security patterns
were arranged into different categories, e.g., by security principles [3,18], by
application domains [4] (software, network, user, etc.), by vulnerabilities [2] or
by attacks [2,15].

© Springer International Publishing AG, part of Springer Nature 2018
N. Cuppens et al. (Eds.): CRiSIS 2017, LNCS 10694, pp. 83–98, 2018.
https://doi.org/10.1007/978-3-319-76687-4_6

Despite the benefits brought by these classifications, they all are confronted to several limitations, which prevent their adoptions in the industry. Firstly, these classifications were manually devised, by directly comparing textual descriptions of different security concepts (patterns, principles, vulnerabilities, attacks, etc.). As these descriptions are generic and have miscellaneous abstraction levels, the categorisation of a pattern can be performed only when there is an evident relation between it and another security property. In addition, as these classifications are not *deterministic* (no strict definition of the classification process [3]), it often becomes delicate to upgrade them. Yskout et al. also reported that the security pattern adoption is limited *possibly due to a sub-optimal quality of the documentation* [19]. We indeed believe that many security pattern classifications lack of Navigability and Comprehensibility, which are quality criteria, proposed in [3] and respectively related to: the ability to direct a software designer among collaborative and related patterns; the ease to understand patterns by both a novice and expert developer.

From these observations, we propose to contribute to the security pattern classification by proposing a strict and precise classification process based on the concept of data integration. To make this classification navigable and comprehensible, we propose to automatically infer attack-defence trees (ADTrees [7]), which illustrate the security pattern combinations that can be used to prevent an attack on an application. More precisely, the contributions of this paper can be summarised by the following points:

- we propose a data integration methodology, built on six steps. These extract data from various Web and publicly accessible sources and store them into a data-store composed of relationships among attacks, attack steps, security principles and security patterns;
- we automatically derive a security pattern classification from the data-store, which can be updated after every data modification. For an attack, the classification expresses the security pattern combinations that can be used in the software design stage to later prevent the attack from being successfully carried out on the application;
- we generate Attack-Defence Trees (ADTrees [7]), which aim at supplementing the classification with illustrations depicting, for a given attack, its (more concrete) sub-attacks, steps and techniques along with defences preventing the attacks expressed here with security patterns combined with logic operations. Such ADTrees aim at improving the navigability and understanding of the previous classification.

We have generated a data-store and a security pattern classification specialised to the Web application domain, which is composed of 215 attacks, 26 security patterns and 66 security principles covering various security aspects. This classification and the ADTree generator are available here[1].

---

[1] http://regainia.com/research/database.html.

The remainder of the paper is organised as follows: Sect. 2 presents some related work and the motivations of our approach. The method, which aims at integrating data to build a data-store, is given in Sect. 3. Section 4 shows how we automatically extract the pattern classification and ADTrees from the data-store. We finally discuss on the resulting classification and conclude in Sects. 5 and 6.

2   Related Work

Several classifications were proposed to ease the pattern choice in the catalogues available in the literature, e.g., [1,19], totalling around 180 patterns. The classifications proposed in [2,12,13,15] focus on the attacker side. This choice of categorisation seems quite interesting and meaningful as attacks are more and more known and examined by designers. Wiesauer et al. initially presented a short taxonomy of security design patterns manually made from links between attack textual descriptions and security pattern purposes [15]. Tondel et al. presented in [12] the combination of three formalisms of security modelling (misuse cases, attack trees and security activity graphs) in order to give a more complete security modelling approach. In particular, they link some activities of attack trees with attacks; they also connect some activities of SAGs (security activity graphs) with security patterns. The relationships among security activities and security patterns are manually extracted from documentation and are not explained. Alvi et al. presented a classification scheme for security patterns putting together attacks and security patterns [2]. They analysed some security pattern templates available in the literature and proposed a new text section for completing the CAPEC classification [9]. After inspection, we observed that this section is seldom available, which limits its interest. Finally, Uzunov et al. proposed a taxonomy of security threats and patterns specialised for distributed systems [13]. This classification includes a library of threats and their relationships with security patterns.

Some papers reviewed these classifications and established a comparative study to point out their positive and negative aspects. Alvi et al. outlined 24 pattern classifications, including security pattern classifications, and established a comparative study to point out their positive and negative aspects [3]. They chose 29 classification attributes (purpose, abstraction levels, life-cycle, etc.) and compared the classifications against a set of desirable quality criteria (Navigability, Comprehensibility, Usefulness, etc.). They observed that several classifications were built in reference to a unique classification attribute, which appears to be insufficient. They indeed concluded that the use of multiple attributes enables the pattern selection in a faster and more accurate manner. Bunke et al. presented a systematic literature review of the papers dealing with security patterns between 1997 and 2012. In addition, they listed a set of classification criteria and compared design pattern and security pattern classifications [4]. They finally proposed a classification based upon the application domains of patterns (software, network, user, etc.).

We observed that the main problem of the above classifications lies in the fact that these all are manually conceived by directly finding relations in textual documents. Justifying these classifications or updating them is difficult. We also observed that they often lack of either Navigability or Comprehensibility or both. Relations among patterns are often not given, yet we noticed that some patterns are compatible together and that others are conflicting. As a consequence, a designer may be still confused about the pattern choice. As in [2], we propose a pattern classification expressing which patterns can be used to counter an attack step. Our classification proposes a more precise and accurate mapping between patterns and attacks. It is more accurate in the sense that we translate the meaning of the patterns and attacks into smaller properties. We establish relations among these properties with respect to security principles, which identify the meaning of these relations. In addition, the classification is completed with inter-pattern relationships. Our data integration process also offers the advantage to justify the pattern classification and reduces the efforts required to update it. Finally, the generation of ADTrees makes the classification precise and readable even for novice in patterns or security.

3   Data Integration

We present below the architecture of the data-store we devised and an example of data integration for attacks and security patterns related to the Web application domain. Beforehand, we recall some basic fact about security patterns.

3.1   Security Patterns

Security patterns provide guidelines for secure system design and evaluation [17]. They often are presented textually or with schema (UML diagrams) and are characterised by a set of structural and behavioural properties.

Several security pattern catalogues are available on the Internet and literature, e.g., [1,19], themselves extracted from other papers. The quality of a pattern and its classification can be established by means of its *strong points*, which are properties expressing pattern key design features. Besides, a security pattern may have different relationships with other patterns. These new properties may noticeably help combine patterns and not to devise unsound composite patterns. Yskout et al. proposed a listing of pattern relations with the following annotations [18]: "depend", "benefit", "impair" (the functioning of the pattern can be obstructed by the implementation of a second one), "alternative", "conflict".

Application Firewall is a security pattern example whose primary objective is to filter out undesired messages given or produced by an application, by means of access control policies. Figure 1 depicts the UML class diagram of this security pattern. This schema shows that it forces to structure an application in such a way that the filtering logic is centralised and decoupled from the functional logic of the application. This also corresponds to a strong point of the pattern.

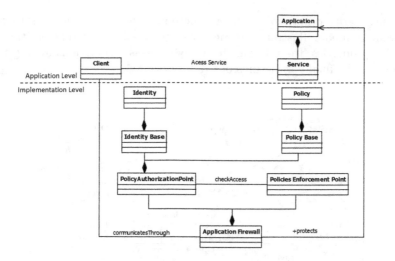

Fig. 1. Security pattern "Application Firewall"

3.2   Data-Store Architecture Presentation

The classification purpose is to ease the design of more secure applications. To do so, we propose to arrange security patterns in such a way that the resulting classification provides the set of patterns that can be used as countermeasures against a given attack (in reference to the security pattern definition of Schumacher [11]) and relations among patterns.

To infer a precise classification, we chose to anatomize attacks and security patterns into more detailed properties that can be interconnected in an explicit manner. After reviewing the literature and some attack bases, we observed that attacks are documented with more concrete attacks, which can be themselves segmented into steps; These steps can be performed with techniques and can be prevented with countermeasures. We did not found smaller properties in the literature. On the other hand, security patterns can be characterised with some sub-properties, e.g., forces, consequences or strong points. A strong point is a pattern key feature that is extractable from its forces or consequences.

In both sides, countermeasures and strong points refer to the notion of attack prevention. But directly finding relations among them is still an obscure task as these properties have different purposes and abstraction levels. To solve this issue, we propose the option of gathering countermeasures into clusters (groups) to reach roughly the same abstraction level as strong points. Indeed, counter-measures are often much more detailed. Then, to link clusters and strong points, we chose to focus on security principles as mediators. We indeed observed that security patterns and strong points are classifiable w.r.t. security principles like most of the security techniques. Since countermeasures aim at preventing attack steps, it sounds natural that countermeasure clusters and strong points belong at least to one principle.

All the security properties considered here and their relations are structured with the meta-model illustrated in Fig. 2 as explained before. The entities refer to security properties, the relations formally express associations among them. This meta-model finally structures our data-store.

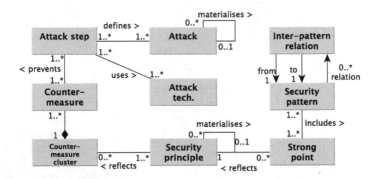

Fig. 2. The proposed mapping metamodel

3.3 Data Integration and Consolidation Steps

We present, in this section, the different steps for integrating security properties into the data-store. The data integration is divided into six steps, which aim at collecting security properties and establishing the different relations presented in Fig. 2. Steps 1 to 5 give birth to databases, and Step 6 consolidates them so that every entity of the meta-model is related to the other ones as expected. These steps offer the strong advantage to semi-automatically achieve a data-store, which can be updated.

We implemented these steps mostly by means of Talend,[2] an ELT (Extraction, Load, Transform) tool that allows an automated processing of data independently from the type of its source or destination. We applied these steps on attacks, patterns and principles related to the Web application context. We provide some quantitative results related to this context with each step. But, these can also be applied to other kinds of systems as long as documentation is available. We integrate data coming from different sources: the CAPEC base [9], several papers dealing with security principles [8,10,14] and the pattern catalogue given in [19].

Step 1: Extraction of attacks, steps, techniques and countermeasures We chose to focus on the CAPEC base to extract information about security attacks. The Common Attack Pattern Enumeration and Classification (CAPEC) is an open database offering a catalogue of attacks in a comprehensive schema. Attack patterns are descriptions of common approaches that attackers take to attack software or systems. An attack pattern, which we refer here as documentation (to avoid the confusion with security pattern), consists of several textual

---

[2] https://talend.com/.

sections. For instance, the section "Related attack patterns" shows interdependence among attacks, having different levels of abstractions.

We extracted attacks of the CAPEC base and organised them into a single tree, which describes a hierarchy of attacks from the most abstract to the most concrete ones so that, we can get all the sub-attacks of a given attack. To reach that purpose, we rely on the relationships among attack descriptions found in the CAPEC section "Related Attack Patterns". By scrutinising all the CAPEC documents, it becomes possible to develop a hierarchical tree whose root node is unlabelled and connected to the attacks of the type "Category". These nodes may also be parent of attacks that belong to the type "Meta Attack pattern" and so on. The leaves are the most concrete attacks of the type "Detailed attack pattern". Then, for every attack, we collected from the CAPEC base (section "Attack Execution Flow") its steps, which may be composed of more concrete sub-steps, and for each step, the corresponding techniques and security controls, which correspond to countermeasures.

This data extraction is automatically performed with a tool, which yields a database DB_1. From the CAPEC base Version 2.8, we extracted these elements for the Web application context and collected 215 attacks, 209 steps, 448 techniques and 217 countermeasures, knowing that attacks can share steps, techniques, etc.

Step 2: Countermeasure hierarchical clustering
The countermeasure number grows quickly while reading the attacks of the CAPEC base. Many of them have a close meaning though, which can be explained by the number of different contributors that added them. These countermeasures can be hence grouped into families to be later associated with a security principle.

We semi-automated this process by applying a hierarchical clustering technique of documents. We firstly used the tool *KHcoder*[3], which is a reputed tool performing quantitative content analysis or text mining. In short, we applied the tool as follows:

1. The Stanford (Part-of-speech) POS tagger is called to sort the keywords found in the countermeasure descriptions (log, input, credentials, etc.) by their frequencies and types (noun, verb, adverb, etc.);
2. From the frequencies, weights are computed and scaled with the Jaccard coefficient (the dissimilarity between sample sets) to measure a distance among countermeasures. The distance between two security controls is minimised when they have more common keywords.

Afterwards, we used the method Ward to automatically yield a hierarchy of countermeasure clusters [16]. We chose Ward because it offers the possibility to merge groups, piece by piece, instead of directly providing big clusters. In our case, this second solution would tend to build big clusters covering too much

---

[3] http://khc.sourceforge.net/en/.

security aspects, which would be later associated with too much security principles. Finally, the level to consider in the cluster organisation (and implicitly the number of clusters to keep) is manually chosen, as the choice of the number of clusters is always supervised with Ward. To get a coherent clustering, we chose the most suitable level after some iterations by checking whether the countermeasures obtained in the clusters refer to the same security principle or set of principles.

The resulting clusters are stored into the database DB_2. The 217 security controls collected by the previous step, are aggregated into 21 clusters.

Step 3: Security patterns and strong points integration

We manually collected security patterns and their strong points from the catalogue given in [19]. Strong points often have to be deduced in the sections referring to the forces and consequences of the patterns. Then, we manually established two relations among patterns and strong points:

1. The first one is a many-to-many relation between security patterns and strong points, each pattern being characterised by a set of strong points that can be shared with other patterns. For example, the patterns "Authorization enforcer" and "Container managed security" share the strong point "Providing the application with authorization mechanism";
2. The second relation is related to the annotations "depend", "benefit", "impair" or "alternative" defined among patterns [18]. With P a set of patterns, this relation is defined as a mapping from P^2 to the annotation set "$depend$", "$benefit$", "$impair$", "$alternative$", which provides for a pair of patterns $(p1, p2)$ an annotation about the relationship between $p1$ and $p2$.

These data and relations, which provide connections among security patterns and between patterns and strong points, are encoded into the database DB_3. For the domain of Web applications, we gathered 26 security patterns and 36 strong points.

Step 4: Security principle integration

We chose to organise security principles into a hierarchy, from the most abstract to the most concrete principles. We collected 66 security principles related to Web applications found in [8, 10, 14] and manually established dependencies in relation to the nature of each security principle, often described with text. The current hierarchy, which has four levels, is certainly not exhaustive. But it covers all the security patterns given in [19]. This security principle hierarchy is stored in the database DB_4.

This principle organisation gives a complete hierarchical view on security mechanisms, which are in the meantime required to prevent an attack step and which are provided by strong points. As principles are hierarchically organised from the most abstract to the most concrete ones, we can find relations between strong points and countermeasure clusters even if they do not exactly have the same level of abstraction.

Step 5: Mapping between strong points, security principles and countermeasure clusters

In this step, we established the many-to-many relation between strong points and security principles. This step was manually done because strong points and principles are mostly presented in an abstract manner. During this step, we observed that the abstraction level of the strong points better fit with the most concrete principles, which are the leaves of our hierarchical organisation.

In the same way, we established the many-to-many relation between countermeasure clusters and security principles. In Step 3, clusters include countermeasures sharing the same security aspects, e.g., Input validation, Authentication or Authorisation. Once these aspects are deduced, linking clusters and security principles becomes straightforward.

These relations are materialised with the database DB_5, which combines 21 clusters, 36 strong points and 66 principles.

Step 6: Data consolidation

This automatic step integrates the previous databases DB_1 to DB_5 into a single one. On the one hand, DB_1, DB_2 and DB_5 store the relations among attacks, steps, countermeasures and principles. On the other hand, DB_3 and DB_5 store the relations among security patterns, strong points and principles. It is now manifest that the security principle hierarchy becomes the central point that helps map attacks onto security patterns.

This step is automatically performed by the tool Talend by means of the meta-model given in Fig. 2. The step produces the final database DB_f.

4   Security Pattern Classification and ADTree Generation

4.1   Security Pattern Classification

The database DB_f holds all the data and relations among attacks, steps, security principles and security patterns allowing to extract a security pattern classification. We have chosen to catalogue the combinations of patterns that are countermeasures against an attack. Given an attack Att, the following data and relations are hence extracted from DB_f:

- the information about Att (name, identifier, description);
- the tree $T(Att)$, whose root is Att, if Att is not a leaf of the attack tree derived in Step 1. For every attack found in $T(Att)$, we also extract its attack steps and techniques;
- for each step st, the complete hierarchy of security principles $Sp(st)$ by means of the successive relations established among st, countermeasure clusters and security principles. $Sp(st)$ represents the complete hierarchy of security principles related to a step, i.e., if a principle sp associated to the step st is not a leaf of our hierarchical organisation, then we also extract all the principle sub-tree whose root is sp;

– for each principle sp in $Sp(st)$, the set of security patterns P_{sp}, the set of patterns $P2_{sp}$ not in P_{sp} that have relations with any pattern of P_{sp}, and the nature of these relations defined for couples of patterns by the annotations in *"depend"*, *"benefit"*, *"impair"*, *"alternative"*, *"conflict"*.

attack_ID	Attack_StepTitle	Attack_Step	tech_desc	Security_pattern	SP_relationship	related_Security_pattern
34	Experiment	Attempt variations on input parameters	Use CRLF characters (encoded or not) in the payloads in order to see if the HTTP header can be split.	Application Firewall	alternative	Input Guard
						Output Guard
				Audit Interceptor	benifits	Secure Service Facade
					depends	Secure Logger
				Input Guard	alternative	Application Firewall
					benifits	Output Guard
				Secure Logger	benifits	Audit Interceptor
						Secure Pipe
			Use a proxy tool to record the HTTP responses headers	Application Firewall	alternative	Input Guard
						Output Guard
				Audit Interceptor	benifits	Secure Service Facade
					depends	Secure Logger
				Input Guard	alternative	Application Firewall
					benifits	Output Guard
				Secure Logger	benifits	Audit Interceptor
						Secure Pipe

Fig. 3. Data extraction for the attack CAPEC-34

Figure 3 depicts an extraction example for the CAPEC attack 34 "HTTP Response Splitting". The first column gives the ID of the chosen attack. This attack belongs to the category "Detailed" of the CAPEC, therefore it has no sub attacks (otherwise, the next columns would list them too). Columns 2 to 4 index the attack steps and techniques. Due to lack of room, we only illustrate the step "Experiment" here. The security patterns allowing to prevent the step are given in Column 5. These four patterns have to be contextualised in the application model and implemented to prevent the attack. The last two columns add the security patterns being associated with the patterns of Column 5 and their relations. For instance, Fig. 3 shows that "Application Firewall" and "Input guard" are alternative patterns, hence using one of them is enough (although using both is not incorrect).

The classification extraction is achieved once all the attacks stored in the database DB_f are covered. This extraction is automatically performed with a tool based upon Talend. This tool can be re-executed every time the data-store is updated. The classification remains up-to-date accordingly.

At this stage, we think that Comprehensibility, which refers to the ability to use the classification by experts or novices, is not yet totally satisfied. Indeed, the classification is given under a tabular form only, which does not appear to be the most user-friendly way to represent a classification. This is why we also propose to generate ADTrees.

4.2 Attack-Defence Tree Generation

Attack Defence Trees *"are graphical representations of possible measures an attacker might take in order to attack a system and the defences that a defender can employ to protect the system"* [7]. We recall that ADTrees have two different kinds of nodes: attack nodes (red circles) and defence nodes (green squares). A node can be *refined* with child nodes using conjunctive or disjunctive refinements. The former is recognisable by edges going from a node to its children. The latter is graphically distinguishable by connecting these edges with an arc. Here, we extend these two refinements with the sequential conjunctive refinement of attack nodes, defined by the same authors in [5]. This operator expresses the execution order of child attack nodes. Graphically, a sequential conjunctive refinement is depicted by connecting the edges going from a node to its children with an arrow.

Keeping in mind that we use ADTrees to help developers design more secure applications, we propose to generate them with the general form illustrated in Fig. 4(a). This ADTree points out how an attack is sequenced with steps and how to prevent them with countermeasures given under the form of security pattern combinations. An ADTree root node is labelled by an attack. If the attack is linked to sub-attacks, the root node is also connected to child attack nodes expressing these sub-attacks. When an attack is defined with steps and techniques, its corresponding node has child nodes expressing them. A node labelled by an attack step has a child defence node, which is the root of a defence sub-tree expressing combinations of security patterns.

We automatically generate ADTrees from the data-store as follows:

1. Every CAPEC attack found in DB_f has its own ADTree whose root node is labelled by its identifier. This root node is linked to other attack nodes with a disjunctive refinement if the attack has sub-attacks. This step is repeated for every sub-attack;
2. For each attack *Att* of the preceding tree, we collect its sequence of steps. The node labelled by *Att* is refined with a sequential conjunction of attack nodes, one for each step. We repeat this process if a step is itself composed of steps. In the same way, for each step *St*, the related techniques are extracted from the classification and are associated to the node labelled by *St* with a disjunctive refinement;
3. For each step *St*, we extract the set *P* of security patterns that are countermeasures of *St*. Given a couple of patterns $(p_1, p_2) \in P$, we illustrate these relations with new nodes and logic operations as follows. If we have:
   - $(p_1 \ R \ p_2)$ with *R* a relation in {*depend, benefit*}, we build three defence nodes, one parent node labelled by $p_1 \ R \ p_2$ and two nodes labelled by p_1, p_2 combined with this parent defence node by a conjunctive refinement;

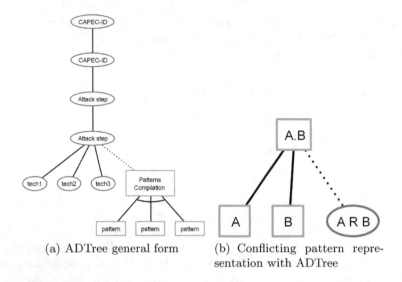

(a) ADTree general form   (b) Conflicting pattern representation with ADTree

Fig. 4. General forms of the ADTrees generated by our approach. (Color figure online)

- (p_1 *alternative* p_2), we build three defence nodes, one parent node labelled by p_1 *alternative* p_2 and two nodes labelled by p_1, p_2, which are linked by a disjunctive refinement to the parent node;
- (p_1 R p_2) with R a relation in $\{impair, conflict\}$. In this particular case, we would want to use the *xor* operation. Unfortunately, the latter is not available with the ADTree model. Therefore, we replace the operator by the classical formula $(A\ xor\ B) \longrightarrow ((A\ or\ B)\ and\ not\ (A\ and\ B))$. The *not* operation is here replaced by an attack node meaning that two conflicting security patterns used together might constitute a kind of attack. The node "Potential attack" expresses a kind of negation. The corresponding sub-tree is depicted in Fig. 4(b);
- p_1 having no relation with any pattern p_2 in P, we add one parent defence node labelled with p_1.

The parent defence nodes, resulting from the above steps, are combined to a defence node labelled by "Pattern Composition" with a conjunctive refinement. This last defence node is linked to the attack node labelled by St.

We implemented the ADTree generation with a tool, which takes as input an attack identifier and yields an ADTree, which is stored into an XML file. These files can be used with the editing tool given in [6]. As a consequence, ADTrees can be modified or updated as the developer wishes.

Figure 5 illustrates the ADTree obtained from the attack CAPEC 34. The root of the tree is the main goal of the attacker. Its second and third levels relate to the attack steps. These nodes are sequential conjunctive refinements of the root node. For instance, the step Exploit is achieved if both steps 3.1 and 3.2 are successfully executed in the right order (from left to right). An attack

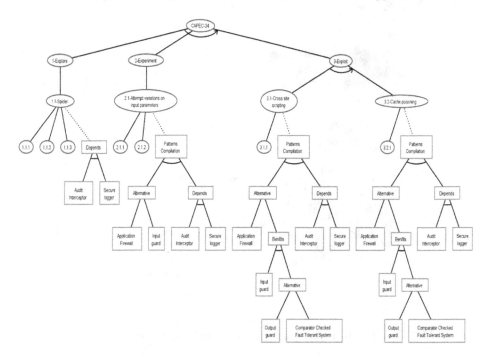

Fig. 5. ADTree of the Attack CAPEC-34

step has a disjunctive refinement of attack nodes labelled by techniques. The step is achieved if one of the attack techniques is applied with success. Defence nodes (square nodes) illustrate security pattern combinations. For instance, the step "1.1 Spider" refers to the Web application exploration through Graphical user interfaces in order to get all the URLs of the application. This step can be prevented by designing the application with both patterns "Audit interceptor" and "Secure logger". "Audit interceptor" can be used to detect the application crawling and to warn an administrator. The audit logs are secured by means of "Secure logger", which guarantees that the audit logs cannot be accessed or altered by unauthorised users. This example illustrates that a designer can easily follow the concrete materialisations of an attack in an ADTree and can directly choose security patterns.

5 Classification Discussion

Our security pattern classification associates attacks, security principles and security patterns in order to help developers in the choice of the most suitable pattern combinations to design and code secure applications. The current classification is founded on 215 CAPEC attacks, 26 security patterns and 66 principles related to the Web application context. It enables multi-attribute based decisions insofar as patterns can be selected according to the provided inter-pattern relations and/or according to the attack steps.

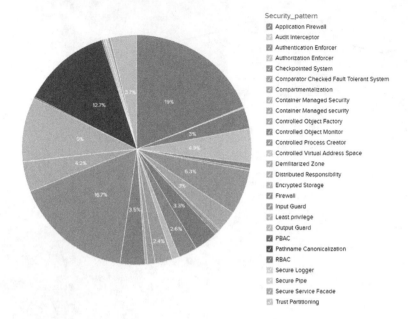

Fig. 6. Percentage of fixed attacks per pattern

Alvi et al. proposed in [3] some criteria for measuring classification quality. Among these criteria, we have noted that our classification meets:

- Navigability: our classification, accompanied by ADTrees, satisfies this criterion as it exhibits the hierarchical refinements of an attack and, for every attack step, the combinations of patterns, which should be integrated in the application model. In addition, the classification provides the relationships among security patterns, which help choose the most appropriate pattern combination;
- Determinism: the classification is clearly defined by means of the method steps. All these steps justify the soundness of the classification;
- Unambiguity/Comprehensibility: patterns are classified w.r.t. defined categories, i.e., attacks, steps, and security principles. This organisation, which is illustrated by means of ADTrees, makes our classification readable and comprehensible even for novices in security patterns;
- Usefulness: we believe the classification can be used in practice since it is based upon a known security pattern catalogue [19] and upon the CAPEC base, which is more and more employed in the industry;
- Repeatability: the classification is generic and can be reused. Furthermore, the data-store and the classification can be updated and generated semi-automatically.

Besides, a variety of statistical information can be automatically extracted from the data-store. For instance, Fig. 6 depicts a pie chart, which shows the ratios of attacks that can be partially prevented per security pattern. These kinds of charts, which are automatically generated from the data-store, seem quite useful to guide designers towards security analysis, good practices and education. For instance, with the above chart, a designer can observe that 2 patterns seem to emerge for partly countering a large part of the 215 attacks covered by the classification, namely "Input Guard" and "Application firewall". It is manifest that if we complete the data-store with more data, e.g., patterns or attack risks, such charts could be more refined and adapted to the developer needs.

Our classification and data integration process present some limitations, which could lead to future works. Firstly, we did not consider the notion of attack combination. Such a combination could be seen as several attacks or as one particular attack. Furthermore, the classification is not yet exhaustive: it includes 215 attacks out of 569 (for any kind of application) and 26 security patterns out of around 180. We also do not take into consideration the ADTree size. This is a strong limitation since large trees are usually unreadable, which contradicts the classification purposes. The ADTree reduction could be a first solution on this problem. But, reducing such trees remains a hard problem as the node meaning must be taken into account in the node aggregating process.

6   Conclusion

We have proposed a security pattern classification method associating attacks, security principles and security patterns in order to help designers understand the inner workings of attacks and choose the most suitable pattern combinations to design secure applications. This method integrates data obtained from various sources and subdivides attacks and patterns into detailed properties, which are associated in accordance with security principles. The pattern classification is then automatically generated from the data-store. The data-store and the classification can be upgraded by following some steps only. We also proposed to portray this classification by means of ADTrees showing attack scenarios (steps, techniques, etc.) and countermeasures given as security pattern combinations.

In future research, we will firstly focus on the automation of some data integration steps. Indeed, it could be relevant to investigate whether some text mining techniques would help partially automate the extraction and integration of the security pattern properties without adding ambiguity. As our ADTrees exhibit concrete attack scenarios composed of sequences of steps, we also intend to use them for the test case generation to check whether an implementation is protected against the attacks given in an ADTree or if security patterns are correctly contextualised and implemented w.r.t. the application context.

Acknowledgement. Research supported by the industrial chair on Digital Confidence http://confiance-numerique.clermont-universite.fr/index-en.html.

References

1. Security pattern catalog. http://www.munawarhafiz.com/securitypatterncatalog/
2. Alvi, A.K., Zulkernine, M.: A natural classification scheme for software security patterns. In: 2011 IEEE Ninth International Conference on Dependable, Autonomic and Secure Computing, pp. 113–120 (2011)
3. Alvi, A.K., Zulkernine, M.: A comparative study of software security pattern classifications. In: 2012 Seventh International Conference on Availability, Reliability and Security, pp. 582–589 (2012)
4. Bunke, M., Koschke, R., Sohr, K.: Organizing security patterns related to security and pattern recognition requirements. International Journal on Advances in Security 5 (2012)
5. Jhawar, R., Kordy, B., Mauw, S., Radomirović, S., Trujillo-Rasua, R.: Attack trees with sequential conjunction. In: Federrath, H., Gollmann, D. (eds.) SEC 2015. IAICT, vol. 455, pp. 339–353. Springer, Cham (2015). https://doi.org/10.1007/978-3-319-18467-8_23
6. Kordy, B., Kordy, P., Mauw, S., Schweitzer, P.: ADTool: security analysis with attack–defense trees. In: Joshi, K., Siegle, M., Stoelinga, M., D'Argenio, P.R. (eds.) QEST 2013. LNCS, vol. 8054, pp. 173–176. Springer, Heidelberg (2013). https://doi.org/10.1007/978-3-642-40196-1_15
7. Kordy, B., Mauw, S., Radomirović, S., Schweitzer, P.: Attack-defense trees. Journal of Logic and Computation p. exs029 (2012)
8. Meier, J.: Web application security engineering. IEEE Secur. Priv. **4**(4), 16–24 (2006)
9. Mitre corporation: Common attack pattern enumeration and classification (2015). https://capec.mitre.org/
10. Saltzer, J.H., Schroeder, M.D.: The protection of information in computer systems. Proc. IEEE **63**(9), 1278–1308 (1975)
11. Schumacher, M.: Security Engineering with Patterns: Origins, Theoretical Models, and New Applications. Springer-Verlag New York Inc., Secaucus (2003)
12. Tøndel, I.A., Jensen, J., Røstad, L.: Combining misuse cases with attack trees and security activity models. In: International Conference on Availability, Reliability, and Security, 2010, ARES 2010, pp. 438–445. IEEE (2010)
13. Uzunov, A.V., Fernandez, E.B.: An extensible pattern-based library and taxonomy of security threats for distributed systems. Comput. Stand. Interfaces **36**(4), 734–747 (2014)
14. Viega, J., McGraw, G.: Building Secure Software: How to Avoid Security Problems the Right Way. Portable Documents, Pearson Education (2001)
15. Wiesauer, A., Sametinger, J.: A security design pattern taxonomy based on attack patterns. In: International Joint Conference on e-Business and Telecommunications, pp. 387–394 (2009)
16. Willett, P.: Recent trends in hierarchic document clustering: a critical review. Inf. Process. Manag. **24**(5), 577–597 (1988)
17. Yoder, J., Yoder, J., Barcalow, J., Barcalow, J.: Architectural patterns for enabling application security. In: Proceedings of PLoP 1997, vol. 51, p. 31 (1998)
18. Yskout, K., Heyman, T., Scandariato, R., Joosen, W.: A system of security patterns (2006)
19. Yskout, K., Scandariato, R., Joosen, W.: Do security patterns really help designers? In: Proceedings of the 37th International Conference on Software Engineering - Volume 1, pp. 292–302. ICSE 2015. IEEE Press, Piscataway (2015). http://dl.acm.org/citation.cfm?id=2818754.2818792

Access Control and Filtering

MA-MOrBAC: A Distributed Access Control Model Based on Mobile Agent for Multi-organizational, Collaborative and Heterogeneous Systems

Zeineb Ben Yahya[1]([✉]) [iD], Farah Barika Ktata[2], and Khaled Ghedira[3]

[1] National School of Computer Science of Tunisia (ENSI),
Complex Outstanding Systems Modeling Optimization and Supervision
(COSMOS), University of Manouba, Manouba, Tunisia
zeineb.benyahya@ensi-uma.tn
[2] Higher Institute of Applied Sciences and Technology of Sousse (ISSATSO),
Complex Outstanding Systems Modeling Optimization and Supervision
(COSMOS), University of Sousse, Sousse, Tunisia
farah.ktata@gmail.com
[3] Complex Outstanding Systems Modeling Optimization and Supervision
(COSMOS), National Agency for Promotion of Scientific Research of Tunisia,
Tunis, Tunisia
khaled.ghedira@isg.rnu.tn

Abstract. Facing the current evolution of networks infrastructure and the expansion of the information system in organizations and businesses, protecting data and resources against unauthorized access and unauthorized disclosure, is an important requirement of any information management system. In this context, diverse security issues are amplified. Particularly, access control seems of main importance because it ensures diverse security services, such as, authentication, identification, confidentiality and integrity. Several works are devoted for designing access control models. In this paper, we work to improve Multi-OrBAC model by introducing a new distributed access control model based on Mobile Agent.

Keywords: Security · Distributed access control · Multi-OrBAC model
Mobile agent

1 Introduction

Recently in this age of dynamic technological change, protecting information and data is a more challenge that an organization or a group of organizations are often called to collaborate with other organizations in order to benefit or provide services, to communicate, to access or deliver information.

Globally, the heterogeneous and distributed environments can be seen as a set of interconnected organizations involving different actors and stakeholders using heterogeneous logical and physical information and communication systems and networks, exhibiting different levels of security threats and protection mechanisms.

© Springer International Publishing AG, part of Springer Nature 2018
N. Cuppens et al. (Eds.): CRiSIS 2017, LNCS 10694, pp. 101–114, 2018.
https://doi.org/10.1007/978-3-319-76687-4_7

One of the most important challenges that needs to be solved throughout this collaboration, is the resources access control, thus we need a lightweight, flexible and scalable method to control the access to data and resources in general.

Offering pertinent services to multiple users at different locations is necessary because any unsecured access may engender numerous critical problems, such as, unauthorized access, loss of governance, divulgation of sensitive data or privacy violation. To avoid these problems, several models have been proposed, like Discretionary Access Control (DAC) [1], Mandatory Access Control (MAC) [2], Role Based Access Control (RBAC) [3], and Organization Role Based Access Control (OrBAC) [4]. However, all these models are not suited for heterogeneous and distributed environments.

In this paper, we propose a modular solution that traces a new access control model using the technology of mobile agents that acts as a portable and secure middleware to interconnect diverse heterogeneous organizations. We initiate a novel research line by adopting mobile agents to model a well-designed access control mechanism that satisfies security requirements of all levels (network, system, application) of an information system. The proposed model takes benefit from the mobility aspect of agents to avoid drawbacks of classical Client/Server communications, and it makes use of cryptographic mechanisms such as encryption and digital signature to ensure authentication, identification, confidentiality and integrity.

For this purpose, the remainder of our paper is organized as follows. We present, in Sect. 2, the necessary background for distributed access control. In Sect. 3 we describe our comparative study of distributed access control strategies. In Sect. 4, we present our access control model based on mobile agent technology: the MA-MOrBAC model. Through this section, we present the motivation for a Multi-organization Access Control Approach and the MA-MOrBAC components. Then, we present the authentication process and a detailed example that aims to clarify our contributions and the functioning of our model.

Finally, in Sect. 5 we conclude the paper and present our future work.

2   Background

Access control [5] is a necessary condition for a variety of services to work together and implement a distributed environment; it is a mechanism that limits the actions that a legitimate user of a computer system can perform.

2.1   Distributed Access Control

In distributed and heterogonous systems, users access to several services after verification of their identity. The access control is to determine what a user can do directly around an object. Compared to traditional systems, the distributed and heterogeneous environment is much more dynamic and distributed, and security for such environment poses many challenges. Therefore, the access control in distributed environments is required to cross the borders of security domains, to be implemented between heterogeneous systems [6]. According to the literature, various strategies have been employed to improve the distributed access control. A comprehensive study of different access control models is presented in Sect. 3.

2.2 Mobile Agent Technology

In open service-oriented systems, it is necessary to establish interactions among several applications through the network. This increases the need of autonomous entities able to resolve the complex problems related to networks. In this context, researchers are gradually more interested in the use of mobile agent technology as it brings significant gains for several application areas.

Ferber has demonstrated in [7] that, Multi-agent systems are systems in which we make cooperation between a set of entities having intelligent behavior called Agents, and that have the power to coordinate their purposes and action plans to solve a problem or achieve an objective. The agents are characterized by certain unique properties to be different from the standard programs; the following are the most important properties [8, 9]: Autonomy, Reactivity, Pro-activity, Communication, Cooperation, Mobility, Learning and Adaptability.

The main advantages of the mobile agent based systems are: 1. Reduce the network load 2. Minimize the network latency 3. Execute in asynchronous and autonomous mode 4. Adapt dynamically and 5. Robust and fault tolerant [10].

3 Related Work

In the literature, several theories have been devoted to the study of access control models, in order to achieve a satisfactory level of security for any environments. Various access control models have been proposed. To describe these models we class them in two main pools: Distributed access control models and Distributed access control models based on mobile agent.

3.1 Distributed Access Control Models

In literature, various strategies have been used to improve the distributed access control. This part, throws light on the research activities in the area of distributed access control, by analyzing the works carried out by the researchers.

The work carried out in [11] presented an adaptive access control algorithm for cloud environments. In this work the authors introduced the concept of trust into cloud computing to decide the access control to the resources using an improved RBAC technique.

The authors in [6] proposed an Attributed and Role Based Access Control model (ARBAC) for service-oriented environment. This model introduces the notion of Service Role (SR) and Business Role (BR) in order to create a flexible, coupled access control solution for service oriented environment. In this work, access negotiation mechanism is not added into ARBAC model.

Sun and Wang, in [12] proposed a semantic access control system to authenticate users of health systems based on anthologies in the distributed environment. Particularly, this system implements a distributed access control system in semantic web environments.

Furthermore, in [4], the authors proposed to use an access control based organization (ORBAC) that is based on the first order logic, which aims to improve inter-organizational access control and provide solutions to specify such contextual security policies. In this work, several issues have not been addressed, such as the fact that conflicts may appear in the security policy and they do not define how to specify security properties in this model.

Then, a hybrid access control model by configuring the functionality of MAC and RBAC has been proposed in [13]. The authors proposed a systematic approach for developing a hybrid access control model using feature modeling with the aim of reducing development complexity and error-proneness.

Moreover, a collaborative access control framework called PolyOrBAC has been proposed in [14]. This approach offers, to each organization taking part in the Critical Information Infrastructure (CII), the capacity of collaborating with the other ones, while maintaining a control on its resources and on its internal security policy. The interactions between organizations participating in the CII are implemented through web services (WS).

3.2 Distributed Access Control Based on Mobile Agent

Other researchers were interested to use the mobile agent technology to improve the distributed access control and are described below.

The most interesting approach of distributed access control based on mobile agent RBAC-MA has been proposed by [15], as a distributed access control model in the inter-organizational environments. They used the RBAC model applied with the mobile agent paradigm to ensure authentication and identification of system entities, as well as to guarantee confidentiality and integrity of data. In this work, several criteria were not dealt: time, performance, persistence and security attacks.

In [16] authors proposed an agent-based approach for the distributed access control in cloud environments for mediating the access requests of cloud consumers, considering the present day requirements of the cloud computing paradigm In this work, they also proposed a workflow model for the proposed agent-based approach for the distributed access control in cloud.

In [17], researchers proposed an intra-organizational access control based on mobile agent in order to improve interoperability and flexibility of RBAC model. They presented a modified RBAC. They proposed a RBAC mobile agent access control model supported by a specially managed public key infrastructure for mobile agent's strong authentication and access control. The main contribution of this work was to guarantee a secure communication channel between health institutions by the means of a strong access control for mobile agents.

In [18], authors discussed the authorization issues in the distributed computing environment. Then, they presented a security agent-based approach for solving these issues. In this work, the security agents are deployed to manage the privileges for the distributed authorization. However, this work does not consider the dynamic nature of the access control. The authors proposed also a distributed access control architecture based on the concept of distributed, active authorization entities [18]. But, this architecture lacks also of the dynamic trust management and the security policy conflict management when various users in the organization access the cloud resources simultaneously.

3.3 Discussion

As is clear from the comparative study presented above, neither of these models is entirely satisfactory the exigencies of communication and collaboration difficulties encountered between or within organizations.

Also, proposed models do not offer mechanism to detect a violation security policy and do not propose the decision to be taken in such case.

Moreover they do not proposed any technique to secure interactions in a collaborative session between users, to satisfy the security requirements identified by all stakeholders of heterogynous environments. Furthermore, the consistency of security policy is not as well checked.

Finally, we believe that a proper solution for the issue of access control in the distributed environments needs extensive research in the area of conflict management of organizational access control policies.

In the following we will decried our proposed approach that deals with these limitations.

4 Proposed Model: MA-MOrBAC Model

4.1 Motivation for Multi-organization Based Access Control

OrBAC model is a centralized approach and many extensions of that model has been developed to address the need for secure collaborations, we cite mainly Multi-OrBAC [19]. Multi-OrBAC is a dynamic and adaptable model of security, allowing one side to specify different security policies in each organization and the other side to impose rules for interactions between organizations that are consistent with the policies of each organization.

Multi-OrBAC keeps the methodology of OrBAC and adapts it to create multi-organizational architectures, cooperative, distributed and interoperable. Multi-OrBAC defines the concepts of role, activity, view and context in relation with organization, giving the organization an important flexibility and scalability.

However, it remains inadequate to secure interaction between users in collaborative systems, and do not meet the security requirements identified in all stakeholders of distributed and collaborative environment.

Moreover, in the context of distributed and collaborative environment, Multi-OrBAC presents several weaknesses. In fact, it offers the possibility to define local rules and accesses for external roles that belongs to another organization, without having any information about who plays these roles and how the rules and the security policies are managed in the remote organization. This causes a serious problem of liability: who is responsible in case of remote abuse of privileges? How can the organization to which belongs the object have total confidence in the organization to which belongs the user? How we manage the assignment permissions in multi-context, multi-user, multi-organization multi-resource to do multi-action at the same time?

The Multi-OrBAC logic is thus not adapted to all kind of heterogeneous and collaborative systems where competitive organizations can naturally be mutually suspicious. Moreover, in Multi-OrBAC the access control decision and enforcement are done by each organization, which means that the global security policy is in fact defined by the set of the organizations security policies. In that case, it is difficult to enforce and maintain the consistency of the global security policy, in particular if each organization's security policy evolves independently.

4.2   MA-MOrBAC Goals

In this context, in our proposed MA-MOrBAC model, collaboration and interactions between organizations are made through the use of the mobile agent technology, which provides platform-independent protocols and standards for exchanging heterogeneous interoperable data services. Software applications written in various programming languages and running on various platforms can use mobile agents to exchange data over computer networks in a manner similar to inter-process communication on a single computer.

In the proposed MA-MOrBAC model, we integrate mobile agent technology and Multi-OrBAC to achieve these objectives:

- Ensure the consistency of different access control policies.
- Improve the detection of violation security policies.
- Facilitate the adaptability of Multi-OrBAC in the distributed and collaborative environments.
- Handle multiple security policies associated to various organizations.
- Provide authentication, integrity and confidentiality of data exchanged in collaborative systems.
- Provide secure interaction with a high level of confidence.

4.3   MA-MOrBAC Functional Architecture

MA-MOrBAC is a new reliable, adaptable, flexible and robust access control model. Our model is intended for multi-organizational systems for distributed environment. Thus, our innovative new access control model is backboned on mobile agent technology.

Owing to the properties of heterogeneous and distributed environment and agent-based systems, and also because of the advantages of an agent-based approach, we consider that it would be an efficient and secure approach to combine the two paradigms so that the access requests could be mediated through the agents.

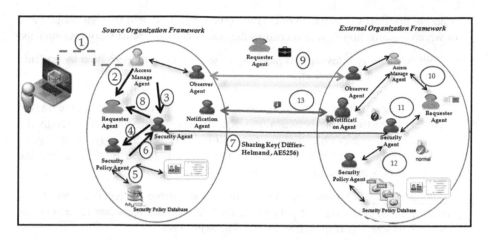

Fig. 1. Functional architecture of MA-MOrBAC

We propose a distributed access control model based on Multi-OrBAC model and mobile agents. Our objective is to have a multi-level access control mechanism that involves many entities and uses a multi-organizational architecture able to manage various security policies, provides an overall level of homogeneous and sufficient security, and guarantees coherence of the various access control policies associated with different organizations.

For this purpose, we adapt the Multi_OrBAC [19] model knowing that it, allows specifying in a homogeneous framework, several security policies for heterogeneous organizations in front to cooperate. This model treated the problem that if a user, in a multi-organizational context, can play multiple roles; it does not necessarily have the right to play them in any of the organizations. Moreover, we use a different mechanism of integrity and flexibility and we apply an algorithm for detecting and managing conflict access control policies in order to achieve the integrity and flexibility of MA-MOrBAC.

In our approach, we use the advantages of mobile agent paradigm to enhance the flexibility and robustness of the Multi-OrBAC model. We simulate the hierarchy architecture of that model using agents that cooperate to achieve the distributed access control purposes.

As represented in Fig. 1, our architecture includes 6 agents:

1. <u>Access Manage Agent:</u> Is the central node of the platform of an organization. This agent is responsible for managing agents of the organizational platform; it is responsible for creating, activating and sending agents. It supervises their operation.
2. <u>Security Policy Agent:</u> Is the agent responsible of the management and the update of policies and security rules for each organization and its sub organizations. It provides control according to the Multi-OrBAC rules. Knowing that a rule can be a permission, prohibition, recommendation or obligation.

The security policy Agent, is the one who will grant or reject an access request after the security policy interrogation, in order to have a response to queries of type "who has privileges (and which ones) on a given object (s), and in what context and for which organization?". It also ensures the consistency of security policies such as:

- Political security rules are contradictory (one action is both permitted by one rule and prohibited by another).
- The operating rules of the system are incompatible with the security rules.
- The management of security policies fusion problems. For example in the context of restructuring between two organizations. A first aspect concerns the definition of compatible organizational roles and structures. Another aspect, relates to the detection of conflicts in the policy obtained by fusion, and the proposal of a method for solving these conflicts.

3. Requester Agent: Is an interface Agent that is responsible for receiving and interpreting queries, preparing and submitting responses to the requester (user, organization). This agent is responsible for the following tasks:

- Treats the queries of requesters.
- Shows to the requester the information about the treatment of the request and follow the execution process of the request.
- Visualizes responses in the format required by the requester.

4. Security Agent: It performs the verification and authentication of the agent requester to ensure its integrity. In fact, a process of sharing key is running between the two "Security Agent" of both Frameworks. This process makes use of Diffie-Hellman Exchange Key Protocol in a novel form that avoids Man-In-Middle attack [20]. This allows it to obtain a common shared key. It is a key of 256 bits introduced in an encryption process between the both sides, using the cryptographic algorithm AES [21].

5. Observer Agent: It is responsible for sending procedures (dispatching) of the agent. It is also responsible for managing and monitoring the changes in the network. Moreover, it reports all events of network occurrences and periodically transmits them to the Access Manage Agent.

6. Notifications Agent: It is an agent that is responsible for automatic notifications of organizations across platforms; it can send a notification to the requester (Organization, User) at the time the recipient organization agrees to process the request. This notification is useful for tracking the mobile agent.

4.4   MA-MOrBAC Authentication Process

In order to easily understand how to apply MA-MOrBAC, we first describe the authentication process of our proposed scheme (Fig. 1). We present the following scenario:

The requester sends a request for access with a set of parameters as its RiO (Role in Organization) and the invoked object. The Access Manager Agent launches the creation of the Requester Agent. The security policy agent interprets this request by interrogating the Security Policy that can be contained in different kind (database, XML file) and generates an evidence of authorization, in order to guarantee its identification at the external organization as shown in Table 1.

Table 1. Evidence of authorization

Parameters	Description
Subject id	The subject id is used to identify the subject who is making the request
Rules details	Is a set of attributes used to inform an external organization of the permissions, obligation, recommendation and Prohibition details that the requester has in his home organization
Data	This attribute is composed by a set of queries that requests the necessary information. The size of this set may varies according to the number of visiting organization. Each one of these queries is ciphered with a respective public key according to its organization's destination
Agent code	This attribute is to identify the visitor agent in the multiple organizations
Emergency level	Represents the emergency level of the request (non-emergency = 0; emergency = 1)
Action deadline	This attribute represents the execution action time, is measured in milliseconds. Once this time expires the mobile agent returns to its home with the obtained results since requested information loses its value after expire date is reached
List of external organizations	This list is composed by a set of attributes that include: the visiting organization, host addresses and their respective certificates
Description	This is an optional open attribute. This attribute should be filled every time the requester considers that an additional justification is required
Requester signature	This is an optional attribute depending on the organization policies
Organization signature	The organization validates the whole set of attributes by signing it. This signature is essential for the mobile agent since external organization only accept signed mobile agent that falls in their circle of trust

After sending the evidence to the Security Agent, a process of sharing key is running between the two Security Agents of both platforms. This process makes use of Diffie-Hellman Exchange Key Protocol in a novel form that avoids Man-In-Middle attack [20]. This allows obtaining a common shared key that we name "Session Key (T)". It is a key of 256 bits, using the cryptographic algorithm AES [21].

Thereafter, the security Agent encrypts the evidence of authorization with the public key of the external organization Security Agent. It supports also the verification and the authentication of the Requester Agent to ensure that did not become a malicious agent. Once the Requester Agent is ready to migrate, the Observer Agent sends it to the external organization. After that, it analyzes network changes and sends a report to the Access Manage Agent.

If the Requester Agent has been accepted, a notification "good received" is sent to the source organization Notification Agent. When the Requester Agent returns at its source place, it goes to state "Hold", and the authentication process will be launched again, to prevent against the fact that behaviors are changed during its mission.

For security reasons, our system must ensure requester access authentication, integrity and confidentiality of security policies. Each agent must be encrypted before migrating by the "Security Agent" and decrypted as soon as it arrives at the sender. All transactions between organizations are encrypted using the "session key" generated by the protocol "Key Exchange protocol (Diffie-Hellman)." Communications between organizations are performed through messages using ACL (Agent Communication Language) with MTP (Message Transport Protocol). The agents's migration process is provided by the ACC (Agent Communication Channel).

4.5   Requester Agent: Creation and Migration Process

In the following, an example of a real practice scenario expressed within a hospital. The example aims, in one hand, to ease the understanding of our model and on the other hand to show clearly the limitations of the Multi-OrBAC model and how our extension helps covering them.

Requester agent creation process

When a user (e.g. healthcare professional, Doctor) requests clinical information from an external health institution, a Requester Agent is created and sent to the external health institution. This agent is associated with several attributes, in the form of evidence of authorization (Table 1) in order to guarantee its identification at the external institution. This evidence of authorization is generated by the Security Policy Agent and encrypted by the Security Agent with the public key of the external organization Security Agent.

Requester agent reception process

When a mobile agent (Requester Agent) arrives at an external health institution the Security Agent decrypt him and checks the mobile agent identity by the usage of the Sharing Key (Diffie-hellman, AES256). After this process the Security Agent verified the mobile agent evidence of authorization in order to define which permissions will be granted to the visitor agent according to the access control policy of the visited health institution.

Depending on the type of request the external access control could need an approval from an internal member (Security Policy Agent) of the institution in order to process the request. In such cases the Security Agent provides to the visitor Agent an identification number that could be used later to query the status of its requirement. This identification number improves the visitor Agent flexibility since this mobile agent could continue his itinerary to other external health institutions and return later to consult the request status.

In special cases where the emergency level is important and an internal member approval is needed the Security Agent will activate a special mechanism known as Break The Glass (BTG) to directly obtain the requested medical information. The BTG mechanism [22] is used to break or override the access controls in a controlled manner. In other words this should allow a user to override the access control rules stated by the access control manager and access what he requests, even thought he was not previously authorized to do it. When this is done, BTG rules come into play reporting the user's actions, thus making him responsible for his requests and oblige him to justify his request.

This is an important mechanism to mobile agents when an emergency scenario happens. For example, when a Requester Agent is in an external health institution and does not have enough permission to access crucial medical information that a healthcare professional needs to save a patient. The BTG also works as a non-repudiation mechanism since the requester is strongly audited after deciding to proceed with the BTG and all involved parties are notified.

Indeed, access control is not a complete solution for securing a system. It must be coupled with auditing. Audit controls concern a posteriori analysis of all the requests and activities of users in a system, this process ensure that authorized users do not misuse their privileges [5]. Thus, extensive auditing is important to ensure traceability of user actions, and in our case actions are mobile agent actions.

4.6   MA-MOrBAC Model Components

MA-MOrBAC is a Multi-OrBAC extension that provide secure collaborations, address the need for dynamic access control and guarantee integrity. MA-MOrBAC keeps the organization as the central entity. MA-MOrBAC is therefore based on its predecessor entities, predicates, language and axioms. In what follows, we keep considering, within Org, s ∈ Subject, r ∈ Role, o ∈ Object, a ∈ ACtivity and c ∈ Contexte.

We describe the new expressions that we introduced to extend MA-MOrBAC.

– **Lorg, Lr, Ls, Lv, La, Lc:** sets of priority levels for, respectively, organization, role, subjects, views, activities and contexts.

In addition, we affect priority levels to the previously identified entities. These parameters are important and needed to determine the priority level to impose on each rules in the security policy.

The modifications are then as follows:

– *Permission (Org, r, v, ay, c)* becomes *Permission (Org, r, v, ay, c, L_p)*,

Where L_p: is the value of the priority level affected to permission predicate. The others access mode predicates [i.e., Obligation(), Recommendation() and Prohibition()] have also get the same modification.

– *Use (Org, o, v)* becomes *Use (Org, o, v, L_u)*, where L_u: is the value of the priority level affected to predicate Use.
– *Consider (Org, ac, ay)* becomes *Consider (Org, ac, ay, L_C)*, where L_C: is the value of the priority level affected to predicate Consider.
– *Empower (Org, s, r)* becomes *Empower (Org, s, r, L_e)*, where L_e: is the value of the priority level affected to predicate Empower.
– *Define (Org, s, o, ac, c)* becomes *Define (Org, s, o, ac, c, L_f)*, where L_f: is the value of the priority level affected to predicate Define.

To Ensure the MA-MOrBAC integrity, we introduce a set of parameters to grant decisions to take into account five major parameters: the predicate priority levels the permission L_p, Use L_u, Consider L_C, Empower L_e and the Define L_f.

Knowing these parameters, we can decide which access requests are appropriate to perform the action, based on the priority level of an access request.

4.7 Case Scenario

As an example of application of MA-MOrBAC, we propose this case scenario: "An old male patient named Ali from Gasrin, has been moved from the regional hospital of Gasrin to undergo urgent surgery on the heart at the university hospital Sahloul. Due to the emergency situation, they forgot his medical records. The Supervisor Dr. Ahmed of the condition's patient applies to the regional hospital of Gasrin to check information on the file (blood analysis, Image of medical scanner and magnetic resonance imaging files). Moreover, he will need to ask for access after the surgery to deposit the results of the operation in the file of this patient in his original hospital".

Figure 1 demonstrates the necessary steps since the agent is created until the agent return.

So the details of access request are:

Org: The Gasrin's regional hospital
Role(r): Doctor
View (v): Medical Record of Ali
Activity (ac): Consulting
Subject (s): Dr. Ahmed
Context (c): Emergency in Sahloul.

Step1: The access request is sent by a subject (Dr. *Ahmed*) and is captured by the Access Manager Agent of University Hospital *Sahloul* platform, which transmit it to the Security Policy Agent. When the doctor triggers this request a Mobile Agent named Requester Agent is created (steps 1, 2 and 3 in Fig. 1).

Step2: The Security Agent then ask the Security Policy Agent about the different rules details associated to the subject (Dr. Ahmed). Whose goal is to have the adequate response to the access request, and to proceed to the encryption process (step 4 in Fig. 1).

Step3: In turn the Security Policy Agent interprets this request by performing the following tasks:

- Interrogates Security Policy (contained in a database or xml file).
- Extracts the rules for deciding in the current cases (which contains the rules RiO sent the query parameters).
- Combines the various possible rule sequences and evaluates the request parameters in these rules.
- Resolves any conflicts.
- Takes a decision (is that the action is allowed, prohibited, obligation or recommended?) and affect a p = 1 as a priority level of rule. Affect a priority to rule will provide more flexibility while developing the policy.
- Generates an evidence of authorization as shown in Table 1, and send it to the Security Agent.

Step4: The Security Agent received the access decision (evidence of authorization). If Dr. Ahmed had sufficient permissions to execute the action, else if he do not have enough permissions, the Security Policy Agent refuse the request.

Then a process of sharing key is running between the two "security Agent" of both platforms. Thereafter it encrypts the evidence of authorization using the public key of the recipient organization Security Agent. Once the Requester Agent is ready to be migrated, the Observer Agent, send it to the recipient organization (Steps 7, 8, 9 in Fig. 1).

Step5: Requester Agent arrives to the recipient organization (Gasrin regional hospital), the latter's Security Agent run the process Authentication, to verify if it have or not the permission to run its code. Since the process Authentication succeeded the recipient organization platform provide it all the resources needed for its action and a notification "Good received" is sent to the university hospital Sahloul platform Notification Agent (10, 11, 12, 13).

Step 6: Once finished, the Requester Agent receives the results of the query and depart from external organization back to its home organization.

5 Conclusion and Future Work

In this paper, we presented an extension of the Multi-OrBAC access control model, called Mobile Agent Multi-OrBAC, which aims to guarantee a secure communication between organizations and satisfy the security requirements. This work is an initial proposal, implementation and evaluation of our proposed model using System for Mobile Agent Jade are in process.

References

1. Lampson, B.: Protection. In: 5th Princeton Symposium on Information Sciences and Systems, pp. 437–443, March 1971
2. Bell, D.E., LaPadula, L.J.: Secure computer systems: unified exposition and multics interpretation. Technical report ESD-TR-73-306, The MITRE Corporation, March 1976
3. Kuhn, D.F.: Role-based access controls. In: 15th National Computer Security Conference, pp. 554–563 (1992)
4. El Kalam, A.A.: ORBAC: un modèle de contrôle d'accès basé sur les organisations (2003)
5. Sandhu, R.S., Samarati, P.: Access controls, principles and practice. IEEE Commun. Mag. **32**(9), 40–48 (1994)
6. Wei, Y., Shi, C., Shao, W.: An attribute and role based access control model for service-oriented environment. In: Proceedings of the Chinese Control and Decision Conference, pp. 4451–4455 (2010)
7. Ferber, J.: Multi-agent Systems An Introduction to Distributed Artificial Intelligence. Addison – Wesley, Boston (1999)
8. Manvi, S.S., Venkataram, P.: Applications of agent technology in communications: a review. Comput. Commun. **27**, 1493–1508 (2004)
9. Magedanz, T., Rothermel, K.: Intelligent agents: an emerging technology for next generation telecommunications. In: Proceedings of the IEEE Globecom, London, UK, pp. 464–472 (1996)

10. Lange, D.B., Oshima, M.: Dispatch your agents; shut off your machine. Commun. ACM **42** (3), 88–89 (1999)
11. Wang, W.: The design of a trust and role access control model in cloud. IEEE (2011)
12. Sun, L., Wang, H.: Semantic access control for cloud computing based on e-Healthcare. In: Proceedings of the 2012 IEEE 16th International Conference on Computer Supported Cooperative Work in Design (CSCWD), pp. 512–518. IEEE (2012)
13. Kim, S.: Building hybrid access control by configuring RBAC and MAC features. Inf. Softw. Technol. **56**, 763–792 (2014)
14. El Kalam, A.A., Deswarte, Y., Baïna, A., Kaâniche, M.: PolyOrBAC: a security framework for critical infrastructures. Int. J. Crit. Infrastruct. Prot. **2**(4), 154–169 (2009)
15. Idrissi, H.: Access control using mobile agents. In: International Conference on Multimedia Computing and Systems ICMCS (2014)
16. Thomas, M.V.: Agent-based approach for distributed access. In: International Conference on Advances in Computing, Communications and Informatics, ICACCI 2013 (2013)
17. Varadharajan, V., Kumar, N., Mu, Y.: Security agent based distributed authorization: an approach. In: Proceedings of the 21st National Information Systems Security Conference (NISSC), USA, pp. 315–328 (1998)
18. Antonopoulos, N., Koukoumpetsos, K., Shafarenko, A.: Access control for agent-based computing: a distributed approach. Internet Res. **11**(1), 55–64 (2001)
19. El Kalam, A.A., Deswarte, Y.: MultiOrBAC: a new access control model for distributed, heterogeneous and collaborative systems. In: IEEE Symposium on Systems and Information Security, Sao Paulo, Brazil (2006)
20. Biswas, B., Basuli, K.: A novel process for key exchange avoiding man-in-middle attack. Int. J. Adv. Res. Technol. (IJOART) **I**(4), 75–79 (2012)
21. Standard NIST-FIPS: Announcing the Advanced Encryption Standard (AES). Federal Information Processing Standards Publication, vol. 197. NIST (2001)
22. Ferreira, A., Chadwick, D., Zao, G., Farinha, P., Correia, R., Chilro, R., Antunes, L.: How securely break into RBAC: the BTG-RBAC model. In: Proceedings from 25th Annual Computer Security Applications Conference - ACSAC (2009)

A Vehicle Collision-Warning System
Based on Multipeer Connectivity
and Off-the-Shelf Smart-Devices

Bogdan Groza$^{(\boxtimes)}$ and Cosmin Briceag

Politehnica University of Timisoara, Timisoara, Romania
bogdan.groza@aut.upt.ro, briceagcosmin@gmail.com

Abstract. Traffic related deaths and injuries take high tolls each year and vehicular collision warning systems can make the future safer. To deploy such systems there are strong efforts from the industry in the development and standardization of Car2X communication technologies, e.g., the 802.11p suite. However, it is unlikely that modern infrastructures will cover all areas of the world and even less likely for all cars to attain communication capabilities in the short term. In this work we study the development of a system that is based on existing off-the-shelf smart-phones and facilitates the creation of ad-hoc networks based on the existing Multipeer technology developed by Apple. This is a non-restrictive approach since similar ad-hoc networking technologies from competitors exists, e.g., WiFi-Direct on Android.

1 Introduction and Motivation

As traffic related deaths and injuries take high tolls each year, vehicular collision warning systems may play a crucial role in the future. To give more motivation some data on road safety from the World Health Organization [11] may be useful. The highest death rates are in countries with less developed infrastructure, e.g., Africa, Asia and the Southern Americas. The distribution of traffic casualties by type of road user shows that even in the most developed countries, e.g., the USA or Western Europe, about half of the casualties occur among the drives and passengers of 4-wheeled vehicles. It is thus clear that more research in this direction and faster introduction of such technologies may be beneficial. Nonetheless, the increasing number of reported attacks on vehicular systems [2,6,7] may bring adversaries that target traffic safety by manipulating vehicle electronics. This should trigger even more attention toward developing more advanced safety mechanisms.

To deploy Car2X communication, i.e., Car2Car and Car2Infrastructure communication, an appropriate network infrastructure is needed. Recently emerged standards, such as the 802.11p, are a proof of the continuous development efforts by the industry. Still, it is unlikely that this infrastructure will quickly cover all areas worldwide and it is hard to forecast an extensive use of modern vehicular communication technologies in less developed parts of the world (this is easier to

© Springer International Publishing AG, part of Springer Nature 2018
N. Cuppens et al. (Eds.): CRiSIS 2017, LNCS 10694, pp. 115–123, 2018.
https://doi.org/10.1007/978-3-319-76687-4_8

project for smartphones which are cheap and available everywhere). Moreover, it is also unlikely for all cars to be equipped with such systems in the short run since cars commonly have lifespans of a decade or more.

Motivated by these, we study the development of a system that is based on existing off-the-shelf iPhones that facilitate the creation of ad-hoc networks based on an existing communication layer, i.e., Multipeer. While this technology is present in all Apple products, alternatives exists for Windows and Android based devices with ad-hoc networking technologies such as WifiDirect. Thus, our proposal is not restricted to the iOS share of the market. We experiment with iPhones only for convenience, but the concepts are general. Mobile phones are cheap and ubiquitous devices while similar capabilities are expressed by after-market infotainment units which are a popular choice among consumers for upgrading older vehicles. Such items cost in the order of several hundred euros and are affordable for most users. Also, they will become even cheaper as production increases. While such gadgets become ubiquitous, the challenge remains in designing suitable solutions. There are numerous constraints both from the existing communication layers, e.g., an ad-hoc networking layer is needed, and also from the computational capabilities of the device. Nonetheless, delays are crucial and the implementation of security mechanisms, which is mandatory for making the solution suitable for real-world needs, comes at a cost. We discuss all these aspects in the forthcoming sections.

1.1 Related Work

A survey on security implications and requirements for Car2X communications can be found in [9]. In our system we do account for basic security objectives such as authentication and cope with real-time needs. Wi-Fi Direct as a communication layer has been previously used for warning systems to avoid collisions with pedestrians and bicyclists in [4]. We believe that the range of Wi-Fi or of the related Multipeer technology, i.e., up to 200 m, is also sufficient for deploying ad-hoc vehicle networks and help in preventing collisions. Another system for collision signaling and avoidance is discussed in [3]. Trajectory predictions has been previously explored by the use of visual information, a survey can be found in [8]. However, the use of visual information requires more demanding algorithms for image processing that we find to be unsuitable for our application setup (image processing requires too much computational time and can also drain the phone's battery). Such algorithms may be of interest as future work in order to corroborate between existing GPS data and also to spot potential malicious reports that contradict visual evidence. A more recent work in [10] provides and excellent survey over intersection monitoring and algorithms for predicting vehicle behaviour. This provides useful information for one of our target scenarios, i.e., a crossroad. In [5] some models are provided for estimating the effectiveness of V2X systems in preventing collisions (in the forthcoming section we briefly discuss the effectiveness of our approach on similar metrics/scenarios).

2   Addressed Scenarios and Constraints

We first discuss on the setup that we address by presenting two relevant scenarios. We also elaborate on the impact of delays which are the most significant constraint of our problem.

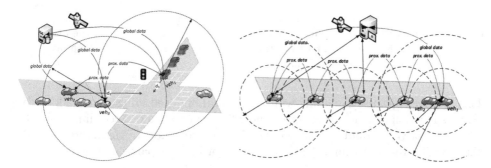

Fig. 1. A vehicle intersection scenario   **Fig. 2.** A highway lane based scenario

2.1   Addressed Scenarios

While we generally target any traffic related scenario, we do theoretically analyze the effectiveness of the mechanism on two target settings: an intersection as depicted in Fig. 1 and a highway as depicted in Fig. 2. These scenarios are useful for assessing the effectiveness of the mechanism (which translates in the number of collisions that can be avoided). Nonetheless, these scenarios provide two of the most prevalent practical setups as crossroads and highways are a common place for vehicle crashes. We now give some metrics on how a collision warning system may help in these scenarios.

Crossroad. For the vehicle crossroad, we consider that the column starting with vehicle veh_1 is departing at green light while vehicle veh_2 is speeding up to takeover the other cars without noticing the red light. The braking distance can be easily computed as: $d = v^2/(2\mu g) + 1.5v$. Here 1.5 s is the driver reaction time and is a standard value in traffic modelling (reaction time may get under 1 s or increase over 2 s depending on driver experience, age, etc.). To provide some hints on the braking distance due to reaction time, in Fig. 3 we show the braking distance due to a reaction time of 2 s at various speeds 5, 10 and 15 km/h and in Fig. 4 the braking distance at 1 s given a speed from 30 to 70 km/h. As depicted in Fig. 3, for a vehicle departing at green light, assuming reaction time of 1.5 s and and a speed of at most 10 km/h, the braking distance d_1 stays in the order of several meters and is below a reasonable 5 m to the center of the intersection. For the second vehicle however, the braking distance d_2 may be well above 30 m even at speed of around 50 km/h. Vehicle veh_3 may easily beacon both vehicles veh_1 and veh_2 to signal the potential collision and thus it can be prevented.

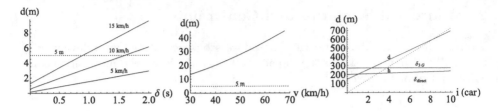

Fig. 3. Braking distance at 0–2 s for speeds of 5, 10 and 15 km/h

Fig. 4. Braking distance in 1 s reaction for speed 3–70 km/h

Fig. 5. Case of the i-th vehicle on the highway lane

This happens because signalling will take several hundred milliseconds added to driver's reaction time which lead to a under 2 s response time. According to Fig. 3 the driver of veh$_1$ could still stop in the 5 m to the center of the intersection if his speed is around 10 km/h (this is realistic for a car departing at green light).

Highway lane. Figure 2 depicts a scenario where a potential chain-collision between vehicles may take place. We assume that for some reason vehicle veh$_1$ slows down and veh$_2$ collides with it due to insufficient distance. In the light of this event, we analyze the impact of a chain-collision due to poor reaction of the rest of the drivers from the lane. The distance between the i-th car in the formation and the front car is ib where b is the recommended 2-s distance between vehicles (at 130 km/h we have b=72 m). The braking distance of the i-th vehicle accounts for the time of the driver to react, that is: $d(i) = 1.5iv + v^2/(2\mu g)$. From Fig. 5 it is easy to see that only vehicle 8 may have sufficient distance to stop until the collision point. However, in case of Multipeer/WiFi-Direct the delay of $1.5i$ becomes $\delta_{direct} = 1.5 + 0.1i$ (which considers the driver reaction time and a 100 s propagation delay between each car) and for 3G considering a 2 s delay δ_{3G} the 3-rd car may stop within safe distance. Consequently, both Multipeer/WiFi-Direct and 3G significantly reduce the number of cars from 7 to 3.

3   Setup and Results

3.1   Practical Considerations and Addressed Setup

Having in mind the required periodicity of 1 status message every 100 ms [9], each vehicle will need to be able to sign/authenticate 10 messages each second for its position alone. In addition, the vehicle must receive and verify messages from the other participants. It is uneasy to estimate the exact number of messages to be verified each second since this is highly dependent on the concrete scenario, but current research places the number of messages that needs to be verified from several hundreds up to 5000 [9].

This leads to a high amount of signing and verification operations each second and we need to adjust to these needs. Since verification is done more often than

Table 1. Computational overhead for authentication tags

Function	Time (ms) for input size (bytes)					
	16	32	64	128	256	512
HMAC-SHA1	0.015	0.002	0.001	0.001	0.001	0.004
HMAC-SHA256	0.004	0.001	0.002	0.001	0.001	0.001

Table 2. Computation time for signing and verification

Function	Time (ms) for input size (bytes)					
	16	32	64	128	256	512
RSA-1024 sign	1.713	1.698	1.843	1.875	1.730	1.713
RSA-1024 verify	0.044	0.045	0.044	0.044	0.044	0.045

signing, RSA seems to be a natural choice due to its higher verification speed. In Table 1 we give some computational timings (in milliseconds) for hash functions and in Table 2 for RSA on an iPhone 6 s. The computational time is short-enough for allowing the requested 5000 signature verifications/second and 10 signatures. Similar collision warning systems, e.g., WiFiHonk [4], do not implement security mechanisms but we believe that the lack of security is not desirable.

We choose to separate between location and authentication data which allows more flexibility in choosing to use (which we recommend) or ignore the authentication data. This leads to a frame having the structure suggested in Fig. 6. The location frame in Fig. 6(i) starts with the length of the frame, followed by the ID of the sender, a fixed value set to 0x00h, a timestamp, current vehicle location. The ID of the other participants follows along with their location. In the authentication frames from Fig. 6(ii) we start again with frame length, sender ID, a fixed value 0xFF to separate from location frames, a timestamp and a signature. Then short Message Authentication Codes (MAC) follow to authenticate data for short-range peers. Moreover, authentication data includes both digital signatures as well as faster MACs which can be used for short-range peers.

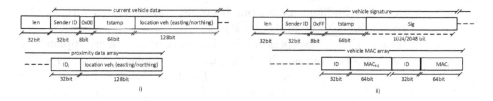

Fig. 6. Structure of location frames (i) and authentication frames (ii)

To save some computational time one can prefer a MAC-based solution but this would require a secret key that is shared between participants. We believe that such a solution may be preferable whenever vehicles clusters are formed, e.g., on a highway. From a security perspective this simply requires an authenticated key-exchange protocol for sharing the key. Coming up with a new authentication protocol per paper is not desirable since it is known that authentication protocols are prone to subtle security flaws. The automotive domain is industry driven and the industry targets standardized solutions which makes it preferable to stay closer to standards. The work in [1] did a careful analysis by formal verification of ISO standardized protocols for key agreement and recommended several fixes. Such protocols can be safely used for sharing keys between two vehicles. Besides these we do of course recommend that the 3G/4G communication with the server is done inside a SSL/TLS channel which is again a standard solution for remote connectivity.

3.2   Implementation and Experiments

The multipeer framework makes the physical transport of data transparent, i.e., switching between both Wi-Fi and Bluetooth. Indeed, once connected over Bluetooth, the range of collision prediction becomes lower than Wi-Fi and thus Wi-Fi is preferable. Connectivity with the server is maintained via 3G and Multipeer facilitates direct connection between 2 peers as soon as they are in close range. According to the documentation up to 8 peers can be connected by Multipeer with rapid switching between these connections.

The development environments that helped us to develop a proof of concept were numerous. Amongst the most used tools were Xcode 8.0 which helped us to design and to implement the application deployed later on iPhone. We also made use of Eclipse CDT which allowed us to implement the server application. The hardware that we used consists in two iPhones (4s respectively 6s), one of them running iOS 9.3 and the other one running iOS 10.3.

Having in mind the requirements for a system able to accomplish V2x communication, we designed two redundant mechanisms in order to eliminate any dead time that could occur during a transmission initiated by one peer and disconnected by an interference. On one side, we have the Multipeer framework which makes possible advertising (broadcast a service to the other traffic participants) and browsing (finding services put by other traffic participants) in the same time without the need of an Access Point.

On the left side of Fig. 7 we present the flowchart of the client application which begins with a fork from which all the others components start. The iOS application is broken into three main blocks: *Location Updater, LTE Handler* and *MP Handler*. Each of these has a well established purpose that is suggested by its: updating the location of the vehicle, handler the LTE or the Multipeer connectivity. The Location Updater updates the coordinates of the current location and converts them from Latitude/Longitude to Easting/Northing since it is more convenient to use such coordinates in 2D Cartesian system. The second one, is specialized in handling both incoming and outgoing packets by LTE, it connects to the server then sends and receives frames. The third block handles the Multipeer connections. The application starts by advertising and browsing for nearby peers. In advertising mode, it exposes v2x-service to other peers and it is waiting for incoming invitations. Once the invitation has arrived, the application checks for its signature and it accepts or denies the invitation. In browsing mode, the application is looking for nearby services. Once found, it sends an invitation for connection and if the invitation was accepted, it starts to send data. The right side of Fig. 7 depicts the server application which takes the incoming frames from the clients and sends back all the neighbors in a range of 200 m.

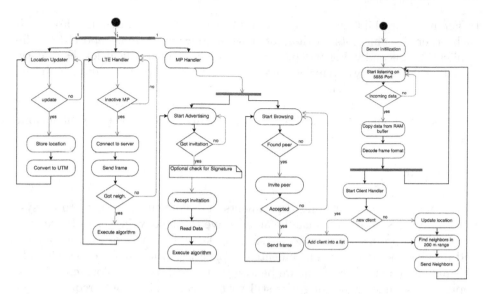

Fig. 7. Flowchart of client (left) and server (right) applications

The server is used for data transfer in LTE mode when the Multipeer connection is not available. The server application starts its life cycle listening on a local port which is set to 5555. For experimental purposes we used port forwarding mechanisms allowing us to run the server on a local machine without the need of having a registered domain. The previously suggested structure for location and authentication frames, i.e., from Fig. 6, can be used for data sent between devices, i.e., by Multipeer connectivity, or received by devices from the server, i.e., by 3G connectivity.

We now discuss experimental results. First, in Fig. 8 we show the trace for two moving persons. We chose this, rather then recording the trace of two cars,

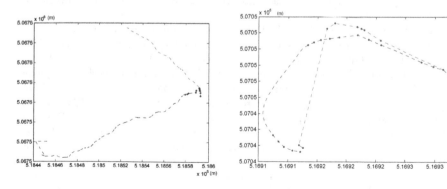

Fig. 8. Trace for two individuals with iPhones (Color figure online)

Fig. 9. Trace for two cars with iPhones (Color figure online)

to get more flexibility in testing the application. As the individuals approach each other the blue dots on the plot mark a collision warning reported by the application. Secondly, Fig. 9 depicts a trace for two moving vehicles. For safety, we run this while two vehicles were moving inside a parking lot. Again the application correctly identifies and signals a potential collision that is marked by red dots. Based on experiments, the accuracy of the GPS localization was very good reaching at around 1 m in some situations which is excellent for our application.

4   Conclusion

Our practical deployment and experiments showed that collision-warning systems based on smart-phones can be an effective technology. In this work we only explored the proposal as a concept, showing key advantages of such a solution and proving that it can be implemented in practice. Our results so far rely only on small scale experiments but we believe that a real-world deployment of such applications while challenging it is still within reach. This would require large-scale simulation/experiments, formal verification of the security suite, interest from car owners and nonetheless cooperation from the industry. We may pursue such direction as future work.

Acknowledgement. This work was supported by a grant of the Romanian National Authority for Scientific Research and Innovation, CNCS-UEFISCDI, project number PN-II-RU-TE-2014-4-1501 (2015–2017).

References

1. Basin, D., Cremers, C., Meier, S.: Provably repairing the ISO/IEC 9798 standard for entity authentication. J. Comput. Secur. **21**(6), 817–846 (2013)
2. Checkoway, S., McCoy, D., Kantor, B., Anderson, D., Shacham, H., Savage, S., Koscher, K., Czeskis, A., Roesner, F., Kohno, T., et al.: Comprehensive experimental analyses of automotive attack surfaces. In: USENIX Security Symposium, San Francisco (2011)
3. Chen, L.-W., Chou, P.-C.: BIG-CCA: Beacon-less, infrastructure-less, and GPS-less cooperative collision avoidance based on vehicular sensor networks. IEEE Trans. Syst. Man Cybern. Syst. **46**(11), 1518–1528 (2016)
4. Dhondge, K., Song, S., Choi, B.-Y., Park, H.: WiFiHonk: smartphone-based beacon stuffed WiFi Car2X-communication system for vulnerable road user safety. In: 2014 IEEE 79th Vehicular Technology Conference (VTC Spring), pp. 1–5. IEEE (2014)
5. Joerer, S., Segata, M., Bloessl, B., Cigno, R.L., Sommer, C., Dressler, F.: To crash or not to crash: estimating its likelihood and potentials of beacon-based IVC systems. In: 2012 IEEE Vehicular Networking Conference (VNC), pp. 25–32. IEEE (2012)
6. Koscher, K., Czeskis, A., Roesner, F., Patel, S., Kohno, T., Checkoway, S., McCoy, D., Kantor, B., Anderson, D., Shacham, H., et al.: Experimental security analysis of a modern automobile. In: 2010 IEEE Symposium on Security and Privacy (SP), pp. 447–462. IEEE (2010)

7. Miller, C., Valasek, C.: A survey of remote automotive attack surfaces. Black Hat, USA (2014)
8. Morris, B.T., Trivedi, M.M.: A survey of vision-based trajectory learning and analysis for surveillance. IEEE Trans. Circ. Syst. Video Technol. **18**(8), 1114–1127 (2008)
9. Schütze, T.: Automotive security: cryptography for Car2X communication. In: Embedded World Conference, vol. 3 (2011)
10. Shirazi, M.S., Morris, B.T.: Looking at intersections: a survey of intersection monitoring, behavior and safety analysis of recent studies. IEEE Trans. Intell. Transp. Syst. **18**(1), 4–24 (2017)
11. World Health Organization: Road traffic deaths. Technical report (2013). http://www.who.int/gho/road_safety/mortality/en/.

Cloud Security

Design and Realization of a Fully Homomorphic Encryption Algorithm for Cloud Applications

Khalil Hariss[1,3]([✉]) [iD], Hassan Noura[1,2], Abed Ellatif Samhat[1], and Maroun Chamoun[3]

[1] Faculty of Engineering - CRSI, Lebanese University, Hadath, Lebanon
hnnoura@gmail.com, samhat@ul.edu.lb
[2] Telecom ParisTech, 46, rue Barrault, 75013 Paris, France
[3] Saint Joseph University, ESIB-CIMTI, Mar Roukoz, Lebanon
khalil.hariss@net.usj.edu.lb, maroun.chamoun@usj.edu.lb

Abstract. Cloud Computing is a kind of internet-based computing that provides shared storage and processing resources. One main drawback of this technique is that users and companies will give the permission to a third party to access their sensitive data. Homomorphic Encryption scheme came as a new cryptographic research topic to resolve the concerned problem by preserving the privacy in the cloud settings. In this paper, we propose a new efficient symmetric lightweight Fully Homomorphic Encryption algorithm, called "NOHE", which profits from the simplicity of the logic *NOT* and the homomorphic behavior of Morgan Theorem. The proposed algorithm is explained in detail and evaluated. The security performance results show an acceptable execution time with no storage overhead and high immunity to attack.

Keywords: Cloud · Storage · Homomorphic encryption

1 Introduction

Cloud Computing is a new efficient and promising technique for storing and processing data, by giving better opportunities for out-sourcing of storage and computation. In this technique all users will allow their data to be stored and processed by a third party. Unfortunately a lot of users retain from risking their own sensitive data to a cloud because not any third party is trusted; the question is: how can we leverage the cryptographic techniques in order to enable the privacy preserving in the cloud settings? Here classical encryption is limited or inefficient, and Homomorphic Encryption (HE) is proposed to achieve this goal.

A Homomorphic Encryption algorithm (HE) is an algorithm that allows processing over the ciphertext. HE is a new cryptographic research topic, that was introduced for resolving the security issues including cloud scenario. It allows

© Springer International Publishing AG, part of Springer Nature 2018
N. Cuppens et al. (Eds.): CRiSIS 2017, LNCS 10694, pp. 127–139, 2018.
https://doi.org/10.1007/978-3-319-76687-4_9

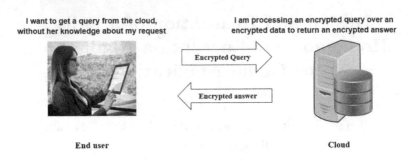

Fig. 1. Secure cloud querying

users to encrypt their data in the cloud, and also allows the cloud to process over encrypted data; the data is kept encrypted in the cloud and there is no need to ship it back to be decrypted. HE also allows users to send encrypted queries to any cloud, which can process encrypted queries over encrypted data to return to the users encrypted answers, then the user can decrypt and get the required result as shown clearly in Fig. 1.

In fact any electrical circuit boolean function is simply a set of additions and multiplications. Thus, the main idea of homomorphic encryption is that any untrusted party should compute $E(x + y)$ and $E(x \times y)$ from $E(x)$ and $E(y)$ without knowing any information about x and y. Two basic properties should be satisfied to build fully homomorphic encryption algorithm, which are described in the following:

$$E_K(x_1) + E_K(x_2) mod N = E_K(x_1 + x_2, mod N) \tag{1}$$

$$E_K(x_2) \times E_K(x_2) mod N = E_K(x_1 \times x_2, mod N) \tag{2}$$

where x_1, $x_2 \in$ ring Z_N, E is the encryption function and K is a secret key.

Several works such as [1–12] have considered the design and the realization of Homomorphic Encryption algorithms. The existing homomorphic algorithms are decomposed into two groups: asymmetric (such as Gentry [5], RSA [6], Pallier [7] and $DGHV$ [8]) or symmetric (such as $MORE$ [9,10], $PORE$ [10] and Domingo Ferrer [11,12]).

In this paper, we propose $NOHE$ (Not Operation for Homomorphic Encryption): a new dynamic lightweight homomorphic scheme that profits from the simplicity of the logic NOT and the homomorphic behavior of the Morgan theorem to build a symmetric FHE (Fully Homomorphic Encryption) that provides efficiency in implementation and high immunity to attacks. The proposed work can be considered as a good candidate for existing homomorphic schemes. The rest of this paper is organized as follows. Section 2 briefly introduces an overview about the two symmetric homomorphic approaches: $MORE$ and $PORE$. In Sect. 3, we present our new symmetric homomorphic algorithm $NOHE$ and its implementation. Security analysis and performances of the resultant algorithm and its comparison with the $MORE$ and the $PORE$ are given in Sect. 4 while conclusions are drawn in Sect. 5.

2   The *MORE* and The *PORE* Approaches

In [9,10] the authors introduced the *MORE* approach (Matrix Operation for Randomization and Encryption) that benefits from the matrix operations for building a FHE algorithm. It is summarized in Table 1.

In [10], the authors explained the *PORE* approach (Polynomial Operations for Randomization and Encryption). The *PORE* Approach is FHE Algorithm that satisfies both properties, Addition and Multiplication. The proposed algorithm is summarized in Table 2. While the Homomorphic behavior of the *MORE* and the *PORE* is proved in [9,10], the two algorithms present high storage overhead and low immunity to attacks.

Table 1. MORE approach

Secret key	Secret invertible matrix K in a ring Z_N
Public parameters	No public parameters
Plain-text space	Set of x in a ring Z_N
Encryption process	$Enc(x) = K \begin{bmatrix} x & 0 \\ 0 & r \end{bmatrix} K^{-1}$, r random
Cipher-text space	Set of matrices $C = [c_{ij}]$, $c_{ij} \in Z_N$
Decryption process	$\begin{bmatrix} x & 0 \\ 0 & r \end{bmatrix} = K^{-1} Enc(x) K$
Fully homomorphic	Verified by a matrix calculations

Table 2. PORE approach

Secret key	$K = (v_1, v_2)$
Public parameters	$b = -(v_1 + v_2) mod(N)$ $c = (v_1 v_2) mod(N)$
Plain-text space	Set of x in a ring Z_N
Encryption process	$Enc(x) = (a, d)$ that satisfies $\begin{aligned} av_1 + d &= x \\ av_2 + d &= r \end{aligned}$ r is a random integer
Cipher-text space	Set of $(a, d) \in Z_N \times Z_N$
Decryption process	$x = (av_1 + d) mod(N)$
Fully homomorphic	b and c should be exposed to the cloud

3   FHE NOHE

3.1   Logic *NOT* and Homomorphic Behavior

Let us define the function f over the bit level

$$f : \{0, 1\} \rightarrow \{0, 1\}$$
$$x \rightarrow \bar{x}$$

The Proposed function f can lead to a homomorphic encryption algorithm based on Morgan theorem:

$$f(x \oplus y) = \overline{x \oplus y} = \overline{\overline{x}y + x\overline{y}} = \overline{\overline{x} \oplus \overline{y}} = \overline{f(x) \oplus f(y)} \tag{3}$$

$$f(x \bullet y) = \overline{\overline{x} \bullet \overline{y}} = \overline{x} + \overline{y} = f(x) + f(y) \tag{4}$$

where ($\oplus$ is Logic XOR), ($\bullet$ is Logic AND) and ($+$ is Logic OR).

3.2   Proposed FHE Algorithm: NOHE

$NOHE$ is built without altering the homomorphic behavior of the f function. The encryption algorithm is divided into three main parts that will be described in detail.

- **Bits Permutation (P-box):** Consider a binary plain-texts vector X of size l. The bits permutation is realized at the message level (all the bits of X) to ensure better resistance against exhaustive research attacks such as chosen plaintext attack.
- **Secret NOT positions:** The binary plain-texts vector X is divided into H blocks, where $H = \lceil \frac{l}{n} \rceil$, n is the block size. The function f (or the logic NOT) is applied over a certain secret bit positions in the blocks of X.
- **Secret Circular Shift operation:** A secret circular shift is applied over the blocks of X.

To ensure higher resistance against attacks, $P-box$, secret NOT positions and circular shifts are renewed for each new session. The diagram of Fig. 2 shows the different steps of $NOHE$ algorithm:

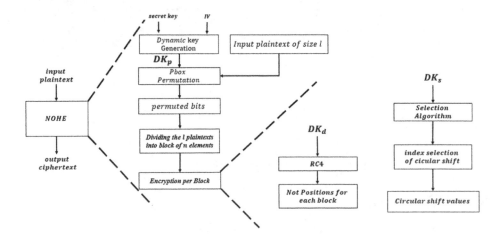

Fig. 2. FHE NOHE flow chart

1. **Dynamic Key Generation:** A Dynamic Key of 64 bytes $(DK) =$ $SecureHash(Secretkey, IV)$ is built, then three secret keys (DK_p, DK_d, DK_s) are picked from it (Fig. 2) to form three cipher layers as follows:
   - DK_p: Dynamic Key for Permutation formed of 23 bytes.
   - DK_d: Dynamic Key for Diffusion formed of 16 bytes.
   - DK_s: Dynamic Key for Selection formed of 23 bytes.
2. **Permutation Box:** Using DK_p, a key dependant $P - box$ is generated and applied over the bit streams to strengthen our implementation as in [13,14], since it preserves the homomorphic properties.
   Suppose that we have $\pi = [p_i]_{1 \leq i \leq N}$, a $P - box$ of dimension N. Two plaintexts X and Y of dimension N are given: $X = [x_i]_{1 \leq i \leq N}$ and $Y = [y_i]_{1 \leq i \leq N}$.
   After permutation $\pi(X) = [x_{p_i}]_{1 \leq i \leq N}$ and $\pi(Y) = [y_{p_i}]_{1 \leq i \leq N}$.
   Suppose that $\odot$ is a law defined over the plain-texts by:
   $X \odot Y = [x_i]_{1 \leq i \leq N} \odot [y_i]_{1 \leq i \leq N} = [x_i \odot y_i]_{1 \leq i \leq N} = [z_i]_{1 \leq i \leq N} = Z$.
   $\pi(X \odot Y) = \pi(Z) = [z_{p_i}]_{1 \leq i \leq N} = [x_{p_i} \odot y_{p_i}]_{1 \leq i \leq N}$.
   And $\pi(X) \odot \pi(Y) = [x_{p_i}]_{1 \leq i \leq N} \odot [y_{p_i}]_{1 \leq i \leq N} = [x_{p_i} \odot y_{p_i}]_{1 \leq i \leq N}$.
   Since $\pi(X \odot Y) = \pi(X) \odot \pi(Y)$, we can deduce the homomorphic behavior of π. As a practical example, an input plain-text $X = [1, 0, 0, 1, 1, 0, 0, 1, 1, 0]$ is taken, and a permutation box $[3, 6, 9, 2, 7, 5, 10, 1, 4, 8]$, the permuted plaintext is $[0, 0, 1, 0, 0, 1, 0, 1, 1, 1]$.
3. **Dynamic Block Encryption:** At this level, the bits permuted plain-texts vector is divided into a block format. For each block, using DK_d and a stream cipher algorithm like $RC4$, a secret sequence of bits having the same length of the block is generated. Each position in the secret sequence with bit equal to 1 is translated into a NOT position in the block. In addition, a circular shift for each block is chosen from a secret bank based on the position index of the block using a dynamic selection algorithm built using DK_s. In the example of the previous section the permuted plain-text $[0, 0, 1, 0, 0, 1, 0, 1, 1, 1]$ is decomposed for example into the following block format: $\begin{bmatrix} 0 & 0 & 1 & 0 & 0 \\ 1 & 0 & 1 & 1 & 1 \end{bmatrix}$.

   Based on the Dynamic encryption implementation suppose that for each block the security parameters are built as in Table 3. The resultant cipher text is: Output Cipher of $X = [0, 1, 1, 1, 1, 1, 0, 1, 1, 0]$.
4. **Dynamic Key Selection Algorithm:** To achieve the circular shift, the dynamic key selection algorithm is creating another permutation box $\Delta = [\delta_i]_{1 \leq i \leq H}$ that has the length of the number of blocks. The circular shift selection is done based on the block number as shown in Fig. 3. Similar to $P - box$ homomorphic behavior, we can show that any circular shift is also homomorphic.

Table 3. Dynamic block encryption

Block Nb	DK_d, RC4	NOT positions	DK_s, selection algorithm
Block 1	[10100]	Not pos. = $(1, 3)$	Secret circular shift $= 3$
Block 2	[01001]	Not pos. = $(2, 5)$	Secret circular shift $= 4$

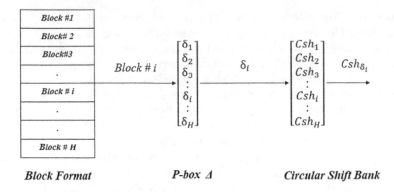

Block Format   P-box Δ Circular Shift Bank

Fig. 3. Dynamic selection algorithm

3.3 Decryption Process

The Decryption process is the inverse of the encryption process listed in Fig. 2 since the scheme is symmetric. The decryption process is based on the following three steps:

1. Inverse Circular shift: The dynamic key selection algorithm is built from DK_s, and using it the receiving end can select for each block the inverse circular shift from the shared circular shift bank.
2. Secret NOT positions: Based on DK_d and $RC4$ algorithm, the same secret bit sequence that represents the secret NOT positions can be generated and the NOT on each block can be removed.
3. Inverse Permutation: The destination produces the inverse secret permutation vector π^{-1} by using DK_p and the following transformation:

$$\pi^{-1}[\pi[X]] = X \tag{5}$$

3.4 FHE NOHE Homomorphic Implementation

Based on the proposed FHE NOHE, we can achieve the homomorphic implementation in two different scenarios: Trusted Cloud or Untrusted Cloud, depending on the level of the trust given to the cloud. The trusted cloud may know the secret NOT positions, but the untrusted one should not know anything about the security parameters. In the following, we give an example to explain the two different implementations. Let X and Y be two plain-texts and their ciphers respectively are $Enc(X)$ and $Enc(Y)$ given using $NOHE$:

1. **Bits Permutation:** let $\pi(X) = [1, 1, 0, 0, 1]$ and $\pi(Y) = [0, 1, 0, 0, 1]$, be the permuted plain-texts vectors for X and Y.
2. **Secret NOT positions:** Suppose that the secret NOT positions are first and fourth positions (1 and 4, shown in bold below), as a result we have:
$f(\pi(X)) = [\mathbf{0}, 1, 0, \mathbf{1}, 1]$ and $f(\pi(Y)) = [\mathbf{1}, 1, 0, \mathbf{1}, 1]$.

3. **Secret Circular Shift operation:** suppose that the secret circular t is 3, in this case we have to apply 3 times a circular shifts and the final cipher-text is given:
   - First circular shift for $f(\pi(X))$ and $f(\pi(Y))$ respectively: $[1, \mathbf{0}, 1, 0, \mathbf{1}]$ and $[1, \mathbf{1}, 1, 0, \mathbf{1}]$
   - Second circular shift: $[\mathbf{1}, 1, \mathbf{0}, 1, 0]$ and $[\mathbf{1}, 1, \mathbf{1}, 1, 0]$.
   - Third circular shift: $Enc(X) = (f(\pi(X)) \quad >> \quad t) = [0, \mathbf{1}, 1, \mathbf{0}, 1]$ and $Enc(Y) = (f(\pi(Y)) >> t) = [0, \mathbf{1}, 1, \mathbf{1}, 1]$.

First Scenario - Trusted Cloud. Since the cloud here is trusted, it is possible to know the bold secret NOT positions. In this case, we define the FHE by these two operations: Homomorphic XOR and Homomorphic AND. **Homomorphic XOR:** The Homomorphic XOR requires the calculation of $Enc(X \oplus Y)$ from $Enc(X)$ and $Enc(Y)$ without knowing any information about X and Y. Given that $\pi(X \oplus Y) = [1, 0, 0, 0, 0]$ after applying FHE NOHE applied on X and Y, we obtain $Enc(X \oplus Y) = [0, 1, 0, \mathbf{0}, 0]$.
$Enc(X) = [0, \mathbf{1}, 1, \mathbf{0}, 1]$ and $Enc(Y) = [0, \mathbf{1}, 1, \mathbf{1}, 1]$ are stored at the cloud side. In this scenario the trusted cloud can distinguish the bold positions (secret NOT) from the normal ones, and it will process the normal $\oplus$ over the normal bits and the homomorphic $\oplus$ over the bold bits as given in this expression:
CloudXORProcess $= [g_1, \boldsymbol{g_2}, g_1, \boldsymbol{g_2}, g_1]$, where $g_1(b_1, b_2) = b_1 \oplus b_2$ and $\boldsymbol{g_2}(b_1, b_2) = \overline{g_1(b_1, b_2)}$ based on Eq. (3). The result of the Cloud processing is given by $[g_1(0, 0), \boldsymbol{g_2}(1, 1), g_1(1, 1), \boldsymbol{g_2}(0, 1), g_1(1, 1)] = [0, 1, 0, \mathbf{0}, 0]$ which is equal to $Enc(X \oplus Y)$. In this Homomorphic XOR we calculate at the cloud side the $Enc(X \oplus Y)$ knowing $Enc(X)$ and $Enc(Y)$ only.

Homomorphic AND: The same operations are repeated in this scenario using the homomorphic AND explained in Eq. (4), the CloudANDProcess $= [g_1, \boldsymbol{g_2}, g_1, \boldsymbol{g_2}, g_1]$, where $g_1(b_1, b_2) = b_1 \bullet b_2$ and $\boldsymbol{g_2}(b_1, b_2) = \overline{b_1 + b_2}$.

Second Scenario - Untrusted Cloud. In this scenario, since the cloud is untrusted, the FHE scheme should be accomplished in a different way to avoid any attacks.
$Enc(X)$ and $Enc(Y)$ are stored at the cloud side, and the bold positions are not known by the cloud. The cloud will process the normal XOR and the homomorphic XOR over the two cipher-texts as shown below:

Homomorphic XOR:

- Normal XOR: $Enc(X) \oplus Enc(Y) = [0, \mathbf{0}, 0, 1, 0]$.
- Homomorphic XOR: $\overline{Enc(X) \oplus Enc(Y)} = [1, \mathbf{1}, 1, \mathbf{0}, 1]$.

The two values of $Enc(X) \oplus Enc(Y)$ and $\overline{Enc(X) \oplus Enc(Y)}$ are shipped back to the host side. The host knows all the cipher layers including the secret NOT positions. Thus the host will choose the normal bits from $Enc(X) \oplus Enc(Y)$ and the bold bit positions from $\overline{Enc(X) \oplus Enc(Y)}$ to get $[0, 1, 0, \mathbf{0}, 0]$ which is equal to $Enc(X \oplus Y)$. In this scenario, we also build $Enc(X \oplus Y)$ from $Enc(X)$ and $Enc(Y)$.

Homomorphic AND:
The same procedure is repeated in this scenario with Homomorphic AND using Eq. (4).

4   Security Analysis and Performances

Security analysis is a set of tests used to evaluate the security performances of the proposed FHE NOHE scheme. Several tests are done as listed in [15], where a set of plain-texts in the ring Z_{256} are picked as integers and then transformed into binary for the $NOHE$ implementation. We compare the execution time and the storage overhead of $MORE$ and $PORE$ with $NOHE$. As for the security analysis, $NOHE$ outperforms $MORE$ and $PORE$ because it is well known that these two FHE algorithms are vulnerable to attacks as shown in [16].

4.1   Resistance Against Statistical Attacks

The independence and uniformity are two important properties should be satisfied by any encryption scheme to ensure high resistance against statistical attacks. Different tests are employed to verify these two properties: Uniformity (Distribution Test, Entropy Test), Independence (Recurrence Test, Difference Test, Correlation Test).

Uniformity

1. **Distribution Test:** To resist statistical attacks, the frequency counts of the cipher-text should be close to the uniform distribution to prevent any useful information that can permit this kind of attacks to break the cipher system. The distribution of a plain-text and its corresponding cipher-text distribution are shown in Fig. 4(a) and (b), respectively. The distribution of the cipher-text after applying $NOHE$ is close to uniform distribution.
2. **Entropy Test:** The information entropy of a source message m is a metric that measures the level of uncertainty in a random variable. The entropy is defined by the following equation:

$$H(m) = \sum_{i=0}^{2^M-1} p(m_i) log_2 \frac{1}{p(m_i)} \tag{6}$$

   where $p(m_i)$ represents the probability of occurrence of symbol m_i and 2^M is the total state of information source. A truly random source entropy is equal to M, since the plain-text is chosen from a ring Z_{256}, the ideal value of the entropy should be equal to 8 ($2^8 = 256$). In Fig. 4(c), the entropy value is calculated for 10000 cipher-texts. The obtained result gives a mean value equal to 7.942 which is very close to 8 with a low standard deviation ($Std = 0.005169$). Therefore, the cipher-text ensures a high entropy value. This confirms the previous result regarding the uniformity and the obtained cipher-text space can be considered as a truly random source.

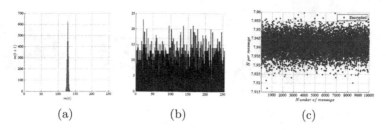

(a)   (b)   (c)

Fig. 4. Distribution test: (a)- Original message, (b)-Cipher message, (c) Entropy test.

Independence Property

1. **Recurrence Test:** The recurrence plot serves to measure the evolution of randomness by estimating the correlations among the data of a sequence as in considering a packet sequence $x_i = x_{(i,1)}, x_{(i,2)}, x_{(i,3)}, ...x_{(i,m)}$, a vector with delay $t \geq 1$ can be constructed by $x_i(t) = x_{(i,t)}, x_{(i,2t)}, x_{(i,3t)}, ...x_{(i,mt)}$. In Fig. 5(a) and (b) the variation between $x_i(t)$ and $x_i(t+1)$ from the original and the encrypted plain-texts respectively are shown. A plain-text is generated using a normal distribution with a mean value equal to 128 and a standard deviation equal to 16 as shown in Fig. 5-(a). After applying the proposed FHE NOHE, one can see in Fig. 5-(b) that the obtained cipher-text presents a non-linearity since no clear pattern is shown after the encryption process. This test demonstrates that the proposed cipher presents a high level of randomness.

2. **Difference Test:** This test is done to calculate the percent of difference at the bit level between the cipher-texts and the plain-texts. Any cipher should ensure a difference percent close to 50% between the cipher-texts and the plain-texts at the bit level to be considered secure. In Fig. 5(c), the difference at bit level between each couple of cipher-text and plain-text is calculated for 10000 times. One can see in Fig. 5(c) that the obtained values are close to the ideal ones with a mean value close to 50 with a low standard deviation equal (0.3095). Consequently, the proposed cipher satisfies the different required cryptographic performances.

3. **Correlation Test:** Any encryption scheme should provide a low correlation between the original and the encrypted plain-texts. The correlation coefficient between the original and the encrypted plain-texts is:

$$\rho_{x,y} = \frac{cov(x,y)}{\sqrt{D(x) \times D(y)}} \text{ where } cov(x,y) = E[\{x - E(x)\}\{y - E(y)\}];$$

$$E(x) = \frac{1}{n} \times \sum_{k=1}^{n} x_i \text{ and } D(x) = \frac{1}{n} \times \sum_{k=1}^{n} \{x_i - E[x]\}^2$$

The correlation test for 10000 iterations is shown in Fig. 5(d), and the obtained results are always close to zero with a mean value equal to 3.107×10^{-5} and a standard deviation equal to 0.01752. The proposed cipher achieves a low correlation between the cipher-texts and the plain-texts and consequently ensures the independence propriety.

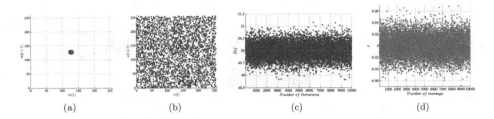

Fig. 5. Recurrence test: (a)- Original message, (b)-Cipher message, (c) Difference test, (d) Correlation test.

4.2   Resistance Against Several Kinds of Key Attacks

The Proposed scheme presents a high immunity against different type of key attacks. The weakness in any dynamic key will not affect the previous and the next processed data since the proposed key derivation function produces a set of dynamic sub-keys with a high degree of randomness. This provides a good resistance degree against the weak keys. In addition the size of the secret key (128,196, 256) bits such as AES and the size of DK 512 bits, are sufficient enough to protect the proposed cipher against the brute force attacks.

Key Sensitivity Test. To confirm resistance against key attacks, this test is used to compute the percent of change in the cipher-text due to a slight change in the encryption key. The cipher should ensure a value of key sensitivity close to 50. Indeed, the sensitivity test for the wth secret key (K'_w) is calculated as follows:

$$KS_w = \frac{\sum_{k=1}^{T} E_{K_w} \oplus E_{K'_w}}{T} \times 100\%, w = 1, 2, \ldots, 1000. \tag{7}$$

where all the elements of K'_w are equal to those of K_w, except a random Least Significant Bit (LSB) of a random byte, and T is the length of the original and cipher plain-text (in bits). The KS test is done for 10000 iterations; the mean value is also close to 50 with a low standard deviation equal to 0.3128 as shown in Fig. 6(a).

4.3   Lack of Avalanche Effect

In any robust cipher, the "Avalanche Effect" property should be ensured to attain the required resistance against chosen/known plaintext/cipher-text attacks. Avalanche effect means that if a one bit change in the plain-text exists, at least half of the cipher-text bits should change. In our proposed algorithm, one bit change in the plain-text will change only one bit in the cipher text.

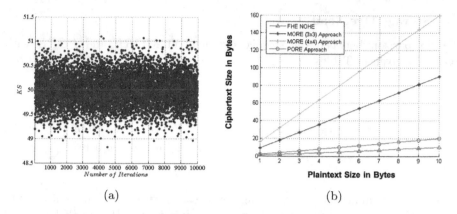

(a)   (b)

Fig. 6. (a) Key sensitivity, (b) Storage overhead comparison.

Overcoming the Lack of Avalanche Effect. Suppose that Trudy is an intruder trying to do a known plain-text/cipher-text attack over our FHE NOHE explained previously. If Trudy sends the input plain-text $= [1, 0, 0, 1, 1, 0, 0, 1, 1, 0]$ to the FHE NOHE the Output cipher-text will be $A = [0, 1, 1, 1, 1, 1, 0, 1, 1, 0]$. If Trudy sends the same plain-text by changing one bit like $[0, 0, 0, 1, 1, 0, 0, 1, 1, 0]$, by applying the same security parameters of the FHE NOHE the Output Cipher in this case is $B = [0, 1, 1, 1, 1, 1, 0, 0, 1, 0]$. To accomplish his attack, Trudy should XOR the two cipher-texts A and B to obtain the following:

$A \oplus B = [0, 1, 1, 1, 1, 1, 0, 1, 1, 0] \oplus [0, 1, 1, 1, 1, 1, 0, 0, 1, 0] = [0, 0, 0, 0, 0, 0, 0, 1, 0, 0]$.

After doing this XOR operation, Trudy can compare the cipher-text and the plain-text to recover the first bit in the plain-text as shown below in Fig. 7. If we examine carefully Trudy attack, we can notice that recovering the 10 bits plain-text from the 10 bits cipher-text requires 10 iterations. In general, recovering a plain-text formed of n bits requires n iterations. To overcome the lack of Avalanche effect, the Dynamic key DK should be used for short encryption sessions in addition to the dynamic key approach and in this case we can avoid Trudy's attack.

Fig. 7. First bit uncover

4.4   Storage Overhead

The comparison between the storage overhead of $MORE$ and $PORE$ with $NOHE$ is given in Table 4.

Table 4. Storage overhead comparison

Input plaintext size	$MORE$	$PORE$	$NOHE$
n bytes	$n \times m \times m$ bytes	$2 \times n$ bytes	n bytes

A simple comparison for the storage overhead between the different encryption algorithms is given in Fig. 6(b). It is very clear that FHE NOHE has a null storage overhead giving a better performance than other FHE algorithms, while the MORE presents the highest one because it is storage overhead is related to the matrix size $(m \times m)$.

4.5   Execution Time

$MORE$ (4×4 matrix), $PORE$ and $NOHE$ implementation are done under MATLAB using Toshiba Laptop having the following specifications: Processor Intel(R) Core(TM) i5-4200U CPU @ $1.60\,GHz$, $2301\,Mhz$, 2 Core(s), 4 Logical Processor(s). The execution time is given for different plain-texts size as shown in Table 5. Based on the execution time, $MORE$ and $PORE$ are better than $NOHE$. However, $MORE$ and $PORE$ are not well secure [16].

Table 5. Execution time in seconds

Plaintext size in bytes	800	3200	5600	8000
NOHE execution time	$0.0302\,s$	$0.1202\,s$	$0.2512\,s$	$0.3106\,s$
MORE execution time	$0.0200\,s$	$0.0544\,s$	$0.0950\,s$	$0.1361\,s$
PORE execution time	$0.0116\,s$	$0.0434\,s$	$0.0762\,s$	$0.1119\,s$

5   Conclusion

In this paper, we present a new lightweight FHE algorithm called $NOHE$. It is based on symmetric primitives to ensure efficiency, robustness in addition to homomorphic proprieties. A practical use of the proposed cipher is for cloud system. $NOHE$ has a dynamic structure and designed to be implemented in two different scenarios, where each one is based on the trust level given to the cloud. The security analysis of the proposed cipher indicates a high level of robustness. Different countermeasures are used to overcome the lack of Avalanche Effect. The main advantage of the FHE NOHE that makes it practical for real world applications is its null storage overhead with an acceptable execution time.

References

1. Aguilar-Melchor, C., Fau, S., Fontaine, C., Gogniat, G., Sirdey, R.: Recent advances in homomorphic encryption: a possible future. IEEE Signal Process. Mag. **30**(2), 108–117 (2013)
2. Chan, AC-F.: Symmetric-key homomorphic encryption for encrypted data processing. In: 2009 IEEE International Conference on Communications, pp. 1–5. IEEE (2009)
3. Fau, S., Sirdey, R., Fontaine, C., Aguilar-Melchor, C., Gogniat, G.: Towards practical program execution over fully homomorphic encryption schemes. In: 2013 Eighth International Conference on P2P, Parallel, Grid, Cloud and Internet Computing (3PGCIC), pp. 284–290. IEEE (2013)
4. Fontaine, C., Galand, F.: A survey of homomorphic encryption for nonspecialists. EURASIP J. Inf. Secur. **2007**(1), 1–10 (2007)
5. Gentry, C.: A fully homomorphic encryption scheme. Ph.D. thesis, Stanford University (2009)
6. Rivest, R., Shamir, A., Adleman, L.: A method for obtaining digital signatures and public-key cryptosystems. Commun. ACM **21**(2), 120–126 (1978)
7. Nassar, M., Erradi, A., Malluhi, Q.M.: Paillier's encryption: implementation and cloud applications. In: 2015 International Conference on Applied Research in Computer Science and Engineering (ICAR), Beirut, pp. 1–5 (2015)
8. van Dijk, M., Gentry, C., Halevi, S., Vaikuntanathan, V.: Fully homomorphic encryption over the integers. In: Gilbert, H. (ed.) EUROCRYPT 2010. LNCS, vol. 6110, pp. 24–43. Springer, Heidelberg (2010). https://doi.org/10.1007/978-3-642-13190-5_2
9. Xiao, L., et al.: An Efficient Homomorphic Encryption Protocol for Multi-User Systems. IACR Cryptology ePrint Archive, Report 2012/193
10. Kipnis, A., Hibshoosh, E.: Efficient methods for practical fully-homomorphic symmetric-key encryption, randomization, and verification. IACR Cryptology ePrint Archive, Report 2012/637
11. Ferrer, J.D.: A new privacy homomorphism and applications. Inf. Process. Lett. **60**(5), 277–282 (1996)
12. Ferrer, J.D.: A provably secure additive and multiplicative privacy homomorphism. In: Chan, A.H., Gligor, V. (eds.) ISC 2002. LNCS, vol. 2433, pp. 471–483. Springer, Heidelberg (2002). https://doi.org/10.1007/3-540-45811-5_37
13. Noura, H., Courroucé, D.: HLDCA-WSN:homomorphic lightweight data confidentiality algorithm for wireless sensor network. Int. Assoc. Cryptogr. Res. IACR **2015**, 928 (2015)
14. Zhang, P., Jiang, Y., Lin, C., Fan, Y., Shen, X.: P-coding: secure network coding against eavesdropping attacks. In: 2010 Proceedings IEEE INFOCOM, pp. 1–9. IEEE (2010)
15. Noura, H., Samhat, A.E., Harkous, Y., Yahiya, T.A.: Design and realization of a neural block cipher. In: 2015 International conference on Applied Research in Computer Science and Engineering (IACR), Beirut, pp. 1–6 (2015). https://doi.org/10.1109/ARCSE 2015.7338131
16. Vizer, D., Vaudenay, S.: Cryptanalysis of chosen symmetric homomorphic scheme. Stud. Sci. Math. Hung. **52**(2), 288–306 (2015)

A Study of Threat Detection Systems and Techniques in the Cloud

Pamela Carvallo[1,2]([⊠]), Ana R. Cavalli[1,2], and Natalia Kushik[1]

[1] SAMOVAR, Télécom SudParis, CNRS, Université Paris-Saclay, Évry, France
{pamela.carvallo,ana.cavalli,natalia.kushik}@telecom-sudparis.eu
[2] Montimage, Paris, France

Abstract. This paper presents a study of existing threat detection techniques in cloud computing, together with an experimental evaluation of a subset of them. We consider the threats defined in the Cloud Security Alliance (CSA) report as well as the techniques for their detection, starting from classical signature-based approaches and finishing with recent machine learning based techniques. This paper also contains an analysis of original results presented in international conferences, published as journal papers, Internet resources, and standards. The main contributions of the study include: 1. providing a closer relationship between top threats in cloud computing and known detection techniques; 2. evaluating existing detection techniques concerning cloud computing principles and security challenges nowadays; and 3. reviewing commonly utilized datasets and their association with threats in the last five years. As existing detection techniques tend to target specific threats (or their groups), we also present the experimental evaluation of the applicability of known detection approaches against non-targeted threat groups.

Keywords: Cloud computing · Security · Cloud-related threats
Detection systems

1 Introduction

Cloud computing opens new possibilities for more flexible and efficient services. However, one of the issues of migrating to the cloud is that it involves a third-party implementation and enforcement of security policies [38]. In such environments, many security aspects must be faced, including risk management, data privacy and isolation, security-by-design applications, vulnerability scans, among others. Besides preventive solutions (e.g., encryption, firewalls), it also becomes necessary to have a system that interrelates all monitored security mechanisms from different points of observation. On the other hand, new attacks emerge every day and thus, threat detection systems start playing a key role in security schemes, identifying possible attacks.

Cloud-based threat detection techniques are commonly divided into three groups, namely pattern-based, behavior-based and hybrid (first two combined).

© Springer International Publishing AG, part of Springer Nature 2018
N. Cuppens et al. (Eds.): CRiSIS 2017, LNCS 10694, pp. 140–155, 2018.
https://doi.org/10.1007/978-3-319-76687-4_10

In the first case, attacks are described as rules or expressions in related grammar (signatures) and the new collected data of the system under test are verified with respect to the set of such signatures. For behavior-based techniques, "normal" system actions are somehow defined, and the monitoring system can later serve for concluding if the monitored environment is differing from the defined behavior. In this case, different statistical models, as well as self-learning techniques, can be effectively utilized. Nevertheless, some proposed algorithms commonly suffer from high false-positive detection rates, encouraging the use of hybrid approaches by companies and academic institutions.

In this paper, we provide a review of existing techniques and tools for effective threat detection in cloud environments. In our study, we have analyzed 47 publications consisting of well-ranked scientific journals and conferences from 2012 up to this year, as well as industry standards and security working groups' guidelines. These scientific publications are indexed by digital scientific databases such as the ACM Digital Library, Elsevier, IEEE Xplore, DBLP and Springer. We assessed the following methodology: We covered the topics of *detection systems* and *detection techniques* in the *cloud*. Also, we specifically searched the mentioned keywords together with each of the threats studied. The selection of works derived in both a systematic review of the detection architectures and the second in a detailed examination of the detection techniques. We note that despite the indirect impact non cloud-specific studies may have, we excluded these works as they do not directly examine any cloud property.

As the topic of providing security in the cloud remains essential, it is worth mentioning that the survey presented in this work is not the first covering this subject. However, existing works (e.g., [22, 24, 26, 34, 35, 37]) mostly focus on either analyzing system requirements and cloud security gaps, or describing detection techniques along with some attacks. It is required then to combine both approaches to provide a broad view of the state of the art of the problem. Below, we briefly sketch some existing works summarizing security issues in the cloud and discuss the motivation for expanding the research on this field.

A systematic review of detection system issues is presented by the authors of [37], comparing advantages and disadvantages of Intrusion Detection System (IDS) components, e.g., type of time detection —*real or non-real time*, data collection types —*distributed or centralized*, node positioning —*network or host based*, response type —*active or passive*, and structural implementation —*individual or collaborative*. Derfouf et al. [9] provided a comparison between the major architectures and proposed a *smart* intrusion detection model, based on the principle of collaboration between many IDSs. Khorshed et al. [26] addressed implementation challenges for threat remediations and applied Naive Bayes, Multilayer Perceptron (MLP), Support Vector Machines (SVMs) and Decision Trees. They used the WEKA data-mining tool for testing against attacks targeting shared memory, Denial of Service (DoS), malicious insiders, phishing and virtual machine side-channels. Additionally, the authors of [35] extensively revised the Distributed DoS (DDoS) and DoS methods following the same detection taxonomy broadly categorized in signature, anomaly and hybrid-based.

Detection techniques have their particular challenges. Therefore different researchers such as Modi et al. [34] and Jouad et al. [22] have studied and compared their advantages and limitations. Modi et al. followed a classification based on signature, anomaly, Artificial Neural Networks (ANN), fuzzy logic, association rule, SVM and hybrid-based approaches. The same classification was also considered in [24] where several detection techniques were described.

Nevertheless, we note the following aspects are missing in the cloud-related surveys listed above, therefore constituting the motivation of this paper: 1. Deeper analysis of the relation between detection techniques and different types of threats; and 2. Experimental evaluation of techniques used for threats of one category, comparing their detection performance against other threat categories.

The structure of the paper is as follows. Section 2 contains preliminaries. Section 3 summarizes existing detection techniques and its discussion (Sect. 3.4). Section 4 shows experimental results on suitable techniques presented in the paper against different types of threats. Finally, Sect. 5 concludes the paper.

2   Preliminaries

2.1   Security Issues in the Cloud

According to the National Institute of Standards and Technology [32], cloud computing is a model for enabling ubiquitous, elastic, on-demand network access to a shared pool of configurable computing resources (e.g., networks, servers, storage, applications, and services). Its service models, known as Software as a Service (SaaS), Platform as a Service (PaaS) and Infrastructure as a Service (IaaS) have specific and shared security challenges. The first provides a Cloud Service Client (CSC) the capability to use applications running on a cloud infrastructure by a Cloud Service Provider (CSP). PaaS provides the CSC with tools to deploy their applications on top of the cloud infrastructure. The latter gives provision to the CSC in processing, storage, networks, and other fundamental computing resources where the consumer can deploy and run arbitrary software, which can include operating systems and applications. Security challenges reside in the coexistence since PaaS, as well as SaaS services, are hosted on top of IaaS.

We further enumerate critical cloud aspects trying to provide the explanations how these elements can influence the design of a cloud-based threat detection system. In particular, we consider:

- **Virtualized environment.** Brings elasticity by allowing multiple Virtual Machines (VMs) management and pooling in the same physical resources.
- **Multi-tenancy.** Enables the use of a single resource by multiple customers that may or may not belong to the same organization.
- **Data life cycle.** Defines no fixed infrastructure and security boundaries on applications and data on the cloud.
- **Network dynamics.** Concerns non-linear, non-stationary and complex dynamical characteristics of the network flows.

- **Access.** Takes into account the fact that data are transmitted using the Internet and may require credentials, authentication, identity management and anonymization.

2.2   Threat Overview

Following the European Network and Information Security Agency [10] we consider a *threat* as an event that can exploit a vulnerability, intentionally or accidentally, and obtain, damage, or destroy an asset. An *attack* is a sequence of components and interfaces that a threat actor or a condition can use to achieve a threat against an asset. The threat actor or actors gain access to the assets via attack vectors and vulnerabilities present in the technology components that host or provide direct access to the targeted assets. *Threat detection systems* are deployed in cloud environments with the intent to prevent, address and mitigate the attacks pursued by the threat actors, thereby protecting the assets.

Common threat guidelines have been proposed reflecting the current concerns among experts [8,10,12,17], resulting in data threats such as breaches or losses, account hijacking, insecure application programming interfaces, DoS, malicious insiders, abuse of cloud services and shared technology. These have been previously reviewed in [43], together with the relevant vulnerabilities and countermeasures analysis [17]. From the preceding sources, we list below the considered group of threats in this work, along with two threat groups gathered from the aforementioned studies: Other attacks (corresponding to known attack patterns from network datasets, such as port scan) and Malware (e.g., Kelihos and Zeus), illustrated in Fig. 1.

- **Data-related threats.** Treated as the top threats among industry experts [8]. A *data breach* is an incident in which protected or confidential information is released, viewed, stolen or processed by an entity not authorized to do so. It concerns IaaS, PaaS and SaaS as they all keep sensitive data.
- **Account Hijacking.** Specified as a process in which an individual or organizations cloud account is stolen or hijacked by an attacker. This threat is relevant to cloud architectures since attackers can often access critical areas of deployed cloud computing services, allowing them to compromise the confidentiality, integrity and availability of IaaS, PaaS and SaaS services.
- **Malicious Insider.** Defined as a threat to an organization occasioned by a current or former employee, contractor, or another business partner who has or had authorized access to an organization network, system, or data. This action intentionally exceeded or misused the access in a manner that negatively affected the confidentiality, integrity, or availability of the organization information or information systems.
- **Denial of Service.** Meant to prevent components from being available in a cloud environment; that concerns, for example addressing to APIs for SaaS outage or specific DDoS at the infrastructural layer [1].
- **Shared Technology threats.** Existent in all delivery models, including multi-tenant architectures (IaaS), re-deployable platforms (PaaS), or multi-customer applications (SaaS) [8].

3   Cloud Threat Detection Systems

Threat detection systems usually correspond to a hardware device or software application that monitors an activity (e.g., from network, VM host, user) for malicious policy violations. Previous works (e.g., [37,44]) have stated several features of detection systems; among those, fault-tolerance, real-time execution, self-monitoring, minimum operational, interoperability, self-adaptiveness, scalability. A multi-criteria analysis of IDSs was presented in [50], following these and other cloud computing requirements such as performance and availability along with CSA-inspired criteria, such as service level expectations, secured and encrypted communication channels, detection methods used and their accuracy.

System architectures may vary if they are distributed, centralized, agent-based [20] or collaborative; the positioning of various observation points also defines different types of architectures. The monitoring layers can be classified as follows: 1. network-based monitor activity of network traffic —mostly IP and transport layer; 2. host-based monitor application or service activities operating on top of VM's operative systems; 3. hypervisor-based monitor virtual machine introspection to gather system-specific features (e.g., process list, threats count, number of open ports); 4. cross layer-based monitor in the form of any combination of the previously mentioned. In general, *data collection and preparation* are performed through a sensor or existing dataset. This information works as an input for the *data analysis and detection*, which corresponds to the module of the algorithms implemented to detect suspicious activities, detailed in the following sections.

3.1   Pattern-Based Approach and Related Techniques

Also known as "signature-based", "knowledge-based" or "misuse-based", this approach operates over a set of rules that define a threat pattern or a known authorized pattern. They are known to have a high level of accuracy [42], but are limited to only known rules and attacks. Therefore, pattern-based techniques cannot detect variants of known or unknown attacks. Moreover, keeping signature or knowledge databases updated may be a hard task.

Latest research focuses on facilitating to cloud administrators the determination of new attack patterns by updating signature databases more efficiently. To assess this automatic and offline analysis, Hamdi et al. [16] proposed Inductive Logic Programming, while Huang et al. [18] used Growing Hierarchical Self Organizing Maps (GHSOM) for the characterization of attack signatures. Other techniques that we further discuss are grouped as so-called *rule-based*.

Rule-based. For known or variants of known attacks, rule-based context methods have been considered in a number of works.

Watermarking was studied for *data breaches* detection by Garkoti et al. [14]. Threats may occur in any stage of the data cycle (Sect. 2.1) and digital watermarking is a reviewed technique for detecting data tampering. Specifically, the authors introduced spatial domain watermarking, encryption and logging modules for clinical data. Concerning insider threats and further potential data-related threats, Kumar et al. [28] considered a method related to the well-known *Bell-LaPadula* model, which aims to determine the organization employee who leaked the data. This model is built on the concept of subjects and objects (i.e., a file). They define levels where subjects have access to objects following security policies. Various cryptographic and watermarking techniques are later applied to identify the internal user involved in the leakage.

Fingerprinting was considered for *malicious insider* threat detection by Gupta et al. [15] through the analysis of commonly used programs by a VM. They assumed that the signature of frequent executions remains reasonably constant and detects malicious modifications of the system call sequences executed from the VM to the hypervisor.

Provable Data Possession (PDP), formalized in [2], is related to *data losses* and preserving data integrity. Basically, a CSC uploads data for storage and keeps meta-data for later verification. The classical idea behind this technique can only be applied to static (or append-only) files. Hence, Erway et al. [11] presented a framework based on Dynamic Provable Data Possession, which extends the PDP traditional approach. It supports provable updates to the stored data, using a new version of authenticated dictionaries based on rank information.

Sequence alignment, commonly used in bioinformatics, was proposed by Kholidy and Baiardi [25] to detect *account or service hijacking* threats, specifically for masquerade attacks. They introduced Heuristic Semi-Global Alignment algorithm, which tests matching patterns of user's session sequences (e.g., mouse movements, system calls, opened windows titles, written commands, opened file names) with the previously stored arrays.

Dependency Graphs were proposed by Yaseen et al. [47]. Based on applying knowledge and dependency graphs one can detect and predict *malicious insiders* in relational databases. The authors considered the network overhead and system performance for variables, including the number of queries per insider, the number of insiders and percentage of accessibility for data items in relational databases.

3.2   Behavior-Based Approach and Related Techniques

Also known as anomaly-based detection, this approach involves the collection of data in order to construct a model of *normal* behavior and then to test newly observed behaviors against potential anomalies. As this is a sophisticated task, some works have proposed a mixed approach (e.g., [23, 36, 46]) where the following statistical and machine learning methods are combined. We have differentiated existing techniques in statistical, machine learning-based and clustering techniques. We hereafter assume that statistical methods mostly use specific formulas or functions to compute the corresponding characteristics of the data attributes; machine learning, on the other hand, "works" when such functions cannot be derived, and thus, it utilizes more complex relationships between the data for further threat prediction.

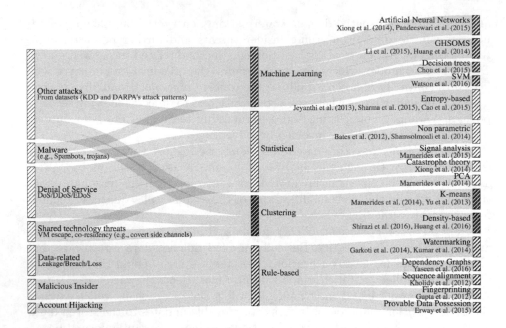

Fig. 1. Relationship between the threats and reviewed detection techniques

Statistical. These approaches are in general predefined by a threshold, first order statistics or probabilities, in order to identify anomalies. As an example one can consider a type of DoS — Economic Denial of Sustainability (EDoS) — issued by [3], where the authors compared user demands against thresholds of duration parameters as the maximum number of requests beyond when the auto-scaling feature is activated.

Non-parametric techniques take place when the system observes the activity of subjects in terms of statistical distribution and creates profiles which represent their behaviors for later similarity comparison. Bates et al. [4] addressed covert-side channel threats by detecting network flow's watermarking. In particular, they modeled packet arrivals by a Poisson distribution and applied the non-parametric Kolmogorov-Smirnov test. DoS was studied by Shamsolmoali et al. [40] in a two-stage detection: extracting the *Time-to-Live* values from incoming IP packets, computing the number of hops the packet had traveled and using Jense-Shannon divergence searching for anomaly in the *normal* trained database.

Entropy-based techniques focus on measuring the uncertainty or randomness associated with a variable. For network flows, comparing the rate of entropy of some packet header fields with other samples of the same nature provides a mechanism for detecting changes in the randomness. For DDoS attack detection, Jeyanthi et al. [21] proposed a cross-layer implementation where the first component analyzes incoming traffic rate and is handed to a Hellinger Distance-based entropy profiler in case it exceeded a threshold. Sharma et al. [41] utilized incoming network packets and studied the entropy of source MAC address also with a threshold-based analysis. Same threat concern and approach were followed in [5] where the authors investigated the VM CPU usage and network interfaces, arguing on the fact that malicious VMs share similar attack patterns.

Principal Component Analysis (PCA) was used by Marnerides et al. [31] for DoS and netscan detection, not only for reducing datasets dimensionality but also to separate the normal data from anomalous.

Signal analysis such as Ensemble Empirical Mode Decomposition was presented in [30]. The authors proposed a data-driven method for malware, motivated by the fact that the algorithm can decompose the data as signals and describe clouds' non-linear and non-stationary network traffic and hypervisor information.

Catastrophe theory studies the way systems respond to the continuous modifications from the variables that control them, producing sudden changes from one system state to another (e.g., from *normal* state to *anomalous*). Xiong et al. [46] introduced a catastrophe function to describe network traffic anomalies in cloud communications.

Machine learning-based. These methods allow improving the performance of their objective by learning from previous results. This subsection is illustrated in Fig. 1, where we group these techniques with their underlying models for detecting security threats in the cloud.

Decision trees are used in [7], where they preprocessed unlabeled data with an unsupervised clustering algorithm. After labeling, a model based in incremental tree inducer is trained, therefore updating itself.

SVM technique for could threat detection was proposed by Watson et al. [45]. The authors studied an online novelty implementation of a supervised one-class SVM algorithm, an extension of traditional two-class SVM which outputs either a known class (VM *normal* behavior) or unknown classes to the classifier, for each particular input vector.

Artificial Neural Networks expose their accuracy based on the configuration of their hidden layers and training phase. Pandeeswari and Kumar [36] preprocessed hypervisor attributes with Fuzzy C-Means clustering and utilized feed-forward neural networks with back-propagation algorithm for each of them. They later combined the results of the ANNs with a fuzzy aggregation module. A Synergetic Neural Network (SNN) was addressed by Xiong et al. [46], given the dynamics of the network's traffic. Their argument relied on the fact that under some situations, the changing trend of the cloud-based network traffic is only determined by a few primary factors and less contribution of others.

GHSOM techniques were also addressed by Li et al. [29], by proposing a cluster system that identified Nmap malicious behaviors in VMs through system call distributions in order to derive rules for SVM detection.

Clustering. These techniques are utilized under the assumption that *normal* data instances lie distance-wise closer to a given centroid of a cluster, whereas *anomalous* data points are recognized due to their much longer distance. Density-based approaches rely on the fact that *normal* data instances belong to large and dense clusters, while *anomalies* either belong to small or sparse clusters.

K-means technique was followed by Marnerides et al. [31], while showing the clustering method is directly affected by live-migrations. In this testbed, they detected DoS and netscan threats successfully when arose, but also achieved high scores when only migration and normal traffic occurred. Additionally, it was utilized for detecting *shared technologies threat*, as seen in Fig. 1. For example, in [48], the authors combined a two-stage detection mode based on statistical similarity tests from the *cache miss times* from hosts, CPU and memory utilization collected from VMs, for later clustering.

Density-based technique was proposed by Shirazi et al. [42] where they divided all measured variables into clusters and evaluated mean and standard deviation, based on the Euclidean distance threshold. The same clustering idea was used with the dimension reasoning technique (based on Local Outlier Factor) for memory leakage and malicious port scan, by Huang et al. [19].

3.3   Hybrid-Based Approach and Related Techniques

Depending on the architecture and a set of threats to be detected, the use of techniques in cloud architecture can require a hybrid approach.

While signature-based approach is more rigorous in its detection, behavior-based methodology is able to "learn" new threats. Therefore, the combination of previously mentioned approaches in Sects. 3.1 and 3.2 may reach a more extensive and accurate detection. As an example, Modi and Patel [33], used SNORT [6] for signature-based detection, whereas for anomaly-based detection they focused on Bayesian, associative and decision tree classifiers. Some of the studies addressing both approaches can be found in [25,33,40,49].

3.4   Discussion

The classification described in the previous sections shows that signature-based methods commonly relate to content-based detection techniques since they test known patterns or accepted actions. Data-related, malicious insider and account hijacking threats (e.g., confidential documents leakage, allowed user behaviors) are mostly studied in this category. For a visual representation of these dependencies, links are depicted in Fig. 1, where rule-based groups only share relations with the previously mentioned threats and are not associated with DoS, shared technology threats or malware.

As usual, detection techniques discussed above have their unique strengths and weaknesses. From the results of this study (Fig. 1 and Sect. 3.2), one can see that the most reviewed group of techniques are the statistical-based and machine learning, often utilized for network traffic and DoS detection. The first relies on the assumption that *normal* data instances fit a statistical model and *anomalies* are compared to this model through inference tests, which may be unhandy for diverse data. Entropy-based techniques offer a deeper examination as they consider the irregularities in the information content of the data being collected. Machine learning algorithms are also efficient due to their self-learning capability. Other approaches such as clustering, add an interesting enhancement since they automatically create and label clusters for future classification.

Also, evaluating the effectiveness of a given detection technique against a particular threat (or a group of them) is mainly performed through corresponding experimentation. For that reason, it is highly relevant building proper datasets that contain heterogeneous *normal* and *abnormal* realistic behaviors with a broad spectrum of threat patterns. Consequently, it may be intuitive to handle combined datasets, as mentioned in the previously cross layer-based system. This implies selecting relevant features, focusing on minimizing used bandwidth during monitoring, improving detection performance and removing redundant data, while keeping lower computational complexity (e.g., machine learning techniques, where the time taken to train the classifier is dataset size dependent).

Literature regarding this matter has used self-generated testbeds [19,21,31, 42,45] while others the well-known datasets: KDD [7,36,40] and DARPA [7,46]. These last two correspond to the group of threats with more references in Fig. 1. However, they suffer from several deficiencies for testing in cloud environments as they do not include behaviors such as stated in Sect. 2.1. Accordingly, a dataset with new malware patterns was used and is presented in the next section.

4   Experimental Evaluation

The aim of the experimental evaluation was to study the missing relation between some threats and a technique of each group. These connections were formerly determined by the reviewed publications where Fig. 1 graphically illustrates which set of techniques have been utilized for detecting different threat categories (from Sect. 2.2). We conducted experiments to estimate the effectiveness of these techniques against other threat types, therefore contributing by adding new links to our study. To the best of our knowledge, such experiments were not performed before for the following detection algorithms against the utilized dataset: SVM, MLP feed-forward Neural Network, and Long Short-Term Memory (LSTM) Recurrent Neural Network, K-means and entropy-based. We have selected one technique of each group to perform a more exhaustive analysis. The first is commonly used as benchmark experiments outperforming in most cases [26,37]; hence, it is of our interest to see how it performs for the chosen dataset's attacks. The second and third techniques enhance the dynamic classification requirement, presented in Sect. 3. Moreover, the study targeted the usage of techniques with self-learning capabilities (i.e., that handle new data after the training phase). Following this idea, MLP and LSTM present relevant characteristics. The last two techniques belong to the clustering and statistical categories, respectively. K-means is a learning algorithm that groups attribute vectors in clusters, based on the notion of similarity. We considered botnets as threats worth of studying since cloud virtualization and service models may allow an

Table 1. Average detection performance for SVM, MLP, LSTM, K-means and entropy-based techniques.

Metric (%)	SVM	MLP	LSTM	K-means	Entropy
Recall	88.255	80.956	81.168	83.431	99.202
Precision	98.506	99.367	79.431	94.071	97.105
FPR	3.773	2.170	4.131	1.547	1.576
Accuracy	89.077	83.530	69.515	65.370	96.407

easier path to their execution. Moreover, we aim to provide another experimental evaluation to the given found studies [31,45] regarding this threat. We utilized the CTU-13 Dataset [13], which comprehends real network traffic capture of more than 5000 hosts labeled in background, normal and botnet behaviors. In particular, this traffic concerns different types of DDoS, port scanning, C&C attacks, among others, there is no single threat vector, and our experimental schema relied on the trial of arbitrary techniques against this range of attack patterns. Training and testing distributions were respectively 83.39% (50.57% and 49.43% for normal and botnet traffic) and 16.61% (13.95% and 86.04% for normal and botnet traffic), accounting more than 90 million packets. Results were analyzed by widely used metrics Precision, Recall, Accuracy and False Positive Rate (FPR).

Data preparation consisted in reading NetFlows[1], selecting and normalizing their attributes in *header-based features* (e.g., source IP address, destination IP address and port, protocol), *content-based features* (e.g., source bytes) and *time-based features* (e.g., session duration). As we are trying to simulate the monitoring of continuous data streaming flows arriving from the cloud, all techniques were implemented using *online learning*, by feeding the algorithms with timely ordered dataset in batches.

In particular, SVM was used as a binary classifier. We applied it with linear kernel, taking into account good experimental results presented in [26]. For MLP, experiments consisted of finding hyper-parameters values and analyzing their impact against the detection metrics mentioned. Given the low standard deviation while changing the number of training iterations, we proceeded experiments with this parameter fixed at 50 epochs. Model setup was a two-layer hidden network, with 36 hidden neurons each. The variability of the latter consisted in increasing the number of neurons, obtaining higher recall and precision values, but also raising the FPR.

For LSTM, we also experimented with various training parameters and topologies. Hidden layer consisted of two LSTM memory blocks, with two cells each and peephole connections. Adam algorithm [27] was considered as the optimizer while MSE as a loss function. We applied an arbitrary exponential learning

---

[1] Network protocol developed by Cisco for the collection and monitoring of network traffic flow data generated by NetFlow-enabled routers and switches.

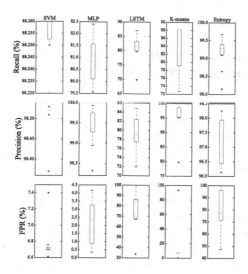

Fig. 2. Experimental results

decay of 0.97. Time step size, batch size and epoch in ranges from [10, 200], [50, 500], [50, 800] respectively, while modifying the learning rate from 0.0001 to 0.1.

For K-means technique we applied the Mini Batches function, a faster approximate version of the more "expensive" K-means clustering [39]. Configuration was set for the algorithm to create two clusters, normal and abnormal (botnet traffic). Given the assumption that normal connections are frequent whereas attacks are very rare, the clustering algorithm should create large clusters for normal connections and small isolated clusters for anomalies.

Lastly, we used an entropy-based detection following an information theoretic perspective. We calculated the entropy $H(i, k)$ for each streaming batch i of k traffic features. Every network flow was treated as a point in a 6-dimensional space with coordinates $\langle \overline{H_i} \rangle = \langle \overline{H}(srcip), \overline{H}(srcbytes), \overline{H}(dstip), \overline{H}(dstport), \overline{H}(proto), \overline{H}(dura) \rangle$. To analyze this multivariate vector in a simpler single-dimension representation, we re-scaled each sample $\langle \overline{H_i} \rangle$ to $\|\langle \overline{H_i} \rangle\|$ in ranges of [50, 2000] samples per batch. Consequently, *normal* behavior is defined as the projection of the data onto this subspace and *abnormal* behavior is defined as any significant deviation of the data from this subspace. The static threshold is defined as the norm of all the calculated $\langle \overline{H_i} \rangle$ training entropies and tried against the testing dataset.

We summarize our experimental results in Table 1 and in Fig. 2. The performance of SVM showed to be more stable than the others for all the metrics, while Artificial Neural Network-based techniques depended on the topology and training parameters. One can see from Table 1 that overall the techniques perform above 79% for Recall and Precision indicators. Nevertheless, LSTM and Entropy techniques do it also by increasing the FPR. The latter is probably due to our static threshold configuration and that chosen features may have dismissed or not fully exploited the dataset threat behavior.

5 Conclusion

In this paper, we studied the relation between security threats and detection techniques in cloud environments. As a result, we conclude that data-related threats and malicious insider activities are mostly pursued by rule-based detection techniques. On the other hand, network-based threats such as DoS and botnet attacks can be effectively tackled with statistical and machine learning techniques. Likewise, whenever behavior-based or hybrid approaches are used, training data phase remains crucial to establish a wide spectrum of *normal* behaviors in cloud architectures. In this sense, more research needs to be performed to correctly discriminate them from real threats.

Through Fig. 1 we have granted a visually synthesized comprehension of which algorithms have been studied for specific threats. However, we noted the absence of some links between them, raising questions regarding the use of certain techniques for threat detection. We think this may be because "well-accepted" methods have proven to be effective to known attack patterns in the past (e.g., SVM and DoS). On the other hand, the existent links are due to the tryout of novel techniques against classic threat patterns or the use of traditional techniques on top of cloud-environment settings.

The latter motivated to study the applicability of existing detection approaches against new threats. Consequently, we attempted at experimenting with an SVM, two ANNs, a statistical and a clustering method; performed an online detection and obtained results to counteract these unseen techniques with a dataset of recent malware vectors. In particular, it was proven that SVM behaves well as an "all-around" classifier, keeping good accuracy while low false alarm rates. In contrast, we observe additional studies should be pursued for neural network detectors as they rely on more parameters. This characteristic adds more complexity at the moment of detecting different types of threats, as they are commonly tuned for a particular testbed.

Also, we note that although many of detection techniques have evaluated their accuracy given FPR, Precision; only a few studies are testing their performance in a holistic approach that contemplates specific cloud computing characteristics (named in Sect. 3), such as scalability or fault-tolerance.

Furthermore, high throughput interfaces and maintainable knowledge database repositories demand a scalable solution. At the same time, cloud-dynamic behavior varies regarding CSC needs, and it can imply the discovery functionality for modified IaaS, PaaS or SaaS configurations. Therefore, it is important to keep in mind a flexible implementation approach that can detect anomalies adapted to each new requirement.

Finally, this survey also proves the absence of a universal approach for identifying various threats of different nature. Additionally, focusing on multiple cloud service features will provide an integral perspective of different behaviors working together. Developing such approach or at least making steps towards deriving a broader yet effective cloud threat detection system, without a doubt, form a group of hot topics for future research work.

Acknowledgment. The project leading to this paper has received funding from the European Union Horizon 2020 research and innovation program under grant agreement No. 644429 - MUSA project.

References

1. Akamai: Akamai's state of the internet/Security Q3 2015 report. Technical report (2015)
2. Ateniese, G., Burns, R., Curtmola, R., Herring, J., Kissner, L., Peterson, Z., Song, D.: Provable data possession at untrusted stores. In: Proceedings of the 14th ACM Conference on Computer and Communications Security, CCS 2007 (2007)
3. Baig, Z.A., Binbeshr, F.: Controlled virtual resource access to mitigate economic denial of sustainability (EDoS) attacks against cloud infrastructures. In: 2013 International Conference on Cloud Computing and Big Data (CloudCom-Asia), pp. 346–353 (2013)
4. Bates, A., Mood, B., Pletcher, J., Pruse, H., Valafar, M., Butler, K.: Detecting co-residency with active traffic analysis techniques. In: CCSW 2012, pp. 1–12. ACM Press, New York (2012)
5. Cao, J., Yu, B., Dong, F., Zhu, X., Xu, S.: Entropy-based denial of service attack detection in cloud data center. In: 2014 Second International Conference on Advanced Cloud and Big Data, pp. 201–207, November 2014
6. Caswell, B., Foster, J.C., Russell, R., Beale, J., Posluns, J.: Snort 2.0 Intrusion Detection. Syngress Publishing, Rockland (2003)
7. Chou, H.H., Wang, S.D.: An adaptive network intrusion detection approach for the cloud environment. In: 2015 International Carnahan Conference on Security Technology (ICCST), pp. 1–6. IEEE (2015)
8. Cloud Security Alliance (CSA): The Notorious Nine: Cloud Computing Top Threats in 2013 (2013)
9. Derfouf, M., Eleuldj, M., Enniari, S., Diouri, O.: Smart intrusion detection model for the cloud computing. In: Rocha, Á., Serrhini, M., Felgueiras, C. (eds.) Europe and MENA Cooperation Advances in Information and Communication Technologies. AISC, vol. 520, pp. 411–421. Springer, Cham (2017). https://doi.org/10.1007/978-3-319-46568-5_42
10. ENISA: ENISA Threat Landscape 2015. Technical report, January 2016
11. Erway, C.C., Küpçü, A., Papamanthou, C., Tamassia, R.: Dynamic provable data possession. ACM Trans. Inf. Syst. Secur. (TISSEC) **17**(4), 15 (2015)
12. Fernandes, D.A.B., Soares, L.F.B., Gomes, J.V., Freire, M.M., Inácio, P.R.M.: Security issues in cloud environments: a survey. Int. J. Inf. Secur. **13**, 113–170 (2014)
13. García, S., Grill, M., Stiborek, J., Zunino, A.: An empirical comparison of botnet detection methods. Comput. Secur. **45**, 100–123 (2014)
14. Garkoti, G., Peddoju, S.K., Balasubramanian, R.: Detection of insider attacks in cloud based e-healthcare environment. In: 2014 International Conference on Information Technology (ICIT), pp. 195–200. IEEE (2014)
15. Gupta, S., Kumar, P., Sardana, A., Abraham, A.: A fingerprinting system calls approach for intrusion detection in a cloud environment. In: 2012 Fourth International Conference on Computational Aspects of Social Networks (CASoN), pp. 309–314. IEEE (2012)

16. Hamdi, O., Mbaye, M., Krief, F.: A cloud-based architecture for network attack signature learning. In: 2015 7th International Conference on New Technologies, Mobility and Security (NTMS). IEEE (2015)

17. Hashizume, K., Rosado, D.G., Fernández-Medina, E., Fernandez, E.B.: An analysis of security issues for cloud computing. J. Internet Serv. Appl. **4**(1), 5 (2013)

18. Huang, S.Y., Suri, N., Huang, Y.: Event pattern discovery on IDS traces of cloud services. In: 2014 IEEE International Conference on Big Data and Cloud Computing (BdCloud), pp. 25–32. IEEE (2014)

19. Huang, T., Zhu, Y., Wu, Y., Bressan, S., Dobbie, G.: Anomaly detection and identification scheme for VM live migration in cloud infrastructure. Future Gener. Comput. Syst. **56**, 736–745 (2016)

20. Idrissi, H., Hajji, S.E., Ennahbaoui, M., Souidi, E.M., Souidi, E.M.: Mobile agents with cryptographic traces for intrusion detection in the cloud computing. Procedia Comput. Sci. **73**, 179–186 (2015)

21. Jeyanthi, N., Iyengar, N.C.S.N., Kumar, P.C.M., Kannammal, A.: An enhanced entropy approach to detect and prevent DDoS in cloud environment. IJCNIS **5**(2), 110 (2013)

22. Jouad, M., Diouani, S., Houmani, H., Zaki, A.: Security challenges in intrusion detection. In: 2015 International Conference on Cloud Technologies and Applications (CloudTech), pp. 1–11. IEEE (2015)

23. Katz, G., Elovici, Y., Shapira, B.: CoBAn: a context based model for data leakage prevention. Inf. Sci.: Int. J. **262**, 137–158 (2014)

24. Kene, S.G., Theng, D.P.: A review on intrusion detection techniques for cloud computing and security challenges. In: 2015 2nd International Conference on Electronics and Communication Systems (ICECS), pp. 227–232. IEEE (2015)

25. Kholidy, H.A., Baiardi, F.: CIDS: a framework for intrusion detection in cloud systems. In: 2012 Ninth International Conference on Information Technology: New Generations (ITNG). IEEE (2012)

26. Khorshed, M.T., Ali, A.B.M.S., Wasimi, S.A.: A survey on gaps, threat remediation challenges and some thoughts for proactive attack detection in cloud computing. Future Gener. Comput. Syst. **28**(6), 833–851 (2012)

27. Kingma, D.P., Ba, J.: Adam: a method for stochastic optimization. CoRR (2014)

28. Kumar, N., Katta, V., Mishra, H., Garg, H.: Detection of data leakage in cloud computing environment. In: 2014 International Conference on Computational Intelligence and Communication Networks (CICN), pp. 803–807. IEEE (2014)

29. Li, Y.H., Tzeng, Y.R., Yu, F.: VISO: characterizing malicious behaviors of virtual machines with unsupervised clustering. In: 2015 IEEE 7th International Conference on Cloud Computing Technology and Science (CloudCom). IEEE (2015)

30. Marnerides, A.K., Spachos, P., Chatzimisios, P., Mauthe, A.U.: Malware detection in the cloud under ensemble empirical mode decomposition. In: 2015 International Conference on Computing, Networking and Communications (ICNC), pp. 82–88. IEEE (2015)

31. Marnerides, A.K., Shirazi, N., Hutchison, D., Simpson, S., Watson, M., Mauthe, A.: Assessing the impact of intra-cloud live migration on anomaly detection. In: 2014 IEEE 3rd International Conference on Cloud Networking (CloudNet) (2014)

32. Mell, P.M., Grance, T.: SP 800-145. The NIST Definition of Cloud Computing. Technical report, Gaithersburg, MD, USA (2011)

33. Modi, C.N., Patel, D.: A novel hybrid-network intrusion detection system (H-NIDS) in cloud computing. In: 2013 IEEE Symposium on Computational Intelligence in Cyber Security (CICS), pp. 23–30 (2013)

34. Modi, C., Patel, D.R., Borisaniya, B., Patel, H., Patel, A., Rajarajan, M.: A survey of intrusion detection techniques in cloud. JNCA **36**(1), 42–57 (2013)
35. Osanaiye, O., Choo, K.K.R., Dlodlo, M.: Distributed denial of service (DDoS) resilience in cloud: review and conceptual cloud DDoS mitigation framework. J. Netw. Comput. Appl. **67**, 147–165 (2016)
36. Pandeeswari, N., Kumar, G.: Anomaly detection system in cloud environment using fuzzy clustering based ANN. Mob. Netw. Appl. **21**, 1–12 (2015)
37. Patel, A., Taghavi, M., Bakhtiyari, K., Celestino Júnior, J.: An intrusion detection and prevention system in cloud computing: a systematic review. J. Netw. Comput. Appl. **36**(1), 25–41 (2013)
38. Rosado, D.G., Gómez, R., Mellado, D., Fernández-Medina, E.: Security analysis in the migration to cloud environments. Future Internet **4**(4), 469–487 (2012)
39. Sculley, D.: Web-scale k-means clustering. In: Proceedings of the 19th International Conference on World Wide Web. In: WWW 2010, pp. 1177–1178. ACM (2010)
40. Shamsolmoali, P., Alam, M.A., Biswas, R.: C2DF: high Rate DDOS filtering method in cloud computing. Int. J. Comput. Netw. Inf. Secur. **6**(9), 43–50 (2014)
41. Sharma, P., Sharma, R., Pilli, E.S., Mishra, A.K.: A detection algorithm for DoS attack in the cloud environment. In: Compute 2015, pp. 107–110 (2015)
42. Shirazi, S.N., Simpson, S., Gouglidis, A., Mauthe, A., Hutchison, D.: Anomaly detection in the cloud using data density. In: 2016 IEEE 9th International Conference on Cloud Computing (CLOUD), pp. 616–623, June 2016
43. Vaquero, L.M., Rodero-Merino, L., Morán, D.: Locking the sky: a survey on IaaS cloud security. Computing **91**(1), 93–118 (2011)
44. Vasilomanolakis, E., Karuppayah, S., Mühlhäuser, M., Fischer, M.: Taxonomy and survey of collaborative intrusion detection. CSUR **47**(4), 33 (2015). Article no. 55
45. Watson, M.R., Shirazi, N., Marnerides, A.K., Mauthe, A., Hutchison, D.: Malware detection in cloud computing infrastructures. TDSC **13**(2), 192–205 (2016)
46. Xiong, W., Hu, H., Xiong, N., Yang, L.T., Peng, W.C., Wang, X., Qu, Y.: Anomaly secure detection methods by analyzing dynamic characteristics of the network traffic in cloud communications. Inf. Sci. **258**, 403–415 (2014)
47. Yaseen, Q., Althebyan, Q., Panda, B., Jararweh, Y.: Mitigating insider threat in cloud relational databases. Secur. Commun. Netw. **9**, 1132–1145 (2016)
48. Yu, S., Gui, X., Lin, J.: An approach with two-stage mode to detect cache-based side channel attacks. In: 2013 International Conference on Information Networking (ICOIN), pp. 186–191. IEEE (2013)
49. Yu, W., Moulema, P., Xu, G., Chen, Z.: A cloud computing based architecture for cyber security situation awareness. In: 2013 IEEE Conference on Communications and Network Security (CNS), pp. 488–492. IEEE (2013)
50. Zbakh, M., Elmahdi, K., Cherkaoui, R., Enniari, S.: A multi-criteria analysis of intrusion detection architectures in cloud environments. In: 2015 International Conference on Cloud Technologies and Applications (CloudTech), pp. 1–9. IEEE (2015)

Cyber-Insurance and Cyber Threat Intelligence

Preventing the Drop in Security Investments for Non-competitive Cyber-Insurance Market

Fabio Martinelli[1], Albina Orlando[2], Ganbayar Uuganbayar[1],
and Artsiom Yautsiukhin[1(✉)]

[1] Istituto di Informatica e Telematica, Consiglio Nazionale delle Ricerche, Pisa, Italy
artsiom.yautsiukhin@iit.cnr.it
[2] Istituto per le Applicazioni del Calcolo "Mauro Picone",
Consiglio Nazionale delle Ricerche, Naples, Italy

Abstract. The rapid development of cyber insurance market brings forward the question about the effect of cyber insurance on cyber security. Some researchers believe that the effect should be positive as organisations will be forced to maintain a high level of security in order to pay lower premiums. On the other hand, other researchers conduct a theoretical analysis and demonstrate that availability of cyber insurance may result in lower investments in security.

In this paper we propose a mathematical analysis of a cyber-insurance model in a non-competitive market. We prove that with a right pricing strategy it is always possible to ensure that security investments are at least as high as without insurance. Our general theoretical analysis is confirmed by specific cases using CARA and CRRA utility functions.

1 Introduction

It is widely recognised that cyber security incidents are much more than just unpleasant events. Such incidents may cause huge losses (e.g., see effect of the latest two data breaches discoveries by Yahoo on its deal with Verizon[1]) and put in danger lives of people (e.g., cyber attacks on critical infrastructures). Therefore, the best risk management practices point out the need of considering cyber risk as a component of the overall risk management routine [6,21,23].

Unfortunately, installation of various countermeasures and adopting best cyber security practices do not guarantee freedom from cyber incidents, regardless their significant cost. In other words, organisations always face some residual cyber risks. The only option which was left for organisations so far was simply to accept this risk, i.e., acknowledge that such a problem may happen and,

---

This work was partially supported by projects H2020 MSCA NeCS 675320 and H2020 MSCA CyberSure 734815.

[1] http://www.euronews.com/2017/02/21/yahoo-pays-the-price-for-massive-data-breaches-in-verizon-deal.

N. Cuppens et al. (Eds.): CRiSIS 2017, LNCS 10694, pp. 159–174, 2018.
https://doi.org/10.1007/978-3-319-76687-4_11

maybe, put some money aside to compensate the losses if the threat occurs (self-insurance). An alternative to these risk treatment options was introduced 20 years ago [12,13]. This alternative is cyber insurance, a risk transfer option which allows insureds to shift their residual cyber risks to insurers.

Cyber insurance is believed to have a number of advantages, next to the obvious one, i.e., covering residual risks and smoothing possible losses. Cyber insurance is a means to collect statistics on cyber events and use it to evaluate security strength of various systems. The assigned premiums may serve as indicators of security strength [1]. Cyber insurance should increase the demand for cyber security standards [5]. Last but not least, cyber insurance is believed to be an intensive for organisations to invest in security in order to get lower premiums [1,12,17]. Unfortunately, some papers [15,16,20] show that without regulatory constraints competitive insurance is not an incentive for self-protection. In fact, the insureds prefer to insure their risks instead of mitigating them with investments. This puts other members of digital society under higher risks [8].

Several proposals were considered to find a solution for the problem and the best option found was "fine and rebate" regulation mechanism, which additionally fines insurers with low security and rebates the ones with high security, next to security discriminating strategy for assigning the premiums [11,16]. These works consider an oversimplified model of security investment: an agent may invest in security a certain amount to get 100% protection of direct attack (but it still can be attacked indirectly, though contagion).

In this work, we propose another way of regulating cyber insurance market looking at the problem from the insured's point of view. We determine the minimal level of insurer's interests (loading factor) which guarantees that investments in insured's protection are as high as in case of no insurance available and insureds are still interested in transferring some (non-zero) part of their risks. Such enforcement may be introduced by the government as a tax for insurer, or by enforcing a law requiring the smallest insurer interest. We use a continuous model of security investments (similar to the one of Ogut et al. [15]) and consider a very generic class of utility functions for modelling insureds' satisfaction.

The result of our theoretical study is a system of two equations with two variables, i.e., it is solvable. On the other hand, because of generality of our approach the unique final formula is very hard to find (if possible at all). Nevertheless, if the utility function is known, it is possible to find the solution. We demonstrate this with our case studies using classical CARA and CRRA functions. In addition, we conduct several experiments to investigate the effect of security interdependence on insurance parameters.

The paper is structured as follows. Section 2 discusses the current achievements in the area and underlines the advantages of our approach. Section 3 introduces the basic insurance model, considering two cases: with cyber insurance available and without it. Section 4 contains our core contribution and describes how security investments can be raised with raise of premium. Section 5 shows two specific examples to confirm the theory. Section 6 outlines conclusions.

2 Related Work

Recently, cyber insurance has gained much attention in the scientific literature [2,13]. Specific attention is devoted to the analysis of the effect of interdependent security on cyber insurance [9,10,15,16,19]. In fact, strong influence of security interdependency is one of the main features that make cyber insurance a specific insurance case.

Ogut et al. [15] provided an analysis in depth of the interdependent security and immaturity of the market on cyber insurance. In particular, the authors investigated how investments in self-protection change. They have found that these investments in self protection reduce with growth of the interdependence and these investments rise with growth of immaturity of insurance market. More-over, the authors considered the effect of enforcement of liability for contagion. They have found, that investments in self-protection in this case rise even higher than the optimal level. The results of the study are limited because of the following assumptions: (1) the authors use only CARA as a utility function; (2) the losses are considered to be too small with respect to the wealth of insureds. The last assumption is particularly dangerous for insurance, since it significantly reduces the effect of risk averseness of insureds. In contrast, we provide a generic approach without the outlined assumptions (we use CARA as the utility function only as an example). Moreover, we show how it is possible to compute the loading factor value to achieve the desired level of self-investment.

A number of authors considered the problem of reducing self-protection level if cyber insurance is available [10,16,19] and whether the optimum level of investments can be reached [18,20]. The solution for the problem found by several authors is additional fines/rebates for the users with low/high security [3,10,11,16]. Naturally, in this case the insurer has to know exactly the level of investments by insureds, i.e., no information asymmetry is allowed (similar to our assumption). Here we should point out that in these cases the authors consider a discrete model of investments, which has two levels (with low protection and fully protected against direct attacks) and specific level of investments required to jump from one level to another one. In reality investments in cyber security have more levels or have continuous impact on probability of an incident.

An interesting method was proposed by Naghizadeh and Liu [14] for specifying the optimal level of investments. In the proposed model the insurer collects the proposals of all its insureds (the whole society) about the desired level of investments and adjusts the policies (i.e., premiums) correspondingly. The authors show that they are able to reach the optimal level with this approach, if participation of all agents in such schema is mandatory. In contrast, we consider voluntary participation and ensure that with specified price of insurance the agents are still interested in buying the policy ($I \geq 0$).

3 Basic Formalisation

Before we go into the discussion of our basic problem, we specify the basic formalisation. We define only the concepts required for our paper and refer the reader interested in the comprehensive definition of basic terms to [13].

Let W^0 be the amount of wealth an agent possesses now. The agent tries to predict its wealth after some period of time (typically, in a year). Naturally, the agent does not know if a threat causing losses to him/her will occur during the considered period, but it may invest some amount of money x to decrease the probability of the incident. Because of the uncertainty about the final outcome, the value is random (and is denoted as $\boldsymbol{W}$), but it is possible to make some predictions about it if the probability of $pr(x)$ and the loss L caused by the incident are known. We see that $pr(x)$ depends on x, i.e., the probability of the incident depends on the amount of investments[2]. It is natural to assume that higher investments lead to lower probability of occurrence: $pr'(x) < 0$; but lower initial investment level requires less additional investments to decrease the probability of occurrence by the same value: $pr''(x) < 0$. The final loss in this case is also a random variable $\boldsymbol{L}$ and is equal either to L, if the threat occurs, or to 0, otherwise.

The expected wealth $E[\boldsymbol{W}]$ after the considered period could be computed as[3]:

$$E[\boldsymbol{W}] = W^0 - E[\boldsymbol{L}] - x = W^0 - pr'(x)(L) + (1 - pr'(x))(0) - x. \quad (1)$$

Let $U(W)$ be a function of wealth, and can be seen as the satisfaction of agents to posses a certain amount of money. The utility function is not linear, and in many situations, increase in satisfaction is lower for higher amount of wealth possessed [22]. Such behaviour of an agent is called risk averseness and can be modelled with a utility function satisfying the following conditions: $U'(W) > 0$ and $U''(W) < 0$. Instead of expected wealth (Eq. 1), we should look now for the expected utility of wealth:

$$E[U(\boldsymbol{W})] = pr(x) * U_L(W^0 - L - x) + (1 - pr(x))U_N(W^0 - x). \quad (2)$$

In this paper, we use a similar formalisation to Ogut et al. [15], which is very generic. Nevertheless, in our work losses could be very high, and the utility function is not bound to be a constant absolute risk aversion (CARA) function only.

3.1   No-Insurance Case

First, we consider the situation when insurance is not available for agents. Let,

$$U_{NN} = U(W^0 - x) \text{ if no incident occurs;} \quad (3)$$

$$U_{NL} = U(W^0 - L - x) \text{ if an incident occurs.} \quad (4)$$

---

[2] We acknowledge that in reality effect of investments on probability of occurrence is more complex and an incident may occur more than once but we would like to underline that this standard (for cyber investment models [7,8,10,13,16] and general insurance [4]) modelling is an approximation of reality which reduces the complexity of computations and allows to analyse the core insights [7].

[3] Although, the Eq. 1 can be simplified, we leave it in this form to underline the similarity with the following step in the discussion.

The expected utility in this case is:

$$E[U(\boldsymbol{W})] = pr(x) * U_{NL} + (1 - pr(x))U_{NN}. \tag{5}$$

We take the first order condition (FOC) for x and look for optimal solution x^N.

$$\frac{\partial E[U(\boldsymbol{W})]}{\partial x}$$

$$= pr'(x^N)U_{NL} - pr(x^N)U'_{NL} - (1 - pr(x^N))U'_{NN} - pr'(x^N)U_{NN} = 0; \tag{6}$$

$$pr'(x^N)(U_{NL} - U_{NN}) = pr(x^N) * U'_{NL} + (1 - pr(x^N))U'_{NN}; \tag{7}$$

$$pr'(x^N) = \frac{pr(x^N) * U'_{NL} + (1 - pr(x^N))U'_{NN}}{(U_{NL} - U_{NN})}. \tag{8}$$

The solution to Eq. 8 will provide us with the optimal amount of money an agent should invest in self-protection if insurance is not available.

3.2   Competitive Insurance Market

Now, we consider the situation when insurance is available to agents. An insurer agrees to bare some part of insured's loss, called an indemnity I ($I \leq L$), in case an incident occurs. An insured pays the premium P as a fee for this service. The premium is usually linked to indemnity by the following relation:

$$P = (1 + \lambda) * pr(x)I; \tag{9}$$

where λ is the degree of market immaturity. This degree can be seen as the amount of money the insurer may ask for the service it provides. If insurance market is mature, i.e., it is a competitive market, it is assumed that no insurers are able to provide a better insurance product than others already do, and $\lambda = 0$.

First we introduce the utility functions for insurance case.

$$U_{IN} = U(W^0 - pr(x)(1 + \lambda)I - x) \text{ if no incident occurs;} \tag{10}$$

$$U_{IL} = U(W^0 - L + I - pr(x)(1 + \lambda)I - x) \text{ if an incident occurs.} \tag{11}$$

The expected utility in this case is

$$E[U(\boldsymbol{W})] = pr(x) * U_{IL} + (1 - pr(x))U_{IN}. \tag{12}$$

In case of a competitive insurance market and using Eq. 12, it is possible to find the optimal level of investment, which is equal to[4]

$$x^I = -\frac{1}{L}. \tag{13}$$

---

[4] See the proof in [15] or [4].

Comparing insurance x^I and no-insurance cases x^N we would like to be sure that security investments will increase the security level of insured. Formally,

$$pr'(x^N) \leq pr'(x^I) \quad or \quad pr'(x^N) \leq -\frac{1}{L}. \tag{14}$$

We see that if this condition holds, security investments, even in case of a competitive market, are higher than in case of no-insurance. On the contrary, many studies [15,16,20] show that cyber insurance tends to reduce the investments and

$$pr'(x^N) > -\frac{1}{L}. \tag{15}$$

In other words, the presence of (competitive) insurance worsens the security investment level for an agent.

Our goal is to investigate the possibility to raise the security investments up to the level of no-insurance, by raising loading factor. The later can be achieved by special taxes applied to insurer to ensure that the loading factor λ is high enough to incentivise insureds to invest in cyber security. Moreover, we will ensure that agents would like to buy insurance regardless the increased price, i.e., the coverage (indemnity) $I > 0$.

4   Raising Security Investment Level with Insurance

Since an insured would like to maximise its utility her/she will set up the best I and x. In other words, we should consider the first order conditions of Eq. 12 for I and x and find the optimal values $I^\star$ and $x^\star$.

$$\frac{\partial E[U(\boldsymbol{W})]}{\partial I}$$
$$= pr(x) * U'_{IL}(1 - pr(x)(1 + \lambda)) - (1 - pr(x))(1 + \lambda)pr(x)U'_{IN} = 0. \tag{16}$$

From Eq. 16 it follows that:

$$\frac{U'_{IL}}{U'_{IN}} = \frac{(1 - pr(x))(1 + \lambda)}{1 - pr(x)(1 + \lambda)} \quad or \tag{17}$$

$$1 + \lambda = \frac{U'_{IL}}{U'_{IN}(1 - pr(x)) + pr(x)U'_{IL}}. \tag{18}$$

We can do the similar analysis for investments.

$$\frac{\partial E[U(\boldsymbol{W})]}{\partial x} = pr'(x^\star) * U_{IL} - pr'(x^\star) * U'_{IL}(pr'(x^\star)(1 + \lambda)I + 1)$$
$$- (1 - pr(x^\star))U'_{IN}(pr'(x^\star)(1 + \lambda)I + 1) - pr'(x^\star)U_{IN} = 0. \tag{19}$$

With some simple transformations, we come to the following form:

$$\frac{(U_{IL} - U_{IN})}{(pr(x^\star)U'_{IL} + (1 - pr(x^\star))U'_{IN})} - \frac{1}{pr'(x^\star)} = (1 + \lambda)I. \tag{20}$$

Our goal is to achieve the same level of security investments as in case of no insurance available, i.e., $x^\star - x^N$. Moreover, in this case the amount of insurance bought must be optimal $I = I^\star$. Naturally, the solution to our problem $(\lambda, I^\star)$ is the solution to the following system of equations:

$$\begin{cases} 1 + \lambda = \frac{U'_{IL}}{U'_{IN}(1 - pr(x^\star)) + pr(x^\star)U'_{IL}}; \\ \frac{(U_{IL} - U_{IN})}{(pr(x^\star)U'_{IL} + (1 - pr(x^\star))U'_{IN})} - \frac{1}{pr'(x^\star)} = (1 + \lambda)I^\star. \end{cases} \tag{21}$$

Although this is a system of two equations with two variables, its solution is not easy to find in the current form. As we will show in the following (see Sect. 5), the solution is not simple (but is possible) even when all functions and values are precisely defined. The main question we would like to answer is whether this system has a non-zero solution for indemnity, i.e., $I^\star > 0$ if $(\lambda, I^\star)$ is the solution for Eq. 21.

Theorem 1. *If the level of investments in self-protection for the competitive cyber insurance market is lower than in case of no insurance available and if the utility function of insured is a of decreasing absolute risk aversion (DARA) type, there is such a setting of λ for non-competitive cyber insurance market which ensures that*

1. the level of investments is equal to the case of no insurance ($x^\star = x^N$);
2. the amount of insurance bought is higher than zero ($I^\star > 0$).

Proof. First, lets put Eq. 18 to Eq. 20:

$$\frac{(U_{IL} - U_{IN})}{(pr(x^\star)U'_{IL} + (1 - pr(x^\star))U'_{IN})} - \frac{1}{pr'(x^\star)} = \frac{U'_{IL}}{U'_{IN}(1 - pr(x)) + pr(x)}I; \tag{22}$$

$$-\frac{1}{pr'(x^\star)} + \frac{(U_{IL} - U_{IN} - I^\star U'_{IL})}{(pr(x^\star)U'_{IL} + (1 - pr(x^\star))U'_{IN})} = f(I^\star) = 0. \tag{23}$$

Now we investigate the function $f(I^\star)$. If we consider $x^\star = x^N$, it is easy to see that $I^\star = 0$ is a solution to the Eq. 23. Trivially, if an agent decides not to buy insurance ($I^\star = 0$) then its optimal investment level is the same as in case when no insurance is available. What we are interested in is *whether there is another solution for* Eq. 23 *on the interval $I^\star \in [0, L]$*.

Another important observation we can make is for the other extreme, when $I^\star = L$, i.e., full insurance case. We see from Eqs. 10 and 11 that in this case: $U_{IL} = U_{IN}$ and the right summand of $f(I^\star)$ is equal to $-L$. Recalling the assumption from Eq. 15, we see that:

$$\frac{1}{pr'(x^\star)} = \frac{1}{pr'(x^N)} < -L. \tag{24}$$

From Eq. 24 it follows that $f(I^\star)|_{I^\star=L} > 0$. Although $I = L$ is not a solution, we get some information about the behaviour of $f(I^\star)$ function.

We have found that $f'(I^\star)|_{I^\star=0} < 0$[5]. Since, we know, that $f(I^\star)|_{I^\star=L} > 0$ and the function is continuous (on the interval $I^\star \in [0; L]$[6]), then according to the Intermediate Value Theorem there *must be at least one more point with* $I^\star > 0$ *which is the solution to* Eq. 23 *(the point, where function* $f(I^\star) = 0$ *for* $I^\star \in (0; L))$.

Insureds prefer to buy insurance. We have shown above that there are at least two solutions to our problem: with $I^* = 0$ and $I^* > 0$.

Insurers, clearly, would like to have $I^* > 0$, and thus, set λ to ensure this choice of the insured. Consider this problem also from the insured point of view. The insured will always select the strategy which maximises its utility $E[U(\mathbf{W})]$. Moreover, since the strategy "do not buy insurance" is always available in our settings, we would like to be sure that the solution for $I^* > 0$ is preferable. Compare these two cases:

$$E[U(W)]|_{I^*\neq 0} - E[U(W)]|_{I^*=0}$$
$$= pr(x^N)U_{IL} + (1 - pr(x^N))U_{IN} - pr(x^N)U_{NL} - (1 - pr(x^N))U_{NN}$$
$$= pr(x^N)(U_{IL} - U_{NL}) + (1 - pr(x^N))(U_{NN} - U_{IN}). \tag{25}$$

Now, we recall that $U_{IL} \geq U_{NL}$ and $U_{NN} \geq U_{IN}$, while the utility function is convex, i.e., $U_{IL} - U_{NL} < U'_{IL}(I^\star(1 - pr(x^N)(1 + \lambda)))$ and $U_{NN} - U_{IN} > U'_{IN}(I^\star pr(x^N)(1 + \lambda))$. Finally, using Eq. 17 we find that the result is greater than 0.

$$E[U(W)]|_{I^*\neq 0} - E[U(W)]|_{I^*=0}$$
$$\geq pr(x^N)U'_{IL}(I^\star(1 - pr(x^N)(1 + \lambda))) - (1 - pr(x^N))U'_{IN}(I^\star pr(x^N)(1 + \lambda)) = 0. \tag{26}$$

We conclude that, for any $I^\star$, $E[U(W)]|_{I^*\neq 0} \geq E[U(W)]|_{I^*=0}$, i.e., an insured always prefers to buy some insurance if the settings are as specified by solution of Eq. 21.

It is easy to see that if $\lambda = 0$ than $I^\star = L$. Now, if $I^\star = 0$, then

$$\lambda = \frac{(U'_{NL} - U'_{NN})(1 - pr(x))}{(U'_{NL} - U'_{NN})pr(x) + U'_{NN}}. \tag{27}$$

Out of Eq. 27, we conclude that the loading factor to force the security level to be equal to x^N belongs to the interval $[0; \frac{(U'_{NL}-U'_{NN})(1-pr(x))}{(U'_{NL}-U'_{NN})pr(x)+U'_{NN}}]$.

---

[5] See the proof in the Appendix.

[6] $f'(I^\star)$ is continuous on the interval $I^\star \in [0; L]$ since neither $pr'(x^\star) = 0$ nor $(pr(x^\star)U'_{IL} + (1 - pr(x^\star))U'_{IN}) = 0$ for realistic values.

Using Eq. 17 for $I \neq 0$ and for $I = 0$ it is easy to find that the loading factor in the first case is always lower:

$$\frac{(1 - pr(x))}{pr(x) + \frac{1}{\frac{U'_{NL}}{U'_{NN}} - 1}} \geq \frac{(1 - pr(x))}{pr(x) + \frac{1}{\frac{U'_{IL}}{U'_{IN}} - 1}}, \; since \; U'_{IL} \geq U'_{NL} \; and \; U'_{IL} \leq U'_{NL}. \quad (28)$$

4.1 Interdependence of Security

Until now we considered only an independent case, i.e., security level of one agent did not depend on the security level of another one. In the cyber world this is not usually the case. Thus, we should change our model of probability to:

$$pr_i(x_i, X_{-i}) = 1 - (1 - \pi_i(x_i)) * \Pi_{-i}. \quad (29)$$

where Π is the degree of the network security. In other words, Π determines the probability that the agent will be compromised indirectly, i.e., through other member of the network. In cyber insurance literature it is usually equals to:

$$\Pi_{-i} = \prod_{\forall j \neq i} (1 - q * \pi_j(x_j)). \quad (30)$$

In this paper, we focus on the effect of the overall network security on a concrete insured. Therefore, in our study insurance (as a risk treatment option) is available only for this insured. Thus, we omit indexes i and $-i$ and skip X_{-i}.

It is easy to see that the procedure for finding I and λ does not change much, we simply should use Eq. 30 instead of simple $pr(i)$.

$$\begin{cases} 1 + \lambda = \frac{U'_{IL}}{U'_{IN}((1 - \pi(x^*)) * \Pi) + (\pi(x^*) * \Pi)U'_{IL}}; \\ \frac{(U_{IL} - U_{IN})}{U'_{IN}((1 - \pi(x^*)) * \Pi) + (\pi(x^*) * \Pi)U'_{IL}} - \frac{1}{\pi'(x^*) * \Pi} = (1 + \lambda)I^*. \end{cases} \quad (31)$$

5 Examples and Analysis of CARA and CRRA

Since the found solution is quite complex in its generic view, in this section we will demonstrate how the finding can be applied in specific cases of the two DARA utility functions most frequently applied for cyber insurance [13]: Constant Absolute Risk Aversion (CARA) and Constant Relevant Risk Aversion (CRRA) functions. We would like to underline that CARA and CRRA utility functions are only useful examples, while the findings from Sect. 4 are valid for any concave utility function.

5.1 CARA Utility Function

Constant Absolute Risk Aversion (CARA) utility function is a function for which the following relation holds:

$$-\frac{U''(W)}{U'(W)} = \sigma; \; \sigma > 0. \quad (32)$$

The unique function satisfying this relation is the exponential function:

$$U(W) = 1 - \exp^{-\sigma W}; \quad U'(W) = \sigma \exp^{-\sigma W}; \quad U''(W) = -\sigma^2 \exp^{-\sigma W}. \quad (33)$$

If we apply this utility function to our Equation system 21, then using the first equation, we can find that:

$$e^{\sigma(L-I^*)} = \frac{(1+\lambda)(1 - pr(x^*))}{(1 - pr(x^*)(1+\lambda))} \quad or \quad (34)$$

$$I^* = L - \frac{1}{\sigma} ln \left[\frac{(1+\lambda)(1 - pr(x^*))}{(1 - pr(x^*)(1+\lambda))} \right]. \quad (35)$$

The second equation from the system can be changed to:

$$\frac{1}{\sigma} \frac{1 - e^{\sigma(L-I^*)}}{1 - pr(x^*) + pr(x^*)(e^{\sigma(L-I^*)})} - \frac{1}{pr'(x^*)} = (1+\lambda)I^* \quad or \quad (36)$$

$$\frac{1}{\sigma} \frac{\lambda}{1 - pr(x^*)} - \frac{1}{pr'(x^*)} = (1+\lambda)I^*. \quad (37)$$

$f(I^*)$ function from Eq. 23 assumes the following form:

$$\frac{1}{\sigma} \frac{\lambda}{1 - pr(x^*)} - \frac{1}{pr'(x^*)} - (1+\lambda)I^* = f(I^*). \quad (38)$$

Now, it is possible to see that the loading factor (λ) we are looking for is the solution of the following equation.

$$\frac{1}{\sigma(1+\lambda)} \frac{\lambda}{1 - pr(x^*)} - \frac{1}{pr'(x^*)(1+\lambda)} = L - \frac{1}{\sigma} ln \left[\frac{(1+\lambda)(1 - pr(x^*))}{(1 - pr(x^*)(1+\lambda))} \right]. \quad (39)$$

Equation 39 is still hard to solve theoretically. Viable approaches are graphic solutions or approximation algorithms.

5.2　CRRA Utility Function

Constant Relative Risk Aversion (CRRA) utility function is a function for which the following relation holds:

$$-\frac{U''(W)}{U'(W)} = \frac{\sigma}{W}; \quad \sigma > 0. \quad (40)$$

The utility function itself can be defined as follows:

$$U(W) = \begin{cases} \frac{W^{1-\sigma}}{1-\sigma} & \text{for } \sigma \neq 1 \\ log(W) & \text{for } \sigma = 1 \end{cases}; \quad U'(W) = W^{-\sigma}; \quad U''(W) = -\sigma \frac{W^{-\sigma}}{W}. \quad (41)$$

Without loss of generality, we assume that $\sigma \neq 1$.

If we apply this utility function to our Equation system 21, then using the first equation, we can find that:

$$\left(\frac{W^0 - pr(x^\star)(1+\lambda)I^\star - x^\star}{W^0 - L + I - pr(x^\star)(1+\lambda)I^\star - x^\star}\right)^\sigma = \frac{(1+\lambda)(1-pr(x^\star))}{(1-pr(x^\star)(1+\lambda))} = \alpha \quad or \quad (42)$$

$$I^\star = \frac{L\sqrt[\sigma]{\alpha} - (W^0 - x^\star)(\sqrt[\sigma]{\alpha} - 1)}{\sqrt[\sigma]{\alpha} - pr(x^\star)(1+\lambda)(\sqrt[\sigma]{\alpha} - 1)}. \tag{43}$$

The second equation from the system can be changed to:

$$\frac{1}{1-\sigma}\frac{(W^0 - pr(x^\star)(1+\lambda)I^\star - x^\star)(\alpha - 1) - \alpha L + \alpha I^\star}{pr(x^\star)\alpha + (1 - pr(x^\star))} - \frac{1}{pr'(x^\star)} = (1+\lambda)I^\star;$$

$$I^\star = \frac{pr'(x^\star)((W^0 - x^\star)(\alpha - 1) - \alpha L) - \beta}{pr'(x^\star)((1+\lambda)\beta + pr(x^\star)(1+\lambda)(\alpha - 1) - \alpha)}, \tag{44}$$

where $\beta = (1-\sigma)(pr(x^\star)\alpha + (1 - pr(x^\star)))$.

$f(I^\star)$ function from Eq. 23 assumes the following form:

$$f(I^\star) = \frac{(W^0 - pr(x^\star)(1+\lambda)I^\star - x^\star)(\alpha - 1) - \alpha L + \alpha I^\star}{(1-\sigma)(pr(x^\star)\alpha + (1 - pr(x^\star)))} - \frac{1}{pr'(x^\star)} - (1+\lambda)I^\star.$$

$$\tag{45}$$

Now, it is possible to see that the loading factor (λ) we are looking for is the solution of the following equation.

$$\frac{L - (W^0 - x^\star)(\sqrt[\sigma]{\alpha} - 1)}{\sqrt[\sigma]{\alpha} - pr(x^\star)(1+\lambda)(\sqrt[\sigma]{\alpha} - 1)} = \frac{pr'(x^\star)((W^0 - x^\star)(\alpha - 1) - \alpha L) - \beta}{pr'(x^\star)(1+\lambda)\beta + pr(x^\star)(1+\lambda)(\alpha - 1) - \alpha}. \tag{46}$$

Equation 46 is still hard to solve theoretically. Viable approaches are graphic solutions or approximation algorithms.

5.3   Numerical Analysis

Finally, we would like to demonstrate the correctness of our theoretical approach with a couple of numerical examples. The initial wealth is assumed to be 20 (thousand) euro, and a possible loss estimated to be around 10 (thousand) euro. In both considered cases (for CARA and CRRA utility functions) we use the same $\sigma = 0.1$. We define the probability function as follows (ensuring that $pr'(x) < 0$ and $pr''(x) < 0$):

$$pr(x) = \frac{0.2}{(1+x)}. \tag{47}$$

With these settings, we are now able to find the resulting λ and I.

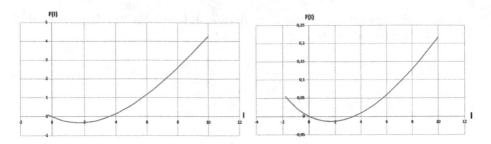

Fig. 1. $f(I)$ for CARA and CRRA examples.

CARA. We start with the example of CARA utility function with $\sigma = 0.1$. First of all we solve Eq. 8 to obtain x^N, which is also our target level of security investments in the insurance case $x^N = x^*$. Now, when the probability function is known (Eq. 47), Eq. 8 can be transformed to a quadratic equation with one solution always negative. The second solution in our case is $x^N \approx 0.69$. If we compute $pr'(x^N)$ we will see that it satisfies condition stated in Eq. 15 $pr'(x^N) \approx -0.07 > -1/10 = -0.1$.

First, consider the auxiliary function $f(I^*)$ and its behaviour (see Eq. 38). The left part of Fig. 1 shows the behaviour of the function. As we found out in our reasoning in Sect. 4, the function crosses the line $f(I^*) = 0$, when $I^* = 0$ and $\lambda \approx 1.26$. Moreover, there is also at least one more intersection with this line for $I^* \approx 3,5946 \neq 0$ and $\lambda \approx 0.7153$.

Naturally, there is no need to consider this auxiliary function looking for the optimal values. It is more convenient to consider Eq. 39 and find the intersection points of left and right parts of the equation. The left part of Fig. 2 shows these functions. In order to find the resulting values of I^* and λ we applied a simply hybrid root-finding algorithm[7].

CRRA. We conducted a similar analysis for CRRA utility function with the same $\sigma = 0.1$. The found level of investment is $x^N \approx 0.43$, which also satisfies condition in Eq. 15 $pr'(x^N) \approx -0,0978 > -1/10 = -0.1$.

Then, we found $f(I^*)$ using Eq. 45 (the right part of Fig. 1) and intersection of left and right hand parts of Eq. 46 (the right part of Fig. 2). This function also crosses the line $f(I^*) = 0$, when $I^* = 0$ and $\lambda \approx 0.063$, plus, there is an intersection for $I^* \approx 3.4586 \neq 0$ when $\lambda \approx 0.0267$.

Effect of Interdependency. Consider now the effect of interdependency (using the degree of network security Π from Eq. 30) on the incentive to buy cyber

---

[7] First, we cut the considered interval into small pieces and found the pieces with border values of different signs. Then, we applied bisection method, cutting the piece in half and checking the signs of the function on border values, always leaving the half with different signs of the function on the border until the last half is shorter than the allowed error.

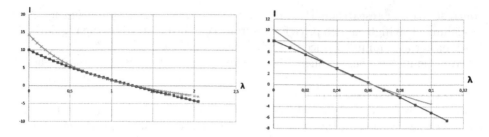

Fig. 2. Intersections of $I(\lambda)$ for Eqs. 39 (left) and 46 (right).

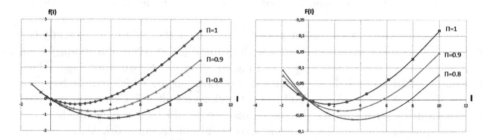

Fig. 3. $f(I)$ for CARA (left) and CRRA (right) examples with different degree of interdependency.

insurance. We conducted an analysis with three coefficients: $\Pi = 1, \Pi = 0.9$, and $\Pi = 0.8$. Figure 3 shows the result.

It is important to note that with the fall of security of the overall network and the growth of the interdependence (causing the fall of Π) the agents are more willing to buy insurance. This can be seen in the graphs, as the point where $f(I)$ line crosses axis I (i.e., $f(I) = 0$) shifts left, and the agent prefers to buy more insurance. Moreover, there is the required increase in the insurance cost (i.e., λ) is lower: for CARA $\lambda = 0.1131$ and for CRRA $\lambda = 0.00947$ if $\Pi = 0.8$ vs. for CARA $\lambda = 0.7153$ and for CRRA $\lambda = 0.0267$ if $\Pi = 1$.

Finally, we see that our function gets lower and lower with increase of inter-dependency effect, and, eventually, its right end gets below 0. This indicates that the optimal investments in case of buying cyber insurance with fair price become higher than in optimal investments in case cyber insurance is not available.

6   Conclusion

In the paper we have studied the possibility to ensure that investment level with available cyber insurance is at least as high as if cyber insurance was not available. This was achieved by the means of increasing the costs of cyber insurance. Our generic analysis have shown that the equal level with no-insurance case is always possible and regardless the higher prices insureds are still interested in buying some portion of insurance. Here we would like to underline, that in contrast to other researchers [15] our analysis has much less assumptions for the modelling. The high enough price for insurance can be enforced by the regulatory body either as a minimal price or with some special tax.

We conducted some numerical experiments with two case studies, where CARA and CRRA functions have been used. The experiments support our findings. Moreover, we were able to find that agents are more eager to buy more insurance with increase of interdependency effect. Furthermore, although the investments in self-protection fall with increase of interdependency effect, agents also become more incentivised by cyber insurance in comparison with no-insurance case. The latest observation requires more thorough theoretical research to prove the dependency for all cases, but we leave it for the future work.

As a future work, we see great potential in the considered model to study the possibility to affect investment level with adjusting the price. For example, we are able to raise investment level even higher than in no-insurance case. Thus, it would be nice to find the maximal value of investments which can be reached. Moreover, currently we considered the network as something that is not affected by available cyber-insurance. In the future, we would like to consider how the security investments change if other participants of the network also have the possibility to insure themselves. Last but not least, we would like to investigate how the analysed mechanism behaves in the models with information asymmetry, i.e., where moral hazard and adverse selection problems have place.

Appendix

We prove that $f'(I^\star)|_{I^\star=0} < 0$.

Proof

$$
\frac{df}{dI^\star}
$$
$$
= \frac{[(1 - (1+\lambda)pr(x^\star) - pr(x^\star)I\frac{d\lambda}{dI^\star})U'_{IL} - U'_{IL}][pr(x^\star)U'_{IL} + (1 - pr(x^\star))U'_{IN}]}{(pr(x^\star))U'_{IL} + (1 - pr(x^\star))U'_{IN})^2}
$$
$$
+ \frac{[(1+\lambda)pr(x^\star) + pr(x^\star)I\frac{d\lambda}{dI^\star})] U'_{IN} [pr(x^\star)U'_{IL} + (1 - pr(x^\star))U'_{IN}]}{(pr(x^\star))U'_{IL} + (1 - pr(x^\star))U'_{IN})^2}
$$
$$
- \frac{I^\star [1 - (1+\lambda)pr(x^\star) - pr(x^\star)I\frac{d\lambda}{dI^\star}] U''_{IL} [pr(x^\star)U'_{IL} + (1 - pr(x^\star))U'_{IN}]}{(pr(x^\star))U'_{IL} + (1 - pr(x^\star))U'_{IN})^2}
$$
$$
- \frac{[U_{IL} - U_{IN} - I^\star U'_{IL}]pr(x^\star) [1 - (1+\lambda)pr(x^\star) - pr(x^\star)I\frac{d\lambda}{dI^\star}] U''_{IL}}{(pr(x^\star))U'_{IL} + (1 - pr(x^\star))U'_{IN})^2}
$$
$$
- \frac{[U_{IL} - U_{IN} - I^\star U'_{IL}]pr(x^\star)(1 - pr(x^\star)) [-(1+\lambda)pr(x^\star) - pr(x^\star)I\frac{d\lambda}{dI^\star}] U''_{IN}}{(pr(x^\star))U'_{IL} + (1 - pr(x^\star))U'_{IN})^2}.
$$
$$(48)$$

What we are interested in is the sign of the first derivative when $I^\star = 0$. Since the divisor is clearly grater than zero, we focus on the dividend only.

$U_{IL}|_{I^*=0} = U_{NL}$ and $U_{IN}|_{I^*=0} = U_{NN}$ and derivatives. We reduce the first part of Eq. 48 by U'_{IL} inside the first brackets. The third part is 0, as well as all subparts with $\frac{d\lambda}{dI^*}$. In the last part we move out $pr(x^*)(1 - (1 + \lambda)pr(x^*))$. We get:

$$(1 + \lambda)pr(x^*)(-U'_{NL} + U'_{NN})(pr(x^*)U'_{NL} + (1 - pr(x^*))U'_{NN})$$

$$+ (U_{NN} - U_{NL})pr(x^*)(1 - (1 + \lambda)pr(x^*))[(U''_{NL} - \frac{(1 - pr(x^*))(1 + \lambda)}{(1 - (1 + \lambda)pr(x^*))}U''_{NN})]$$

$$= (1 + \lambda)pr(x^*)(-U'_{NL} + U'_{NN})(pr(x^*)U'_{NL} + (1 - pr(x^*))U'_{NN})$$

$$+ (U_{NN} - U_{NL})pr(x^*)(1 - (1 + \lambda)pr(x^*))[(U''_{NL}U'_{NN} - U''_{NN}U'_{NL})]\frac{1}{U'_{NN}}.$$

$$(49)$$

We know, that $U'_{NL} > U'_{NL}$ and the first derivative is positive. Thus, the first summand is negative. Also $U'_{NL} < U'_{NL}$ and utility function is always positive. Also, $1 > (1 + \lambda)pr(x^*)$, otherwise an insured should pay more premium than the identity it gets in case of an incident. The only part left for consideration is $(U''_{NL}U'_{NN} - U''_{NN}U'_{NL})$.

We would like to recall that for the utility functions in use a *coefficient of absolute risk aversion* is defined as:

$$A(\boldsymbol{W}) = -\frac{U''(\boldsymbol{W})}{U'(\boldsymbol{W})}. \tag{50}$$

Moreover, the experimental and empirical evidence mostly confirm the decreasing absolute risk aversion (DARA). For the sake of generality, here we assume non-increasing risk aversion (CARA and DARA):

$$\frac{\partial A(\boldsymbol{W})}{\partial \boldsymbol{W}} \leq 0. \tag{51}$$

In other words $A(W_{NL}) \geq A(W_{NN})$, where W_{NL} is the financial position of an insured in case of incident, while W_{NL} is the financial position of an insured in case no incident happens.

Thus, $(U''_{NL}U'_{NN} - U''_{NN}U'_{NL}) = U'_{NN}U'_{NL}[A(W_{NN}) - A(W_{NL})] \leq 0$ and the second summand in the overall formula is negative or zero.

References

1. Anderson, R., Böhme, R., Claytin, R., Moore, T.: Security economics and the internal market, January 2008. https://www.enisa.europa.eu/publications/archive/economics-sec/at_download/fullReport. Accessed 15 Jan 2016
2. Böhme, R., Schwartz, G.: Modeling cyber-insurance: towards a unifying framework. In: Proceedings of the 9th Workshop on the Economics in Information Security (2010)
3. Bolot, J., Lelarge, M.: A new perspective on internet security using insurance. In: Proceedings of the 27th IEEE International Conference on Computer Communications, Phoenix, AZ, USA, pp. 1948–1956, April 2008

4. Ehrlich, I., Becker, G.S.: Market insurance, self-insurance, and self-protection. In: Dionne, G., Harrington, S.E. (eds.) Foundations of Insurance Economics, pp. 164–189. Springer, Dordrecht (1992). https://doi.org/10.1007/978-94-015-7957-5_8

5. ENISA: Incentives and barriers of the cyber insurance market in Europe, June 2012. goo.gl/BtNyj4. Accessed 12 Dec 2014

6. EY: Global insurance outlook (2015). goo.gl/uyFzQ4. Accessed 11 Aug 2015

7. Gordon, L., Loeb, M.: The economics of information security investment. ACM Trans. Inf. Syst. Secur. **5**(4), 438–457 (2003)

8. Laszka, A., Felegyhazi, M., Buttyan, L.: A survey of interdependent information security games. ACM Comput. Surv. **47**(2), 23:1–23:38 (2014)

9. Laszka, A., Johnson, B., Grossklags, J., Felegyhazi, M.: Estimating systematic risk in real-world networks. In: Christin, N., Safavi-Naini, R. (eds.) FC 2014. LNCS, vol. 8437, pp. 417–435. Springer, Heidelberg (2014). https://doi.org/10.1007/978-3-662-45472-5_27

10. Lelarge, M., Bolot, J.: Network externalities and the deployment of security features and protocols in the internet. SIGMETRICS Perform. Eval. Rev. **36**(1), 37–48 (2008)

11. Lelarge, M., Bolot, J.: Economic incentives to increase security in the internet: the case for insurance. In: Proceedings of the 28th IEEE International Conference on Computer Communications, Rio de Janeiro, pp. 1494–1502, April 2009

12. Majuca, R.P., Yurcik, W., Kesan, J.P.: The evolution of cyberinsurance. The Computing Research Repository, pp. 1–16 (2006)

13. Marotta, A., Martinelli, F., Nanni, S., Orlando, A., Yautsiukhin, A.: Cyber-insurance survey. Comput. Sci. Rev. **24**, 35–61 (2017)

14. Naghizadeh, P., Liu, M.: Voluntary participation in cyber-insurance markets. In: Proceedings of the 2014 Workshop on Economics in Information Security (2014)

15. Ogut, H., Menon, N., Raghunathan, S.: Cyber insurance and it security investment: impact of interdependent risk. In: Proceedings of the 4-th Workshop on the Economics of Information Security (2005)

16. Pal, R., Golubchik, L., Psounis, K., Hui, P.: Will cyber-insurance improve network security? A market analysis. In: Proceedings of the 2014 INFOCOM, pp. 235–243. IEEE (2014)

17. Schneier, B.: Insurance and the computer industry. Commun. ACM **44**(3), 114–115 (2001)

18. Schwartz, G., Shetty, N., Walrand, J.: Cyber-insurance: missing market driven by user heterogeneity. In: WEIS (2010)

19. Schwartz, G.A., Sastry, S.S.: Cyber-insurance framework for large scale interdependent networks. In: Proceedings of the 3rd International Conference on High Confidence Networked Systems, HiCoNS 2014, pp. 145–154. ACM (2014)

20. Shetty, N., Schwartz, G., Walrand, J.: Can competitive insurers improve network security? In: Acquisti, A., Smith, S.W., Sadeghi, A.-R. (eds.) Trust 2010. LNCS, vol. 6101, pp. 308–322. Springer, Heidelberg (2010). https://doi.org/10.1007/978-3-642-13869-0_23

21. Vaughan, E.J., Vaughan, T.M.: Fundamentals of Risk and Insurance, 11th edn. Wiley, Hoboken (2014)

22. von Neumann, J., Morgenstern, O.: Theory of Games and Economic Behaviour, 3rd edn. Princeton University Press, Princeton (1953)

23. World Economic Forum: Global risks 2014. 9th edn (2014). http://www.droughtmanagement.info/literature/WEF_global_risks_report_2014.pdf. Accessed 3 Jan 2017

Towards an Anonymity Supported Platform for Shared Cyber Threat Intelligence

Thomas D. Wagner[✉][iD], Esther Palomar, Khaled Mahbub,
and Ali E. Abdallah

Birmingham City University, Birmingham, West Midlands B4 7XG, UK
{thomas.wagner,esther.palomar,khaled.mahbub,ali.abdallah}@bcu.ac.uk

Abstract. Over the last few years, cyber defense strategies in large organizations have gradually shifted from being reactive to being increasingly
pro-active. In the latter mode threats are anticipated and corresponding mitigations are actionable. An essential component of this strategy
is the ability to share threat intelligence from multiple sources ranging
from crowd sourcing to closed circles of trusted stakeholders and their
supply chains. This paper presents a collaborative platform that supports sharing of cyber threat intelligence in which anonymity is a key
component. The component has been compared to existing threat intelligence sharing solutions. The design of the component is examined and
a prototype of the supporting tool has been implemented.

Keywords: Advanced persistent threat · Cyber threat intelligence
Threat sharing · Anonymity

1 Introduction

A more systematic response to Advanced Persistent Threats (APT) and timely
response to new attacks is required [14]. The sharing of Cyber Threat Intelligence (CTI) can significantly benefit organizations (and also states) as a way to
understand where risk events are occurring and realize their financial implications. Indeed, threat sharing revolutionizes current risk management procedures
by improving situational awareness exchange and hence, mitigating attacks [8].
Situational awareness achieved through cyber threat intelligence enhances the
collective understanding of threats and how to remedy vulnerabilities.

This work pays special attention to the prototype implementation of the
anonymizing tool for anonymous and automated sharing of threat intelligence.
We also introduce the implementation decisions of the aforementioned tool,
within a preliminary working prototype of a collaboration platform based on
the Malware Information Sharing Platform (MISP).

The rest of the paper is organized as follows. Section 2 introduces our generic
collaborative platform for CTI sharing. Section 3 presents the anonymity prototype. Section 4 shows an analysis and, compares and evaluates our model to
existing solutions. Section 5 concludes our work.

© Springer International Publishing AG, part of Springer Nature 2018
N. Cuppens et al. (Eds.): CRiSIS 2017, LNCS 10694, pp. 175–183, 2018.
https://doi.org/10.1007/978-3-319-76687-4_12

2   A Generic Cyber Threat Sharing Platform

In this section we overview the building block of the proposed platform, namely the anonymity prototype (Fig. 1).

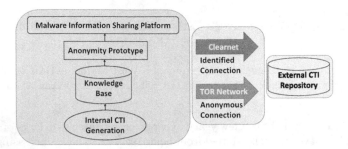

Fig. 1. TIP architecture

The open-source and community driven MISP (2.4.55) is used to manage and exchange CTI in human and machine readable form [16]. The platform is installed on Oracle's Virtual Box with Linux Ubuntu Server (14.04) and stores CTI in the Structured Threat Information Expression (STIX) format. To develop a Threat Intelligence Platform (TIP) independent function, the tool is developed outside the MISP environment and connects remotely to MISP's SQL database. This gives us the option to scale and apply the tool to other TIP's in the future.

2.1   Anonymity Filter

Generated CTI is stored in a local knowledge base and then anonymized through the prototype which uploads it to the MISP instance for sharing. To anonymize the content, regular expressions in Java are used to mask confidential details that could reveal Personal Identifiable Information (PII). A properties file stores the regular expressions which can be expanded and modified. Table 1 lists some truncated regular expressions that have been used for testing. The full list of regular expressions can be found here[1]. For example, the regular expression for e-mails ensures that only real e-mail addresses are anonymized. CTI could contain an "@" sign instead of having "at" written out and will ergo not be anonymized.

Exceptions to the regular expressions are implemented to avoid that core information of CTI is anonymized. For instance, information about Phishing sites and SPAM contain IP addresses which should not be anonymized. We are using MISP's tagging system for Phishing (ID 35), and SPAM (ID 31) to create exceptions for these types of information. Other exception or tagging id's can be added and customized to stakeholder preferences.

---

[1] https://github.com/X2018X/CTISharing/wiki.

Events

Id	Info
546	IP ****6 **** ****3 **** ****5 **** **** **** **** ****0 ***
547	OSINT - Odinaff: New Trojan used in high level financ
548	Spam 2016-10-12 (mule acquisition) - probably relate
549	OSINT - How Stampado Ransomware Analysis Led 1
550	Threat Spotlight: GozNym
551	RIG exploit kit takes on large malvertising campaign
552	Phishing attack client telephone number ****
553	Credit card fraud 423456****
554	Identity fraud with SSN ****
555	@@@@
556	Online fraud with NI ****

Fig. 2. Anonymity tool

Table 1. Regular expressions

Type	Regular expression
IP addresses	(([0–1]?[0–9]{1,2} \\)?\\
NI numbers	(([a-zA-Z]){2}( )?([0–9])
E-mail	(?:[a-z0-9!#$%& '*+/=?^
Credit cards	\\+?1?*\\(?-*\\
SSN	((?!000—666)[0–9][0–9]
UK postcodes	([A-PR-UWYZ](([0–9]((
US zip codes	([0-9]5(?:-[0–9]4

PII is masked with four asterisk characters as shown in Fig. 2. The anonymity prototype uses the Traffic Light Protocol (TLP) to define the anonymity level where white has the highest anonymity level because it is publicly shared. Anonymity for green, amber, and red labeled CTI has to be defined according to the stakeholders and groups exchange policy. Repositories such as "Hail-a-Taxii"[2] allow anonymous connections without the need for authentication. Masking PII is imperative but not enough to provide sufficient anonymity. To enhance the anonymity of CTI we also have to anonymize the path. We therefore tunnel the connection through the TOR network[3] to hide our identity and connect to the repositories where white labeled CTI is shared. Applications can also be routed through TOR to allow anonymous connections. We use the Whonix gateway[4] to connect to the network. Tunneling the data through the TOR network will avoid service providers and stakeholders to identify the location or origin of the stakeholder.

Our prototype provides a masking function before the content is shared outside of a stakeholder's premises, which mitigates the risk of revealing PII to the service provider, if any, and stakeholder. Exceptions to the anonymization process avoid that core information is being hidden. Results of accuracy are shown in Table 2.

The anonymization rules are based on the regular expressions and the TLP presented in the previous subsection. For instance, the regular expression to anonymize e-mails is enabled when the TLP ID is white. If it is green, amber, or red, the regular expression is disabled. E-mail addresses are not anonymized when the tag ID is 43 which stands for Phishing. The reason is that the Phishing e-mail is a core attribute of the CTI. The rational behind the set of rules is that the depicted attributes are a common set of PII that should never be shared. The anonymization rules can be modified according to individual requirements. I.e., regular expressions may be added or disabled, the TLP anonymity level

---

[2] http://hailataxii.com.
[3] https://www.torproject.org.
[4] https://www.whonix.org.

Table 2. Anonymity results

Anonymization	Data sets	Accuracy	False negatives
E-mail addresses	1,110	1,105 (99.54%)	5
IP addresses	1,003	1,002 (99.9%)	1
Credit card numbers	1,002	1,002 (100%)	0
Social security numbers	1,001	1,001 (100%)	0
National insurance numbers	100	82 (82%)	18
UK postcodes	1,000	1,000 (100%)	0
US zip codes	1,002	1,002 (100%)	0

may be modified. The test run of the prototype has shown a high percentage of successfully anonymized PII. Ergo, the prototype has proven a high degree of anonymity in our test environment.

3   Anonymity Filter: First Prototype

Most of the platforms are typically tied to specific security product lines, service offerings, or community-specific solutions. Nonetheless, there are ongoing efforts to create and refine the community-based development of sharing and structuring cyber threat information. For instance, the MITRE Corporation is engaging organizations and experts across a broad spectrum of industry, academia, and government towards the provision of standardized, structured representations of this information. The Structured Threat Information Expression (STIX), Cyber Observable Expression (CybOX), and Trusted Automated Exchange of Indicator Information (TAXII) represent the most recognized languages in the threat information sharing community [3–5,9]. In particular, STIX aims to extend indicator sharing to enable the management and exchange of significantly more expressive sets of indicators as well as other full-spectrum cyber threat information [2]. Software solutions should provide intuitive user interface masking back-end STIX and TAXII complexities according to the high acceptance of these languages by the community like government, organizations, and vendors.

The common desire of many organizations to exchange information automatically as much as possible but yet not lose the human judgment and control is largely a phenomenon of many information sharing programs [13].

3.1   A Note on Anonymity Techniques

Information about vulnerabilities can contain sensitive attributes like client or organizational data. Therefore, CTI has to be anonymized to avoid reputation deterioration which is a drawback in information sharing [7]. Even internally shared information should not reveal any PII to employees who do not possess adequate permission. Stakeholders have to analyze which information is sensitive and should be masked [12]. Privacy techniques for data anonymization have been presented in k-anonymity where data records are indistinguishable from other records. For example, the age of a patient only shows that they are younger or older than 40 years [15]. l-diversity was presented in [11] which successfully defends anonymity against diversity and background knowledge attacks. l-diversity uses a 3-diverse version of a table which makes it impossible to exactly know which information relates to which identity. t-closeness was presented in [10] to provide anonymity beyond k-anonymity and l-diversity by reducing the granularity of a data representation. The authors correctly identified that most privacy-preserving methods assume that all attributes are categorical. Another technique for sanitation is pseudonymized data which sanitizes data before its release [1]. The work is presented as a general approach to data anonymization, nevertheless, this work could be used to anonymize CTI in our model. Further research is presented in [6] as a prototype implementation called PRACIS, a protocol that provides privacy-preserving and aggregatable CTI sharing and uses STIX as its standard message format. This protocol is very useful for encrypting CTI and could extend our anonymity model for trusted sharing.

3.2 System Model

Generated CTI is stored in the local knowledge base in STIX format. The stakeholder decides whether to share the information and labels the information according to the TLP. The anonymity prototype anonymizes the information according to the color of TLP synchronized with the MISP tagging system where the color white has the ID 1 in the "tags" table, green has ID 3, amber ID 44, and red ID 45. As an example we chose the TLP color white which has the highest anonymity level because the consuming stakeholder can share the information publicly. The information is processed through the anonymity prototype which detects the ID 1 in the "tags" table and therefore applies a pre-defined set of regular expressions, discussed in Subsect. 2.1 to mask confidential attributes. The regular expressions are accessed from a properties file which makes requirement adjustments simpler instead of modifying the Java code. Some attributes are critical to the usefulness of the intelligence such as e-mails in Phishing attacks. The prototype has therefore exceptions implemented which allows the filtering process to ignore specific attributes. We implemented 2 exceptions for SPAM with the ID 31 and Phishing with the ID 35 from the MISP "tags" table. If the prototype encounters these ID's then the anonymization process for e-mails is disabled. Untagged information is ignored by the prototype, hence full disclosure of the intelligence. The MISP instance connects to the repositories through the TOR network utilizing the Whonix gateway to establish an anonymous connection for information sharing.

3.3 Preliminary Evaluation and Threat Model

The evaluation of the tool was set up in the test environment and run with various data sets. The tool was tested against accuracy and false negatives. The first test run of the prototype had satisfactory results regarding the accuracy of masking PII shown in Subsect. 2.1. More exceptions have to be added in the future to render the tool more accurate and powerful. The TOR connection provides anonymous connections which makes it difficult for consuming stakeholders to re-identify our identity. Our system has shown to be vulnerable to background knowledge attacks. For example, if an adversary knows that an organization was breached with a 0-day attack, then shared information about that particular event can reveal the identity of the providing stakeholder. The acquisition of the background knowledge could have been gained through the media.

Attacks on anonymity such as de-anonymization can reveal personal information even after the anonymization process. The literature in Subsect. 3.1 discusses various anonymity techniques and attacks. If the hacker has background knowledge of the stakeholder then she can correlate the knowledge with the visible information. Background attacks such as infeasibility and probabilistic attacks are described in [1]. k-anonymity provides anonymity by obfuscating table attributes to render it impossible to identify an entity. Nevertheless, successful homogeneity and background knowledge attacks on k-anonymity were proven by [11].

4 Analysis of Threat Intelligence Platforms

30 threat intelligence platforms have been analyzed and compared, to the best of our knowledge, pertaining to anonymity (Table 3). The methods used for the evaluation were direct testing where possible. We did not have access to all platforms, therefore we analyzed the academic literature, white/gray literature such as technical reports, and company websites for the evaluation.

We have identified 3 platforms that enable different approaches to anonymity in threat intelligence sharing. Alien Vault's anonymity function does not identify stakeholders identity including system's data and internal IP traffic. If a contribution is made, external IP addresses, traffic patterns, timestamps, and Indicator of Compromise (IOC) activity data are collected. Therefore, in this hub-to-spoke model an anonymity function is provided. Nevertheless, it does not provide any anonymity pertaining to the content. I.e., removing or masking of PII which has to be conducted manually before CTI is shared.

The HP Threat Central platform enables a preprocessing of the data as to remove specific information before it is being shared with the community. Although, stakeholders have to advise HP which information should be anonymized. The platform encrypts the communication channel over HTTPS. Moreover, it provides a comprehensive policy setting to decide with whom to share.

Table 3. Threat intelligence platforms: [a]denotes direct access, [b]denotes white/gray literature.

Threat intelligence platforms	Anonymity
Malware Information Sharing Platform (MISP)[a]	—
NC4 CTX/soltra edge[a]	—
ThreatConnect[a]	—
Microsoft interflow[b]	—
HP threat central[b]	X
Facebook threat exchange[b]	—
IBM X-force exchange[a]	—
Alien vault Open Threat Exchange (OTX)[a]	X
Anomali Threat Stream (STAXX)[b]	—
LookingGlass ScoutPrime (Cyveillance)[b]	—
Cisco talos[b]	—
Crowd strike falcon platform[b]	—
Norm shield[b]	—
ServiceNow - bright point security[b]	—
NECOMAtter (NECOMAtome)[b]	—
Splunk[a]	—
CyberConnector[b]	—
Last Quarter Mile Toolset (LQMT)[b]	—
Health information trust alliance - Cyber Threat XChange (CTX)[b]	—
Defense security information exchange[b]	—
Retail cyber intelligence sharing Center (R-CISC) intelligence sharing portal[b]	—
Accenture cyber intelligence platform[b]	—
Anubis networks cyberfeed[b]	—
Comilion[b]	X
McAfee threat intelligence exchange[b]	—
ThreatQuotient[b]	—
ThreatTrack ThreatIQ[b]	—
Eclectic IQ[b]	—
Infoblox threat intelligence data exchange[b]	—
Cyber-security information sharing partnership[a]	—

By contrast, Comilion provides anonymization at the architecture level making the sender untraceable. This is a valuable and imperative function, nevertheless, the sharing stakeholder could be de-anonymized by analyzing the unmasked

PII. We conclude that only HP Threat Central provides a content masking function which is conducted on site.

Our tool provides a content anonymity and connection function which has not been found, in such form, in any of the analyzed platforms.

5 Conclusion

In this paper, we introduced a generic cyber threat sharing platform that enables sharing of cyber threat intelligence. There is currently a lot of interest in developing systems that automate the exchange of security information as well as in the need of standards to develop as to ensure machine-readability and interoperability. The building base for our model is anonymity. An analysis was conducted of 30 threat sharing platforms regarding anonymity. Immediate work focused on the implementation and evaluation of the anonymity prototype as proof-of-concept for automation of the processes involved in real-time.

References

1. Bagai, R., Malik, N., Jadliwala, M.: Measuring anonymity of pseudonymized data after probabilistic background attacks. IEEE Trans. Inf. Forensics Secur. **12**(5), 1156–1169 (2017)
2. Barnum, S.: Standardizing cyber threat intelligence information with the structured threat information eXpression (STIX). MITRE Corp. **11**, 1–22 (2012)
3. Burger, E.W., Goodman, M.D., Kampanakis, P., Zhu, K.A.: Taxonomy model for cyber threat intelligence information exchange technologies. In: Proceedings of the 2014 ACM Workshop on Information Sharing & Collaborative Security, pp. 51–60. ACM (2014)
4. Connolly, J., Davidson, M., Richard, M., Skorupka, C.: The trusted automated eXchange of indicator information (TAXII) (2012)
5. Fransen, F., Smulders, A., Kerkdijk, R.: Cyber security information exchange to gain insight into the effects of cyber threats and incidents. e & i Elektrotechnik und Informationstechnik **132**(2), 106–112 (2015)
6. de Fuentes, J.M., González-Manzano, L., Tapiador, J., Peris-Lopez, P.: PRACIS: privacy-preserving and aggregatable cybersecurity information sharing. Comput. Secur. **69**, 127–141 (2016)
7. Garrido-Pelaz, R., González-Manzano, L., Pastrana, S.: Shall we collaborate?: A model to analyse the benefits of information sharing. In: Proceedings of the 2016 ACM on Workshop on Information Sharing and Collaborative Security, pp. 15–24. ACM (2016)
8. Goodwin, C., Nicholas, J.P., Bryant, J., Ciglic, K., Kleiner, A., Kutterer, C., Sullivan, K.: A framework for cybersecurity information sharing and risk reduction. Technical report, Microsoft Corporation, Technical report (2015)
9. Kampanakis, P.: Security automation and threat information-sharing options. Secur. Priv. IEEE **12**(5), 42–51 (2014)
10. Li, N., Li, T., Venkatasubramanian, S.: t-closeness: privacy beyond k-anonymity and l-diversity. In: Proceedings of the 23rd International Conference on Data Engineering, ICDE 2007, The Marmara Hotel, Istanbul, Turkey, April 15–20, 2007, pp. 106–115 (2007)

11. Machanavajjhala, A., Kifer, D., Gehrke, J., Venkitasubramaniam, M.: L-diversity: privacy beyond k-anonymity. TKDD **1**(1), 3 (2007)
12. Mohaisen, A., Al-Ibrahim, O., Kamhoua, C., Kwiat, K., Njilla, L.: Rethinking information sharing for actionable threat intelligence. CoRR abs/1702.00548 (2017)
13. Philip, R., et al.: Enabling Distributed Security in Cyberspace. Department of Homeland Security (2011)
14. Sigholm, J., Bang, M.: Towards offensive cyber counterintelligence: adopting a target-centric view on advanced persistent threats. In: 2013 European Intelligence and Security Informatics Conference (EISIC), pp. 166–171. IEEE (2013)
15. Sweeney, L.: k-anonymity: a model for protecting privacy. Int. J. Uncertainty Fuzziness Knowl. Based Syst. **10**(5), 557–570 (2002)
16. Wagner, C., Dulaunoy, A., Wagener, G., Iklody, A.: MISP: the design and implementation of a collaborative threat intelligence sharing platform. In: Proceedings of the 2016 ACM on Workshop on Information Sharing and Collaborative Security, pp. 49–56. ACM (2016)

Human-Centric Security and Trust

Phishing Attacks Root Causes

Hossein Abroshan$^{(\boxtimes)}$ (iD), Jan Devos, Geert Poels (iD),
and Eric Laermans (iD)

Ghent University, 9000 Ghent, Belgium
{hossein.abroshan, jang.devos,
geert.poels, eric.laermans}@ugent.be

Abstract. Nowadays, many people are losing considerable wealth due to online scams. Phishing is one of the means that a scammer can use to deceitfully obtain the victim's personal identification, bank account information, or any other sensitive data. There are a number of anti-phishing techniques and tools in place, but unfortunately phishing still works. One of the reasons is that phishers usually use human behaviour to design and then utilise a new phishing technique. Therefore, identifying the psychological and sociological factors used by scammers could help us to tackle the very root causes of fraudulent phishing attacks. This paper recognises some of those factors and creates a cause-and-effect diagram to clearly present the categories and factors which make up the root causes of phishing scams. The illustrated diagram is extendable with additional phishing causes.

Keywords: Phishing · Scam · Root causes · Behaviour

1 Introduction

Human life has significantly changed as a result of online services including e-shopping and e-banking, etc. Although these services offer great convenience, they are accompanied by an increase in cybercrimes and present new security threats. An online phishing is a cybercrime to steal credentials from users, such as login and credit card details, "by masquerading as trustworthy entities in electronic communication" [1]. Then the attacker usually uses the collected information to sign into the genuine reputable website, such as those that are used for internet banking, to steal from the victim's online account [2]. In recent years, many researchers have focused on phishing attacks in order to offer an anti-phishing solution for protecting sensitive financial data from phishers. However, phishing still works, and every day brings with it new phishing websites and techniques which steal personal credentials.

By reviewing the existing anti-phishing techniques, we understand that most of them are trying to technically detect and/or prevent phishing attacks. We are of the opinion that focusing on the human psychological and sociological factors that attackers use to scam people would be an effective way to fundamentally tackle phishing attacks. We believe that current anti-phishing solutions are useful though insufficient, as phishers always use people's psychological weaknesses to design new types of phishing attacks. Several studies [3, 4] have already identified some of the

© Springer International Publishing AG, part of Springer Nature 2018
N. Cuppens et al. (Eds.): CRiSIS 2017, LNCS 10694, pp. 187–202, 2018.
https://doi.org/10.1007/978-3-319-76687-4_13

above-mentioned factors, but none of them have carried out a root cause analysis to list all the possible psychological factors at play and the tricks that scammers use to fool people.

The objective of this research is to identify human and psychological factors which phishers can use to scam people and make a successful phishing attack. Listing and categorising these root causes will enable us to develop improvement programmes for each factor. If we know that a psychological reason, for instance gullibility, is one of the root causes of phishing attacks then we can detect users' gullibility level, for example by using a psychological test and/or a trust game, as well as develop some improvement and treatment programmes, in the form of specific trainings for example, to improve gullibility level of to those who easily trust others. We hope that such programmes could help reduce the number of successful phishing attacks by treating the phishing root causes as identified in this paper. It is possible to systematically identify users' behaviour by monitoring their online activities, using online tests, and providing them relevant trainings based on the detected weaknesses. Therefore, these anti-phishing solutions can be automated.

For this purpose, we initially reviewed anti-phishing solutions to find out which techniques are being applied to deal with phishing attacks. We also used anti-phishing studies to figure out how the targeted phishing attacks work and what phishing tactics are being used by attackers. We then reviewed other studies, especially scam-related psychological articles, to identify which cognitive factors can be used by phishers to fool people and to design phishing attacks. We then identified tricks that a phisher might use to scam people. We focused on a selection of tricks from the reviewed studies, particularly anti-phishing studies. Finally, we illustrated the root causes, including the identified human factors and the tricks used via a cause-and-effect diagram. Such a diagram presents a clear and easily comprehensible picture of the issue at hand.

For conducting our literature review we used the Webster and Watson [5] structured approach. We therefore started with searching Phishing Attacks, Anti-phishing techniques, Social Engineering Attacks and Online Scam literatures. We performed our queries on journal databases such as Science Direct, Google Scholar, and WorldCat, and browsed seventy journals such as MIS Quarterly, ACM Transactions on Information and System Security, International Journal of Security and Its Applications, Journal of Personality and Social Psychology, etc. We also queried and examined related conference papers. We selected articles that explained and defined phishing methods, root causes, and other useful information and references for our study. Then we went through the citations of the selected articles to determine whether there were more publications that we should review. In the last stage, we used the Web of Science to identify more articles citing the key articles we had identified in our earlier stage.

The paper starts with reviewing the existing anti-phishing techniques. It then presents several phishing attacks. Next, it explains psychological factors which can influence a phishing process and describes tactics scammers use to trick people. Finally, it comes up with a cause-and-effect diagram and provides concluding remarks.

2   Anti-Phishing Techniques

The existing anti-phishing approaches are classified as either server based and/or client based [6], where most of the client side anti-phishing systems are plug-ins or web browser toolbars. In recent years, many research efforts have been conducted in developing anti-phishing systems to detect and prevent phishing emails and/or websites. Table 1 indicates some existing anti-phishing techniques and grouped them into five anti-phishing categorises based on their technical and/or non-technical approaches to detect or prevent Phishing. Those techniques which are using webpage features like URL and web ranking to detect phishing attacks are not able to recognise all phishing websites. Heuristics and machine learning methods use webpage features for phishing detection, however they mostly have "high complexity" and "high false positive rates" issues [7]. The blacklists and whitelists need to be frequently updated. Blacklists are only useful to detect the detected phishing websites and emails and are not agile in responding to "zero-hour attacks" [8]. Using time-sensitive tokens works until the criminals implement real-time attacks.

Table 1. Anti-phishing categories and techniques.

Category	Techniques	
Phishing emails (Detection and prevention)	Features processing [11–15] Identification and authentication [16]	Heuristics method [13, 17] Hybrid methods [18, 19]
Phishing websites (Detection and prevention)	Content-based detection [20] Visual and layout similarity [21–24] Heuristics [25, 26] URL evaluation [27, 28]	User activities [29] Evaluation and ranking [30] Whitelists [31–33] Blacklists [34, 35] Hybrid [36, 37]
Network-based (Detection and prevention)	Authentication [38–41] Network security elements [42] Password management tools [41, 43]	Fraudulent activity detection (Transaction and log analysis) [44–46] Honeypot/phisher tracer [42, 47, 48]
Improvement of user knowledge	Knowledge evaluation and training systems [49, 50] Warning effectiveness [51]	
Prosecution	**Sending phishing messages** [52]: CAN-SPAM Act (18 U.S.C. § 1037) (US) E-Privacy Directive (EU) General Data Protection Regulation (GDPR) (Regulation (EU) 2016/679) [53] Directive (EU) 2016/680 [53] Anti-phishing Act of 2005 [54] Fraud Act 2006 (UK) [55] **Deterrence of identity theft** [52]: Crime Ordinance (Cap. 200) (HK) Theft Ordinance (Cap. 210) Identity Theft and Assumption Deterrence Act (18 U.S.C. § 1028) (US) Credit card fraud (18 U.S.C. § 1029) (US) Bank fraud (18 U.S.C. § 1344) (US) Computer fraud (18 U.S.C. § 1030(a)(4)) (US) Computer-related fraud (Article 8, Convention on Cybercrime) Fraud Act 2006 (UK) [55]	**Data privacy** [52]: Personal Data (Privacy) Ordinance (Cap. 486) (HK) Telecommunication Ordinance (Cap. 106) (HK) Telecommunication Privacy Directive (EU) E-Privacy Directive (European Union) Data Interference (Article 4, Convention on Cybercrime) System interference (Article 5, Convention on Cybercrime) General Data Protection Regulation (GDPR) (Regulation (EU) 2016/679) [53] Directive (EU) 2016/680 [53] Fraud Act 2006 (UK) [55] Rundschreiben 4/2015 (BA) (Germany) [56] **Fake websites** [52]: Copyright Ordinance (Cap. 528) (HK) Wire fraud (18 U.S.C. § 1343) (US) Infringements of copyright (Article 10, Convention on Cybercrime)

The phishing attacks will not disappear with "one solution" and at "one level" [9]. A study shows that even by utilising modern anti-phishing techniques, over 11% of users read the spoofed messages and enter their credentials [10].

3 Phishing Attacks

In recent years, researchers and organisations have categorised phishing attacks in similar or sometimes in different ways. Some examples of the mentioned categorisations of phishing tactics are "Deceptive Phishing" [57], "Malware-based Phishing" [11, 57–59], "Key-loggers" and "Screen-loggers" [57, 58], "Session Hijacking" [57], "Web Trojans" [57], "Hosts File Poisoning" [57], "System Reconfiguration" attacks [57, 59], "Data Theft" [57], "DNS-based Phishing" (Pharming) [57–59], "Content-injection Phishing" [57, 58], "Man-in-the-Middle Phishing" [57, 58], "Search Engine Phishing" [57, 59], "Website Forgery" [58], "Social Engineering" [11], "Mimicry" [11], "Email Spoofing" [11], "URL Hiding" [11], "Invisible Content" [11], "Image Content" [11].

By using the above tactics, scammers try to gain access to victims' sensitive information by masquerading as a reputable organisation or person. Figure 1 presents an example of a spear phishing attack. In this example, the phisher obtains basic information such as the name and email address of the targeted users by creating a real website that looks like the genuine website, or by hacking a real website. The fake or real website could be, for example, a promotional website, a lottery website, an e-shop, or any other website which asks for a user's personal information. Phishers can also obtain basic user information via public data or social media. In that case, the phisher uses the obtained information to create a phishing email.

Thus, a phisher relies on building trust, so that the victim believes that s/he is in contact with a reputable entity. A phisher might use tricks, persuasion, visceral influence, and/or any other technique to gain a user's trust.

4 The Influence of Cognitive Factors in the Phishing Process

Social engineering and technical tricks are two mechanisms phishers use to steal personal and financial credentials [60]. Social engineering targets individuals and the result of attacks depends on human decision, trust, and other cognitive factors. "Fraud is a human endeavor, involving deception, purposeful intent, intensity of desire, risk of apprehension, violation of trust, rationalization, etc. So, it is important to understand the psychological factors that might influence the behavior of fraud perpetrators" [61]. Therefore, to analyse the root causes of phishing attacks, we should study psychological and sociological factors to find out the main reasons why a user gets caught in a phishing net.

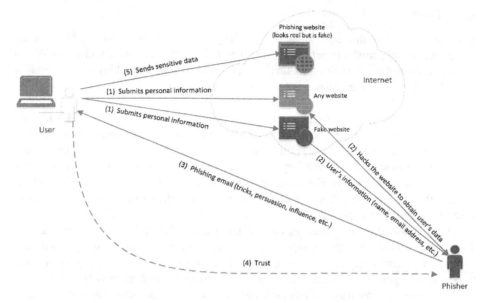

Fig. 1. Example of a phishing attack flow

4.1 Suspicion

A recent study [4] shows that suspicion is one of the determinative factors in the email phishing attacks. The study also indicated that the users determine suspicion based on how they process emails, systematically or heuristically.

If the users believe that their cyber action is risky then they will systematically process the email but in case the users believe that their cyber action is safe then they will heuristically process it.

The heuristic-systematic model [62] proposes two information processing modes. In systematic processing, independent variables such as "source factors" directly impact on "argument acceptance process". In heuristic processing, on the other hand, those independent variables may directly impact on accepting the message itself without paying enough attention to the arguments.

Based on the heuristic-systematic model, we conclude that people who highly involve the received email messages usually employ a "systematic processing" strategy which cause high suspicion about the phishing emails, whereas those who weakly involve the messages usually employ a "heuristic processing" strategy which cause low suspicion about the phishing emails.

For instance, a user who think that cyber activities are very risky usually has focus on the email's message cues, where a user who think that cyber activities are quite safe usually has not enough focus on content cues.

4.2 Trust

Trust is defined in this context as the "willingness of taking a risk", which means sometimes people trust a beneficiary when they believe that this trust will be beneficial for them, even though they know that it is possible to lose something in this relation [63]. That is one of the reasons why a victim trusts a scammer.

Moreover, characteristics of both the trustor and the beneficiary and the situation of trustor are several important factors of trust. People with different cultural background, experiences, and personal character have different propensity to trust. Some people trust others more easily, whereas others do not trust people or entities in many situations [63]. However, the beneficiary's previous behaviour as well as his/her character are crucial factors [64, 65]. For instance, if someone had positive experiences with an e-shop, then the person will trust that e-shop much more than an e-shop associated with a negative previous experience.

As mentioned above, trust is one of the factors that affect a phishing attack. Therefore, it is crucial to consider the conditions of trust, which are "availability, competence, consistency, fairness (perceived equity), integrity, loyalty (perceived benevolence), openness, overall trust, promise fulfilment, and receptivity" [65].

Sometimes people trust a predictable person or entity, more than they would others. However, predictability is not enough to build trust, as maybe the reason of that predictability was something else, such as "controls" [63]. In addition, we cannot necessarily expect that a person is being fully rational when s/he trusts people or organisations, as people might trust entities based on limited information and in many cases "biased information" [66]. People usually trust a source of information which they perceive to be similar to themselves, such as family members or friends for example [64]. Thus, people cannot be sure that their trust in an email or on a website is completely justified. Phishers might use affective trust factors and as conditions to encourage victims to trust them.

4.3 Decision-Making

A phishing attack, especially in the case of spear phishing, is a scamming process. Usually there are at least two steps in this process where a victim makes decisions. Figure 2 illustrates an example of the role of decision-making in a phishing attack. In some cases, people decide "either to trust or not trust" others [67, 68], so the first step is when the victim decides to trust the attacker and the second step is right before sharing sensitive information with the attacker.

There are several parameters which influence the victim's decision to trust an attacker, including beliefs, values, and behaviours [69]. Decision-making is a process in itself and a sub-process of a phishing attack. Decision-making consists of the following phases: "perception activity", "mental representation", "data processing", "problem solving", and "choice of solution" [70]. Thus, a user's abilities in each phase can affect the result of the decision and eventually, affect the outcome of a phishing attack. For instance, a user with better data processing knowledge and skill is more likely to make a wiser decision. However, sometimes the decision-making process does not play a major role in a phishing attack. In some cases, users do not have enough awareness of the risks of sending personal information to a phisher, or they are not sensitive to potential losses. In such cases, phishing (A) is neutral, but making some money (B) is considerable. When a phisher tries to attract a victim by offering an impressive result, the user evaluates B-A as earned money [71]. Based on a previous study [71], we can define the following possible effects of the decision-making factor in a phishing attack:

- If the person believes that the probability of gain is high, then the effect of the decision is low.
- If the person believes that the probability of loss is high, then the individual most likely will not go for it, so the effect of the decision is low.
- If the person believes that the probability of gain or loss is low, then the effect of the decision is high.

Hence, decision-making can play a major role in a phishing attack when the user believes that the chance of either utility or loss is low.

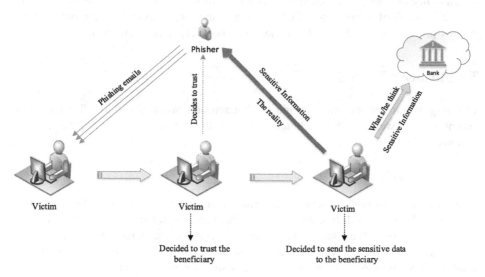

Fig. 2. Decision-makings in phishing attacks

4.4   Prediction

Phishers increase their resemblance with the targeted organisation in order to encourage the victim to believe that the phisher is who s/he claimed. This happens because people "predict by similarity" [72].

The individual's previous experience, as well as the person's knowledge, information, and/or experience with this particular type of phishing or the phisher, will affect the user's prediction in a given phishing attempt. However, the level of individual's "expected accuracy of prediction" will affect the effectiveness of evidences and his/her prior information about the particular phishing attack/attacker [72]. For instance, if the user's opinion or guess about a specific phishing is that it probably is not an attack, then the person might predict that it is a normal communication, even when the user has a degree of knowledge about phishing attacks. When a user is at the stage of making a decision to share or not to share sensitive data with a phisher, then some examples of the individual's prior information and other factors which can affect his/her prediction can be considered to be:

- Previous awareness and information about cybercrimes, especially phishing attacks, previous phishing experience, level of trust to the entity, knowledge about sensitive data, and risks of sharing the sensitive information with others.
- Similarity of the phisher to the claimed person or entity, how attractive is the phisher's offer, the phisher enforcement, real-time information, the user's impression of the offer, and the user's Emotional Quotient (EQ).

Where descriptions of what may influence a person's prediction are not available or are very limited, it is possible that the person makes a prediction based on a base rate information [72]. If a person does not receive any awareness about phishing attacks or no guidance or alarm is provided to warn of a phishing attack, or this person does not take advantages of a safeguard which is in place, then the individual might only rely on her/his prior understanding and knowledge of phishing attacks and/or the attacker.

5   Phisher's Tactics

Phishing scammers use an individual's behavioural weaknesses to offer attractive promotions as well as other techniques to trick the person into fulfilling the desired actions.

5.1   Scams and Tricks

The root causes of digital social engineering scams are very similar to the scams that happen in the real world. In both cases, the scammers use techniques and tricks to gain the victim's trust. They target the victims' psychological behaviours, and use the weaknesses of those behaviours to build a strong trust. They use the discovered psychological behaviours to design and create a scam. For instance, a phisher may find out that the victim is a person who usually tends to help others, then the scammer running a scam by feigning that they need a person to help them [73].

One of the reasons why phishing still works is because some people desire to take a gamble [74]. Therefore, an attractive prize or promotion could be enough to get them into a trap.

There are some "motivational and cognitive sources of errors" when people assess a phishing or a phisher. A phisher can use errors such as "visceral influences", "reduced motivation for information processing", "preference for confirmation", "lack of self-control", "mood regulation and phantom fixation", "sensation seeking", "liking and similarity", "reciprocation", "commitment and consistency", "reduced cognitive abilities", "positive illusions", "background knowledge and overconfidence", "norm activation", "false consensus", "authority", "social proof", "alter casting" [74], to phish.

5.2 Persuasion and Influence

There are individuals who usually desire to say yes to demands made by others, because they like reacting to "assertions of authority" [75]. They respond to others' demands even to someone who does not have the related authority. They prefer to fulfil a request or a demand, instead of investigating and verifying the authenticity of the demander. That is why when a phisher sends a fake email, e.g. from a bank, and informs them that "you need to change your password", then they do exactly what the phisher told them to do.

Moreover, "people have a natural tendency to think that a statement reflects the true attitude of the person who made it", and also some people usually tend to do what others do or to say what others say, which "may prompt them to take actions that is against their self-interest without taking the time to consider them more deeply" [75].

There are two ways that a phisher may choose to push a victim to fulfil the demand [75]:

- "Central route to persuasion"
  The phishing message contains very "systematic and logical" reasoning which motivates the victim to rationally think and cogitate on the statements, and in the end to do whatever the phisher wants. The phisher has carefully designed the scenario and the argument, and knows the victim's conclusion.
- "Peripheral route to persuasion"
  A phisher leads the victim to do the request without thinking about it. The phisher uses "mental shortcuts to bypass logical argument". For example, the victims receive an email informing them that they won thousands of dollars and a very expensive laptop in a recent lottery promotion. This fantastic prize would stimulate many people to give personal information about themselves and can cause people to fall into the phishing trap.

5.3 Visceral Influence

A visceral motivation can cause less thinking about the legitimacy of transactions, as the person's focus is on activities that could satisfy the visceral needs. In this situation, instead of rationally thinking about a given situation and analysing it accordingly, people usually do not care about the outcomes of their actions and make gut-feeling decisions. The influences of visceral factors are categorised to "low-level, middle-level, and high-level" [76] as defined below:

- Low-level: reasonable behaviour;
- Middle-level: people behaving in an opposite way to their actual interests, leading to them being upset with what they did, as they believe that they made an unreasonable decision;
- High-level: not making reasonable decisions.

Phishers create messages containing a scam reward and scam cues. Two types of scam rewards are "reward proximity" and "vividness" [77]:

- Reward proximity: if the phisher offers an easily and quickly-achievable reward, then it makes the individual hungrier than when a reward is not quickly-achievable, even if the value of the reward which is not quickly-achievable is higher.
- Vividness: when the phisher offers a very tangible reward, then it will be highly attractive for the victim. Professional phishers create different rewards for different targets groups to make each reward more clear and understandable for the related group of victims.

A person with low visceral influence is more likely to focus on scam cues, whereas one with high visceral influence is more likely to focus on the scam rewards. A victim who has high focus on the scam reward might get hooked by the phishing attack if s/he has low self-control, for example, and a victim who focuses on scam cues might get hooked if s/he has a low attention to the cues, in addition to having a high level of "social isolation", "cognitive impairment", "gullibility", "susceptibility to interpersonal influence", and/or low level of "skepticism", and/or "scam knowledge" factors [77].

However, even people with enough scam knowledge may follow a phishing cue if they enjoy activities such as gambling, for example. One of the reasons why those who have scam knowledge may still fall into a phishing trap is that sometimes experience is in opposition to knowledge, and that abnormal conditions may increase the effect of feelings on judgments [78]. That is a reason why some people process all the received emails even when they know about phishing attacks. It is therefore important to focus on the conditions which lead to decision-making. It is of crucial importance to keep in mind that visceral factors can influence behaviour even without "conscious cognitive mediation" [79]. For example, a person who is not hungry but starts eating just because someone is eating a sandwich in front of them [80].

6   Discussion

One of the techniques that scammers utilise to obtain individuals' sensitive data is social engineering [60]. The focus of this article is on the root causes of social engineering subterfuge in phishing attacks. A series of potential psychological and sociological effects have been identified.

There are several methods for root-causes analysis such as "Events and Causal Factors Charting", "Tree Diagrams", "Why-Why Chart", "Storytelling", and "Realitycharting" [81]. The Ishikawa Fishbone diagram [82] is a cause and effect analysis technique, which is useful for arranging the causes of a problem by focusing on potential factors in an organised way [83]. All the root cause analysis techniques and methods have useful features, however the Ishikawa Fishbone diagram was chosen to present the root causes of phishing attacks, which have been identified in this paper, as it is deemed to be a suitable technique to structure, categorise, as well as clearly illustrate all the extracted root causes.

Figure 3 presents the recognised root causes of phishing scams. This diagram consists of a main body, seven branches, and three sub-branches representing the grouped causes that are investigated in this paper. The presented extendable cause-and-effect diagram is a starting point, and future phishing causes could be added to the diagram.

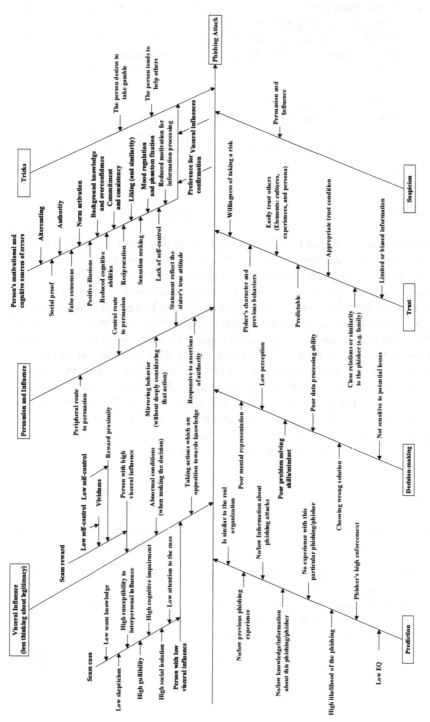

Fig. 3. Fishbone diagram of phishing attacks

Mitigating the identified causes will reduce the probability of phishing scams. Thus, focusing on the root causes to find and utilise appropriate mitigating techniques and solutions is fundamental to tackle phishing attacks from the root.

By using a psychological test, we can measure a specific cognitive behavior of a user. Then we can test the user's vulnerability to a simulated phishing attack which is founded on one of the listed root-causes. By choosing a sample of random internet users and testing different root-causes, we can describe the degree of relationship between different types of phishing attacks and their related cognitive behaviors.

If we identify an individual's weaknesses, for example by measuring his/her behaviors on one or some root-causes, then we would be able to design and provide improvement programs, such as specific trainings, to immune the person against that type of phishing attacks.

7   Conclusion

Many techniques, solutions, and tools have been developed to prevent or at least reduce the number of successful phishing attacks. Some of these techniques try to stop phishing emails or websites, whereas others try to notify or alert the user. There are also other solutions available, such as improving people's awareness of phishing scams. However, none of these solutions have so far managed to prevent phishing attacks a hundred per cent. Phishers are always developing new scams that the current anti-phishing techniques cannot detect and/or stop. Furthermore, they use human cognitive and behavioral attributes to design new tricks. This paper has identified and attempted to categorise some of the factors that phishers might use to phish the victims.

Future studies may recognise other root causes of phishing which can then be added to the cause-and-effect diagram presented in this paper. Meanwhile, the root causes identified can already be used to develop new anti-phishing techniques which can proactively prevent the future phishing scam, whether focused on the tools used by phishers or on the users who ultimately make the decisions.

References

1. Chang, E.H., Chiew, K.L., Sze, S.N., Tiong, W.K.: Phishing detection via identification of website identity. In: International Conference on IT Convergence and Security (ICITCS), pp. 1–4 (2013)
2. Li, S., Schmitz, R.: A novel anti-phishing framework based on honeypots. In: eCrime Researchers Summit, eCRIME 2009, pp. 1–13 (2009)
3. Harrison, B., Vishwanath, A., Rao, R.: A user-centered approach to phishing susceptibility: the role of a suspicious personality in protecting against phishing. In: 2016 49th Hawaii International Conference on System Sciences (HICSS), pp. 5628–5634. IEEE (2016)
4. Vishwanath, A., Harrison, B., Ng, Y.J.: Suspicion, cognition, and automaticity model of phishing susceptibility. Commun. Res. (2016). https://doi.org/10.1177/0093650215627483
5. Webster, J., Watson, R.T.: Analyzing the past to prepare for the future: writing a literature review. MIS Q. **26**, xiii–xxiii (2002)

6. Tayade, P.C., Wadhe, A.P.: Review paper on privacy preservation through phishing email filter. Int. J. Eng. Trends Technol. (IJETT) **9**, 4 (2014)
7. Zhuang, W., Jiang, Q., Xiong, T.: An intelligent anti-phishing strategy model for phishing website detection. In: 2012 32nd International Conference on Distributed Computing Systems Workshops, pp. 51–56 (2012)
8. Hong, J.: The state of phishing attacks. Commun. ACM **55**, 74–81 (2012)
9. Lynch, J.: Identity theft in cyberspace: crime control methods and their effectiveness in combating phishing attacks. Berkeley Technol. Law J. **20**, 259 (2005)
10. Jakobsson, M., Ratkiewicz, J.: Designing ethical phishing experiments: a study of (ROT13) rOnl query features. In: Proceedings of the 15th International Conference on World Wide Web, pp. 513–522. ACM, Edinburgh (2006)
11. Bergholz, A., De Beer, J., Glahn, S., Moens, M.-F., Paaß, G., Strobel, S.: New filtering approaches for phishing email. J. Comput. Secur. **18**, 7–35 (2010)
12. Chandrasekaran, M., Karayanan, K., Upadhyaya, S.: Towards phishing e-mail detection based on their structural properties. In: New York State Cyber Security Conference (2006)
13. Rigoutsos, I., Huynh, T.: Chung-Kwei: a pattern-discovery-based system for the automatic identification of unsolicited E-mail messages (SPAM). In: CEAS: First Conference on Email and Anti-Spam (2004)
14. Fette, I., Sadeh, N., Tomasic, A.: Learning to detect phishing emails. In: Proceedings of the 16th International Conference on World Wide Web, pp. 649–656. ACM, Banff (2007)
15. Toolan, F., Carthy, J.: Phishing detection using classifier ensembles. In: eCrime Researchers Summit, eCRIME 2009, pp. 1–9 (2009)
16. Herzberg, A.: DNS-based email sender authentication mechanisms: a critical review. Comput. Secur. **28**, 731–742 (2009)
17. Yu, W.D., Nargundkar, S., Tiruthani, N.: PhishCatch - a phishing detection tool. In: 33rd Annual IEEE International Computer Software and Applications Conference, COMPSAC 2009, pp. 451–456 (2009)
18. Hamid, I.R.A., Abawajy, J.: Hybrid feature selection for phishing email detection. In: Xiang, Y., Cuzzocrea, A., Hobbs, M., Zhou, W. (eds.) ICA3PP 2011. LNCS, vol. 7017, pp. 266–275. Springer, Heidelberg (2011). https://doi.org/10.1007/978-3-642-24669-2_26
19. Ma, L., Ofoghi, B., Watters, P., Brown, S.: Detecting phishing emails using hybrid features. In: Symposia and Workshops on Ubiquitous, Autonomic and Trusted Computing, UIC-ATC 2009, pp. 493–497 (2009)
20. Zhang, Y., Hong, J.I., Cranor, L.F.: Cantina: a content-based approach to detecting phishing web sites. In: Proceedings of the 16th International Conference on World Wide Web, pp. 639–648. ACM, Banff (2007)
21. Chen, T.-C., Dick, S., Miller, J.: Detecting visually similar web pages: application to phishing detection. ACM Trans. Internet Technol. **10**, 1–38 (2010)
22. Rosiello, A.P., Kirda, E., Ferrandi, F.: A layout-similarity-based approach for detecting phishing pages. In: Third International Conference on Security and Privacy in Communications Networks and the Workshops, SecureComm 2007, pp. 454–463. IEEE (2007)
23. Liu, W., Deng, X., Huang, G., Fu, A.Y.: An antiphishing strategy based on visual similarity assessment. IEEE Internet Comput. **10**, 58 (2006)
24. Zhou, Y., Zhang, Y., Xiao, J., Wang, Y., Lin, W.: Visual similarity based anti-phishing with the combination of local and global features. In: 2014 IEEE 13th International Conference on Trust, Security and Privacy in Computing and Communications, pp. 189–196 (2014)
25. Chen, T.-C., Stepan, T., Dick, S., Miller, J.: An anti-phishing system employing diffused information. ACM Trans. Inf. Syst. Secur. (TISSEC) **16**, 16 (2014)
26. Chou, N., Ledesma, R., Teraguchi, Y., Mitchell, J.C.: Client-side defense against web-based identity theft. In: NDSS. The Internet Society (2004)

27. Garera, S., Provos, N., Chew, M., Rubin, A.D.: A framework for detection and measurement of phishing attacks. In: Proceedings of the 2007 ACM Workshop on Recurring Malcode, pp. 1–8. ACM, Alexandria (2007)
28. Nguyen, L.A.T., To, B.L., Nguyen, H.K., Nguyen, M.H.: A novel approach for phishing detection using URL-based heuristic. In: International Conference on Computing, Management and Telecommunications (ComManTel), pp. 298–303 (2014)
29. Wu, M., Miller, R.C., Little, G.: Web wallet: preventing phishing attacks by revealing user intentions. In: Proceedings of the Second Symposium on Usable Privacy and Security, pp. 102–113. ACM (2006)
30. Kim, Y.-G., Cho, S., Lee, J.-S., Lee, M.-S., Kim, I.H., Kim, S.H.: Method for evaluating the security risk of a website against phishing attacks. In: Yang, C.C., et al. (eds.) ISI 2008. LNCS, vol. 5075, pp. 21–31. Springer, Heidelberg (2008). https://doi.org/10.1007/978-3-540-69304-8_3
31. Cao, Y., Han, W., Le, Y.: Anti-phishing based on automated individual white-list. In: Proceedings of the 4th ACM Workshop on Digital Identity Management, pp. 51–60. ACM, Alexandria (2008)
32. Dong, X., Clark, J.A., Jacob, J.L.: Defending the weakest link: phishing websites detection by analysing user behaviours. Telecommun. Syst. **45**, 215–226 (2010)
33. Likarish, P., Eunjin, J., Dunbar, D., Hansen, T.E., Hourcade, J.P.: B-APT: Bayesian anti-phishing toolbar. In: International Conference on Communications, ICC 2008, pp. 1745–1749. IEEE (2008)
34. Prakash, P., Kumar, M., Kompella, R.R., Gupta, M.: PhishNet: predictive blacklisting to detect phishing attacks. In: 2010 Proceedings IEEE, INFOCOM, pp. 1–5 (2010)
35. Whittaker, C., Ryner, B., Nazif, M.: Large-scale automatic classification of phishing pages. In: NDSS. The Internet Society (2010)
36. Bo, H., Wei, W., Liming, W., Guanggang, G., Yali, X., Xiaodong, L., Wei, M.: A hybrid system to find & fight phishing attacks actively. In: Proceedings of the 2011 IEEE/WIC/ACM International Conferences on Web Intelligence and Intelligent Agent Technology, vol. 1, pp. 506–509. IEEE Computer Society (2011)
37. Marchal, S., Armano, G., Grondahl, T., Saari, K., Singh, N., Asokan, N.: Off-the-Hook: an efficient and usable client-side phishing prevention application. IEEE Trans. Comput. **PP**, 1 (2017)
38. Braun, B., Johns, M., Koestler, J., Posegga, J.: PhishSafe: leveraging modern JavaScript API's for transparent and robust protection. In: Proceedings of the 4th ACM Conference on Data and Application Security and Privacy, pp. 61–72. ACM, San Antonio (2014)
39. Dhamija, R., Tygar, J.D.: The battle against phishing: dynamic security skins. In: Proceedings of the 2005 Symposium on Usable Privacy and Security, pp. 77–88. ACM, Pittsburgh (2005)
40. Huang, C.-Y., Ma, S.-P., Chen, K.-T.: Using one-time passwords to prevent password phishing attacks. J. Netw. Comput. Appl. **34**, 1292–1301 (2011)
41. Yee, K.-P., Sitaker, K.: Passpet: convenient password management and phishing protection. In: Proceedings of the Second Symposium on Usable Privacy and Security, pp. 32–43. ACM, Pittsburgh (2006)
42. Husák, M., Cegan, J.: PhiGARo: automatic phishing detection and incident response framework. In: 2014 Ninth International Conference on Availability, Reliability and Security, pp. 295–302 (2014)
43. Ross, B., Jackson, C., Miyake, N., Boneh, D., Mitchell, J.C.: Stronger password authentication using browser extensions. In: Usenix Security, pp. 17–32. Baltimore (2005)

44. Bignell, K.B.: Authentication in an internet banking environment: towards developing a strategy for fraud detection. In: International Conference on Internet Surveillance and Protection (ICISP 2006), p. 23 (2006)
45. Steel, C.M., Lu, C.-T.: Impersonator identification through dynamic fingerprinting. Digit. Investig. **5**, 60–70 (2008)
46. Ramachandran, A., Feamster, N., Krishnamurthy, B., Spatscheck, O., Van der Merwe, J.: Fishing for phishing from the network stream. Technical report (2008)
47. Li, S., Schmitz, R.: A novel anti-phishing framework based on honeypots. In: 2009 eCrime Researchers Summit, pp. 1–13 (2009)
48. Han, X., Kheir, N., Balzarotti, D.: PhishEye: live monitoring of sandboxed phishing kits. In: Proceedings of the 2016 ACM SIGSAC Conference on Computer and Communications Security, pp. 1402–1413. ACM (2016)
49. Alnajim, A., Munro, M.: An evaluation of users' anti-phishing knowledge retention. In: International Conference on Information Management and Engineering, ICIME 2009, pp. 210–214. IEEE (2009)
50. Kumaraguru, P., Rhee, Y., Acquisti, A., Cranor, L.F., Hong, J., Nunge, E.: Protecting people from phishing: the design and evaluation of an embedded training email system. In: Proceedings of the SIGCHI Conference on Human Factors in Computing Systems, pp. 905–914. ACM (2007)
51. Yang, W., Xiong, A., Chen, J., Proctor, R.W., Li, N.: Use of phishing training to improve security warning compliance: evidence from a field experiment. In: Proceedings of the Hot Topics in Science of Security: Symposium and Bootcamp, pp. 52–61. ACM, Hanover (2017)
52. Bose, I., Leung, A.C.M.: Unveiling the mask of phishing: threats, preventive measures, and responsibilities. Commun. Assoc. Inf. Syst. **19**, 24 (2007)
53. European Commission: Reform of EU data protection rules (2016)
54. https://www.congress.gov/bill/109th-congress/senate-bill/472/text. Accessed 11 May 2016
55. UK Legislation: Fraud Act 2006. UK Legislation (2006)
56. BaFin: Rundschreiben 4/2015 (BA): Bundesanstalt für Finanzdienstleistungsaufsicht (BaFin) (2015)
57. PCWorld. http://www.pcworld.com/article/135293/article.html. Accessed 09 Nov 2015
58. Suryavanshi, N., Jain, A.: Phishing detection in selected feature using modified SVM-PSO. IJRCCT **5**, 208–214 (2016)
59. Chaudhry, J.A., Chaudhry, S.A., Rittenhouse, R.G.: Phishing attacks and defenses. Int. J. Secur. its Appl. **10**, 247–256 (2016)
60. Anti-Phishing Working Group: http://docs.apwg.org/reports/apwg_trends_report_q2_2016.pdf. Accessed 11 Aug 2106
61. Ramamoorti, S., Olsen, W.: Fraud: the human factor; many discount behavioral explanations for fraud, but as the incidence of fraud continues to grow, placing the spotlight on behavioral factors may be an important approach not only to detection, but to deterrence as well. Financ. Exec. **23**, 53–56 (2007)
62. Chaiken, S.: Heuristic versus systematic information processing and the use of source versus message cues in persuasion. J. Pers. Soc. Psychol. **39**, 752–766 (1980)
63. Mayer, R.C., Davis, J.H., Schoorman, F.D.: An integrative model of organizational trust. Acad. Manag. Rev. **20**, 709–734 (1995)
64. Alesina, A., La Ferrara, E.: Who trusts others? J. Public Econ. **85**, 207–234 (2002)
65. Butler, J.K.: Toward understanding and measuring conditions of trust: evolution of a conditions of trust inventory. J. Manag. **17**, 643–663 (1991)
66. Khodyakov, D.: Trust as a process a three-dimensional approach. Sociology **41**, 115–132 (2007)

67. Klein, D.B.: Knowledge and Coordination: A Liberal Interpretation. Oxford University Press, Oxford (2011)
68. Huang, J., Nicol, D.: A Formal-Semantics-Based Calculus of Trust. IEEE Internet Comput. **14**, 38–46 (2010)
69. Oliveira, A.: A discussion of rational and psychological decision making theories and models: the search for a cultural-ethical decision making model. Electron. J. Bus. Ethics Organ. Stud. **12**, 12–13 (2007)
70. Bezerra, S., Cherruault, Y., Fourcade, J., Veron, G.: A mathematical model for the human decision-making process. Math. Comput. Model. **24**, 21–26 (1996)
71. Tversky, A., Kahneman, D.: Rational choice and the framing of decisions. J. Bus. **59**, S251–S278 (1986)
72. Kahneman, D., Tversky, A.: On the psychology of prediction. Psychol. Rev. **80**, 237 (1973)
73. Mitnick, K.D., Simon, W.L.: The Art of Deception: Controlling the Human Element of Security. Wiley, Hoboken (2011)
74. Lea, S., Fischer, P., Evans, K.: The psychology of scams: provoking and committing errors of judgement. Report for the Office of Fair Trading (2009). www.oft.gov.uk/shared_oft/reports/consumer_protection/oft1070.pdf
75. Rusch, J.J.: The "social engineering" of internet fraud. In: Internet Society Annual Conference (1999). http://www.isoc.org/isoc/conferences/inet/99/proceedings/3g/3g_2.htm
76. Loewenstein, G.: Out of control: visceral influences on behavior. Organ. Behav. Hum. Decis. Process. **65**, 272–292 (1996)
77. Langenderfer, J., Shimp, T.A.: Consumer vulnerability to scams, swindles, and fraud: a new theory of visceral influences on persuasion. Psychol. Mark. **18**, 763–783 (2001)
78. Strack, F., Neumann, R.: "The spirit is willing, but the flesh is weak": beyond mind-body interactions in human decision-making. Organ. Behav. Hum. Decis. Process. **65**, 300–304 (1996)
79. Bolles, R.C.: Theory of Motivation. HarperCollins Publishers, New York (1975)
80. Pribram, K.H.: Emotion: a neurobehavioral analysis. In: Approaches to Emotion, pp. 13–38 (1984)
81. Gano, D.L.: Comparison of common root cause analysis tools and methods. In: Apollo Root Cause Analysis-A New Way of Thinking (2007)
82. Ishikawa, K.: Introduction to Quality Control. Productivity Press, Cambridge (1990)
83. Juran, J.M., Godfrey, A.B.: Quality Handbook. Republished McGraw-Hill, New York (1999)

Domain Name System Without Root Servers

Matthäus Wander(✉), Christopher Boelmann, and Torben Weis

University of Duisburg-Essen, Duisburg, Germany
matthaeus.wander@uni-due.de

Abstract. We present a variation to the infrastructure of the Domain Name System (DNS) that works without DNS root servers. This allows to switch from a centralized trust model (root) to a decentralized trust model (top-level domains). By dropping DNS root in our approach, users have one entity less that they must trust. Besides trust issues, not relying on DNS root means that DNS root servers are no longer a central point of failure. Our approach is minimally invasive, builds on established DNS architecture and protocols and supports the DNS Security Extensions (DNSSEC). Furthermore, we designed our approach as an opt-in technology. Thus, each top-level domain operator can decide whether to support rootless DNS or not.

The challenge of a rootless DNS is to keep track of changing IP addresses of top-level domain servers and to handle key rollovers, which are part of normal DNSSEC operation. Top-level domains opting in to rootless DNS must follow constraints regarding the frequency of changes of IP addresses and DNSSEC keys. We conducted a four-year measurement to show that 82% respectively 72% of top-level domains fulfill these constraints already.

Keywords: Domain Name System · DNSSEC · Infrastructure security

1 Introduction

The Domain Name System (DNS) is a critical infrastructure for the whole Internet. In order to resolve a domain name, clients iterate through the hierarchical namespace from root to the leaf. The availability of the DNS thus depends on a reliable operation of the root. With the DNS Security Extensions (DNSSEC), the root also serves as trust anchor for authorizing cryptographic keys that are used for signing domain name entries. The security of DNSSEC thus depends on a trusted and proper root key management.

In this paper we explore the design of a rootless Domain Name System. The objective of this system is to have independent top-level domains (TLDs), which do not depend on a root authority. The trust is distributed to coequal TLD operators, whose control is limited to their respective namespace. We argue that the dependency on root can be eliminated with little technical changes for

© Springer International Publishing AG, part of Springer Nature 2018
N. Cuppens et al. (Eds.): CRiSIS 2017, LNCS 10694, pp. 203–216, 2018.
https://doi.org/10.1007/978-3-319-76687-4_14

most TLDs and without introducing new attack vectors. The two components of this approach—*priming* and *trust anchor updates*—have been originally designed to work on root level, but we show that they are also applicable for TLDs. The proposed approach is minimally invasive and reuses the existing network protocol, methods and infrastructure. Unlike peer-to-peer-based approaches, this allows for an incremental deployment and shares the performance and usability characteristics of the proven-in-practice DNS.

2   Motivation

Trust. This work is motivated by removing the trust dependency upon root without lessening the security guarantees of DNSSEC. The DNS root has the technical authority to answer any domain or to delegate any domain to another organization. The root key is configured as trust anchor in validating DNSSEC clients. A compromised root key thus allows an attacker to fabricate malicious responses with a valid DNSSEC signature, e.g. as part of a man-in-the-middle attack. Apart from the threat of key theft, the organizations handling the root key are entrusted not to misuse the key for actions that are not in accordance with objectives of the global DNS community. This includes not to use the root authority as a political instrument for influencing Internet governance. Name resolution without root removes this burden of trust in influential institutions.

Reliability. Another factor is reliability, as the availability of DNS depends on the availability of the root. Techniques like caching and anycast [1] are used to reduce the load on root or add redundancy. Though this cushions the impact of malfunctions or denial of service attacks, the threat remains in principle. A rootless name resolution can serve as backup mechanism to ensure DNS service availability in case of severe failures of the root.

Use case. One of the possible use cases of a rootless DNS are redundant domain names. For example, consider the name "`www.example.br+pl+cz`" as three distinct names `www.example.br`, `www.example.pl` and `www.example.cz` that should all evaluate to the same IP address. Whenever a client resolves a redundant name, e.g. in a weblink or in the configuration of an email client, the client performs a majority voting over all three domains. With rootless DNS and redundant domain names, there is no single entity that has the power to misdirect the name resolution.

3   Background

3.1   DNS and DNSSEC

The DNS architecture consists of resolvers (clients) and name servers. The hierarchical namespace is structured as a tree, which is cut into non-overlapping zones. A *zone* is a collection of domain names below a particular part of the namespace, e.g. `com` or `example.net`. Zones contain either the actual data entities or delegate subparts of the namespace to other name servers. The root of the

Root

Top-level

2nd level

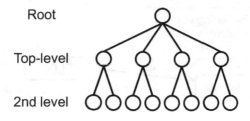

Fig. 1. DNSSEC trust model.

DNS tree comprises the root zone, which delegates TLDs like com or uk to the corresponding TLD name servers. A *delegation* consists of a set of authoritative name servers for the child zone and their IP addresses.

The DNS Security Extensions (DNSSEC) introduce public-key cryptography into that system. The trust model builds on top of the hierarchical namespace, as shown in Fig. 1. Domain name records are signed with the private key of the zone administrator and resolvers verify the signature after the corresponding public key has been authenticated. Delegations additionally contain the fingerprint (hash value) of the public key of the child zone. Thus, resolvers authenticate zone keys by following the chain of keys up to the root, which is signed by a key known to the resolver. Such a well-known key serves as *trust anchor*.

3.2   Root Zone Management

Several entities are involved in the management and operation of the root zone. TLD operators request changes of TLD delegations from the *Internet Corporation for Assigned Names and Numbers* (ICANN) respectively its close affiliate *Public Technical Identifiers* (PTI), who manages the TLD contacts and delegations [2]. ICANN/PTI vets change requests for technical and formal correctness and forwards them to Verisign, who implements the change in the root zone and distributes it to the operators of the 13 root name servers. ICANN is a U.S.-based non-profit organization and Verisign is a U.S.-based corporation. 7 root name servers are operated by U.S.-based organizations, 3 are operated by U.S. governmental or military agencies, and the operators of the remaining 3 servers are located in Sweden, the Netherlands and Japan, respectively. Historically, the U.S. government oversaw the root zone operation, but stepped back from this role in October 2016.

There are two root DNSSEC keys: the root *Key Signing Key* (KSK) is configured as trust anchor on DNSSEC validators worldwide. ICANN stores the private part of the root KSK at two redundant colocation facilities and uses it for authorization of the root *Zone Signing Key* (ZSK), which is replaced regularly in the root zone. Verisign owns the private part of the root ZSK and uses it for signing the root zone contents, which have been provided and approved by ICANN respectively its affiliate PTI. Both the root KSK and ZSK are technically eligible for signing and authenticating any domain or any TLD delegation.

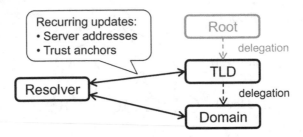

Fig. 2. Name resolution without asking root. Resolvers query TLD servers regularly for the current TLD server set (*priming*) and the current TLD key set (*trust anchor update*).

4   Approach

The name resolution that we intend in our approach is shown in Fig. 2: resolvers skip the root and start name resolution at top level, which is one level below root. The resolvers must hold the information that would be otherwise served by root: the names of the TLDs, the set of authoritative name servers and their IP addresses, and the copy or a secure fingerprint of the TLD public key. The challenge of our approach is for resolvers to keep this information up-to-date, as TLD delegations occasionally change. We show that it is possible to update the TLD server addresses (Sect. 4.2) and trust anchors (Sect. 4.3) without asking or trusting root.

4.1   Bootstrapping

Bootstrapping is the process of initializing a rootless resolver with the TLD del-egation data required for resolving domain names. The secure retrieval of trust anchors is sensitive in particular because a successful attack at this point com-promises the security of DNSSEC. The bootstrapping must be performed once at the installation time of a DNS resolver. At this point the user or system administrator relies on their operating system vendor or a DNS software vendor to retrieve the resolver software. This is a trusted path to ensure that the behav-ior of the resolver is not manipulated, otherwise this would nullify any security mechanisms like DNSSEC validation. In present-day DNS, the resolver software is shipped with the IP addresses of the root name servers and the root KSK as trust anchor. Our approach complements this existing bootstrapping channel with a list of TLDs, each with an initial set of TLD servers and a TLD trust anchor. The system can bootstrap from aged data within certain limitations (cf. Sect. 4.4), e.g. from a USB stick or another physical storage medium obtained from a software vendor.

An alternative bootstrapping channel is by manual intervention, i.e. a person inspects and copies the TLD trust anchor and server addresses from a source deemed to be trusted. TLD operators should foster the dissemination of their

TLD delegation data over several publication channels, e.g. on their website, by sending changes via email or snail mail to subscribers, or by offering voice message via telephone. Though none of these individual methods is inherently secure, each of them contributes to a human decision whether the data is sufficiently trusted. Manual bootstrapping is cumbersome and we expect that the general user base will not use it, though individual operators of high-value resolvers e.g. in industry or government networks have the possibility to do so. The target audience of manual bootstrapping are vendors of DNS software and network appliances, who redistribute the TLD data over their automated software update mechanisms.

4.2   Priming

Resolvers perform priming to initialize an empty cache after startup with information about which server to ask first during name resolution. In present-day DNS, resolvers send priming queries to one of the root name servers [3], with the IP addresses given in a configuration file `root.hints` or built into the resolver software. The query asks for the set of authoritative name servers for the root domain (". IN NS"). The response contains the root server names together with their IPv4 and IPv6 addresses (so called *glue records*). In our approach, resolvers skip root and ask each TLD for their authoritative name servers ("tld IN NS"). The TLD server addresses have been initially retrieved during bootstrapping. When the priming query times out due to an IP address change in the meantime, the resolver retries with another known TLD server address. The priming response will be cached for the time interval indicated by the Time-to-Live (TTL) field. Subsequent queries for another name under the same TLD will be thus served without priming. When different TLDs are being queried, each TLD will be primed once and remain in cache until the TTL times out or the resolver shuts down.

The priming response contains the set of name servers that are currently authoritative for the TLD, together with the glue records of these servers. In our approach, priming responses are supposed to be signed with DNSSEC and are validated with the trust anchor for the respective TLD, which has been retrieved during bootstrapping. Though the server names are signed, the IP addresses are not because DNSSEC does not sign glue records by design. Our approach does not intend to change the DNSSEC signing or validation semantics; instead, resolvers emit follow-up resolution attempts for each server name to one of the TLD servers. Thus, resolvers will validate all contents of the priming response, including the authenticity of the name-to-IP-address mapping at the cost of additional network queries (one per each server name).

Once the priming response has been received and all server names have been resolved and validated, resolvers store the new server addresses locally for later access. Whenever the TLD operator adds or replaces a server IP address, the change will be distributed to all resolvers with the next priming query and response. Thereby the TLD server addresses, which may change over time, are kept up-to-date with an in-band update mechanism.

4.3   Updating Trust Anchors

In the rootless approach, resolvers use locally stored TLD public keys as trust anchors. DNSSEC-signed responses are validated by authenticating the chain of keys from some leaf domain `www.example.tld` up to a TLD trust anchor. In normal operation, trust anchors and other keys must be replaced periodically to avoid that a key is broken eventually. The key replacement procedure is called *key rollover* and does not replace keys at an instant of time, but gradually introduces a new key and then withdraws the old key. RFC 5011 [4] specifies an automated update mechanism for trust anchors, which we utilize to keep the TLD trust anchors up-to-date. Resolvers regularly retrieve the set of all TLD keys by querying for "`tld IN DNSKEY`". The TLD operator may introduce new keys into the set, as long as the set is signed by the established TLD trust anchor. The new key cannot be used for signing zone data for a hold-down time of 30 days while resolvers learn of the new key soon to be used. The resolver will thus store two redundant trust anchors for a TLD, both authorized for signing operations. In order to remove a deprecated trust anchor, the TLD operator sets a revocation flag in the key set to indicate which key is ought to be deleted. Resolvers check the integrity and authenticity of the revocation flag during DNSSEC validation.

4.4   Opt-In and Commitment

The rootless name resolution is designed as opt-in service for both, TLD operators and resolver operators. Our motivation for an optional service is as follows:

- It allows gradual and parallel deployment in the existing DNSSEC ecosystem.
- TLD operators that opt-in are making a commitment to serve stable parameters over an extended period of time. If they cannot or do not want to commit, they should not opt-in.
- Resolver operators decide whether the rootless approach is useful to them, e.g. subject to a trust assessment in root.

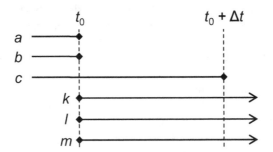

Fig. 3. IP address update scheme for TLDs.

TLD operators indicate support by setting a flag in a special-purpose DNS record in the TLD zone, e.g. by reutilizing the TXT record or by specifying a dedicated AUTONOMOUS record type. Furthermore, TLD operators cooperate with DNS software vendors to publish their bootstrapping data. When the opt-in flag is set, the TLD operator commits to operate long-lived name servers and trust anchors. The commitment period Δt is configurable per TLD in the above-mentioned record. The commitment applies to server IP addresses and trust anchors so that resolvers will know when to refresh a TLD before potential expiration.

When a TLD operators intends to replace all server **IP addresses**, they must continue to operate at least one server on an old IP address for at least Δt. However, with n server addresses, up to $n - 1$ addresses can be removed or replaced without any special considerations. An example is shown in Fig. 3: addresses a and b are removed, while address c is held back for Δt. Thus the priming succeeds and resolvers will learn of newly introduced server IP addresses k, l and m, which they can subsequently use.

TLD operators must retain a **trust anchors** for signing for at least Δt (though different Δt values can be used for IP addresses and trust anchors). Unlike server IP addresses, there is typically only one established trust anchor for a domain, but otherwise the same considerations as above apply. When replacing trust anchors periodically, there must be an overlap of Δt of the old and new key so that resolvers will authenticate newly introduced keys with the trust anchor previously known to them.

We can formalize the commitment period as

$$\exists x \in RESP : active(x) > \Delta t, \tag{1}$$

where $RESP$ is the set of parameters publicly released in priming or trust anchor responses, $active(x)$ is the lifetime of a parameter x (IP address or trust anchor) before changing or removing it. The rootless approach will be self-sustaining if resolvers manage to run the priming and trust anchor update every $\Delta u \leq \Delta t$. Our recommendation is to specify an ample commitment period of $\Delta t = 1$ year to account for extended offline times of resolvers running on end-user devices. Most TLDs already fulfill this commitment as we show in the feasibility study in Sect. 6. If a resolver is offline for $> \Delta t$, it may miss an update and will need to bootstrap the TLD data from scratch.

5   Security Discussion

Trust. By cutting off root, we have eliminated a single point of trust. The trust model is still a hierarchical one, separately for each TLD. Each TLD is a point of trust on its own, because each operator is able to tamper with their registered domains. However, this has been true before, thus our approach does not create any new attack vector. The authority of a TLD operator is limited to their own namespace, whereas the authority of root includes all TLDs. Domain registrants can choose between several operators independent of each other, which are based in different countries and jurisdictions. This allows for decentralized domain setups, e.g. redundant domains under different TLDs.

TLD or resolver operators do not need to cooperate with root to deploy the rootless approach. A trusted bootstrapping channel is required to securely initialize a TLD, which constitutes a weak point of our approach. We suggest to involve the operating system or DNS software vendor for this purpose because we can reuse the existing trust relationship and communication channel that is used for distributing software security updates. Again, this does not introduce a new attack vector in addition to potential attacks that are already possible. Once bootstrapped, the system will update in-band via DNSSEC-secured communication with TLD servers. The approach is designed as opt-in service, which means that resolvers will continue to rely on root for those TLDs that have not opted-in, but the influence of root is confined to those TLDs.

Key rollovers. The commitment period Δt limits the frequency of trust anchor rollovers for TLDs. For those TLDs, which roll the key more often, this imposes a security degradation. With appropriately sized keys, a rollover every one or two years is sufficiently secure. Unscheduled emergency rollovers, though, will lead to a service degradation and resolvers will have to bootstrap that TLD again. Unscheduled key rollovers are exceptional events that should not occur on a regular basis. However, they potentially degrade the availability compared to using the root as backup authority.

Privacy. As a side effect, omitting root accounts for one fewer authority that is able to inspect query contents. This slightly improves the privacy of clients, albeit to a small degree, because queries are still transmitted in cleartext to TLDs. The effect is not identical but roughly comparable to DNS query name minimization [5], which also attempts to hide the query name from root, amongst others.

6   Feasibility Study

In this section we provide a feasibility study for our approach to a rootless DNS by analyzing the root zone development over a time period of 4 years from April 2013 to May 2017. We collected data almost daily by downloading the root zone from ICANN servers and querying TLD servers directly to gather the TLD Key Signing Keys (KSK), which are our trust anchors. The measurement period overlaps with ICANN's introduction of new generic TLDs [6]; out of 1549 TLDs in our data, the majority has been introduced since October 2013. We discard TLDs that appeared for less than one year in our data because we require longer periods of time for evaluation of long-term behavior. This yields a data set of 1317 TLDs for this study, composed of 306 old and 1011 new TLDs.

6.1   Frequency of IP Address Changes

First we determine the period after when a TLD has replaced all of their server IP addresses. This enables us to approximate a threshold of how long a resolver may be offline until it will be unable to find the servers of a TLD using priming when

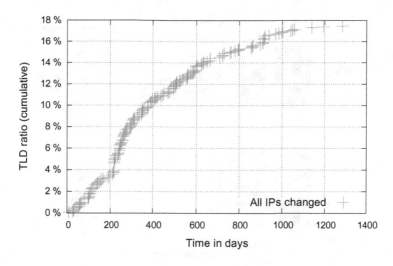

Fig. 4. Duration after when TLDs replaced all IP addresses ($N = 1317$).

getting back online. If the resolver looses track of the current server IP addresses, it will need to bootstrap again with the mechanism explained in Sect. 4.1.

Figure 4 shows the cumulated amount of TLDs, whose set of IPv4 and IPv6 addresses had completely changed after a period shown on the x-axis. Altogether 233 TLDs (17.7%) changed their server IP addresses completely during the measurement. Most of these were new TLDs, whose operations may not have matured yet; 26 old TLDs (2%) changed their whole server address set. For the other 1084 TLDs (82.3%) at least one IP address lasted for the whole measurement duration. The majority of TLDs would have thus been reachable with rootless DNS even without any recurring priming queries during our measurement period.

Considering the lifetime of IP addresses, 943 TLDs (71.6%) kept *each* of their addresses for ≥ 1 year. Thus, the majority overfulfills our requirement of committing to at least *one* IP address for $\Delta t \geq 1$ year.

Whether a TLD becomes unavailable for a rootless resolver depends on its update interval Δu. The update interval limits the maximum tolerable offline time of a resolver, since the device must be powered on and connected to the Internet to perform the update. We now simulate different intervals $\Delta u \in \{365, 90, 14, 7, 1\}$ (in days) for the periodic priming queries. The simulation is driven with our real-world measurement data and checks all possible offsets, e.g. for $\Delta u = 14$ days we conduct 14 simulations starting on day $1, 2, \ldots,$ 14. We consider the worst-case result, i.e. a TLD is unavailable if at least one of simulation offsets looses track of the server IP addresses.

Figure 5 shows the result subject to different Δu. Running priming once in year slightly improves the availability over running no updates at all, but 221 TLDs (16.8%) become unavailable eventually. Reducing the update interval steadily decreases the amount of TLDs that the resolver would have lost track of. However, even with daily priming 147 TLDs (11.2%) would have become

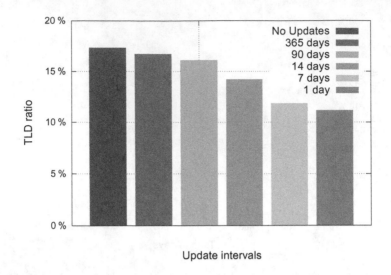

Fig. 5. Ratio of unavailable TLDs subject to resolver update intervals.

unavailable because they replaced all server IP addresses at once. Note that these are conservative estimations because our data does not cover whether the TLD operator continued to serve the old IP addresses after switching to new addresses. It is good operational practice to maintain servers on both IP address sets for a transition period (e.g. used by the D-root server operator [7]) and this might actually mitigate an outage of our rootless approach.

6.2   Frequency of Trust Anchors Rollover

In the following study we analyze how often TLD operators replaced the trust anchor (i.e. the public *Key Signing Key* or KSK) within our 4-year observation.

Note that not all TLDs are already signed with DNSSEC: we consider 1174 TLDs (89.1%) in this study that were signed for at least part of our observation period.

Figure 6 shows the average lifetime of a KSK before being replaced. The first thing to notice is that 351 TLDs (29.9%) never replaced the KSK during our observation period. An additional 488 TLDs (41.6%) replaced the KSK, but less often than once a year, i.e. maintained one key for more than one year on average. Thus, 839 TLDs (71.5%) satisfy our proposed commitment period Δt in our observation on average.

A minority of TLDs rolls their keys very frequently: 175 TLDs (14.9%) replaced their KSK every 90 days or less. These operators would have to roll their KSK less often if they chose to opt-in. Instead, the operators could increase the KSK bit length to compensate for long-lived keys.

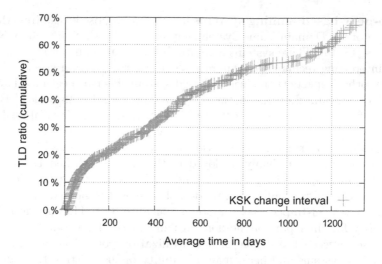

Fig. 6. KSK change interval of TLDs ($N = 1174$).

6.3 Efficiency

The rootless approach requires periodic retrieval of TLD server IP addresses and trust anchors. However, regular domain name lookups below a TLD require these queries anyway. When a TLD is in active use, the message overhead for the rootless approach will be insignificant compared to regular DNS operations. We leave it to future studies to validate this claim with a quantification.

The message size of TLD trust anchors increases because the rootless approach requires a continuous overlap during the commitment period when intending to replace keys regularly. This disadvantage can be mitigated by using elliptic-curve signatures, which are considerably shorter than RSA signatures with a similar level of security [8].

7   Related Work

Alternative DNS roots have emerged in the past, which were operated independently from the ICANN-coordinated root. Mueller [9] explained in 2002 that competing DNS roots were caused by a disjunction between the demand for and supply of new TLDs. ICANN introduced 15 new generic TLDs in 2000, 2004 and 2011 and is in the process of introducing more than thousand new TLDs [6] since 2013. The Open Root Server Network (ORSN) [10] is an alternative DNS root that was created explicitly for strategical reasons only and without serving any other data than the ICANN root. The objective of ORSN is to create a counterpart, independent of any influence from the ICANN root. Our approach differs from the concept of competing roots by eliminating the need for a central root authority.

Peer-to-peer-based naming systems have been proposed to address the centralization of the Domain Name System, e.g. CoDoNS [11], Namecoin, GNS [12] and others [13–15]. These systems are entirely different than the DNS, allowing to take interesting technological approaches to improve certain aspects, but are weaker in other aspects than a server-based system. Peer-to-peer-based systems require a decentralized overlay network, e.g. a distributed hash table (DHT), to achieve its function cooperatively without a central instance. Typical weak spots of DHT-based systems are higher lookup latency, loss of locality and loss of resistance against sybil attacks. Our solution in this paper is a small improvement but one that can be gradually deployed in the well-established DNS, sharing the existing namespace, infrastructure and performance characteristics. While we omit the central root authority, we do not achieve the same degree of decentralization like peer-to-peer-based systems, because each TLD operator is still an authority for their part of the domain namespace. Thus, our approach is a compromise between the degree of decentralization/control achieved by peer-to-peer-based systems and performance/stability of the existing Domain Name System.

Massey et al. [16] identified that the tree-based DNSSEC trust model is detrimental due to a single point of failure and undesirable trust relationships. They discussed the web of trust and mesh of trust approaches, which allow for trust relationships that do not follow the hierarchical namespace.

Malone [17] suggested to distribute a copy of the root zone to resolvers for improving performance and scalability. There is no trust improvement because the root zone is copied from the root authority without changes.

Kuerbis and Mueller [18] proposed to distribute the root signing authority to different actors to increase transparency and eliminate the threat of political interference. ICANN is using a centralized root signing procedure instead, but they invite community representatives to participate as independent bystanders or recovery key holders [2] for the sake of transparency. With our rootless approach, the power of the root authority is inherently distributed to independent TLD operators.

8   Conclusions

Our analysis has shown that a rootless DNS/DNSSEC can be implemented with minimal changes to the existing infrastructure. Already today, most TLD operators are handling IP address updates (82%) and key rollovers (72%) in sufficiently large intervals. Those TLD operators who change IP addresses or keys more frequently could continue to do so, because our approach is entirely opt-in. Both, TLD providers and client-side resolver operators can decide whether or not to use the rootless name resolution. This allows a smooth phase-in of our proposed approach and coexistence in the same DNS ecosystem without having to switch to another naming system.

The benefit of rootless DNS is that we moved from a centralized to a decentralized trust model. That means there is no longer a single entity controlling the entire namespace. The primary stakeholders are providers and users of country-code TLDs, who are able to operate a stable naming infrastructure autonomously without potential interference from root. Though we are focusing on top-level providers, the rootless approach could be used on lower levels in the DNS hierarchy as well.

In a next step, we want to evaluate how such a system performs when the DNS resolvers are located on end-user devices. As of today, clients typically rely on their network operator to resolve and validate domain names. Name resolution on user devices allows end-to-end security with DNSSEC, for example when authenticating digital certificates via *DNS-Based Authentication of Named Entities* (DANE). However, this increases the load on TLD servers since each client has to run the update procedure as described in this paper. It would be interesting to quantify the efficiency of the rootless approach with practical evaluations.

References

1. Abley, J., Lindqvist, K.: Operation of Anycast Services. RFC 4786 (Best Current Practice), Internet Engineering Task Force, December 2006. http://www.ietf.org/rfc/rfc4786.txt
2. Root Zone KSK Policy Management Authority: DNSSEC Practice Statement for the Root Zone KSK Operator, October 2016. https://www.iana.org/dnssec/icann-dps.txt
3. Koch, P., Larson, M., Hoffman, P.: Initializing a DNS Resolver with Priming Queries. RFC 8109, March 2017. http://www.ietf.org/rfc/rfc8109.txt
4. St.Johns, M.: Automated Updates of DNS Security (DNSSEC) Trust Anchors. RFC 5011, Internet Engineering Task Force, September 2007. http://www.ietf.org/rfc/rfc5011.txt
5. Bortzmeyer, S.: DNS Query Name Minimisation to Improve Privacy. RFC 7816 (Experimental), Internet Engineering Task Force, March 2016. http://www.ietf.org/rfc/rfc7816.txt
6. Internet Corporation For Assigned Names and Numbers: New Generic Top-Level Domains. https://newgtlds.icann.org
7. Lentz, M., Levin, D., Castonguay, J., Spring, N., Bhattacharjee, B.: D-mystifying the D-root address change. In: Proceedings of the 2013 Conference on Internet Measurement Conference, IMC 2013, pp. 57–62. ACM, New York (2013)
8. van Rijswijk-Deij, R., Sperotto, A., Pras, A.: Making the case for elliptic curves in DNSSEC. SIGCOMM Comput. Commun. Rev. **45**(5), 13–19 (2015). http://doi.acm.org/10.1145/2831347.2831350
9. Mueller, M.L.: Competing DNS roots: creative destruction or just plain destruction. J. Netw. Ind. **3**, 313 (2002)
10. Open Root Server Network. http://www.orsn.org
11. Ramasubramanian, V., Sirer, E.G.: The design and implementation of a next generation name service for the internet. In: ACM SIGCOMM Computer Communication Review, vol. 34, no. 4, pp. 331–342. ACM (2004)
12. Wachs, M., Schanzenbach, M., Grothoff, C.: A censorship-resistant, privacy-enhancing and fully decentralized name system. In: Gritzalis, D., Kiayias, A., Askoxylakis, I. (eds.) CANS 2014. LNCS, vol. 8813, pp. 127–142. Springer, Cham (2014). https://doi.org/10.1007/978-3-319-12280-9_9

13. Cox, R., Muthitacharoen, A., Morris, R.T.: Serving DNS using a peer-to-peer lookup service. In: Druschel, P., Kaashoek, F., Rowstron, A. (eds.) IPTPS 2002. LNCS, vol. 2429, pp. 155–165. Springer, Heidelberg (2002). https://doi.org/10.1007/3-540-45748-8_15

14. Theimer, M., Jones, M.: Overlook: scalable name service on an overlay network. In: Proceedings of the 22nd International Conference on Distributed Computing Systems, pp. 52–61 (2002)

15. Danielis, P., Altmann, V., Skodzik, J., Wegner, T., Koerner, A., Timmermann, D.: P-DONAS: a P2P-based domain name system in access networks. ACM Trans. Internet Technol. **15**(3), 11:1–11:21 (2015). http://doi.acm.org/10.1145/2808229

16. Massey, D., Lewis, E., Gudmundsson, O., Mundy, R., Mankin, A.: Public key validation for the DNS security extensions. In: Proceedings of the DARPA Information Survivability Conference & amp; Exposition II, DISCEX 2001, vol. 1, pp. 227–238. IEEE (2001)

17. Malone, D.: The root of the matter: hints or slaves. In: Proceedings of the 4th ACM SIGCOMM Conference on Internet Measurement, IMC 2004, pp. 15–20. ACM, New York (2004)

18. Kuerbis, B., Mueller, M.: Securing the root: a proposal for distributing signing authority. Paper IGP07-002 (2007)

Data Hiding on Social Media Communications Using Text Steganography

Hung-Jr Shiu[1], Bor-Shing Lin[2], Bor-Shyh Lin[3], Po-Yang Huang[1],
Chien-Hung Huang[4(✉)], and Chin-Laung Lei[1]

[1] DCNS Laboratory, Graduate Institute of Electrical Engineering,
National Taiwan University, Taipei 10617, Taiwan
[2] Department of Computer Science and Information Engineering,
National Taipei University, New Taipei City 23741, Taiwan
[3] Institute of Imaging and Biomedical Photonics,
National Chiao Tung University, Tainan 71101, Taiwan
[4] Department of Computer Science and Information Engineering,
National Formosa University, Huwei 63201, Yunlin County, Taiwan
chhuang@nfu.edu.tw

Abstract. This research work proposes a steganography on social media communications. Nowadays, people frequently use messenger or social network such as Skype, Line, Facebook, Whatsapp and Twitter, etc. to communicate with other people and these platforms become popular to be used to exchange secrets or preserve personal information. Personal information like accounts and passwords might not be seen and embedded to cover objects when two clients communicate to each other. Those objects shall be pictures, music, or text messages. The proposed scheme will be deployed on the cover text. A strategy is designed to increase the capacity of hidden data and try to make any simple piece of text to be the cover text; such as letters, article of news or the common messages. The new approach – Extended Line will be adopted, and then together with White Space between to increase the capacity of a text. The simulation results disclose that the algorithm not only increases the capacity, but also increases the efficiency of decoding. Moreover, it still works on any kind of cover text.

Keywords: Information protection · White space · Extended line
Text steganography · Social media

1 Introduction and Related Work

Data hiding schemes are used to hide secrets in cover media, producing stego-media. The approach enables users to discover attempts by intruders to replace original messages with fabricated content. The objective of data hiding is to increase hiding capacity while reducing the likelihood that intruders identify anything is hidden [1, 2].

Numerous researchers prefer to use popular multimedia as cover media because they are always being transmitted over the Internet and so their use minimizes the risk that intruders become aware of the stego-media that are generated from them [3]. Popular multimedia includes images, audio, video and text [4–7].

© Springer International Publishing AG, part of Springer Nature 2018
N. Cuppens et al. (Eds.): CRiSIS 2017, LNCS 10694, pp. 217–224, 2018.
https://doi.org/10.1007/978-3-319-76687-4_15

In the past years, there are many strategies proposed for text steganography [8–13]. All of them suffer OCR programs. Roy and Manasmita proposed a new hybrid model using special character, line shifting and word shifting coding techniques of text steganography [14]: for each line of the test, if two spaces exist simultaneously in the text, there are "01" embedded; if there is a special character is present after a space in the text, there are "10" embedded; if line size is smaller than the standard line size, there are "00" embedded; if line size is larger than the standard line size, there are "11" embedded. According to this method, it could be used to hide two bits for each line of a text, however, it still suffer the destruction of using OCR programs on the stego-text. Another drawback is that this method will fully depend on a structure of the cover text: it always uses the cover texts which are one sentence per line, but these texts are not so common in our daily life.

2   Methods and Algorithms

This section introduces the methodologies and algorithms of the proposed scheme. First, White-Space and Extended-Line will be described and then the steganography is provided. Finally, an example will be illustrated to understand.

2.1   White Space and Extended-Line

The White-Space has always been used to hide information by adding extra space in the text. White spaces could be placed between words, at the end of a line, or the end of a paragraph. Figure 1 demonstrates an example of White-Space method. The above is cover text and the following is stego text with white spaces added in the end of the text.

Extended-Line is a new method to hide data in text by comparing the length of a line. Suppose the text is n-bits wide, the length of each line could be longer of shorten than n bits for hiding information in text. Consider Fig. 2, the line which longer than a length c, there is a bit '1' embedded inside; and there is a bit '0' embedded inside if the line is shorter than c.

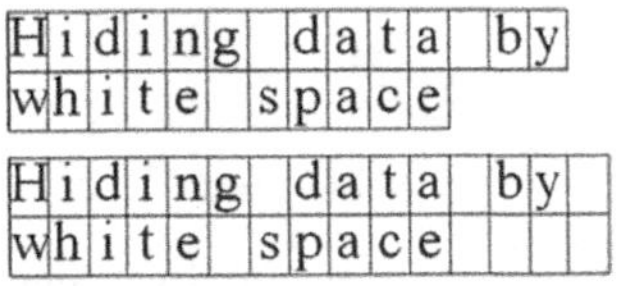

```
As you know I'll get married next   1
week and will be moving to London   1
with  my husband, I wanna thank     0
all of you for  your good wishes    0
and blessings. You've been source   1
of large joy and support in that    0
most difficult times and it deeply  1
```

Hidden message: 1100101

Fig. 1. An example of white space method. 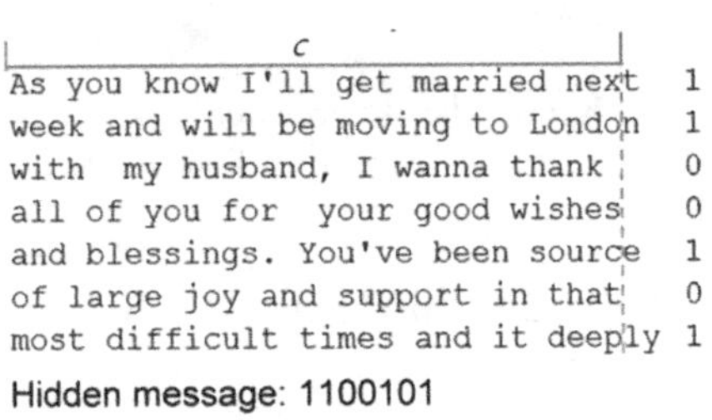   **Fig. 2.** An illustration of extended line.

2.2   Algorithms

The algorithms will be presented under a detail form as a program like. Algorithm 1 presents the embedding algorithm and Algorithm 2 presents the extracting algorithm.

Algorithm 1. The data embedding algorithm.
Input: cover text, secret message, L: bits of a line
Output: Stego-text
Variables: array pw[], array word[], done = 0, lengthOfLine = 0
Step 1.   transform the secret message into binary code by referencing ASCII;
Step 2.   check whether the stego text is done.
              if done == 1, goto Step 11;
Step 3.   if the message is end of file
                  set all pw[] = 0;
              else
                  store the first three bits of secret message in array pw[0], pw[1], and
                  pw[2];
Step 4.   if pw[0] == 1, then L = bits of a line – 1;
Step 5.   read a word from the cover text, store it in word[i], and lengthOfLine =
              lengthOfLine + length of word[i] + 1;
Step 6.   if lengthOfLine > 1
                  temp = word[i];
              else
                  go to Step 5;
Step 7.   if pw[0] == 1
                  Print the array word[] sequentially with original whitespace, and add
                  an extra whitespace between words;
              else
                  print word[] sequentially with original whitespace;
Step 8.   if pw[1] == 1
                  print temp at the end of line; lengthOfLine = 0; i = 0;
              else
                  word[0] = temp; i = 1; lengthOfLine = length of word[0];
Step 9.   if pw[2] == 1
                  add an extra space to the end of line and wrap to the next line;
              else
                  wrap to the next line;
Step 10.   If the cover text is end of file
                  done = 1;
              go to step 2;
Step 11.   end;

Algorithm 2. The data extracting algorithm
Input: Stego-text, default length of a line L
Output: Secret message
Step 1.   set pw[0] = 0, pw[1] = 0, pw[2] = 0
Step 2.   read the line from the stego text;
Step 3.   If the last character of the first line is white space, then pw[2] = 1;
Step 4.   If the length of the line is larger than L, then pw[1] = 1;
Step 5.   if there is a white space between two words, the pw[0] = 1;
Step 6.   write the pw[] array in to the password file;
Step 7.   if the stego text is not end of file, then goto step 1;
Step 8.   transfer the password file from binary code to character by ASCII table;

3 Results

This section demonstrates a real example of the proposed scheme by using the Facebook messenger. Figure 3 is the original cover text. Figure 4 is the original cover text after setting the default length of a line.

```
As you know I'll get married next week and will be moving
to London with my husband, I wanna thank all of you for
your good wishes and blessings.
You've been source of large joy and support in that most
difficult times and it deeply saddens me to leave you all.
I will remember the days in college, all that mischief we
did in that hostel and how we're there for each in times
of crisis. I wish you all the best for your future, and
hope that I can find more good friends like you in London
too. See you next summer.
```

Fig. 3. The original cover text.

In this section, the secret message "NTUEE" is going to be hidden. Use ASCII to transform "NTUEE" to 0100111001010100010101 with 'N' = 78 = 01001110, 'T' = 84 = 01010100 and 'U' = 85 = 01010101, 'E' = 69 = 01000101. Figure 5 presents the stego-text after embedding the secret messages.

The detail data embedding goes as follows.

1. The binary value of the secret values are calculated and concatenated to 0100111001010100010101010100010101000101.
2. Check the binary text three bits at once, e.g., 010.
3. Read the cover text, and set the value L (the bits of a line), e.g., the cover text, $L = 32$.
4. If the first bit is '1', then it will add an extra white space at the random place between two words at the line.
   If the second bit is '1', then it will read one more word from cover text to let the length of line larger than L.
   If the third bit is '1', then it will add a white space at the end of line.
   Otherwise, the line of the cover text will output normally, in the other word, there are no extra white spaces in the line, and the length of the line will be less than L.

The corresponding extraction procedure goes as follows.

1. The stego file is take as Fig. 6.
2. Read the line from the stego text.
3. If the last character of the first line is white space, then pw[2] = 1. e.g. pw[2] = 0 at first time.
4. If the length of the line is larger than L, then pw[1] = 1. e.g. pw[1] = 0 at first line.
5. If there is a white space between two words, the pw[0] = 1. e.g. pw[0] = 0.
6. Save the first three bits according to pw[0], pw[1], and pw[2]. e.g. the first three bits are "010".

7. Go to step 2 until the stego text is end of file.
8. Transfer the binary code to character by ASCII table and print out.

```
As you know I'll get married
next week and will be moving to
London with my husband, I wanna
thank all of you for your good
wishes and blessings. You've
been source of large joy and
support in that most difficult
times and it deeply saddens me
to leave you all. I will
remember the days in college,
all that mischief we did in that
hostel and how we're there for
each in times of crisis. I wish
you all the best for your
future, and hope that I can find
more good friends like you in
London too. See you next summer.
```

Fig. 4. Cover text.

```
As you know I'll get married next
week and will be moving to London
with  my husband, I wanna thank
all of you for  your good wishes
and blessings. You've been source
of large joy and support in that
most difficult times and it deeply
saddens me to leave  you all. I
will remember the days in college,
all that mischief we did in that
hostel and how we're there for each
in times  of crisis. I wish you
all the best for your future, and
hope that I  can find more good
friends like you in London too.
See you next summer.
```

Fig. 5. Stego-text after embedding "NTUEE"

```
As you know I'll get married next
week and will be moving to London□
with  my husband, I wanna thank
all of you for  your good wishes□
and blessings. You've been source
of large joy and support in that□
most difficult times and it deeply
saddens me to leave  you all. I□
will remember the days in college,
all that mischief we did in that□
hostel and how we're there for each
in times  of crisis. I wish you□
all the best for your future, and
hope that I  can find more good
friends like you in London too.
See you next summer.
```

Fig. 6. Stego text with white space and *L*.

We exploited the technology on Facebook, which is one of the most popular social media communication tools. The experiment is implemented using Sikuli script. The transmitted cover text is the same of the above example and the secret messages are also "NTUEE". The developed script procedures go as follows. Figure 7 demonstrates the stego transmission of the Facebook messager.

Moreover, the application does not need to transfer the stego-text to image file such that it can be deployed on social media messenger or communication tools. Also, without using OCR, the efficiency of encoding and decoding would be higher and the disadvantages of using OCR will no longer exist.

Fig. 7. An experimental example of the proposed scheme on Facebook messenger.

4 Discussions

This section provides performance analysis and comparisons to related works. At first, suppose that the average number of letters per word is 5, and the average number of words per sentence is 15, thus the average number of characters per sentence is as follows: the average number of characters per sentence = the average number of letters per word × the average number of words per sentence + the average number of white space between words per sentence + the size of new line character = 90. The data rate is as follow: data rate = *the number of hidden bits per sentence*/the average number of bits per sentence = *the number of hidden bits*/(8×90). According to some existing algorithms [10] based on White-Space between words or White-Space at the end of line, the drawback of the algorithm is inefficient because it needs a large amount of text to encode a few bits and then one bit per sentence is equal to the data rate of one bit per 720 bits approximately. Algorithms proposed in [14] is a hybrid mode using special character, Line-Shifting and Word-Shifting coding techniques of text steganography. They are used to hide two bits per sentence. Algorithms proposed here are used to hide two bits in a sentence while the data rate will perform better than other methods when the length of a line is small. Table 1 presents the data rate between [10, 14] and the proposed scheme. Figure 8 illustrates the differences between data rate and the number of words in a line. The proposed algorithm hides two bits per line, not two bits per sentence. It means that if L (the number of characters per line) is smaller, the capacity of the same cover text will be larger. Just like the example provided, the L is assign roughly 32, and the data rate will be raised to 2 bits per 256 bits which is almost 8 times to 1 bit per 720 bits. In general, assume that the number of words per line is n, and the capacity of the proposed algorithm is as follows: data rate = *the number of hidden bits per line*/*the number of bits per line* = $2/(8 \times$ *the average number of characters per line*) = $3/8(6n-1)$. By changing the number of words per line, obviously, the data rate increases when the number of words per line decreases.

Table 1. The capacity comparison of the proposed and related

Method	Shahreza et al. [13]	Roy et al. [14]	Proposed method
data rate (*bits/bits*)	1/720	2/720	2/720 (minimum)

Distortion issues such as PSNR are often provided to evaluate the performance of the proposed research works, however, the application here does not based on image. Text steganography will also consider the distortion evaluation of digital media because some stego-texts are finally transformed to images. Here the proposed scheme does not output image but purely text files. In order to evaluate the same concepts of distortion, another measurement is provided here, that is, the change of size between cover text and stego-text. Suppose the number of words per line in cover text is 15, so the number of white spaces between words per line in cover text is $15 - 1$; the size of new-line character is one byte. Hence, the file size of cover text is $(5 \times 15 + (15 - 1) + 1) \times h = 90h$, where h is the number of lines in the cover text. Assume the probability of adding a white space between words each line and adding a white space end of line each line are both ½, the expected value of an extra space is 1, i.e. $\frac{1}{2} \times 2$. Thus, the file size of stego-text is: $\left(\frac{1}{2} \times 2 + (5 \times n + (n - 1) + 1)\right) \frac{15}{n} h = \frac{15(6n+1)h}{n}$, where n is the number of words per line in stego-text. Finally, the change rate of file size is as follows: the change rate of file size = *the file size of stego-text/the file size of cover text* = $\frac{\frac{15(6n+1)h}{n}}{90h} = 1 + \frac{1}{6n}$. By changing the number of words per line, obviously the change rate of file size decreases when the number of words per line increases as shown in Fig. 9.

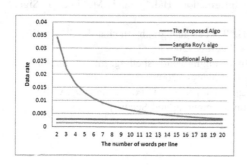

Fig. 8. Data rate comparisons.

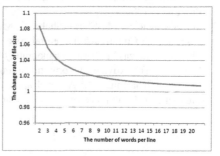

Fig. 9. Change rate curve.

5 Conclusions

In this paper, a new approach for text steganography is proposed. A binary bitstream transformed from secret messages by referencing ASCII is embedded in a cover text. Adopting White-Space between words and Extended-Line makes the capacity high and flexible under modifying the length per line. Experiments demonstrate the feasibility of the scheme and the performance is analyzed and compared between related works. The results disclose that the proposed scheme performs better than others under short line of a cover text.

References

1. Katzenbeisser, S., Petitcolas, F.A.P.: Information Hiding Techniques for Steganography and Digital Watermarking. Artech House, Norwood (2000)
2. Petitcolas, F.A.P., Anderson, R.J., Kuhn, M.G.: Information hiding: a survey. Proc. IEEE (Spec. Issue) **87**, 1062–1078 (1999)
3. Li, B., He, J., Huang, J., Shi, Y.Q.: A survey on image steganography and steganalysis. J. Inf. Hiding Multimedia Signal Process. **2**, 142–172 (2011)
4. Bender, W., Morimoto, N., Lu, A.: Techniques for data hiding. IBM Syst. J. **35**, 313–336 (1996)
5. Shiu, H.J., Tang, S.Y., Huang, C.H., Lee, R.C.T., Lei, C.L.: A reversible acoustic data hiding method based on analog modulation. Inf. Sci. **273**, 233–246 (2014)
6. Shiu, H.J., Lin, B.S., Cheng, C.W., Huang, C.H., Lei, C.L.: High-capacity data-hiding scheme on synthesized pitches using amplitude enhancement-a new vision of non-blind audio steganography. Symmetry **9**(6), 92–111 (2017)
7. Shiu, H.J., Ng, K.L., Fang, J.F., Lee, R.C.T., Huang, C.H.: Data hiding methods based upon DNA sequences. Inf. Sci. **180**, 2196–2208 (2010)
8. Rafat, K.F.: Enhanced text steganography in SMS. In: 2nd International Conference on Computer, Control and Communication (2009)
9. Shirali-Shahreza, M., Shirali-Shahreza, M.H.: A new approach to Persian/Arabic text steganography. In: 5th IEEE/ACIS International Conference on Computer and Information Science (2006)
10. Shirali-Shahreza, M., Shirali-Shahreza, M.H.: Text steganography in SMS. In: 2007 International Conference on Convergence Information Technology (2007)
11. Shirali-Shahreza, M., Shirali-Shahreza, M.H.: A new synonym text steganography. In: International Conference on Intelligent Information Hiding and Multimedia Signal Processing (2008)
12. Shirali-Shahreza, M., Shirali-Shahreza, M.H.: Text steganography in chat. In: 3rd IEEE/IFIP International Conference in Central Asia on Internet (2007)
13. Shirali-Shahreza, M.: Test steganography by changing words spelling. In: 10th International Conference on Advanced Communication Technology (2008)
14. Roy, S., Manasmita, M.: A novel approach to format based text steganography. In: 2011 International Conference on Communication, Computing and Security (2011)

Risk Analysis

Privacy Scoring of Social Network User Profiles Through Risk Analysis

Sourya Joyee De[2](✉) and Abdessamad Imine[1,2](✉)

[1] Lorraine University, Nancy, France
abdessamad.imine@loria.fr
[2] LORIA-INRIA Nancy Grand-Est, Villers-lès-Nancy, France
sourya-joyee.de@inria.fr

Abstract. The social benefit derived from online social networks (OSNs) can lure users to reveal unprecedented volumes of personal data to a social graph that is much less trustworthy than the offline social circle. Although OSNs provide users privacy configuration settings to protect their data, these settings are not sufficient to prevent all situations of sensitive information disclosure. Indeed, users can become the victims of harms such as identity theft, stalking or discrimination. In this work, we design a privacy scoring mechanism inspired by privacy risk analysis (PRA) to guide users to understand the various privacy problems they may face. Concepts, derived from existing works in PRA, such as privacy harms, risk sources and harm trees are adapted in our mechanism to compute privacy scores. However, unlike existing PRA methodologies, our mechanism is user-centric. More precisely, it analyzes only OSN user profiles taking into account the choices made by the user and his vicinity regarding the visibility of their profile attributes to potential risk sources within their social graphs. To our best knowledge, our work is the first effort in adopting PRA approach for user-centric analysis of OSN privacy risks.

Keywords: Online social networks (OSN) · Privacy harms
Privacy score · Harm trees · Privacy risk analysis (PRA)

1 Introduction

Users reveal personal data, build their social graphs and affiliate to groups to derive various social benefits (such as connecting to offline friends, establishing new connections) from their online social network (OSN) profiles. It is possible to infer various personal data of a user not only from the values of the OSN profile attributes (such as birth year, home address, work place, education) revealed by the user himself, but also from those revealed by his friends and from group affiliations [2,14,24]. Moreover, members of the social graph may be complete strangers, future employers, colleagues, relatives, etc., from whom various privacy risks may arise. For example, in his workplace, an employee may withhold

This work is partially funded by MAIF Foundation.

© Springer International Publishing AG, part of Springer Nature 2018
N. Cuppens et al. (Eds.): CRiSIS 2017, LNCS 10694, pp. 227–243, 2018.
https://doi.org/10.1007/978-3-319-76687-4_16

some information about himself and maintain an image that is different from his personal life [11]. An OSN profile may reveal these otherwise hidden information to colleagues leading to poor impression or hurting professional growth. Users can also become the victims of harms such as identity theft, stalking, discrimination, or sexual predation. In the absence of additional support, the privacy settings provided by OSNs are not enough to mitigate these privacy problems. So, there is a need to guide users to: (1) understand the privacy problems they may face due to their actions on OSNs (such as the personal data they reveal, the social circle they build) and (2) adopt suitable preventive measures. Designing such a guidance tool is our broad aim. In this work, we focus on the first step, i.e., design a privacy scoring mechanism to compute for the users the privacy risks of their OSN profiles and social graphs.

Computation of the privacy level of an OSN user's profile in terms of privacy metrics has recently drawn the attention of researchers [13,15,17,18,20,22]. In contrast to these works, our privacy scoring mechanism is inspired by privacy risk analysis (PRA) [3–5,9]. A PRA methodology helps service providers to assess the privacy risks of information systems that process personal data. Such methodologies are gaining focus as the EU General Data Protection Regulation (GDPR) mandates the conduction of a data protection impact assessment[1] for service providers with certain categories of personal data processing.

In this work, we adopt the PRA approach in designing our privacy scoring mechanism to assist users (instead of the service provider), borrowing concepts like privacy harms, risk sources and harm trees from [5–7]. Unlike existing PRA methodologies, we do not consider the entire OSN system or risk sources like hackers or the service provider and ignore privacy weaknesses [5] introduced by the service provider's choices during system design and implementation. Instead, we focus on the choices made by the user and his friends regarding the visibility of their profile attributes to potential risk sources already in their social graph. To the best of our knowledge, our work is the first effort in utilizing PRA concepts for user-centric analysis of OSN privacy risks based on the visibility of attribute values.

We introduce the main ingredients of our privacy scoring mechanism in Sect. 2 and discuss attribute visibility from an OSN user profile in Sect. 3. In Sect. 4 we present our privacy scoring mechanism. Finally, in Sect. 5 we discuss related works and conclude with future directions in Sect. 6.

2   Model Ingredients

Users may publish various personal data in their OSN profiles. Various actors in the OSN may become *risk sources* processing the revealed personal data to cause a variety of *threats* that ultimately lead to *privacy harms* for the user. In what follows, we define these concepts, which form the building blocks of our privacy scoring mechanism, more formally and provide appropriate examples.

---

[1] The technical details of a privacy impact assessment (PIA) are referred to as privacy risk analysis (PRA) [5,6].

We represent the OSN as a graph $G = (V, E)$, where V is the set of nodes representing the users of the OSN and E is the set of edges representing the friendship links among the users. $e_{i,j} \in E$ represents a friendship link between the nodes v_i and v_j. The *target user*, denoted by v_T, represents the OSN user for whom the privacy score is being computed. We also assume that the target user has at least one friend.

Attributes and Other Personal Data. Some personal data are made available by the target user and his friends in their OSN profiles. We call these personal data *user attributes* that can be defined as:

Definition 1. *A **user attribute** is a personal data[2] item considered as a part of the user profile information. It helps to present this user to other users of the same OSN.*

Each user has a set A of profile attributes. We consider the following elements of set A: 1. Birth year (B.Yr); 2. Birthday (B.Dt); 3. Gender (Gen); 4. Phone number (Ph); 5. Gender interests (G.Int); 6. Home address (H.Add); 7. Workplace (W.Pl); 8. Work designation (W.desig); 9. Political views (Pol); 10. Religious views (Rel); 11. Relationship status (RStat); 12. Interests (Int). Each user attribute may assume different values. Other personal data such as work locality (W.Loc) can be obtained by inference from these attributes. Other attributes may also be revealed in different OSNs, but we consider only this set for the current discussion. We also assume that providing a name is mandatory and can be seen by everyone on the OSN. So we do not consider it as an attribute.

Privacy Harms. We adapt the definition of privacy harm from [5–7] in the context of an OSN.

Definition 2. *A **privacy harm** is the negative impact of the use of an OSN on the target user as a result of one or more privacy breaches.*

Over the years, many types of privacy harms have been observed in real life as well as found to be possible by different research works [10–12,16,21] from the data revealed from OSNs. In this work, we consider two harms: (1) stalkers use the target user's profile to assess him as a potential victim (H.1) and (2) identity fraud/theft (H.2). Of course, the harms presented here are not exhaustive and only involve a subset of the user attributes provided above. Other harms, involving different user attributes, are possible and can be analyzed in the same way as we will show in the next sections for these representative harms.

Risk Sources. We adapt the definition of risk sources from [5–7] in the context of an OSN.

Definition 3. *A **risk source** is any entity (individual or organization) that may process (legally or illegally) data belonging to the target user and whose actions may directly or indirectly, intentionally or unintentionally lead to privacy harms.*

---

[2] According to the GDPR (General Data Protection Regulation) of European Union.

In this work, we focus on the user's social graph to find out the relevant risk sources which include: (1) friends of the target user $(A.1)$; (2) the friends of friends of the target user $(A.2)$; (3) the friends of friends of friends of the target user $(A.3)$; (4) the strangers to the target user (degrees of relationships higher than 3) $(A.4)$. These risk sources only process data already made visible to them by the user leading to various harms. For example, the colleagues of the user who are his friends in the OSN $(A.1)$ can form a negative impression about him based on his political and/or religious views or based on his interests, sexual orientation, etc., which may negatively affect him at his work-place. We ignore risk sources such as the OSN service provider, the government and hackers.

Threats. We define threats in the context of an OSN as:

Definition 4. *A **threat** is an action of a risk source with respect to one or more pieces of personal data resulting in a privacy harm.*

In the context of an OSN, threats include unintended inference of data (FE.1) (e.g., strangers infer the gender of the target user from the genders of his friends), direct access to data by unintended audiences due to similar attributes revealed by the user (FE.2) (e.g., friends of friends come to know the user's phone number), and the undesirable reactions from intended audiences (FE.3) (e.g., colleagues respond negatively to the target user's political views) [11,16,21]. We only consider threats resulting from inappropriate privacy settings used by the target user and his friends for their attributes and ignore threats originating from the service provider's design and/or implementation choices (e.g., lack of anonymization, poor protection of data stores) as we only focus on the analysis of the OSN user profile and not the entire system.

Inference of Personal Data. The attributes revealed by the target user or his friends can reveal other personal data of the target user. The attributes used for the inference could be of the same type. For example, the gender (Gen) of the target user's friends can be used to infer the gender (Gen) of the target user. It is also possible to use other types of attributes to reveal a particular personal data. For example, the work place (W.Pl), a data about the user's profession, is an indicator of the target user's work location (W.Loc), which is a location data. Sometimes, multiple attributes can be used to infer a personal data item. For example, the sexual orientation (SO) of a target user can be inferred from his gender interests (G.Int) and gender (Gen). These different types of inference methods can thus be categorized based on three criteria as follows: (1) whether the personal data is inferred *directly*, i.e., from attribute(s) revealed by the target user himself or *indirectly*, i.e., from attribute(s) revealed by the friends of the target user; (2) whether a *single* or *multiple* attribute(s) are used for the inference; (3) whether the attribute(s) used for the inference constitutes a *similar* type of personal data as the one that is being inferred or are completely *different*. Here, we only consider direct/indirect, single and similar attribute inference for user attributes and direct/indirect, single/multiple and similar/different attribute inference for other personal data not included as user attributes.

Table 1 presents the attributes that can be used to infer various types of personal data through some of the above inference methods[3]. The types of personal data (such as contact data, location data, identification data) we use are inspired from [6]. A particular personal data can be inferred using one or more inference methods. The choice of inference method depends on the availability of attribute values and the desired accuracy of inference.

Table 1. Inferring user attributes and other personal data

Personal data type	Code	User attribute or other personal data	User attribute (Target user)	User attribute (Friends)	Inference Types
Contact data	M.1	Phone no. (Ph.)	Phone no. (Ph.)	×	Direct, single, similar attribute
	M.2	Home address (H.Add)	Home address (H.Add)	×	Direct, single, similar attribute
Location data	M.3	Home locality (H.Loc)	Home address (H.Add)	Home address (H.Add)	Direct/indirect, single, different attribute
	M.4	Work locality (W.Loc)	Workplace (W.Pl)	Workplace (W.Pl)	Direct/indirect, single, different attribute
Identification data	M.5	Gender (Gen)	Gender (Gen)	Gender (Gen)	Direct/indirect, single, similar attribute
	M.6	Age (Age)	Birth year (B.Yr)	Birth year (B.Yr)	Direct/indirect, single, similar attribute
	M.7	Date of birth (DoB)	Birth year (B.Yr), Birth day (B.Dt)	×	Direct, multiple, similar attribute

3   Attribute Visibility

After assigning values to the attributes in their OSN profiles, users can select from a range of privacy settings to ensure that the attribute values are visible to desirable audiences in their social graph. Here, we consider that the user can choose from the following privacy settings, inspired from those used in Facebook:

1. *"private"*: makes an attribute value visible to no one;
2. *"friends"*: makes an attribute value visible to friends only;
3. *"friends of friends"*: makes an attribute value visible to friends and friends of friends;
4. *"public"*: makes an attribute value visible to all users of the OSN.

---

[3] In Table 1, neither the list of inference methods nor the personal data that can be inferred from the given set of attributes nor the personal data types that must be considered is exhaustive. Other inferred personal data, personal data types and inference methods can be easily incorportaed in our framework.

The visibility matrix $\mathbf{M}$ of a target user v_T displays the visibility values of all the attributes in A (the set of user attributes, see Definition 1) as given by their privacy settings chosen by v_T and his friends. Each element of the matrix is a set that denotes the members of the OSN to whom the jth attribute a_j is visible. These members are assigned based on the privacy setting of the attribute selected either by v_T or a friend of v_T. Entry $\mathbf{M(1,j)}$ represents the visibility of the jth attribute, $v_T.a_j$, as set by v_T. As for $\mathbf{M(i,j)}$, with $i > 1$, it represents the visibility of the jth attribute, $v_i.a_j$, as set by the ith friend ($i \neq 1$) of v_T (but, with respect to v_T and not themselves)[4]. Other types of privacy settings used in other OSNs can also be used to fill in $\mathbf{M}$.

For $i = 1$, i.e., for v_T himself, $\mathbf{M(i,j)}$ is assigned values as follows:

1. $\mathbf{M(i,j)} = \{\}$, if the privacy setting of $v_T.a_j$ is "private";
2. $\mathbf{M(i,j)} = \{A.1\}$, if the privacy setting of $v_T.a_j$ is "friends";
3. $\mathbf{M(i,j)} = \{A.1, A.2\}$, if the privacy setting of $v_T.a_j$ is "friends of friends";
4. $\mathbf{M(i,j)} = \{A.1, A.2, A.3, A.4\}$, if the privacy setting of $v_T.a_j$ is "public".

For $i > 1$, i.e., for the friends v_i of v_T, $\mathbf{M(i,j)}$ is assigned values as follows:

1. $\mathbf{M(i,j)} = \{\}$, if the privacy setting of $v_i.a_j$ is "private";
2. $\mathbf{M(i,j)} = \{A.1, A.2\}$, if the privacy setting of $v_i.a_j$ is "friends"[5];
3. $\mathbf{M(i,j)} = \{A.1, A.2, A.3\}$, if the privacy setting of $v_i.a_j$ is "friends of friends";
4. $\mathbf{M(i,j)} = \{A.1, A.2, A.3, A.4\}$, if the privacy setting of $v_i.a_j$ is "public".

The true visibility $Vis_{true}(v_T.a_j)$ of a target user's attribute is the same as $\mathbf{M(1,j)}$. However, its observed visibility $Vis_{obs}(v_T.a_j)$ depends on the values of $\mathbf{M(i,j)}$, for all i. For our purpose, we assume that $Vis_{obs}(v_T.a_j)$ is the set $\mathbf{M(i,j)}$ that has the maximum number of risk sources for a given attribute a_j over all i, i.e., the observed visibility is the same as the weakest privacy setting among all the privacy settings assigned to the attribute by the target user and his friends. For some attributes whose value cannot be inferred from the attribute values of the friends due to the nature of the attribute (for example, birth day (B.Dt), phone no. (Ph), etc.), $Vis_{obs}(.) = Vis_{true}(.)$.

We now show how the visibility matrix and the true and observed visibility values are computed for a target user Ana, for the attribute B.Yr, given her friendship network and the disclosure of this attribute by her and her friends in Fig. 1.

Figure 2 presents Ana's visibility matrix. The first row of the matrix, $\mathbf{M(1,B.Yr)}$, corresponds to Ana's privacy setting for B.Yr. The subsequent rows represent the privacy settings of her friends (but, with respect to her) for B.Yr. For example, Fig. 1 shows that Ana's friend Emma reveals her B.Yr to her friends. Thus, apart from Ana herself and her mutual friends with Emma, Emma's B.Yr is

---

[4] Notation wise, for simplicity, we assume that the target user is the first friend for himself, i.e., when $i = 1$, $v_i = v_T$.

[5] $A.2$ is included because a friend of v_i ($i \neq 1$) is a friend of friend of the target user.

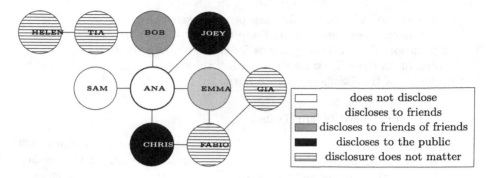

Fig. 1. The target user and its vicinty for the revelation of the attribute B.Yr

visible to Emma's friends who are friends of friends with respect to Ana. Therefore, in the visibility matrix, we fill up the row corresponding to Emma for B.Yr
with the value $\{A.1, A.2\}$ (and not $\{A.1\}$, because it is filled up from Ana's point
of view). Ana's friend Bob reveals his B.Yr to his friends of friends. From Ana's
point of view, Bob's B.Yr is visible to Ana's friends of friends of friend. So we fill
up the corresponding cell in the visibility matrix with the value $\{A.1, A.2, A.3\}$.
Ana's friend Joey reveals his B.Yr to the public (i.e., beyond friend of friend),
i.e., $\{A.1, A.2, A.3, A.4\}$ with respect to Ana. The true visibility of Ana's B.Yr is
given by $Vis_{true}(v_{Ana}.B.Yr) = \{\}$ and the observed visibility of Ana's B.Yr is
given by $Vis_{obs}(v_{Ana}.B.Yr) = \{A.1, A.2, A.3, A.4\}$.

$$
\begin{array}{r}
\text{Ana} \\
\text{Bob} \\
\text{Chris} \\
\text{Emma} \\
\text{Joey} \\
\text{Sam}
\end{array}
\begin{array}{c}
\text{B.Yr} \\
\left(\begin{array}{c}
\{\} \\
\{A.1, A.2, A.3\} \\
\{A.1, A.2, A.3, A.4\} \\
\{A.1, A.2\} \\
\{A.1, A.2, A.3, A.4\} \\
\{\}
\end{array}\right)
\end{array}
$$

Fig. 2. Visibility matrix for the target user Ana for B.Yr

4   Privacy Scoring Mechanism

The discussions in Sects. 2 and 3 form the basis of the privacy scoring mechanism
that we describe in this section. As discussed in the Introduction, the mechanism
ultimately informs users of an OSN about the privacy risks of their profiles and
social graphs. In brief, the privacy scoring mechanism consists of the following
steps, each of which we discuss in details with appropriate examples in the rest
of this section:

1. Construction of a harm tree for each privacy harm.
2. Pruning harm trees based on attribute visibilities.
3. Computation of the accuracy values for each attribute value.
4. Pruning harm trees based on the accuracy values.
5. Evaluation of the likelihood of each harm.

4.1   Construction of Harm Trees

The first step in deriving the privacy score is to construct the harm tree for each privacy harm. A harm tree [5–7] describes the relationship among the privacy harms, threats, risk sources and the personal data/attributes of the target user. The root node of a harm tree denotes a privacy harm. Leaf nodes represent the exploitation of personal data (user attributes or other personal data) by risk sources. Intermediate nodes represent the threats caused by the risk sources. Child nodes can be connected by: (1) an AND node if all of them are necessary to give rise to the parent; (2) an OR node if any one of them is sufficient to give rise to the parent and (3) a k-out-of-n node if any k of the n child nodes are sufficient to give rise to the parent node.

In case of some harms, the personal data that can be exploited may vary from risk source to risk source or a particular occurrence of the harm to another one. For example, a potential employer may assess the target user's profile based on political views, religious views, sexual orientation, interests and relationship status or a subset of these data. In such cases, we present n of the most probable attributes leading to the harm in the harm tree. Out of these n attributes, any k may be used by the risk source leading to the harm.

The harm tree for H.1 in Fig. 3 represents that a target user's profile can be assessed for suitability for stalking by a friend of a friend of a friend ($A.3$) or a stranger ($A.4$). The stalker can use either the gender (Gen) or the age (Age derived from the attribute B.Yr) or both of a target user to assess the profile. The risk source also needs to know a more or less precise location data for the user given by the home locality (H.Loc derived from H.Add) or the work locality (W.Loc derived from W.Pl). These data can be either accessed directly (FE.2) or can be inferred (FE.1). Figure 4 presents the harm tree for H.2.

The harm trees can be constructed by privacy experts beforehand and stored in a database. The latter can be updated when new harms are discovered. Existing harm trees can also be modified based on new information. This step can be performed once (and the database can be updated once in a while) and can be reused for each target user.

4.2   Pruning Harm Trees Based on Attribute Visibility

The observed visibilities $Vis_{obs}(.)$ of the target user's attributes are derived from the visibility matrix $\mathbf{M}(i, j)$. Table 2 represents the true and the observed visibilities (derived from the visibility matrix of the corresponding user) of an example target user T (accuracy is discussed in Sect. 4.3 and the column for accuracy is used in Sect. 4.5). The branches of the harm trees using the attributes for

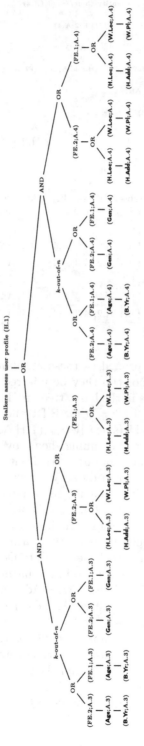

Fig. 3. Harm tree for H.1

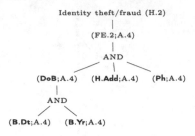

Fig. 4. Harm tree for H.2

Table 2. True and observed visibility sets and the accuracy values for T

Attribute $(v_T.a_j)$	True visibility $Vis_{true}(v_T.a_j)$	Observed visibility $Vis_{obs}(v_T.a_j)$	Accuracy
B.Dt	{}	{}	$A.1, A.2, A.3, A.4 : 0$
B.Yr	{}	$\{A.1, A.2, A.3, A.4\}$	$A.1, A.2 : 0.45; A.3 : 0.4; A.4 : 0.4$
Gen	{}	$\{A.1, A.2, A.3, A.4\}$	$A.1, A.2 : 0.8; A.3 : 0.7; A.4 : 0.6$
Ph	{}	{}	$A.1, A.2, A.3, A.4 : 0$
H.Add	{}	{}	$A.1, A.2, A.3, A.4 : 0$
W.Pl	{}	$\{A.1, A.2, A.3, A.4\}$	$A.1, A.2 : 0.45; A.3 : 0.4; A.4 : 0.3$

which $|Vis_{obs}(.)| = 0$ can be pruned as these attributes or personal data are neither disclosed by the user nor can they be inferred from his friends. So, for the target user T, the branches in the harm tree for H.2 (see Fig. 4) corresponding to DoB (since $|Vis_{obs}(T.B.Dt)| = 0$ for B.Dt and both B.Dt and B.Yr are required to obtain DoB), H.Add (since $|Vis_{obs}(T.H.Add)| = 0$) and Ph (since $|Vis_{obs}(T.Ph)| = 0$) can be pruned (pruning shown by $\times$ in Fig. 5).

Next, a second level of pruning can be carried out based on whether a harm tree uses the exploitation of personal data by a risk source who does not have access to it. For example, suppose that for the attributes B.Dt, H.Add and Ph of another target user T', $Vis_{obs}(.) = \{A.1\}$, implying that the risk sources $A.2$, $A.3$ and $A.4$ do not have access to these attribute values nor can they infer the required personal data (e.g. DoB) to cause the harm. In the harm tree for H.2 (see Fig. 4), the risk source $A.4$ must have access to DoB, Ph. and H.Loc. So, for T', the corresponding branches are pruned in the harm tree for H.2. In contrast, if the observed visibility values of B.Dt, B.Yr, H.Add and Ph for a target user T'' are given by $Vis_{obs}(.) = \{A.1, A.2, A.3, A.4\}$, the corresponding branches of the harm tree for H.2 cannot be pruned.

The harm tree for H.2 becomes non-existent for the target users T and T' as the personal data necessary to cause H.2 are not available to the risk source $A.4$. So the privacy settings of T and T' and those of their friends protect them from H.2 but the privacy settings of T'' and his friends do not. The harm tree for H.1 (given in Fig. 3) can be pruned similarly (see Fig. 6).

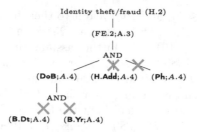

Fig. 5. Pruning of harm tree for H.2 for T and T' based on visibility (Color figure online)

4.3 Accuracy of Attribute Values

The accuracy of an attribute in having a particular value depends on the true and the observed visibility of the attribute(s) from which it can be derived. If for an attribute, $|Vis_{true}| > 0$, the target user has himself revealed the attribute. So, when the target user reveals an attribute to his friends (i.e., $Vis_{true} = \{A.1\}$), to his friends of friends (i.e., $Vis_{true} = \{A.1, A.2\}$) and to strangers (i.e., $Vis_{true} = \{A.1, A.2, A.3, A.4\}$), then the corresponding risk sources know the value of the corresponding attribute with full accuracy[6]. When there is a difference in the observed and the true visibility sets, then at least some risk sources do not know the value with full accuracy and therefore infer the value with some accuracy. We consider a simple measure of accuracy for the jth attribute of the target user v_T as derived by the kth risk source $A.k$ given as:

$$Acc(v_T.a_j)_{A.k} = Max_l(Pr[v_T.a_j = s_l | \forall i, i > 1, v_i.a_j = s_l, e_{T,i} \in E, A.k \in \mathbf{M(i,j)}])$$

$$= Max_l(\frac{|v_i.a_j|_{v_i.a_j=s_l,i>1,A_k \in \mathbf{M(i,j)}}}{|v_i.a_j|_{i>1}})$$

where, s_l is the lth value that can be assumed by the attribute a_j of the target user v_T or his friend v_i, $\mathbf{M}$ is the visibility matrix and A_k is the kth risk source. $|v_i.a_j|_{i>1}$ denotes the total number of friends v_i (we assume that the target user has at least one friend) and $|v_i.a_j|_{v_i.a_j=s_l,i>1,A_k \in \mathbf{M(i,j)}}$ denotes the number of friends v_i for whom $v_i.a_j = s_l$ and $A_k \in \mathbf{M(i,j)}$. The range of values (s_l for all l) assumed by an attribute can be obtained from the values assigned to the attribute by friends of v_T or from an accepted set of values (e.g., cities in France).

The above formula can be used to compute the accuracy value for attributes that assume a categorical value. For example, Gen can assume a value from {Male, Female}, RStat can assume a value from {Single, Married, Divorced} etc. For some attributes such as B.Yr, instead of inferring the exact value, the risk source may infer the range within which the value lies.

We illustrate the computation of accuracy values with an example. Suppose the target user T' does not reveal his B.Yr. He has a 100 friends and 60 of those friends reveal their B.Yr to strangers (i.e., $\mathbf{M(i,B.Yr)} = \{A.1, A.2, A.3, A.4\}$, $1 < i \le 61$), 5 of them reveal it to their friends of friends (i.e., $\mathbf{M(i,B.Yr)} =$

---

[6] The accuracy values lie between 0 (no accuracy) and 1 (full accuracy).

$\{A.1, A.2, A.3\}$, $61 < i \le 66$) and 10 reveal it to their friends (i.e., $\mathbf{M(i, B.Yr)} = \{A.1, A.2\}$, $66 < i \le 76$). The rest, i.e., 25 do not reveal it at all (i.e., $\mathbf{M(i, B.Yr)} = \{\}$, $76 < i \le 101$). We further assume that of the first 60 friends, 70% are in the range of 1980 to 1990, 20% are earlier than 1980 and remaining later than 1990. For all the other groups, 20% are in the range of 1980 to 1990, 40% earlier than 1980 and remaining later than 1990. Then the accuracy with which $A.1$ (mutual friends) can infer about the B.Yr of T' is:

$Acc(v_{T'}.\text{B.Yr})_{A.1} = Max(Pr[1980 \le v_{T'}.\text{B.Yr} \le 1990|\forall i, 1980 \le v_i.\text{B.Yr} \le 1990, e_{T',i} \in E, A.1 \in \mathbf{M(i, B.Yr)}], Pr[v_{T'}.\text{B.Yr} < 1980|\forall i, v_i.\text{B.Yr} < 1980, e_{T',i} \in E, A.1 \in \mathbf{M(i, B.Yr)}], Pr[v_{T'}.\text{B.Yr} > 1990|\forall i, v_i.\text{B.Yr} > 1990, e_{T',i} \in E, A.1 \in \mathbf{M(i, B.Yr)}]) = Max(0.45, 0.18, 0.12) = 0.45$.

The computation of the accuracy value is inspired by the friend-aggregated model in [24]. However, as discussed in [24], other types of computations of the accuracy value are also possible, depending upon the inference method being used. Different risk sources may choose different inference methods based on their capabilities. The computation method presented above provides a lower bound to the achievable accuracy values – risk sources, using better inference methods, can achieve better accuracy. Our aim is to provide the user with a base level for the score (improving the inference method is not our focus), implying that the privacy risk is at least equal to the privacy score that we present.

4.4 Pruning the Harm Trees Based on Accuracy

Once the accuracy values are known, a third stage of pruning can be carried out based on which attributes in the harm trees are known with full accuracy and which ones are to be inferred. We show this step for T and the harm H.1 in Fig. 7. For T, the attributes B.Yr and Gen have to be inferred from what T's friends reveal by the risk sources $A.3$ and $A.4$ (FE.1) as similar attributes have not been disclosed by T himself (FE.2). So the branches of this harm tree for these attributes and FE.2 are pruned. Similarly, H.Add and W.Pl must be inferred from what T's friends have disclosed (FE.1) as similar attributes have not been disclosed by T himself (FE.2), by both risk source $A.3$ and $A.4$. So whenever an attribute value is known with full accuracy[7] by a risk source, the corresponding branch (FE.2) in the tree is left untouched while the branch for inferring the value of the attribute (FE.1) by that risk source is pruned. Otherwise branches with FE.1 are retained and those with FE.2 pruned. We also fix the values for k and n. In the worst case (for the user), each risk source uses only the attribute having the maximum accuracy for the harm. Then, we substitute all nodes with k-out-of-n by OR nodes [23]. In the best case (for the user), each risk source uses all the attributes for the harm. In this case, we substitute all k-out-of-n nodes by AND nodes. There may be intermediate cases, where risk sources use different number and combinations of attributes. For example, one intermediate scenario is where the attributes with the top k accuracy values are used by the risk source.

---

[7] The value of an attribute is known with full accuracy only when the value is disclosed by the target user himself, i.e., only for some cases of direct, similar attribute inferences (e.g., a risk source comes to know v_T's gender because v_T reveals it).

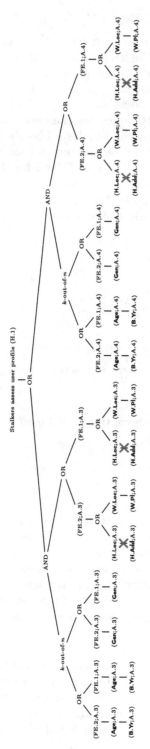

Fig. 6. Pruning of harm tree for H.1 for T based on visibility

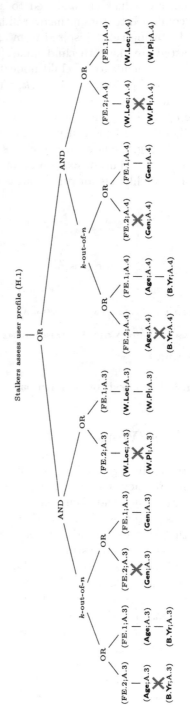

Fig. 7. Pruning of the harm tree for H.1 for T based on accuracy

4.5 Evaluation of Harm Likelihoods

Once accuracy values are assigned to all the leaf nodes in a harm tree, they must be combined to obtain the overall likelihood of the harm. The combination uses the following rules, inspired from [23], where Acc_i is the accuracy value of the ith attribute (i.e., ith child node):[R1.] AND node: $\prod_i Acc_i$, $i = 1, \ldots, n$ (assuming independence of child nodes); [R2.] OR node: $Max_i(Acc_i)$; [R3.] k-out-of-n node: $\prod_i Acc_i$, $i = 1, \ldots, k$, where the k attributes are the ones with the top k accuracy values (assuming independence of child nodes). The above rules are applied bottom-up on the harm tree. We illustrate the computation of the likelihood of H.1 for T using the example accuracy values in Table 2 for the worst case in Fig. 8. The accuracy values and the likelihood value for the relevant nodes are presented inside curly brackets beside each node. The likelihood of H.1 is 0.28. The likelihoods for other harms can be similarly computed.

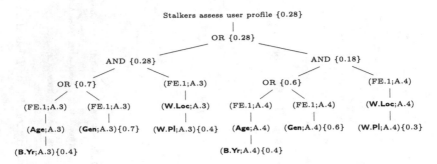

Fig. 8. Likelihood computation based on worst case harm tree for H.1 for T

5 Related Works

One of the earliest privacy scoring models is the one by Liu and Terzi [13]. In their work, privacy score is a monotonically increasing function of the visibility of attribute values and their sensitivity. It has been assumed that the privacy settings assigned to an attribute depend on its sensitivity and hence a response matrix that records the privacy settings of different attributes by a number of users has been used to estimate the value of sensitivity of each attribute. The visibility of the attribute value is influenced by the privacy setting of the user and his position in the network. The probability that an attribute is truly visible is estimated using the observed visibility values (i.e., the privacy settings) recorded in the response matrix using the Item Response Theory. In contrast, we do not assume that users consider the "sensitivity" of personal data when they specify their privacy settings, nor do we use sample data to compute the privacy scores.

Wang and Nepali [20] introduce the privacy index as a measurement of the exposure of the privacy of a participant in an OSN based on known attributes. In [15, 22], they use it for their social network model for privacy monitoring and ranking. Both sensitivity and visibility of attributes are taken into account in the computation of the privacy index. We only consider visibility of attribute values as a contributor to the computation of privacy scores. The sensitivity of the attributes are implicitly revealed by their popularity in the harm trees. In the recent PScore framework [18], the scoring mechanism can be linked to any inference algorithm. Any inference algorithm could also be plugged into our method and the only adjustment required while doing so is to update the calculation of the accuracy value. However, in contrast to [18], our mechanism is concrete yet simple.

Some works [1,17,19] also focus on the rating of the user's OSN friends based on their attitudes towards privacy, helping him to make an informed decision of sharing information with them. We do not consider the ranking of the user's friends or the active disclosure of the target user's data by the risk sources, but rather focus on privacy risks that arise from what the target user or his friends willingly disclose about themselves. In our approach, the user does not need to provide any input that may require any awareness about privacy problems.

In most works, the implicit assumption is that if the user prefers to disclose or has no problems in allowing the propagation of some data then it is less sensitive to him than if he prefers otherwise. We assume that the user is not a privacy expert and may end up disclosing data that may cause him a lot of harm. Therefore, our privacy scores serve to warn the user about the imminent dangers of revealing personal data on the OSN. None of the previous works on privacy scores draw inspiration from privacy risk analysis.

Privacy harms, threats and risk sources specific to OSNs and their relationship with various personal data must be obtained from previous research. Information disclosed in OSNs can significantly affect others' impression of the user [16] and hiring decisions [12,16]. Other harms include thieves or sexual predators tracking, monitoring, locating and identifying a user as a potential victim, political parties targetting a user through ads and data mining [12] and identity theft [10]. OSN users often regret sharing information on alcohol and drug use, sex, religious and political opinions, personal and family issues, work etc., chiefly due to undesirable reactions from other users and unintended audience [21].

Our work is inspired by privacy risk analysis (PRA), a review of which can be found in [5,6]. Harm trees linking privacy weaknesses and risk sources to harms, via feared events have been introduced and widely used in [5–7]. Here, we adopt these concepts to our setting. PRA methodologies help the service provider to evaluate systems processing personal data for privacy risks, thus helping to design and implement these systems in the least privacy invasive way. Deng et al. [8] provide an example of using their LINDDUN risk analysis framework [9] for analyzing social networks. Our mechanism differs from these PRA methodologies in a number of ways: (1) our aim is to guide users instead of service providers; (2) we analyze each user's OSN profile and social graph to uncover the privacy risks, instead of the entire OSN system; (3) we consider risk sources that are already within the user's social graph and who process personal data that are already made visible to them by the user and do not consider hackers, OSN service providers, the government etc.; (4) we consider only the choices made by the user and his friends regarding the visibility of their profile attributes, but not privacy weaknesses [5,6] originating from the service provider's choices during system design and implementation (such as insufficient protection of data store, lack of anonymization techniques) (5) since OSN profiles are user-specific, counter-measures suggested based on the privacy scores will differ from user to user, based on privacy risks of their profiles and their requirements regarding social benefit. In addition, unlike [7], the harm trees do not consider system components (generic or specific) but only the data elements and the risk sources and the pruning of harm trees takes place based on attribute visibility and the accuracy of the inferred attribute values rather than system architectures and the implementation context. To our best knowledge, our work is the first effort in utilizing PRA concepts for user-centric analysis of privacy risks of OSN profiles.

6   Conclusion and Future Works

We designed a privacy scoring mechanism for OSN profiles inspired by privacy risk analysis (PRA). The privacy scores can be used to inform the user about the privacy risks of his OSN profile. Our model can form the basis of designing a user interface to effectively communicate privacy scores and conduct a usability study to understand their effect on the user's privacy awareness. Based on the scores, we can also suggest counter-measures to users, taking into account the trade-off between the privacy risks and the social benefits of using OSNs. Such counter-measures include: (1) the selection of the right privacy setting for each profile attribute; (2) a decision on which friendships to continue based on their effects on the user's privacy scores and/or the negotiation of a privacy setting allowing both the user and his friends to maintain privacy and derive the social benefits of using an OSN. We leave these as future work.

References

1. Akcora, C., Carminati, B., Ferrari, E.: Privacy in social networks: how risky is your social graph? In: 2012 IEEE 28th International Conference on Data Engineering (ICDE), pp. 9–19. IEEE (2012)
2. Al Zamal, F., Liu, W., Ruths, D.: Homophily and latent attribute inference: inferring latent attributes of Twitter users from neighbors. In: ICWSM, vol. 270, pp. 387–390 (2012)
3. Commission Nationale de l'Informatique et des Libertes (CNIL): Privacy Impact Assessment (PIA) Methodology (How to Carry Out a PIA) (2015)
4. Commission Nationale de l'Informatique et des Libertes (CNIL): Privacy Impact Assessment (PIA) Tools (templates and knowledge bases) (2015)
5. De, S.J., Le Métayer, D.: PRIAM: a privacy risk analysis methodology. In: 11th International Workshop on Data Privacy Management (DPM). IEEE (2016)
6. De, S.J., Le Métayer, D.: Privacy risk analysis. In: Synthesis Series. Morgan & Claypool Publishers (2016)
7. De, S.J., Le Métayer, D.: A Risk-based Approach to Privacy by Design (Extended Version). Number RR-9001, December 2016

8. Deng, M., Wuyts, K., Scandariato, R., Preneel, B., Joosen, W.: LINDDUN: running example-Social Network 2.0
9. Deng, M., Wuyts, K., Scandariato, R., Preneel, B., Joosen, W.: A Privacy threat analysis framework: supporting the elicitation and fulfilment of privacy requirements. Requirements Eng. **16**(1), 3–32 (2011)
10. Gross, R., Acquisti, A.: Information revelation and privacy in online social networks. In: Proceedings of the 2005 ACM Workshop on Privacy in the Electronic Society, pp. 71–80. ACM (2005)
11. Huang, L., Wang, D.: What a surprise: initial connection with coworkers on Facebook and expectancy violations. In: Proceedings of the 19th ACM Conference on Computer Supported Cooperative Work and Social Computing Companion, pp. 293–296. ACM (2016)
12. Johnson, M., Egelman, S., Bellovin, S.M.: Facebook and privacy: it's complicated. In: Proceedings of the Eighth Symposium on Usable Privacy and Security, p. 9. ACM (2012)
13. Liu, K., Terzi, E.: A framework for computing the privacy scores of users in online social networks. ACM Trans. Knowl. Disc. Data (TKDD) **5**(1), 6 (2010)
14. Mislove, A., Viswanath, B., Gummadi, K.P., Druschel, P.: You are who you know: inferring user profiles in online social networks. In: Proceedings of the Third ACM International Conference on Web Search and Data Mining, pp. 251–260. ACM (2010)
15. Nepali, R.K., Wang, Y.: SONET: a social network model for privacy monitoring and ranking. In: 2013 IEEE 33rd International Conference on Distributed Computing Systems Workshops (ICDCSW), pp. 162–166. IEEE (2013)
16. Ollier-Malaterre, A., Rothbard, N.P., Berg, J.M.: When worlds collide in cyberspace: how boundary work in online social networks impacts professional relationships. Acad. Manag. Rev. **38**(4), 645–669 (2013)
17. Pergament, D., Aghasaryan, A., Ganascia, J.-G., Betgé-Brezetz, S.: FORPS: friends-oriented reputation privacy score. In: Proceedings of the First International Workshop on Security and Privacy Preserving in e-Societies, pp. 19–25. ACM (2011)
18. Petkos, G., Papadopoulos, S., Kompatsiaris, Y.: PScore: a framework for enhancing privacy awareness in online social networks. In: 2015 10th International Conference on Availability, Reliability and Security (ARES), pp. 592–600. IEEE (2015)
19. Vidyalakshmi, B.S., Wong, R.K., Chi, C.-H.: Privacy scoring of social network users as a service. In: 2015 IEEE International Conference on Services Computing (SCC), pp. 218–225. IEEE (2015)
20. Wang, W., Zhuo, L.: Cyber security in the Smart Grid: survey and challenges. Comput. Netw. **57**(5), 1344–1371 (2013)
21. Wang, Y., Norcie, G., Komanduri, S., Acquisti, A., Leon, P.G., Cranor, L.F.: I regretted the minute I pressed share: a qualitative study of regrets on Facebook. In: Proceedings of the Seventh Symposium on Usable Privacy and Security, p. 10. ACM (2011)
22. Wang, Y., Nepali, R.K., Nikolai, J.: Social network privacy measurement and simulation. In: 2014 International Conference on Computing, Networking and Communications (ICNC), pp. 802–806. IEEE (2014)
23. Yager, R.R.: OWA trees and their role in security modeling using attack trees. Inf. Sci. **176**(20), 2933–2959 (2006)
24. Zheleva, E., Getoor, L.: To Join or not to join: the illusion of privacy in social networks with mixed public and private user profiles. In: Proceedings of the 18th International Conference on World Wide Web, pp. 531–540. ACM (2009)

A Method for Developing Qualitative Security Risk Assessment Algorithms

Gencer Erdogan$^{(\boxtimes)}$ and Atle Refsdal

SINTEF Digital, Oslo, Norway
{gencer.erdogan,atle.refsdal}@sintef.no

Abstract. We present a method for developing qualitative security risk assessment algorithms where the input captures the dynamic state of the target of analysis. This facilitates continuous monitoring. The intended users of the method are security and risk practitioners interested in developing assessment algorithms for their own or their client's organization. Managers and decision makers will typically be end users of the assessments provided by the algorithms. To promote stakeholder involvement, the method is designed to ensure that the algorithm and the underlying risk model are simple to understand. We have employed the method to create assessment algorithms for 10 common cyber attacks, and use one of these to demonstrate the approach.

Keywords: Security risk assessment · Risk assessment algorithms
Qualitative risk assessment

1 Introduction

Decision makers need to understand security risks to determine how to deal with them. Many managers, particularly at the business level, expect quantified assessments of risks in terms of estimated likelihood and monetary loss. Unfortunately, providing trustworthy numbers is very difficult. This requires not only insight into the systems, threats, vulnerabilities and business processes of the organization, but also access to good empirical data and statistics to serve as a foundation for quantified estimates. Such data is often unavailable. Even if we can obtain it, analyzing the data to understand its impact on the assessment is a major challenge [15].

This means that providing good quantitative assessments is not always feasible. In such cases, a qualitative approach can be a good alternative. By qualitative, we mean that we use ordinal scales, for which the standard arithmetic operators are not defined, to provide assessments. Each step is usually described by text, such as {Very low; Low; Medium; High; Very high}. More informative descriptions of each step can of course be given. Ordinal scales allow us to order values, thereby making it possible to monitor trends. Since security risk assessment is costly when performed manually, we need to find ways to reduce the effort required to update assessments.

© Springer International Publishing AG, part of Springer Nature 2018
N. Cuppens et al. (Eds.): CRiSIS 2017, LNCS 10694, pp. 244–259, 2018.
https://doi.org/10.1007/978-3-319-76687-4_17

The contribution of this paper is a *method for creating executable algorithms* for qualitative security risk assessment. The input to the algorithms captures the current state of the target of analysis, such as the presence of vulnerabilities, suspicious events observed in the application or network layer, and the potential consequence of security incidents for the business processes. The output from the algorithms is an assignment of qualitative risk values to all identified risks. Hence, an updated risk assessment can be obtained by rerunning the algorithms with new input. This facilitates continuous monitoring of the risk level.

Our goal is to create a method that does not require programming skills or extensive effort, ensures that the underlying risk models are documented in a comprehensible format, and results in transparent algorithms that can be understood by all stakeholders. We combine a graphical risk modeling technique, extended with a construct to capture dynamic factors, with a decision modeling technique to define the algorithm. The novelty of our approach lies in the integration of these techniques in an overall method that exploits their strengths. Both techniques are well-established, supported by freely available tools, and designed to provide models that can be easily understood.

In Sect. 2, we give an overview of the method, which consists of three steps. The next three sections explain each step. We then relate our method to other approaches in Sect. 6. Finally, in Sect. 7, we discuss the approach and report on initial experiences before concluding in Sect. 8.

2   Method Overview

Our method is illustrated in Fig. 1. In relation to the general security risk management process documented in ISO 27005 [10], the method starts at the risk assessment phase. That is, we assume that the context has been established, including purpose, scope, and target of analysis.

Fig. 1. Method overview.

Step 1 takes as input a description of the target of analysis, which may be in the form of system diagrams, use case documentation, system manuals etc. Based on the description, we create a risk model to identify and document the assets, risks, threats and vulnerabilities of relevance for the target of analysis. At this point, estimates of likelihood and consequence values are represented by parameters. We also identify indicators that capture dynamic factors influencing the risk level, such as the presence or absence of a certain vulnerability, or the expected consequence for an asset if a given incident occurs. The indicators represent the input to the final security risk assessment algorithm, as each indicator will define one input variable. The output from Step 1 is a security risk model with indicators, as well as parameters representing likelihood and consequence estimates.

In Step 2, we develop the security risk assessment algorithm based on the security risk model. This is done in a modular fashion. We exploit the structure of the risk model developed in Step 1 and transform each part of the risk model to a corresponding part of the algorithm. The output of this step is an initial version of the security risk assessment algorithm.

In Step 3, we validate the risk assessment algorithm based on expert judgment to check if it produces correct output, and adjust as necessary. The output of this step is a validated security risk assessment algorithm.

3   Step 1: Create Security Risk Model

For creating security risk models, we have chosen to use CORAS [12], which is a graphical risk modeling language that has been empirically shown to be intuitively simple for stakeholders with very different backgrounds [18]. Moreover, CORAS comes with a method that builds on established approaches, in particular ISO 31000 [9]. The method includes detailed guidelines for creating CORAS models, which can be applied to carry out Step 1.

Figure 2 illustrates a CORAS risk model, which we use as a running example throughout the rest of this paper. This risk model is one of 10 risk models we developed in the WISER project [20]. These models were primarily intended for an arbitrary European SME. The risk model describes a Hacker carrying out an HTTP Verb tampering attack or a reflection attack in the authentication protocol to gain access to restricted files/folders. The risk is that the server provides access to restricted files/folders, which in turn has an impact on confidentiality. The dashed arrows, which are not themselves part of the CORAS model, are used to point out the different model elements. The unbroken arrows are relations in CORAS. There are three kinds of relations used to connect different nodes. The *initiates* relation goes from a threat to a threat scenario or an unwanted incident. The *leads to* relation goes from a threat scenario or an unwanted incident to a threat scenario or an unwanted incident. The *impacts* relation goes from an unwanted incident to an asset.

Notice that the risk model represents likelihoods, conditional likelihoods, and consequences as parameters. For example, the likelihood $LS2$ represents the likelihood of threat scenario $S2$. Our naming convention for parameters and other risk model elements is provided in Appendix A. We use the parameters later in the process to create the assessment algorithm.

Having created the risk model, next we identify indicators and attach them to the relevant risk model element. An indicator may be assigned to any risk-model element. We distinguish between four different types of indicators: *business configuration* (represented by the color blue in Fig. 2), *test* (green), *network-layer*

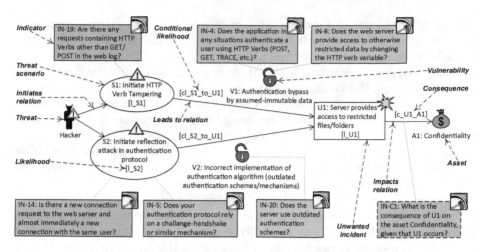

Fig. 2. CORAS risk model. (Color figure online)

monitoring (yellow, not included in the example), and *application-layer monitoring* (red). Values for the *business configuration* indicators are obtained by asking business related questions. The indicator values are thus based on expert knowledge. Values for the *test* indicators are obtained by carrying out vulnerability tests. Values for the *network-layer monitoring* indicators and the *application-layer monitoring* indicators are obtained by monitoring the network layer and the application layer, respectively. However, all indicator types are treated the same in the guidelines presented in the next section.

4   Step 2: Develop Security Risk Assessment Algorithm

In this section, we show how to build an assessment algorithm from a CORAS model. But first we introduce the tool we use for algorithm definition and execution.

4.1   A Brief Introduction to DEXi

DEXi [7] is a computer program for development of multi-criteria decision models and the evaluation of options. We use DEXi because it has been designed to produce models that are comprehensible to end users [6]. The comprehensibility of DEXi seems to be confirmed by the fact that it has been applied in several different domains, involving a wide range of stakeholders [4–6]. For a detailed description, we refer to the DEXi User Manual [3].

A multi-attribute model decomposes a decision problem into a tree (or graph) structure where each node in the tree represents an attribute. The overall problem is represented by the top attribute. All other attributes in the tree represent sub-problems, which are smaller and less complex than the overall problem.

Each attribute is assigned a value. The set of values that an attribute can take is called the *scale* of the attribute. DEXi supports definition of ordinal scales; typically, each step consists of a textual description.

Every attribute is either a basic attribute or an aggregate attribute. *Basic attributes* have no child attributes. This means that a basic attribute represents an input to the DEXi model, as its value is assigned directly, rather than being computed from child attributes. When using DEXi as a standalone tool, the user manually selects values for all basic attributes.

Aggregate attributes are characterized by having child attributes. The value of an aggregate attribute is a function of the values of its child attributes. This function is called the *utility function* of the attribute. The utility function of each aggregate attribute is defined by stating, for each possible combination of its child attribute values, what is the corresponding value of the aggregate attribute. The DEXi tool automatically computes the value of all aggregate attributes as soon as values have been assigned to the basic attributes. Hence, a DEXi model can be viewed as an algorithm where the basic attribute values constitute the input and the values of the aggregate attributes constitute the output. A java library and a command-line utility program for DEXi model execution is also available [7], meaning that functionality for executing DEXi algorithms can be easily integrated in software systems.

Figure 3 shows an example of a DEXi model which consists of three aggregate attributes and three basic attributes; the latter are shown as triangles. The top attribute, which is an aggregate attribute, is named *Risk* and has two child attributes (*Likelihood* and *Consequence*) that are also aggregate attributes. The *Likelihood* attribute has in turn two basic attributes as child attributes (*Likelihood indicator 1* and *Likelihood indicator 2*), while the *Consequence* attribute has one basic attribute as child attribute (*Consequence indicator 1*).

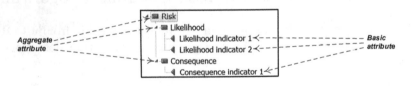

Fig. 3. DEXi model.

In the remainder of Sect. 4, we show how to build a security risk assessment algorithm, in the form of a DEXi model, based on a CORAS model. We use the model in Fig. 2 as an example. This means that the decision problem represented by the top attribute in the DEXi model concerns deciding the risk level. We start by explaining how each fragment of the CORAS model can be schematically translated to a corresponding fragment of the DEXi model in Subsects. 4.2 to 4.7. A summary of the schematic translation is provided in Appendix A. Having thus shown how to build the DEXi model structure, we provide guidelines for defining scales and utility functions in Subsect. 4.8.

4.2 Risk

CORAS representation. For any risk, the risk level depends on the likelihood of the unwanted incident and its consequence for the asset in question. A risk corresponds to a pair of an unwanted incident and an asset, including the *impacts* relation from the incident to the asset. In Fig. 2, this corresponds to the unwanted incident *U1* and the *impacts* relation to asset *A1*. The likelihood of *U1* is denoted by $LU1$, while the consequence of *U1* for asset *A1* is denoted by c_U1_A1.

DEXi representation. A risk is represented as a top (i.e. orphan) attribute that has two child attributes, one representing the likelihood of the incident and one representing the consequence for the asset in question. Figure 4(a) shows the corresponding DEXi-representation of the CORAS fragment described above. We use the variable/node names in the risk model to express the corresponding DEXi fragment to make it easier to understand the connection between a CORAS risk model and its corresponding representation in DEXi. Hence, the top attribute *R1* in Fig. 4(a), which represents the risk, has the two child nodes $LU1$ and c_U1_A1. Notice that *R1* does not occur as a separate name in the CORAS diagram, as a risk is represented by the combination of the incident, the asset, and the relation between them, rather than by a separate node.

4.3 Node with Incoming *Leads-to* Relations

CORAS representation. Figure 2 shows that the unwanted incident *U1* has two incoming *leads-to* relations, one from *S1* and one from *S2*. This means that the likelihood of *U1* depends on the likelihood contributions from *S1* and *S2*.

DEXi representation. The likelihood of a node with incoming *leads-to* relations[1] is represented by an attribute with one child attribute for every incoming *leads-to* relation. The attribute $LU1$ in Fig. 4(b), which represents the likelihood of *U1*, therefore has two child attributes, $LS1\_to\_U1$ and $LS2\_to\_U1$, representing the likelihood contributions from *S1* and *S2* via their outgoing *leads-to* relations.

4.4 Node with Outgoing *Leads-to* Relation

CORAS representation. The contribution from a *leads-to* relation to a target node depends on the likelihood of the source node and the conditional likelihood that an occurrence of the source node will lead to an occurrence of the target node. The latter is assigned to the *leads-to* relation. Figure 2 includes two *leads-to* relations, one from *S1* to *U1* and one from *S2* to *U1*. The likelihood contribution from the relation from *S1* depends on the likelihood of *S1* and the conditional likelihood that *S1* leads to *U1*, and similarly for *S2*.

---

[1] Recall from Sect. 3 that threat scenarios and unwanted incidents are the only node types that may have incoming *leads-to* relations.

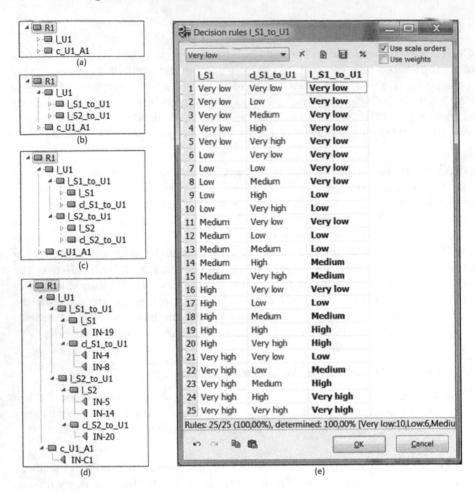

Fig. 4. Screenshots from the DEXi tool.

DEXi representation. The likelihood contribution from a *leads-to* relation is represented by an attribute with two child attributes, one representing the likelihood of the source node and one representing the conditional likelihood that an occurrence of the source node will lead to the target node. As illustrated in Fig. 4(c), the attribute *LS1_to_U1* representing the likelihood contribution from *S1* to *U1* therefore has two child attributes, *LS1* representing the likelihood of *S1* and *cl_S1_to_U1* representing the conditional likelihood of *S1* leading to *U1* (and similarly for *LS2_to_U1*).

4.5   Node with Attached Indicators

CORAS representation. Indicators can be attached to a node to show that the indicators are used as input for assessing the likelihood of the node.

Figure 2 shows that indicator *IN-19* is attached to threat scenario *S1*, while indicators *IN-5* and *IN-14* are attached to threat scenario *S2*.

DEXi representation. Indicators attached to a node are represented as basic attributes under the attribute representing the node. Figure 4(d) shows the complete DEXi tree structure derived from the CORAS risk model in Fig. 2. The basic attributes in Fig. 4(d) correspond to the indicators in Fig. 2. As shown in Fig. 4(d), we add the indicator *IN-19* as a child attribute of *LS1* and the indicators *IN-5* and *IN-14* as child attributes of *LS2*.

Notice that we may have cases where a node has incoming *leads-to* relations in addition to attached indicators. In such cases, the attribute representing the node can have child attributes representing the incoming branches, as explained in Subsect. 4.3, as well as the child attributes representing indicators.

4.6 *Leads-to* Relation with Attached Indicators

CORAS representation. Indicators can be attached to a *leads-to* relation from one node to another to show that the indicators are used as input for assessing the conditional likelihood of an occurrence of the source node leading to the target node. This is typically done by attaching the indicators to a vulnerability on the relation, as such indicators normally say something about the presence or severity of the vulnerability.

Figure 2 shows that indicator *IN-20* is attached to vulnerability *V2* and thus on the *leads-to* relation going from *S2* to *U1*. Similarly, indicators *IN-4* and *IN-8* are attached to vulnerability *V1*.

DEXi representation. Indicators attached to a *leads-to* relation are represented by basic attributes under the attribute representing the conditional likelihood assigned to the relation. For example, two basic attributes representing IN-4 and IN-8 are children of *cl_S1_to_U1*. Hence, the conditional likelihood *cl_S1_to_U1* depends on the indicators *IN-4* and *IN-8*.

4.7 Other CORAS Model Fragments

We have not provided separate guidelines for threats, *initiates* relations, and indicators attached to *impacts* relations. For the latter, the reason is that a CORAS model does not provide any support for consequence assessment beyond the assignment of a consequence value to the *impacts* relation from an unwanted incident to an asset. All indicators relevant for consequence assessments are therefore represented as basic attributes directly under the attribute representing the consequence, as illustrated by *c_U1_A1* in Fig. 4(d). In our example, the single indicator attached to the *impacts* relation from *U1* actually provides the consequence value directly, which means that the *IN-C1* attribute could have been attached directly under *R1*, without the intermediate *c_U1_A1* attribute. We chose to include *c_U1_A1* to illustrate the general structure.

Concerning threats and *initiates* relations, we rarely assign likelihoods to these CORAS elements in practice, as estimating threat behavior is very difficult. Instead, we assign a likelihood directly to the target node of the *initiates* relation. An indicator assigned to a threat or to an *initiates* relation can therefore be handled as if it was assigned directly to the target node, following the guidelines of Sect. 4.5.

4.8   Defining Scales and Utility Functions

Before defining utility functions, we need to define scales for the attributes. We strongly recommend using ordered scales consistently such that increasing the value implies increasing the (contribution to) the risk level, as this simplifies the definition of the utility functions. For all aggregate attributes in our running example, we use the scale {Very low; Low; Medium; High; Very high}.

We also make sure to follow the same scale order for the basic attributes representing the indicators. For example, consider the indicator *IN-19: Are there any requests containing HTTP Verbs other than GET/POST in the web log?* attached to *S1*. Since this is a yes/no question, the scale for the indicator only has two steps: Yes and No. A positive answer may indicate that someone has tried to prepare for an attack, and hence an increased likelihood. Therefore, for this indicator scale, the order from lowest to highest value should be {No; Yes}.

Assuming we have ordered all scales in this manner, increasing the value of a child attribute should never lead to a decrease in the value of its parent. The following restriction therefore guides the definition of utility functions:

Utility function restriction 1. *The value of an attribute should be monotonically increasing in all its child attributes. It does not have to be strictly increasing.*

For example, the risk *R1* should be monotonically increasing in the likelihood *L_U1* and the consequence *c_U1_A1*. Figure 5 illustrates an example of how a utility function fulfilling this restriction might be defined.

For the likelihood contribution from a *leads-to* relation, we also need to consider that the conditional likelihood of the source node leading to the target node will only affect the target node to the extent that the source node actually occurs. We therefore add the following restriction:

Utility function restriction 2. *The value of the attribute representing the likelihood contribution from a leads-to relation should not be higher than the value of the attribute representing the likelihood of the source node.*

For example, *L_S1_to_U1* should never be higher than *L_S1*. The screenshot from the DEXi tool in Fig. 4(e) shows a definition of the utility function of *L_S1_to_U1* that respects both utility function restrictions presented above.

For a threat scenario or unwanted incident with incoming *leads-to* relations, the likelihood can clearly not be lower than the highest contribution from the incoming relations. We therefore add the following restriction:

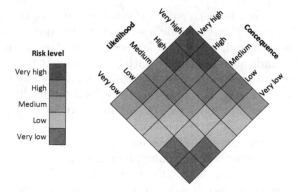

Fig. 5. Example of risk level defined as a monotonically increasing function of likelihood and consequence.

Utility function restriction 3. *The value of an attribute representing the likelihood of a node with one or more incoming leads-to relations should be at least as high as the highest value of the attributes representing the contributions from the incoming leads-to relations.*

For example, L_U1 should be at least as high as the highest of $L\_S1\_to\_U1$ and $L\_S2\_to\_U1$. Restrictions 2 and 3 apply under the assumption that the same scale is used for the attributes representing likelihood of nodes.

If a node has several incoming *leads-to* relations and/or attached indicators, combinatorial explosion can make it very hard to define the utility function for the attribute representing the node, due to the number of child attributes. In such cases, we recommend reducing the granularity of the scales of the child attributes or restructuring the model, as further explained in [3].

5   Step 3: Validate Security Risk Assessment Algorithm

Before putting the algorithm produced in Step 2 in operation, it should be validated to verify that its output correctly reflects reality. This can be done in many ways, depending on the data and resources available. When dealing with the kind of security risk assessment addressed in this paper, we typically need to rely on expert judgment. We first select a set of validation scenarios and then validate each of these with a team of experts.

A validation scenario is a set of indicator values representing one possible snapshot of the dynamic factors that influence the risk level. Thus, the number of possible scenarios is the product of the number of possible values for each indicator. This often results in many possible scenarios, which may be infeasible to validate. We therefore need to select a reasonable number of scenarios depending on the available effort. As a minimum, we suggest selecting validation scenarios based on the following two criteria: (1) cover the extreme scenarios (yielding the minimum and maximum risk values), and (2) cover each path in the CORAS risk model, meaning that for each path p (from the threat to the unwanted incident) in the risk model, there must be a scenario where one or more indicators along the path is triggered and the indicators for all other paths are not triggered unless these indicators also affect path p. By triggered, we mean that the indicator value contributes to the increase of likelihood. For the reasons given in Sect. 4.7 concerning consequence assessment, we focus on likelihood validation.

Our example in Fig. 2 includes six Boolean indicators affecting the likelihood assessment (as well as one affecting the consequence). This gives 64 possible scenarios. Table 1 gives an example of four scenarios fulfilling the criteria mentioned above. This represents the absolute minimum number to fulfill the coverage criteria, and we recommend using more validation scenarios. The Scenarios SC1 and SC4 satisfy the first coverage criterion. SC1 is the minimum risk scenario where no indicators are triggered, and SC4 is the maximum risk scenario where all indicators are triggered. The Scenarios SC2 and SC3 satisfy the second coverage criterion, where SC2 covers the top path of the risk model (involving "Initiate HTTP Verb Tampering") and SC3 covers the bottom path of the risk model (involving "Initiate reflection attack in authentication protocol"). The column L_U1 shows the resulting likelihood value of $U1$ for each scenario.

Table 1. Example of validation scenarios.

Scenario	IN-19	IN-4	IN-8	IN-14	IN-5	IN-20	LU1
SC1	No	No	No	No	No	No	Very low
SC2	Yes	Yes	Yes	No	No	No	High
SC3	No	No	No	Yes	Yes	Yes	Medium
SC4	Yes	Yes	Yes	Yes	Yes	Yes	Very high

With respect to validating the selected scenarios, we recommend using a well-established approach such as the Wide-band Delphi method [1]. The Wide-band Delphi method is a forecasting technique used to collect expert opinion in an objective way, and arrive at consensus conclusion based on that. Another similar estimation approach is the Constructive Cost Model (COCOMO) [2].

6   Related Work

Most security risk approaches aim to provide assessments capturing the risk level at a single point in time, rather than continuous monitoring. However, there are also approaches that address dynamic aspects and offer support for updating assessments based on new information, such as the ones proposed by Poolsappasit and Ray [14], Frigault et al. [8], Liu and Liu [17], and Krautsevich et al. [11]. Common for all these is that they offer quantitative assessments based on variants of Bayesian Networks or Markov Chains. Building and understanding the models therefore requires specialized expertise. Many security and risk practitioners, and most managers and decision makers, do not possess this expertise. Our qualitative approach based on CORAS and DEXi is designed to be simple and aimed at a broader user group.

DEXi is one of many approaches within the field of multi-criteria decision making (on which there is huge literature [19]), and has been tried out in a wide range of domains, such as health care, finance, construction, cropping systems, waste treatment systems, medicine, tourism, banking, manufacturing of electric motors, and energy [6,7]. To the best of our knowledge, DEXi has not been used for security risk assessment. However, it has been applied to assess safety risks within highway traffic [13] and ski resorts [5]. Although they focus on safety risks, the approaches provided by Omerčević et al. [13] and Bohanec and Delibašić [5] are similar to our approach in the sense that they use DEXi models as the underlying algorithm to compute an advice based on relevant indicators. Unlike our approach, they do not employ any dedicated risk modeling language to provide a basis for developing the DEXi models.

CORAS is a comprehensive framework for model-driven risk analysis. In addition to the risk modeling language, the framework consists of a tool and a comprehensive method [12]. However, CORAS focuses on quantitative assessment and does not address development of executable algorithms. Roughly speaking, what we have done in the work presented here is to insert the DEXi approach into the risk estimation step of the CORAS method and add indicators to capture dynamic aspects. The first use of measurable indicators as dynamic input to provide risk level assessments based on CORAS was presented in [16]. This is a quantitative approach aimed at developing mathematical formulas for assessing risk levels, where indicators are represented by variables in the formulas.

7 Discussion of the Approach and Initial Experiences

Our experience from applying the presented method to develop CORAS models and corresponding DEXi models for 10 common cyber attacks indicates that the method is easy to use. Therefore, our hypothesis is that most security and risk practitioners can adopt it without extensive additional training. In future work, we hope to test this hypothesis empirically with practitioners who have not been involved in developing the method.

This work was done in the context of the WISER project [20], which offers a framework for real-time security risk assessment where values for the basic attributes are automatically assigned from test tools, monitoring infrastructure and user interfaces. The risk assessment results (i.e. the output of the algorithms) are presented in a dashboard, which is part of the WISER framework. The DEXi models constitute the qualitative assessment algorithms offered by the framework, and will be tested on three pilots as part of the validation of the WISER framework. Notice that the method presented here does not require adoption of the WISER framework. It is possible to use only the DEXi tool to run the algorithms and view the results, if one is willing to manually feed the indicator values by assigning values to all basic attributes.

The effort required to apply the method obviously depends on several factors, including the complexity of the attack to be captured, the chosen abstraction level for the risk model, the number of indicators, and the choice of validation approach. As a rough rule of thumb, we estimate that applying the method will typically take from 20 to 40 h of work. This estimate is based on our experience from the WISER models and applies for general attacks that are already well understood, such as the one presented here. If a more complex CORAS model needs to be developed from scratch in Step 1, the effort may be significantly higher. Due to the guidelines provided for Step 2, we can reasonably assume that the effort required to develop the DEXi model will grow more or less in proportion to the number of elements in the CORAS model.

While the schematic translation to obtain the DEXi model structure is straightforward and could even be automated, the definition of scales and utility functions is based on subjective judgment. Here we see a potential for more extensive guidelines. These could, for example, provide guidance on the degree of impact on parent nodes for different types of indicators.

An inherent limitation of the approach is that new threats and attack types can only be addressed by creating new risk models and algorithms. The reason is that the only dynamic aspects that can be captured by the algorithms are those covered by the identified indicators. Periodic evaluations should therefore be performed to decide whether new or updated models and algorithms are required. This limitation applies for all approaches that rely on human experts.

8 Conclusion

We have presented a method for developing security risk assessment algorithms, using ordinal scales with textual descriptions for risk level assessments. Indicators constitute the input to the algorithms and capture the current state of the target of analysis, such as the presence of vulnerabilities, suspicious events observed in the infrastructure or the potential impact of security incidents on business processes. By producing an algorithm, rather than an assessment capturing the risk level at a single point in time, the method facilitates continuous assessment and monitoring of trends.

The method is designed to provide risk models documented in a comprehensible format and transparent assessment algorithms that can be understood by all stakeholders, without requiring programming skills or extensive effort. This promotes user involvement, critical scrutiny and improvement, and helps build trust in the results. Based on our initial experiences, we believe our work can contribute to enhanced security and better decision making by helping organizations to obtain transparent and comprehensible security risk assessments.

Acknowledgments. This work has been conducted as part of the WISER project (653321) funded by the European Commission within the Horizon 2020 research and innovation programme.

A   Schematic Translation from CORAS to DEXi

Table 2 shows the naming convention for risk model elements including likelihood and consequence parameters. The lower-case letters x and y in the table represent integers.

Table 2. Naming convention.

Name	Meaning
Ax	Asset x
Rx	Risk x
Sx	Scenario x (threat scenario)
Ux	Incident x ('U' stands for unwanted incident)
Vx	Vulnerability x
l_Ux	Likelihood of Ux
l_Sx	Likelihood of Sx
c_Ux_Ay	Consequence of Ux for Ay
cl_Sx_to_Sy	Conditional likelihood of Sx leading to Sy
cl_Sx_to_Uy	Conditional likelihood of Sx leading to Uy
cl_Ux_to_Sy	Conditional likelihood of Ux leading to Sy
cl_Ux_to_Uy	Conditional likelihood of Ux leading to Uy
l_Sx_to_Sy	Likelihood contribution from Sx to Sy
l_Sx_to_Uy	Likelihood contribution from Sx to Uy
l_Ux_to_Sy	Likelihood contribution from Ux to Sy
l_Ux_to_Uy	Likelihood contribution from Ux to Uy
IN-x	Indicator x
IN-Cx	Consequence indicator x

Figure 6 shows an overview of risk model fragments and their schematic translation from CORAS to DEXi. In all except the "Risk" row, we have used threat scenarios to illustrate nodes. However, these threat scenarios may also be replaced by unwanted incidents. The lower-case letters x, y, z, u, v, and n in Fig. 6 represent integers.

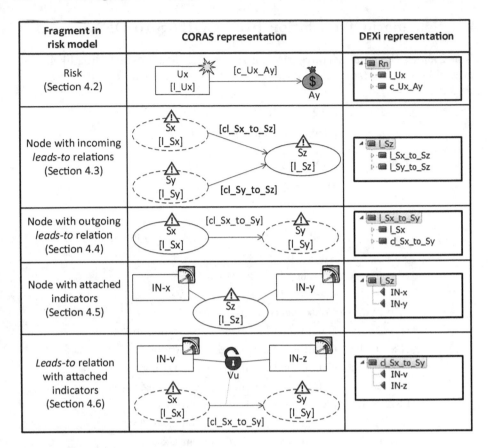

Fig. 6. Schematic translation from CORAS to DEXi

References

1. Boehm, B.W.: Software Engineering Economics. Prentice Hall, Upper Saddle River (1981)
2. Boehm, B.W., Abts, C., Brown, A.W., Chulani, S., Clark, B.K., Horowitz, E., Madachy, R., Reifer, D.J., Steece, B.: Software Cost Estimation with COCOMO II. Prentice Hall, Upper Saddle River (2000)
3. Bohanec, M.: DEXi: program for multi-attribute decision making. User's Manual v 5.00 IJS DP-11897. Institut "Jožef Stefan", Ljubljana, Slovenija (2015)
4. Bohanec, M., Aprile, G., Costante, M., Foti, M., Trdin, N.: A hierarchical multi-attribute model for bank reputational risk assessment. In: DSS 2.0 - Supporting Decision Making with New Technologies, pp. 92–103. IOS Press (2014)
5. Bohanec, M., Delibašić, B.: Data-mining and expert models for predicting injury risk in ski resorts. In: Delibašić, B., Hernández, J.E., Papathanasiou, J., Dargam, F., Zaraté, P., Ribeiro, R., Liu, S., Linden, I. (eds.) ICDSST 2015. LNBIP, vol. 216, pp. 46–60. Springer, Cham (2015). https://doi.org/10.1007/978-3-319-18533-0_5

6. Bohanec, M., Žnidaršič, M., Rajkovič, V., Bratko, I., Zupan, B.: DEX methodology: three decades of qualitative multi-attribute modeling. Informatica (Slovenia) **37**(1), 49–54 (2013)
7. DEXi: A Program for Multi-Attribute Decision Making. http://kt.ijs.si/MarkoBohanec/dexi.html. Accessed 9 Jan 2017
8. Frigault, M., Wang, L., Singhal, A., Jajodia, S.: Measuring network security using dynamic Bayesian network. In: Proceedings of the 4th ACM Workshop on Quality of Protection (QoP 2008), pp. 23–30. ACM (2008)
9. International Organization for Standardization: ISO 31000:2009(E), Risk management - Principles and guidelines (2009)
10. International Organization for Standardization: ISO/IEC 27005:2011(E), Information technology - Security techniques - Information security risk management (2011)
11. Krautsevich, L., Lazouski, A., Martinelli, F., Yautsiukhin, A.: Risk-aware usage decision making in highly dynamic systems. In: Proceedings of the 5th International Conference on Internet Monitoring and Protection (ICIMP 2010), pp. 29–34. IEEE (2010)
12. Lund, M.S., Solhaug, B., Stølen, K.: Model-Driven Risk Analysis: The CORAS Approach. Springer, Heidelberg (2011). https://doi.org/10.1007/978-3-642-12323-8
13. Omerčević, D., Zupančič, M., Bohanec, M., Kastelic, T.: Intelligent response to highway traffic situations and road incidents. In: Proceedings of the Transport Research Arena Europe, pp. 21–24 (2008)
14. Poolsappasit, N., Ray, I.: Dynamic security risk management using Bayesian attack graphs. Int. J. Adv. Intell. Syst. **9**(1), 61–74 (2012)
15. Refsdal, A., Solhaug, B., Stølen, K.: Cyber-Risk Management. Springer, Cham (2015). https://doi.org/10.1007/978-3-319-23570-7
16. Refsdal, A., Stølen, K.: Employing key indicators to provide a dynamic risk picture with a notion of confidence. In: Ferrari, E., Li, N., Bertino, E., Karabulut, Y. (eds.) IFIPTM 2009. IAICT, vol. 300, pp. 215–233. Springer, Heidelberg (2009). https://doi.org/10.1007/978-3-642-02056-8_14
17. Liu, S.-C., Liu, Y.: Network security risk assessment method based on HMM and attack graph model. In: Proceedings of the 17th IEEE/ACIS International Conference on Software Engineering, Artificial Intelligence, Networking and Parallel/Distributed Computing (SNPD), pp. 517–522. IEEE (2016)
18. Solhaug, B., Stølen, K.: The CORAS language - why it is designed the way it is. In: Proceedings of the 11th International Conference on Structural Safety & Reliability (ICOSSAR 2013), pp. 3155–3162. Taylor and Francis (2013)
19. Velasquez, M., Hester, P.T.: An analysis of multi-criteria decision making methods. Int. J. Oper. Res. **10**(2), 56–66 (2013)
20. Wide-Impact cyber SEcurity Risk framework (WISER). https://www.cyberwiser.eu/. Accessed 8 Feb 2017

An Empirical Analysis of Risk Aversion in Malware Infections

Jude Jacob Nsiempba[✉], Fanny Lalonde Lévesque,
Nathalie de Marcellis-Warin, and José M. Fernandez

École Polytechnique de Montréal, Montréal, QC, Canada
{jude-jacob.nsiempba, fanny.lalonde-levesque,
nathalie.demarcellis-warin, jose.fernandez}@polymtl.ca

Abstract. We present in this paper the results from a field study we conducted over a 4-month period. The experience aimed at evaluating the impact of the technological and human factors on the risk of getting infected by malware.

In this article, we applied the economic concept of risk aversion in order to study the behaviour of users towards the risk of malware infection. Our results show that younger users and men in particular, with a higher level of expertise in computer science are more susceptible to open multiple web accounts and install more software from the Internet. Furthermore, the increase in the level of expertise in computer science, creates in men a negative attitude towards alert messages of antivirus; while in women, the opposite happens.

Keywords: Computer security · Risk aversion · Human factors

1 Introduction

Studies published over the last decade have demonstrated the importance of human factors such as users' characteristics, demographic factors, and behaviors, in the success or failure of defense mechanisms in computer security. So far, many studies have investigated how socio-demographic factors relate to the risk of cyberattacks; only few have focused on malware attacks [6, 9, 10]. Their overwhelming evidence essentially suggest that socio-demographic factors (age, gender, income, education, etc.) are significant correlates for malware attack. However, these studies have mostly focused on the identification of key predictors rather than the origins of these associations, i.e. their causality. We believe a better understanding of socio-demographic differences in the risk of malware attack could enable practitioners, researchers, and policy makers to better design interventions in cybersecurity. It is therefore essential to perform research of malware attack to investigate the underlying causes behind these socio-demographic differences.

As a first attempt, we conducted a field study designed to examine the interactions between users, anti-malware software, and malware attacks as they occur on deployed systems [4, 5]. The 4-month study involved 50 participants whose computers were instrumented to monitor potential malware attacks and gather data on user behavior. Although the population size was limited, this initial study produced some interesting, non-intuitive insights into how socio-demographic factors and user behavior relate to

© Springer International Publishing AG, part of Springer Nature 2018
N. Cuppens et al. (Eds.): CRiSIS 2017, LNCS 10694, pp. 260–267, 2018.
https://doi.org/10.1007/978-3-319-76687-4_18

the risk of malware attack. In particular, we found evidence that users with a high (self-declared) level of computer expertise are more likely to be exposed to malware than users with a low (self-declared) level of computer expertise [4]. Although one could expect users who have more knowledge and expertise in computer to be less at-risk, prior work shown that this may not always be the case [1–3, 6].

On the one hand, it is conceivable that users with high computer expertise differ in their type and frequency of computer usage, which could contribute to increase, intentionally or not, their likelihood of malware attack. On the other hand, the psychological traits and level of knowledge of users can affect their decision making in the context of computer security. In the first case, previous research [6–8] support the existence of a relationship between type and frequency of computer usage and the risk of malware attack. In the second case, there is sufficient evidence from prior research [2, 3] to believe that users with higher computer and security knowledge are more likely to exhibit insecure behavior. For these reasons, it is plausible that users with higher level of computer expertise could be more prone to engage in computer behaviors that may increase their risk of malware attack.

In order to investigate this hypothesis, we applied the concept of *risk aversion* to the risk of malware attack. In economics, someone is referred as a risk-seeker, or risk-lover, if he prefers to accept a bargain with an uncertain payoff rather than a bargain with more certain, but possibly lower expected payoff. Applied to our study, a risk-seeker would prefer to adopt risky behavior even if there is an uncertain outcome associated with the action. For example, deliberately using peer-to-peer (P2P) networks to download movies at the risk of being infected by malware, or clicking on a link sent by an unknown sender to see exclusive images of celebrities.

In this paper, we extends the preliminary results already presented in earlier work [4] by investigating the potential mediator effect of risk aversion between (self-declared) level of computer expertise and the risk of malware attack. The rest of the paper is organized as follows. Section 2 presents a review of the related work. The research methodology and the analysis framework are detailed in Sect. 3. The results are presented in Sect. 4 followed by an analysis and a discussion in Sect. 5. A conclusion on future perspectives completes the article in Sect. 6.

2 Related Work

Some researchers have investigated the relationship between computer knowledge and expertise and the risk of malware attack. For example, Ovelgönne et al. [1] leveraged 2009–2011 telemetry data from the Symantec's Worldwide Intelligence Network Environment (WINE) project [7] to study the relationship between user behavior and cyberattacks. They created four user profiles (gamers, professionals, software developers, and others), and studied how seven machine features (number of binaries; fraction of unsigned, downloaded, low prevalence, and unique binaries; number of ISPs to which the user connected) correlate with the number of attempted malware attacks by host. The authors found all features to be significant contributing factors, and identified software developers to be the most prone to malware attacks. Similarly, Yen et al. [6] conducted a study of malware encounters in a large, multi-national enterprise.

They coupled malware encounters with web activities, users' characteristics and demographic factors. Their results suggested that users' characteristics, demographic factors, and behavior can be used to infer the likelihood of malware encounters. More particularly, they found people with technical expertise to be more at risk of encountering malware. In another study, Ngo and Paternoster [10] applied the general theory of crime and lifestyle/routine activities framework to assess the effects of individual and situational factors on seven types of cybercrime victimization, including computer virus infection. They conducted a self-assessment survey on a sample of 295 college students, and found no significant relationship between computer skills and computer virus infection. While some of these studies [1, 6] support our previous finding, that computer expertise is positively associated with the risk of malware attack, they offer little discussion on how the results should be interpreted in terms of causality.

Other researchers have focused on how expert and non-expert users differ in their security behavior. Using online surveys, Ion *et al.* [2] compared the (self-reported) security practices of security expert and non-expert users. Their results shown discrepancies between how security experts and non-experts behave. For instance, security experts were found to be more prone to open emails from unknown sender, visit unknown we sites, and less likely to install an antivirus software in comparison to non-expert users. Finally, De Luca *et al.* [3] also conducted an online survey to investigate how IT security expert and non-expert differ in their attitudes towards secure instant messaging. Their analysis revealed that while experts are more aware of potential risks, the extent to which they exhibit insecure behavior is similar to that of non-experts.

In light of this discussion, we believe it is plausible that users with higher expertise in computer are more prone to malware attack because they are more *risk-seeking*. Our main contribution is therefore to investigate this potential underlying cause by applying the economic concept of risk aversion to malware attack.

3 Methodology

3.1 Study Design

Inspired by the medical approach, we designed a *computer security clinical trial* to monitor real-world computer usage through diagnostics and logging tools, monthly interviews and questionnaires, and in-depth investigation of any potential malware infections. The 4-month field study involving 50 participants was conducted at the École Polytechnique de Montréal from November 2011 to February 2012. This first experiment of its kind aimed at (i) developing an effective methodology to evaluate antivirus (AV) software in a real-world environment, (ii) determining how malware infects computer systems and identify source of malware infections, and (iii) determining how technological and human factors affect the risk of malware infection.

3.2 Data Collection

Users were required to attend 5 in-person sessions: an initial session and 4 monthly sessions. The aim of the initial session was to provide the laptop to users and collect general information, such as gender, age group, status, etc. During the monthly meetings, users were invited to complete an online questionnaire about their computer usage and experience, while we were collecting local data compiled by our automated scripts.

The dependent variable, users' self-declared expertise in computer, was computed based on six tasks: (i) configuring a firewall, (ii) configuring a home wireless network, (iii) securing a wireless network, (iv) creating a web page, (v) changing the default security settings of a web browser, and (vi) installing an operating system (OS) on a computer. Each user was monthly assigned a level of computer expertise ranging from 0 to 6 based on the number of tasks they reported having previously completed.

Risk aversion was measured based on user's attitude and behavior regarding the AV and potential risky situations. Each month, users were asked about their feelings (Q1) and behavior (Q2) when a window appears from the AV. Answers for question Q1 were coded with two dummy variables. The first one (Q1a) could either be 1 or 0, whether the user answered that he feels annoyed that the AV software is interrupting him. The second variable (Q1b) could either be 1 or 0, depending if the user answered that he feels comforted to know that the AV software is working. Similarly, we created one dummy variable (Q2a) to evaluate users' behavior when a window appears from the AV. The variable could either be 1 or 0, where 1 means that the user is reading and following the instructions from the AV, and 0 means that the user is not following the instructions.

Users' behavior was monthly assessed based on six factors that may increase, intentionally or not, the risk of malware infection: (i) clicking on links and attachments of email from unknown sender (Q3), (ii) using P2P networks (Q4), (iii) number of web accounts protected by password (Q5), (iv) number of password used (Q6), (v) installing applications from the Internet (Q7), and (vi) downloading audio or video files from the Internet (Q8). Following a similar approach to that of Q1 and Q2, question Q3 was coded with two dummy variables (Q3a and Q3b). Q3a could either be 1 or 0, if the user answered that he clicks on to links and attachments of any email he receives provided that he is interested in viewing the content. The other dummy variable (Q3b) could either 1 or 0, whether the user said that he only clicks on to links and attachments of emails from known senders. All other questions (Q4 to Q8) were considered as ordinal discrete variables for the purpose of our analysis.

3.3   Statistical Analysis

Bivariate and stratified analysis by socio-demographic factors was performed to assess the association between computer expertise and risk aversion. Given the nature of our data and the small sample size, we used the Spearman rank correlation, a non-parametric statistical test, to study the relationship between the level of computer expertise and risk aversion. The statistical analysis was conducted with SPSS (V.21).

4   Results

4.1   Computer Expertise and Risk Aversion

We started by analyzing the relationship between the level of self-declared computer expertise and the 10 risk aversion variables selected by using Spearman's correlation month after month. Results in Table 1 presents the correlation coefficients (rho) and the associated p-value. Items in bold were considered statistically significant at p-value = 0.05.

Table 1. Spearman correlation coefficients (rho (p-value))

	Nov. (N = 47)	Dec. (N = 47)	Jan. (N = 46)	Feb. (N = 47)
Q1a	0.031 (0.419)	−0.008 (0.479)	−0.133 (0.189)	−0.039 (0.398)
Q1b	0.052 (0.363)	0.005 (0.486)	0.004 (0.491)	0.108 (0.235)
Q2a	−0.51 (0.367)	0.160 (0.142)	0.032 (0.416)	0.133 (0.187)
Q3a	0.197 (0.092)	0.049 (0.371)	0.163 (0.140)	0.068 (0.324)
Q3b	−0.177 (0.117)	−0.238 (0.054)	−0.224 (0.067)	−0.098 (0.256)
Q4	0.134 (0.185)	−0.027 (0.428)	0.234 (0.059)	**0.326 (0.013)**
Q5	**0.350 (0.008)**	**0.440 (0.001)**	**0.258 (0.042)**	**0.370 (0.005)**
Q6	−0.029 (0.425)	0.096 (0.260)	−0.001 (0.498)	0.163 (0.136)
Q7	**0.374 (0.005)**	**0.394 (0.003)**	0.206 (0.085)	0.228 (0.062)
Q8	0.225 (0.064)	0.156 (0.147)	**0.253 (0.045)**	0.096 (0.260)

The first observation from Table 1 is that none of the variables related to the AV (Q1 and Q2) were significant correlates of the level of computer expertise. When looking at behaviors (Q3 to Q8), variables related to links and attachments of email from unknown sender (Q3a and Q3b) and the number of password (Q6) were not found to be significant. Interestingly, using P2P networks (Q4), installing applications from the Internet (Q7), and downloading video or audio files from the Internet (Q8) were only significant for one or two months. One potential explanation is that users did not sufficiently engaged in these activities for some months, which could result in non-significant correlations. Only one variable, the number of web accounts (Q5), was found to be significant every month. The overwhelming evidence, however, is that all significant correlations are positive. This suggests that higher self-declared level of computer expertise is associated with higher adoption of online behaviors (Q4, Q5, Q7, Q8) that may contribute to increase, intentionally or not, the likelihood of malware infection.

4.2   Stratified Analysis by Socio-Demographic Factors

We also analyzed the correlations between the self-declared level of computer expertise and risk aversion by socio-demographic factors. For the purpose of our research, we restricted our analysis to gender and age, as both factors are known to affect how someone response to computer security-related risk [6, 9–14].

Gender. Our results in Table 2 show that male and female with computer expertise differ in their response to risk. As the level of computer expertise increases, male reported being less prone to read and follow the instructions suggested by the AV (Q2a). To the opposite, female were more likely to read the message from the AV and follow its suggestions (Q2a) as their level of computer expertise increases. Regarding users' behavior, only the variables related to the number of web accounts (Q5) and the number of video or audio files downloaded from the Internet were statistically significant. Similarly to our previous analysis in Sect. 4.2, they were both positively associated with the level of computer expertise.

Table 2. Total number of significant correlations by gender

	Male		Female	
	(+)	(−)	(+)	(−)
Q1a	0	0	0	0
Q1b	0	0	0	0
Q2a	0	2	2	0
Q3a	0	0	0	0
Q3b	0	0	0	0
Q4	0	0	0	0
Q5	3	0	0	0
Q6	0	0	0	0
Q7	0	0	0	0
Q8	0	0	4	0

Age. Results in Table 3 show no significant correlation between the level of computer expertise and the variables related to the AV (Q1a, Q1b, Q2a). In young people aged 18 to 24, we observed that the more the level of expertise in computer sciences increases, the less they are inclined to click on link and attachments in emails coming from unknown senders (Q3b), compared to others. On the other hand, as it pertains to their behaviour online, they use more accounts than all other users and install just as many software as people aged 35 and above. People aged 25 to 34 have a tendency to use P2P networks and have less passwords than others when their level of expertise in computer science increases.

Table 3. Total number of significant correlations by age groups

	18–24		25–34		35+	
	(+)	(−)	(+)	(−)	(+)	(−)
Q1a	0	0	0	0	0	0
Q1b	0	0	0	0	0	0
Q2a	0	0	0	0	0	0
Q3a	0	0	0	0	0	0
Q3b	0	1	0	0	0	0
Q4	0	0	1	0	0	0
Q5	3	0	1	0	1	0
Q6	0	0	0	2	0	0
Q7	2	0	0	0	2	0
Q8	0	0	0	0	1	0

5 Discussion

We found that women with an expertise in computer science are more likely to read antivirus messages and to follow suggestions (Q2a). As for men, they use more web accounts than women, thus multiplying the sources of vulnerability. The explanation we can provide for these results is that expertise in computer science seems to create a false sense of confidence that leads men to adopt more at-risk attitudes contrary to women, for whom computer science expertise seems to cause a greater awareness to threats. Such an attitude stems from what Luhmann calls assured confidence [15]; meaning that the Internet user is assured (confident) that his/her high level of computer expertise guarantees him a high level of protection. Faced with contingent events, the idea that his/her expectations are not met does occur to him. And because of this state of mind infections are more common compared to someone who does not master computer science.

We also realised that users in general, even though they have a higher level on computer science expertise, continue to multiply the number of web accounts and to download application software from the Internet. The explanation we found is that the proportion of youth aged 18 to 24 was higher (38%) and furthermore, 60% of our total sample was made up of men. It was mentioned in our results above that 18 to 24 year olds use more web accounts than others, and install just as many applications downloaded, with men being more likely to do so, than women. A double handicap that could partly explain the result of our previous research [11].

6 Conclusion of Future Perspectives

We presented the results of our analysis of the field study that aimed at studying the impact of the level of expertise in computer science on the attitude of the Internet users towards risk. Our hypothesis was that users with a higher level of computer science expertise are more likely to adopt behaviours susceptible to increase the risk of them getting infected by malware. Our results supported our initial hypothesis. We found that users with a higher self-reported level of expertise in computer science are more likely to have multiple web accounts and to install the application software from the Internet and in so doing, they contribute to increasing their risk of infection. Also, high level of computer expertise was associated with a negative attitude towards the AV for men, and with a positive attitude for women. Our study has a number of limitations, specifically the size and composition of our sample. For example, young people and students were overrepresented in our sample. Our study can therefore not be generalised. We believe that a broader study on computer science expertise and risk aversion with a more representative sample should be performed in order to confirm our conclusions.

References

1. Ovelgönne, M., Dumitras, T., Prakash, B.A., et al.: Understanding the relationship between human behavior and susceptibility to cyber attacks: a data-driven approach. ACM Trans. Intell. Syst. Technol. (TIST) **8**(4), 51 (2017)
2. Ion, I., Reeder, R., Consolvo, S.: No one Can Hack My Mind: comparing expert and non-expert security practices. In: SOUPS, pp. 327–346 (2015)
3. De Luca, A., Das, S., Ortlieb, M., et al.: Expert and non-expert attitudes towards (secure) instant messaging. In: Symposium on Usable Privacy and Security (SOUPS) 2016
4. Lalonde Lévesque, F., Nsiempba, J., Fernandez, J.M., et al.: A clinical study of risk factors related to malware infections. In: Proceedings of the 2013 ACM SIGSAC Conference on Computer & Communications Security, pp. 97–108. ACM (2013)
5. Lalonde Lévesque, F., Davis, C.R., Fernandez, J.M., Chiasson, S., Somayaji, A.: Methodology for a field study of anti-malware software. In: Blyth, J., Dietrich, S., Camp, L.J. (eds.) FC 2012. LNCS, vol. 7398, pp. 80–85. Springer, Heidelberg (2012). https://doi.org/10.1007/978-3-642-34638-5_7
6. Yen, T., Heorhladi, V., Oprea, A., et al.: An epidemiological study of malware encounters in a large enterprise. In: Proceedings of the 2014 ACM SIGSAC Conference on Computer and Communications Security, pp. 1117–1130. ACM (2014)
7. Carlinet, Y., Me, L., Debar, H., et al.: Analysis of computer infection risk factors based on customer network usage. In: Second International Conference on Emerging Security Information, Systems and Technologies, 2008, SECURWARE 2008, pp. 317–325. IEEE (2008)
8. Canali, D., Bilge, L., Balzarotti, D.: On the effectiveness of risk prediction based on users browsing behavior. In: Proceedings of the 9th ACM Symposium on Information, Computer and Communications Security, pp. 171–182. ACM (2014)
9. Bossler, A.M., Holt, T.J.: On-line activities, guardianship, and malware infection: an examination of routine activities theory. Int. J. Cyber Criminol. **3**(1), 400 (2009)
10. Ngo, F.T., Paternoster, R.: Cybercrime victimization: an examination of individual and situational level factors. Int. J. Cyber Criminol. **5**(1), 773 (2011)
11. Lévesque, F.L., Fernandez, J.M., Batchelder, D.: Age and gender as independent risk factors for malware victimisation. In: Proceedings of the 31th International British Human Computer Interaction Conference. ACM, Sunderland, UK (2017)
12. Oliveira, D., Rocha, H., Yang, H., et al.: Dissecting spear phishing emails for older vs young adults: on the interplay of weapons of influence and life domains in predicting susceptibility to phishing. In: Proceedings of the 2017 CHI Conference on Human Factors in Computing Systems, pp. 6412–6424. ACM (2017)
13. Grimes, G.A., Hough, M.G., Signorella, M.L.: Email end users and spam: relations of gender and age group to attitudes and actions. Comput. Hum. Behav. **23**(1), 318–332 (2007)
14. Sheng, S., Holbrook, M., Kumaraguru, P., et al.: Who falls for phish?: a demographic analysis of phishing susceptibility and effectiveness of interventions. In: Proceedings of the SIGCHI Conference on Human Factors in Computing Systems, pp. 373–382. ACM (2010)
15. Luhmann, N:. Confiance et familiarité. Réseaux (4), 15–35 (2001)

Author Index

Printed in the United States
By Bookmasters